P9-BZZ-521

Enthusiasm! Be an irresistible force of nature! **Exuberance!** Vibrate—cause earthquakes! **Execution!** Do it! Now! Get it done! Barriers are baloney! Excuses are for wimps! Accountability is gospel! Adhere to the Bill Parcells doctrine: "Blame no one! Expect nothing! Do something!" **Empowerment!** Respect and appreciation rule! Always ask, "What do you think?" Then listen! Then let go and liberate! Then celebrate! **Edginess!** Perpetually dancing at the frontier, and a little or a lot beyond. **Enraged!** Determined to challenge and change the status quo! Motto: "If it ain't broke, break it!" **Engaged!** Addicted to MBWA/Managing By Wandering Around. In touch. Always. **Electronic!** Partners with the world 60/60/24/7 via electronic community building of every sort. **Encompassing!** Relentlessly pursue diverse opinions—the more diversity the merrier! Diversity per se "works"! **Emotion!** The alpha. The omega. The essence of leadership. The essence of sales. The essence of marketing. The essence. Period. Acknowledge it. **Empathy!** Connect, connect, connect with others' reality and aspirations! "Walk in the other person's shoes"— until the soles have holes! **Ears!** Effective listening: Strategic Advantage Number 1! **Experience!** Life is theater! Make every activity-contact memorable! Standard: "Insanely Great"/Steve Jobs; "Radically Thrilling"/BMW. **Eliminate!** Keep it simple! **Errorprone!** Ready! Fire! Aim! Try a lot of stuff and make a lot of booboos and then try some more stuff and make some more booboos—all of it at the speed of light! **Evenhanded!** Straight as an arrow! Fair to a fault! Honest as Abe! **Expectations!** Michelangelo: "The greatest danger for most of us is not that our aim is too high and we miss it, but that it is too low and we reach it." Amen! **Eudaimonia!** Pursue the highest of human moral purpose—the core of Aristotle's philosophy. Be of service. Always. **EXCELLENCE!** Never an exception! *If not Excellence, what?*

The Little BIG Things

ALSO BY TOM PETERS

In Search of Excellence:
Lessons from America's Best-Run Companies
(with Robert H. Waterman, Jr.)

A Passion for Excellence:
The Leadership Difference (with Nancy K. Austin)

Thriving on Chaos:
Handbook for a Management Revolution

Liberation Management:
Necessary Disorganization for the Nanosecond Nineties

The Tom Peters Seminar:
Crazy Times Call for Crazy Organizations

The Pursuit of WOW!
Every Person's Guide to Topsy-Turvy Times

The Circle of Innovation:
You Can't Shrink Your Way to Greatness

The Brand You50:
*Fifty Ways to Transform Yourself from an "Employee" into a Brand
That Shouts Distinction, Commitment, and Passion!*

The Project50:
Fifty Ways to Transform Every "Task" into a Project That Matters!

The Professional Service Firm50:
*Fifty Ways to Transform Your "Department" into a Professional
Service Firm Whose Trademarks Are Passion and Innovation!*

Re-imagine!
Business Excellence in a Disruptive Age

Essentials:
Leadership: Inspire, Liberate, Achieve

Essentials:
Design: Innovate, Differentiate, Communicate

Essentials:
Trends: Recognize, Analyze, Capitalize (with Martha Barletta)

Essentials:
Talent: Develop It, Sell It, Be It

Sixty:
This I Believe

The Little BIG Things

163 Ways to Pursue EXCELLENCE

TOM PETERS

harperstudio

An Imprint of HarperCollinsPublishers

Grateful acknowledgment is made to John Wiley & Sons, Inc., BMW, and The Penguin Press for excerpts used in this book.

Excerpts from "Planners Versus Searchers," from *The White Man's Burden* by William Easterly, copyright © 2006 by William Easterly. Used by permission of The Penguin Press, a division of Penguin Group (USA) Inc.

THE LITTLE BIG THINGS. Copyright © 2010 by Thomas J. Peters. All rights reserved. Printed in the United States of America. No part of this book may be used or reproduced in any manner whatsoever without written permission except in the case of brief quotations embodied in critical articles and reviews. For information address HarperCollins Publishers, 10 East 53rd Street, New York, NY 10022.

HarperCollins books may be purchased for educational, business, or sales promotional use. For information please write: Special Markets Department, HarperCollins Publishers, 10 East 53rd Street, New York, NY 10022.

For more information about this book or other books from HarperStudio, visit www.theharperstudio.com.

FIRST EDITION

Designed by Joy Panos Stauber

Library of Congress Cataloging-in-Publication Data

Peters, Thomas J.
   The little big things : 163 ways to pursue excellence / by Tom Peters.—1st ed.
     p. cm.
   ISBN 978-0-06-189408-4
  1. Industrial management—United States. 2. Excellence—United States.
I. Title.
   HD70.U5P4245 2010
   658.4'09—dc22

                                    2009051160

10 11 12 13 14 DIX/RRD 10 9 8 7 6 5 4 3 2 1

For Warren Bennis

MENTOR, COLLEAGUE, FRIEND

Courtesies of a small and trivial character are the ones which strike deepest in the grateful and appreciating heart.

—Henry Clay, American statesman (1777–1852)

Contents

CUSTOMERS

ACTION

CHANGE

SPECIAL SECTION: YOU, ME, AND CHARLIE WILSON'S WAR

PASSION

Introduction

On July 28, 2004, I made my first blog post at tompeters.com. The topic was then Illinois state senator Barack Obama's speech to the 2004 Democratic Convention in Boston. In an apolitical post, I said that it had been one helluva speech—take it from someone who knows a good speech when he hears one. (Me.) Since then I've made over 1,700 posts, and with the help of many friends the blog has prospered—even bagging a "Top 500" designation in 2007!

On September 18, six weeks after beginning my blogging adventure, I happened by a particularly messy chain-store branch in the Natick Mall outside of Boston. I followed the visit with a spur-of-the-moment, throwaway post that I called "100 Ways to Succeed/Make Money #1": "THE CLEAN & NEAT TEAM! (TEAM TIDY?)"; I suggested that the store's blatant disarray screamed . . .

"We don't care."

I said that stores, and even accounting offices, were judged as much or more on appearance as on "substance." The appearance is a nontrivial part of the overall assessment of the "substance"—in fact, a part of the substance.

I promised that I'd proceed to supply 100 such "success tips"—God alone knows why!

I enjoyed the process, and by July 2009 we'd posted precisely 176 of the promised 100! Somewhere along the way, Bob Miller, first boss of the publisher Hyperion, and currently launching HarperStudio, ran (surfed) across the tips, got in touch with us, and said, in effect, "You've inadvertently written a book." He sent along a contract—and we signed, despite my prior vow, recorded in blood, that I'd never write another book. But, hey, why not, a few books sold, a little publicity—and no work!

Ha!

I have a very low "dissatisfaction threshold," and don't think a book is a book until it's been through about a dozen major redrafts—and this one has been no exception. I more or less sacrificed the full summer of 2009 on my glorious farm in Vermont to editing and editing and editing—and you'll see the product here. (For better or for worse.)

All of which is to say that in some respects this is not a "normal" book—or I guess it probably is, circa 2010. That is, it is derived from a blog—even if now the original is barely recognizable. Among other things, that means that the structure does not follow a tidy plotline. We have organized "stuff" in appropriate "pots," but what you see is what you get. It's a book of tips or notions or suggestions or actionable ideas, more or less as they arrived at tompeters.com. They were based on observations that flowed from my travels (mainly international these days), the news of the day, exchanges with some of the tens of thousands of people who've attended my seminars, from Bucharest to Shanghai to Tallinn, and things large and mostly "small" that have pissed me off along the way. (I argue here and elsewhere that the *only* effective source of innovation is pissed-off people! Hence, bite your tongue and cherish such misfits! I, in fact, have been tolerated—or not—along the way. Cf. "McKinsey and Me, 1974–1981"; "McKinsey and Me Part Company," circa 1981.)

Not many of these more or less "tips" are oceanic. That is, they are mostly, as the book's title suggests . . . "little BIG things." "Little BIG things" such as my reaction to the messy store—or, alternatively, a spectacularly clean bathroom, complete with several decades of family photos, at the Wagon Wheel Country Drive-in restaurant in Gill, Massachusetts. They *are* "little"—a "mere" restroom at a smallish restaurant in a wee town you've doubtless never heard of. (Applicability in Tallinn?) But they are also, indeed, BIG—including in Tallinn. That is, the restaurant's "We care so much we can taste it" or the chain store's "We don't care," "We can't be bothered" is at the heart of the BIG idea of so-called experience marketing—which in turn is the heart of "value-added" in a crowded marketplace for damn near everything damn near everywhere that insists on such value-added for survival.

In general, I am a sucker for a little, comprehensible, compelling nugget of a life experience that is representative of a BIG and Potent Idea; I prefer such an illustration to some elaborate example in a pithy tome from the Harvard Business School Press—complete with charts and graphs! (I suppose this predilection means I've traveled a long way from my engineering training, my MBA, and that McKinsey stint—in all of which complex analysis rules; something that you *can* understand is considered a less-than-powerful "strategic insight." Whoops—I think I just inadvertently explained the super-super-senior-derivates-that-defied-comprehension problem that brought you and me and the global economy to our collective knees.) But I *am*, in my passion for little stories with real people as the principal players, being consistent with my approach and fervent and guiding belief about effective enterprises first exhibited in public in 1982 in a book I cowrote with Bob Waterman called *In Search of Excellence*.

The main "takeaway" from that book, as I still see it almost three decades later, was a "simple" ("little BIG thing") assertion that was our de facto six-word motto:

"Hard is soft. Soft is hard."

Search was to a significant extent a response to the Japanese challenging American economic hegemony and beating the hell out of us in the auto market in the 1970s, based not on "a sophisticated analysis of the U.S. market" concocted by a brigade of MBAs, but . . . on offering up cars that worked. (Better quality.) So Bob and I slapped the regnant "strategy-first" mavens in the face and said that "the 'hard' numbers" were the *true* "soft stuff"—encompassing a ridiculously limited slice of reality. And such purportedly "soft" things as "quality," "people and relationships," "core values," "closeness to the customer," and, thank you Hewlett-Packard, Managing By Wandering Around, or "MBWA," were the *true* "hard stuff"—these aspects of business were not "fluff"-"soft," as disdainfully portrayed by the likes of McKinsey and the B-schools, including mighty Stanford, from which both Bob and I had graduated with an MBA. (We were also both engineers and both McKinsey partners.)

We tried our best—to, alas, I must ruefully admit, little avail.

The Enron fiasco, crafted by Harvard B-School- and McKinsey-trained Jeff Skilling, was a classic case, circa 2001, of the lingering "reality" of "numbers" over "good sense." And, God knows, the mega-crash of 2007++ was led by phony-"soft" numbers and delusional advanced math and a total lack of good sense.

Well, this book is another effort to right the ship!

In fact, an inbred and determined "back-to-basics" streak has engulfed me in the last couple or so years. In part, it's in reaction to the entirely preventable financial madness that surrounds us, but it's also, perhaps, a result of a modest pushback against the hyper-hyped-over-the-top-breathlessly-breathless "absolutely everything we know about everything has changed" air surrounding the likes of Google, iPhones, Facebook, and Twitter.

I do blog, and blog assiduously; hence, this book. And I do in fact tweet and enjoy it and find it powerful and useful as well as pleasurable—so I hardly merit a Luddite badge.

But still . . .

Oddly, the icing on the cake, the motivational engine, the final flash of re-realization about those "eternal basics" can be traced to a single, slim volume I read in 2008, at the height of the endless Vermont winter, while on vacation in New Zealand. The book, by David Stewart, is titled *The Summer of 1787*. It is a day-to-day account of the writing of the U.S. Constitution, a grand happening and a landmark in human history, which occurred during a mercilessly hot and humid summer in a hopelessly stuffy, closed-windows room in Philadelphia. (I know of what I speak when I assert that the weather was dispiriting—I grew up near neighboring Baltimore.) I underscore the heat and humidity, because it per se was one of those "little BIG things" that had an enormous impact on the final outcome.

The delegates would often break early to escape the elements, turning over the writing of some key clause to a little subcommittee that would in turn retire to a Philly pub to do their monumental (as we now see it) work. The subcommittee members rarely included grandees such as old Ben Franklin or young James Madison; instead the group likely consisted of four delegates from God knows where with God knows what qualifications (in many cases, not many qualifications) who had simply raised their hands and gotten the mostly unwanted assignment, a "little BIG" assignment, as it turned out, to shape some essential part of the workings of what has ended up becoming the most powerful nation in world history.

But it was more than the weather "basic" that shaped the outcome. Hard as it may be to swallow today, some states simply didn't bother to send delegates, not thinking the whole exercise was of much import. And the New York delegation, for example, never had a quorum present in the hall—hence never cast a single vote. Furthermore, states that did bother to come could determine the size of their contingent, and wee (then and now) Delaware showed up big time *and* sent five representatives—*and* the five were present every damn day from the opening bell to the closing bell. *And* they voted on every-damn-thing, *and* because of their numbers—5 out of just 30 on the floor on average that summer—ended up volunteering for many, many a crucial sub-committee assignment. Wee Delaware's impact on the final document is stratospheric.

There's the "little BIG thing" called "showing up," Delaware style, and then there's, um, "showing up": Yet another "mundane" but potent-beyond-measure determinant of the final document came via delegates and delegations that showed up in Philadelphia with rough drafts of parts of the proposed document in hand; for lack of better guidance (Madison's soaring rhetoric was a bit over the top for a sizable chunk of this oft ordinary gang), numerous rough drafts carried to the Convention got tidied up a bit, and became pillars of the final product.

And then there was plain-old-down-and-dirty-with-us-through-the-ages horse trading, where the toughest or most wily bargainers prevailed. To a large extent, success at *that* "eternal basic" is the reason slavery remained intact in the final document. The Northerners won the rhetoric battle—and the Southerners, South Carolinians in particular, were the tougher and more persistent and stubborn and sometimes devious horse traders.

The frequently tawdry affairs chronicled in Mr. Stewart's book made me laugh out loud at several occasions, despite the gravity of the topic; and it reminded me of the decisive role in anything, including the drafting of the U.S. Constitution, of numerous "little BIG things"—like showing up, and showing up with a draft document in tow, and then sticking around from the opening to the closing bell. And bringing the right temperament to the party: One of the most apparently powerful delegates played an inconsequential role—because he was deemed by his peers to be a "windbag" and given to "bombast"; hence, his mates refused to accept him as a member of any subcommittee. They wanted to be done and go home—and not linger, thanks to our windy forebear, in a stuffy little room in swampy Philly in August.

Economists and strategy gurus ordinarily . . . just don't get it. ("It" being this "mundane" "soft," "Philadelphia-flavor" stuff.) So I have been determined here to produce what, as subtext, emphasizes the "stuff that really matters" in getting things done—the "little BIG things."

My colleagues and I mostly expect you to read the book while sitting on the toilet. (Literally or figuratively.) That is, we hardly imagine that you'll breathlessly read what follows from start to finish—John le Carré or Alan Furst I am not. Instead, I imagine you'll look at this idea or that—and I obviously hope that a few will be compelling enough to induce you to take action, to try out one of these "little BIG things," maybe even eventually include it in your canon.

Which is hardly to suggest that because these ideas are apparently "simple"—that they are therefore "no-brainers" to incorporate in your daily affairs. For example, the day I finished off this introduction, I also presented a seminar in Manchester, England. At one point I had a lengthy exchange with a technically trained and disposed chap who ran an engineering-services company. The topic was "the power of expressed appreciation"—more specifically, saying "Thank you" with some regularity, or great regularity, which so graphically acknowledges the value of the recipient, maid or manager. Like many, many others, especially men, my engineer-leader not only doesn't say those two words often, but actually doesn't understand how to. His "how to" question to me was obviously from the heart—and a brave heart indeed to broach the personal and emotional subject in a public setting. The point is, he "got it," at least intellectually, and "got" the point of the *power* of this sort of gesture, regularized. It was a fine discussion—underscoring "little BIG," and also the fact that there is a genuine discipline, worthy of a methodical engineer's careful consideration, associated with this flavor of apparently "mundane" activity. From one "just-the-facts" engineer to another, I wish him well, and if he does enter "appreciation" into his canon, that alone will have made my 6,000-mile round-trip across the Atlantic and back worthwhile.

There are, derivative of the anecdote about my engineer colleague just mentioned, two other essential themes I want to note before whisking you on your way. First, I wish to be crystal clear about one essential aspect of the . . . "Hard is soft," "Soft is hard" . . . notion that de facto animates the entire book. Ideas like conscientiously showing appreciation are matchless signs of humanity—and the practice thereof, in my opinion, doubtless makes you a better person, a person behaving decently in a hurried and harried world. But, to the principal point of this book, such acts also result in dramatically improved organizational effectiveness—and goals more readily achieved; whether those goals involve profitability or provision of human services by nonprofits, NGOs, or government agencies. Acts of appreciation, to stick with my theme of the moment, are masterful, even peerless, ways of enthusing staff and partner and client alike, and, hence, greasing the way to rapid implementation of damn near anything. That is, "Soft is hard" is wholly pragmatic—and more often than not, effectively implemented, makes the bottom line blossom!

Second, obviously you learn to fly-fish or play the piano or build cabinets by working your butt off and valiantly attempting to master the craft. So, too, to do financial analysis or plan marketing campaigns. Well, in this book I argue that "the stuff that matters" is the likes of intensive and engaged listening and showing appreciation of the work and wisdom of others, any and all others. And I argue and fervently believe that you can *study* these full-blown disciplines and *practice* these full-blown disciplines and become, say, a full-fledged "*professional* listener." I suggest, for example, that "effective strategic listening" is a key, perhaps *the* key, to lasting, "strategic" customer relationships—and top-flight "professional" "mastery" of listening per se beats, on the power scale, quantitative marketing analysis tools pretty much every time, from the world of that little restaurant in Gill, Massachusetts, to the world of an Airbus sale to Emirates Air, or the eradication of malaria in some part of Africa.

That's my story, and I'm sticking to it. I hope you enjoy—and I hope you ponder and then work diligently on some of the "little BIG things" that overwhelmingly determine effective project implementation and career success and customer contentment and employee engagement and business profitability and the shape of the likes of the U.S. Constitution!

> A BLINDING FLASH OF THE OBVIOUS

Alas, I confess to having begun this introduction with a lie. (Not a very good start.) I said I'd begun the "success tips," as we initially called them, on September 18, 2004. That was true—that is, the tips—but the book actually began on about August 9, 1966. That's 44 years, 1 month, and 26 days ago as I write.

On August 9 I boarded a U.S. Air Force C-141 in San Bernardino County, California, and began the journey to Danang, Republic of Vietnam—there was a stop in Guam along the way. I was a U.S. Navy "combat engineer," or Seabee, to use our ID.

It was my first real job.

(Besides summer stuff, including waiting tables, for nine years in high school and college, and the like.)

This book is up close and personal—and it took all damned 44 years to write. There were those "incidents and accidents" (thank you, Paul Simon) that triggered many of the "tips" at the blog. But mostly, it is a reflection of the Seabees, the Pentagon, the White House and Office of Management and Budget, Stanford, McKinsey, my own company, decades of off-and-on research—and contact with some of the roughly 3,000,000 thoughtful-curious people who've attended my seminars in 67 countries since about 1980.

I've learned a lot of stuff. Well, maybe, maybe not. I've *seen* a lot of stuff—and perhaps learned a little along the way. For example, I've met great leaders—from 2-person companies and 200,000-person companies and government agencies and elementary schools; and I've met some, let's say, real beauts! (Both sorts abet the learning process. Here's to the jerks as well as the saints.)

Truth be known, engineering training and German bloodline notwithstanding, I'm not much of a linear thinker—so "my secret" is that I run into stuff I care like hell about, and make it into one of "Tom's passions," as my wife calls them, for a year or two or 10 or even 20. It need not fit tightly into a framework, like Michael Porter's work—it's just "stuff that's damned important that people are foolishly paying little or no attention to," according to me.

That stuff includes: Germany's Mittelstand (mid-sized companies) that often lead the world in exports; Design (!!); execution (I call it "doin' stuff—the 'missing last 98 percent' ") ("they" say I wrote the first ever Stanford dissertation on implementation—most of the faculty was busy creating the intellectual foundation for derivatives—whoops, it's the intro—hold the cynicism for now, Tom); women as leaders (more of, *lots* more of) and the opportunity associated with developing products and services tailored to women's abundant needs (world's biggest and most underserved market); scintillating customer service (I pretty much had that "space" all to myself in the mid-1980s, believe it or not—"everybody" was doing quality, I was doing service); patient safety (grappling with a monster in the closet); and, always, always, always, the bedrock beneath every iota of my work, "people first, people second, people third, people ad infinitum" (still news—do you really think Ken Lewis at Bank of America gave two hoots about his staff? Well, maybe two, but sure as hell not three).

I lied again, at the beginning of *this* riff. "It" didn't start in Danang—it started in Severna Park, Maryland, in about 1946—that makes "all this" *63* years in the making. My Virginia-born mom was a stickler's stickler on the subject of manners. (You know, that Southern thing!) I bridled, naturally, but in these last 40+ years I've learned just how far a "thank you" and a "yes, sir" and a "yes, ma'am" can take you—at age 67, I still "yes, sir/ma'am" 19-year-old 7-Eleven clerks in inner cities. (You'll see a helluva lot in this book about civility and thoughtfulness and manners—it was George Washington's forte and "competitive advantage," and it's worked for me in far, far, far more humble settings.)

Manny Garcia, Burger King's top franchisee at the time, attended a Young Presidents' Organization seminar of mine in the mid-1980s. At wrap-up time, he said it was great, his best seminar ever, in fact, but he added that he'd learned nothing new. Instead he called it an all-important "blinding flash of the obvious."

I *loved* that.

I *love* that.

Well, here goes. You're going to get 63 years' worth of my experience, starting with Mom Peters's blasts from the Chesapeake past (and could she blast!), from my fourth birthday on, lessons from my bosses and sailors and U.S. Marine Corps customers during two Vietnam tours, and the insights of those three million people I've hung out with in my more or less three thousand seminars in Siberia and Estonia and India and China and Omaha and Oman and York, Pennsylvania.

Yup, here it comes—stuff I've long, long, long been itching to say.

Yup, and almost all of it is as obvious as the end of your or Manny Garcia's nose.

Enjoy the ride.

The Little BIG Things

1. 2. 3. 4. 5. 6. 7. 8. 9. 10. 11. 12. 13. 14. 15. 16. 17. 18. 19. 20. 21. 22. 23. 24. 25. 26. 27. 28. 29. 30. 31. 32. 33. 34. 35. 36. 37. 38. 39. 40. 41. 42. 43. 44. 45. 46. 47. 48. 49. 50. 51. 52. 53. 54. 55. 56. 57. 58. 59. 60. 61. 62. 63. 64. 65. 66. 67. 68. 69. 70. 71. 72. 73. 74. 75. 76. 77. 78. 79. 80. 81. 82. 83. 84. 85. 86. 87. 88. 89. 90. 91. 92. 93. 94. 95. 96. 97. 98. 99. 100. 101. 102. 103. 104. 105. 106. 107. 108. 109. 110. 111. 112. 113. 114. 115. 116. 117. 118. 119. 120. 121. 122. 123. 124. 125. 126. 127. 128. 129. 130. 131. 132. 133. 134. 135. 136. 137. 138. 139. 140. 141. 142. 143. 144. 145. 146. 147. 148. 149. 150. 151. 152. 153. 154. 155. 156. 157. 158. 159. 160. 161. 162. 163.

Little

1. It's All About the Restrooms!

I usually fly to my next seminar in the Great City of Wherever from Logan Airport. The trip from Tinmouth, Vermont, to Boston passes through Gill, Massachusetts. It's exactly halfway, the 87-mile mark on my odometer—hence, the perfect place for a pit stop. With choices aplenty, I am nonetheless firm in my habit of stopping at the Wagon Wheel Country Drive-in. It's, in fact, a smallish coffee shop–diner. The food, including the fresh muffins that are about a foot away as you enter (typically at dawn's early light, in my case), is boffo. The attitude is boffo, too. But make no mistake, my custom is well and truly earned, three or four times a month by . . .

the restroom!

It's clean-to-sparkling. (Come to think of it, despite the invariably crowded shop, I have never seen even the tiniest scrap of paper on the bathroom floor.) Fresh flowers are the norm. And best of all, there is a great multigenerational collection of family pictures that cover all the walls; rushed though I typically am, I invariably spend an extra minute examining one or another, smiling at a group photo from a local company dinner, or some such, circa 1930 I'd guess.

To me, a clean and attractive and even imaginative loo is the best . . .

"We care"

sign in a retail shop or professional office—and (ATTENTION! ATTENTION! ATTENTION!) it goes double when it comes to *employee* restrooms!

So . . .
Step #1: Mind the restrooms!

> ## ▶ NOT A "TRIVIAL PURSUIT"

Today (fall 2009 as I drafted this), the recession's tentacles continue to cling. If possible, an abiding obsession with "the basics" beat "brilliance" more handily than ever, and I can't think of a better place to start than in the loo.

(Or a better person to put in the crosshairs than the owner or manager! Reverting to my Navy days: Owner! Owner! Man your swab!)

To do, more generally: I suggest that you devote most of your "morning meeting" or "weekly phone call" (or whatever) to the "little" things—from clean restrooms to deliveries made or missed to thank-you calls to a customer for her business after an order ships to flowers acknowledging "lower-level" staff excellence.

Keep on each other! How about a designated nag:

"Little Things" Lunatic.

Or: **"Tiny Touch" Maniac-in-Chief.**

(Micro-Maestro.)

(Wizard of Wee.)

(Whatever.)

And be very very **very** liberal with the public kudos for those who go an extra *millimeter* to do a "trivial" job especially well.

2. "Small Stuff" Matters. A Lot!

Fix your voice message now!

"If you claim to be different from your competition, a GREAT place to start is your recorded message."
—Jeffrey Gitomer, *The Little Red Book of Selling*

What other little things might you do today to make a **big difference** in your business?

Action item: *At* . . . **every** . . . *weekly team meeting, have each and* . . . **every** . . . *honored invitee (that is, employee upon whom Excellence wholly depends) bring in and present "a little thing" that could become a Big Thing.*

Select at least one.
Implement.
Now.*

(*This item is very, very short—and I hope very, very sweet. And I know very, very doable. Hence . . . **zero** . . . excuses for not putting it into effect. Now.)

3. Flower Power!

(1) Put flowers all over the place (!) in the office—especially in winter and especially in places like Boston or Minneapolis or Fargo or New York or London or Bucharest. Or Vermont (!).

(2) **Let it be known that the "flower budget" is unlimited.**

(3) In the next **24 hours,** send flowers to . . . **four people** . . . who have supported you inside or outside your organization—including, and this is mandatory, at least one person in another function.*

*I am simply, unabashedly insane about enhancing cross-functional communication, arguably business's issue #1, via the "soft arts," such as sending flowers, not just, or mainly, via sexy software!! (Be prepared for me to be repetitive on this topic, coming at it from any angle I can conjure up.)

4. Master the Fine Art of . . . Nudgery!

My mostly dormant but longtime interest in "little things" with enormous impact was rekindled after the recent publication of *Nudge* (Richard H. Thaler and Cass R. Sunstein), *Sway* (Ori Brafman and Rom Brafman), and a couple of other like books. I had studied their principal antecedent, the work of Nobel laureate Daniel Kahneman and his partner Amos Tversky, in the mid-1970s. They unearthed dimension after measurable dimension of human "irrationality" in a world where the myth of rationality and the likes of hyperrational "economic man" held center stage—and damn near every other part of the stage as well. Kahneman and Tversky again and again observed dramatic human overreaction to some tiny thing—and underreaction to some big thing. It was especially eye-opening to an engineer—me.

The central idea of the books just enumerated—and this book—is powerfully simple (as well as simply powerful): "Little" things can make enormous—**staggering**—BIG differences in situations of the utmost importance; situations that can, in health care, for example, save thousands and thousands of lives. Consider this tiny sampling of examples that I've collected from hither and thither in my wanderings:

- Put geologists (rock guys) and geophysicists (computer guys), typically at war over dramatically different views of the world, in the same room, and . . . **find more oil** . . . than your "separate room" competitors.

- Stanford University works to increase significantly the number of multidisciplinary research grants that it receives. That's the basis for solving the world's most important problems, the president contends. In fact, he calls it nothing less than the linchpin of that Great University's future. One **(big)** part of the answer to this big issue is a "mere" building, a research building wholly and exclusively dedicated to multidisciplinary research—put the whole, diverse team cheek by jowl and watch the miracles of collaboration pour forth!

- People whose offices are more than 100 feet apart might as well be 100 miles apart, in terms of frequency of direct communication.

- Walmart increases shopping cart size—and sales of big items (like microwave ovens) go up . . . **50 percent!**

- Use a round table instead of a square table—and the percentage of people contributing to a conversation leaps up!

- If the serving plate is more than **6.5 feet** from the dining room table, the number of "seconds" goes down **63 percent,** compared with leaving the serving plates on the table.

- Want to make a program "strategic"? Put it at the top of *every* agenda. Make asking about "it" your *first* question in *every* conversation. Put the person in charge in an office next to the Big Boss. Etc. (Talk about powerful messages!)

- Want to save lives? Issue everyone who checks into the hospital **compression stockings** to reduce the risk of deep vein thrombosis. Doing so could save **10,000 lives** in the United Kingdom alone.
- Want to save lives? One survivor of 9/11 had walked downstairs from a top floor—about once a month. Such "trivial" "drills" could have saved innumerable lives.
- Frito-Lay adds new bag sizes, suffers no cannibalization of current offerings, and ends up creating totally new (and enormous) markets—racking up, eventually, billions in revenues.
- Get rid of wastebaskets under desks—recycling leaps up.
- Simply put hand-sanitizer dispensers all over a dorm, with no signs asking students to use them—and the number of sick days and missed classes per student falls **20 percent.** (University of Colorado/Boulder.)
- Let patients see greenery through their windows—and their average post-op stay duration drops 20 percent.
- Go *white* (that is, paint roofs, roads, etc., white)—and reduce CO_2 emissions by 44 billion tons.
- **"Broken windows":** Clean up trash, fix broken windows, stop miscreants for trivial offenses such as loitering or having open alcohol containers—and increase neighborhood safety dramatically. (Using this approach, Chief Bratton and Mayor Giuliani had spectacular success on a pretty big stage—New York City.)
- If signing up to join a 401(k)-style tax-enhanced savings plan is the *default option* in a computer-based sign-up process . . . **86** percent of people will "join." If they must "opt *in*" . . . just **45** percent choose to join. (This is a staggering, almost two-to-one difference—*in a decision of enormous personal significance*—and it's based on a "trivial" difference in the design of the process.)

The preceding examples are merely indicative of the sorts of things (of which there are, more or less, a gazillion) that one can concentrate on. **The toughest part of this message is that to do much with the idea you need an "attitude."** An attitude that this sort of thing *can* work, and a willingness to screw around and screw around and then screw around until you get "it" (whatever is under consideration) more or less "right"—and then keep fine-tuning, eternally.

❯ LET ME NUDGE YOU . . . TO BE A NUDGE

Make Nudgery the centerpiece of your change strategy in almost all, if not all, circumstances. (The world may become your oyster—even if you are a junior oysterman.)

Here's the good news about the Art of Nudgery:

(1) Amenable to rapid experimentation/failure.

(2) Quick to implement/Quick to roll out.

(3) Inexpensive to implement/Inexpensive to roll out.

(4) Huge multiplier.

(5) An "Attitude" required—not a one-off "program."

(6) Does **not,** by and large, require a "power position" from which to launch experiments—this is mostly "invisible stuff," below the radar, that most people don't care about on the front end.

Consider:

Study* the Art of Nudgery!

Practice* Nudgery!

Become a **Professional*** Nudgist!

(*As always, "even with" these so-called small things, the words *"study," "practice," and "professional"* are key, the sine qua non, without which there is . . . nothing. Thus, this not so little idea—nudgery—becomes no less than a true "calling.")

1. 2. 3. 4. **5. 6. 7. 8.** 9. 10. 11. 12. 13. 14.
15. 16. 17. 18. 19. 20. 21. 22. 23. 24. 25.
26. 27. 28. 29. 30. 31. 32. 33. 34. 35.
36. 37. 38. 39. 40. 41. 42. 43. 44. 45.
46. 47. 48. 49. 50. 51. 52. 53. 54. 55. 56.
57. 58. 59. 60. 61. 62. 63. 64. 65. 66. 67.
68. 69. 70. 71. 72. 73. 74. 75. 76. 77. 78.
79. 80. 81. 82. 83. 84. 85. 86. 87. 88.
89. 90. 91. 92. 93. 94. 95. 96. 97. 98. 99.
100. 101. 102. 103. 104. 105. 106. 107.
108. 109. 110. 111. 112. 113. 114. 115.
116. 117. 118. 119. 120. 121. 122. 123.
124. 125. 126. 127. 128. 129. 130. 131.
132. 133. 134. 135. 136. 137. 138. 139.
140. 141. 142. 143. 144. 145. 146. 147.
148. 149. 150. 151. 152. 153. 154. 155.
156. 157. 158. 159. 160. 161. 162. 163.

Excellence

5. If Not Excellence, What? If Not Excellence Now, When?

I'm here in this place on your palpable or electronic bookshelf because of . . .

Excellence.

That is, back in 1982 I cowrote a book called *In Search of Excellence*.

A lot of people were kind enough to buy it.

And I've been "talking Excellence" for the subsequent 25+ years.

(NB: Never write the word *Excellence* without capitalizing the **"E."** This I command—not that I have the power to do so.)

I love "Excellence"—and not just because it paid for the farm I bought in Vermont in 1984.

I love EXCELLENCE—truth is, I think you should capitalize *all* the letters—because Excellence is soooooo Cool. (Cap "C.")

It's so *cool*.

It's so *heartening*.

It's so *soaring* & *inspiring*.

It's so worth *getting out of bed* for.

(Even in the winter in Vermont.)

It's so *healthy.*

It's so *helpful* to others.

(The *striving* more than the arriving.)

It's so good for your *morale*—even on the shittiest of days.

(*Especially* on the shittiest of days.)

And, over the mid to long term (and in the short term, too), it *turns on your customers* and is . . . **profitable as hell.**

Professional driver Bill Young says:

"Strive for excellence. Ignore success."

Amen. (Love it!)

(Excellence is a "way of life," a "way of being"—not a steady state to be "achieved.")

Anon* says:

"Excellence can be obtained if you:

". . . care more *than others think is wise;*

". . . risk more *than others think is safe;*

". . . dream more *than others think is practical;*

". . . expect more *than others think is possible.*"

(*Posted by K. Sriram at tompeters.com.)

Amen. (Love it!)

Your "takeaway": Asked how long it took to achieve Excellence, IBM's legendary boss Tom Watson is said to have answered more or less as follows: **"A minute.** *You 'achieve' Excellence* by promising yourself right now that you'll never again knowingly do anything that's* not Excellent—*regardless of any pressure to do otherwise by any boss or situation.*"

(*I don't really know whether or not Watson insisted on the cap **"E"**—from what I've learned, I wouldn't be surprised. I *do* know he loved the word.)

TP: Amen. (Love it!)

Regardless of the location (China, Lithuania, Miami) or industry (health care, fast food), I title all of my presentations:

Excellence. Always.
If Not Excellence, What?
If Not Excellence Now, When?

I *hate* the word "*motivation*"—surely I've indicated that before.

I hate it because the idea of *me* "motivating" *you* is so outrageous—and arrogant.

To state the obvious . . .

. . . only *you* can motivate *you*.

What I *can* do (as boss or even "guru") is to Paint Portraits of Excellence.

And then we can imagine ourselves in those portraits—in Pursuit of Excellence.

"Pursuit": Excellence, I repeat, is not a "goal"—it's the way we live, who we are.

EXCELLENCE. Always.
If Not EXCELLENCE, What?
If Not EXCELLENCE Now, When?

› WHEN THE GOING GETS TOUGH . . . GET EXCELLENT

Excellence in (Today's) Tough Times.
Now.
More Than Ever.
In tough times, the pressure is such that there is often a temptation to cut corners.

Think "Excellence."
Don't cut corners.

In tough times, your morale is often shot, and it's hard to get out of bed.

Think "Excellence."
Set the alarm a half hour earlier than usual.

In tough times, it's really tough to be a boss.

Think "Excellence."
It *is* tough to be a boss in tough times—but tough times are the Ultimate Test for you and your team— EXCELLENCE is a more worthy aspiration than ever before.

6. Whither Excellence? Or: Asleep at the Wheel.

One of our best business analysts, James B. Stewart, offered this "simple" commentary on the precipitous decline of General Motors (in the June 3, 2009, *Wall Street Journal*):

"It has been long in coming, this slow death of what was once the greatest and biggest corporation in the world. The myriad causes of its demise have been thoroughly chronicled, but to my mind one stands out: The custodians of GM simply gave up trying to build the best cars in the world. **To accommodate a host of competing interests, from shareholders to bondholders to labor, they repeatedly compromised on excellence.** Once sacrificed, that reputation has proved impossible to recapture. . . . Can anyone say GM builds the best cars in any category?" (My emphasis. Note that the "e" in "excellence" is **not** capitalized.)

And you?

Try this: Consider the three (or two or five) meetings you've been to *today*. Consider the three project milestones just buttoned up—or the three on the near horizon:

Has the word "Excellence" *per se* been used as a basis for evaluating your actions? Could you personally call the outcome of each meeting or the nature of the milestone/s achieved "Excellent"?

Key idea: The "Excellence Standard" is not about Grand Outcomes. In Zenlike terms, all we have is today. If the day's work cannot be assessed as Excellent, then the oceanic overall goal of Excellence has not been advanced. Period.

That is, the "Excellence Watch" must be a daily affair—or you simply are not serious about the overall . . .

Aspiration of Excellence.

7. "Quality": You'll Know It When You See It.

Six Sigma is "good stuff"—great stuff. No doubt whatsoever about it. From a more encompassing standpoint, the quality "movement" added billions upon billions of dollars to the bottom line in the USA alone.

Only . . . Whoops! Better car quality—which we surely got from GM and Ford—was supposed to have saved the U.S. automotive industry from the Japanese automotive onslaught.

As I said: Whoops.

Am I suggesting you scrap traditional quality programs? Hardly! But "quality," as it's commonly understood, is Six Sigma–flavored and readily measured. And there's more to it. Much more. I believe that "quality," like "Excellence," is primarily one of those . . . **"I'll know it when I see it"** . . . words. So quantify quality all you want (please do, please do!) . . . but don't forget that quality is equally—nay, primarily—determined by something that is elusive, mysterious, emotional, indefinable. *And* . . . in the eye of the beholder.

Get smart!

Give the "soft side" of quality the respect it deserves!

8. Excellence Is . . .

Excellence is the best defense.

Excellence is the best offense.

Excellence is the answer in good times.

Excellence is the answer in tough times.

(Excellence is the answer in tough times.)

Excellence is about the big things.

Excellence is about the little things.

Excellence is a relationship.

Excellence is a philosophy.

Excellence is an aspiration.

Excellence is immoderate.

Excellence is a pragmatic standard.

Excellence is execution.

Excellence is selfish.

Excellence is selfless.

Excellence is what keeps you awake.

Excellence is what lets you sleep well.

Excellence is a moving target.

Excellence is that which . . . knows no bounds.

EXCELLENCE. Always.

If not EXCELLENCE, what?

If not EXCELLENCE now, when?

Guru Gaffes

I contend that something is badly out of whack. Consider the world of "business gurus" (myself included, to be sure) and their-*our* obsessions versus "the rest of us" and "life-in-the-real-world":

Guru Focus (GF): Big companies and attendant first-order, industry-redefining strategic issues.

> **Real World (RW): Most of us, still, in 2010 don't work for Big Companies; we labor in "SMEs," Small and Medium-sized Enterprises. (Or the likes of government agencies.) And if we *are* in a big company or agency, most of our focus is the 17-person department in which we labor. (As to "SMEs," Germany has been, ahead of China, the planet's #1 exporter, thanks mainly to focused, high-end, middle-sized companies, the "Mittelstand" enterprises.)**

GF: Public corporations.

> **RW: Most of us work in privately owned companies. (Or in those government agencies.)**

GF: Cool industries.

> **RW: Most of us aren't in "Cool" industries, we do pretty ordinary stuff—like my pal, Larry Janesky, who makes a buck, and then another ($60 million, actually), creating "dry basements" that are free of toxic mold and can be used as a spare room or for a playroom or storing anything and everything.**

GF: "Excellence" is reserved for GE and GE and GE (maybe Google and Apple, too).

> **RW: "Excellence," bar none, is the fabulous, friendly, informative, instantly responsive pharmacy next door that takes on docs and insurance companies with vigor and usually victory. (Gary Drug Company on Charles Street in Boston, for me.)**

GF: Boss-less, flat, friction-free, self-defining organizational settings.

RW: Most of us have "bosses." Most of us are assigned tasks.

GF: "Getting ahead" means becoming a "Brand You," in a world where what our peers think of us is more important than the boss's evaluation.

RW: While "lifetime employment" may indeed be D.O.A., at any point in time most of us still must cater to our bosses to get ahead.

"Most of us try to use everyday language such as 'the way we make a buck' (instead of 'business model'), 'let's grow this sucker' (not 'Is it scalable?'), 'hire good people and treat 'em well and give 'em a chance to shine and thank 'em for the stuff they do' (rather than 'strategic talent management'), 'bust our asses to keep our customers happy and keep 'em coming back' (instead of 'customer-retention management'), and 'share the stuff you learn with everybody ASAP, don't hoard it' (rather than 'executing a knowledge-management paradigm')."

GF: "Cover boy" CEOs with G4s, trophy wives, and the kids from all three marriages in prep schools with tuitions starting at $70K.

RW: Most of us work for government agencies or in schools or fire departments, or in private companies perhaps run by the "millionaire next door," who owns two suits, a 2006 Lexus, stops in the coffee shop on the way to work, and sends his kids to public school or the local private school.

GF: New "virtual organization" forms of doing business; workplaces with hierarchy are "so yesterday."

RW: Most of us work amid a rather clear "hierarchy" as depicted on a standard organization chart. (Though there are probably a few less layers than there were a few years ago.)

GF: Creative right-brain weirdos, "with it" in these odd times.

RW: The majority of us are not "New Age creatives," but are occasionally quite clever . . . and pretty good at "blocking and tackling" in order to "get done what needs to be done."

GF: The immediate threat, to millions upon millions, of being "outsourced."

RW: Most of us aren't especially threatened by the prospect of having our jobs outsourced to India or China or Romania.

GF: Global enterprises "playing in the big league," in a "flat world."

RW: Many (most) of us are only marginally affected by globalization, and our firms don't sell more than a modest share of their products or, especially, services beyond our national borders. (The primary reach of the 18-person accountancy in a midsized city of 84,000 is perhaps three miles.)

GF: A world where "the Web is everything, changes everything."

RW: Most of us haven't had our world turned anything like "upside down" by the Web, though the Web has surely had a significant impact. (We communicate with the plumber by BlackBerry email from our car, but he's still five hours late!)

GF: Our ability to be in instant communication with anyone, anywhere.

RW: We use email, but still practice MBWA—Managing By Wandering Around—if our head's screwed on right.

GF: An encompassing IS-IT strategy, with everything wired to everything else.

RW: While integrating IS is very important, most of us muddle through, trying to ensure that the IT-enhanced bits (the frontline subsystems) are marvels of simplicity that deliver the goods for those frontline folks and their internal-external customers.

GF: Strategic planners and CEOs desperately seeking "blue oceans."

RW: Most of us don't spend much or any of our day making grand plans. Never have. Never will.

"Many (most) of us are only marginally affected by globalization, and our firms don't sell more than a modest share of their products or, especially, services beyond our national borders. (The primary reach of the 18-person accountancy in a midsized city of 84,000 is perhaps three miles.)"

GF: Thinking "outside the box," of course.

RW: Most of us obsess on "doing," pretty much inside the box. (There are enough damn problems *in* the box—pissed-off customers of long standing, etc.)

GF: Complex "systemic change."

RW: Most of us believe in and spend our time doing on-the-cheap, rapid experimentation, picking off the "low-hanging fruit," muddling our way through to big change.

GF: Imposing words-phrases such as "business models," "scalable," "strategic talent management," "customer-retention management," and "knowledge-management paradigm."

RW: Most of us try to use everyday language such as "the way we make a buck" (instead of "business model"), "let's grow this sucker" (not "Is it scalable?"), "hire good people and treat 'em well and give 'em a chance to shine and thank 'em for the stuff they do" (rather than "strategic talent management"), "bust our asses to keep our customers happy and keep 'em coming back" (instead of "customer-retention management"), and "share the stuff you learn with everybody ASAP, don't hoard it" (rather than "executing a knowledge-management paradigm").

GF: Best database + sexiest algorithms win in our customer-centric enterprise.

RW: Most of us spend our time on "trivial" acts of relationship building with customers, suppliers, leaders in our community, etc.

GF: The relentless pursuit of "synergies."

RW: Most of us focus, focus, focus in order to stand a chance of succeeding in the marketplace. (Those astounding German Mittelstand companies again, or Larry Janesky, the dry-basement guy.)

GF: Marketing sleight of hand!

RW: Sales! Sales! Sales!

GF: Put the customer first!

RW: Put the frontline employee and the frontline manager co-first! (In order to maximize the odds of repeat business driven by turned-on employees.)

GF: Acquisitions and mergers aimed at expanding our "reach" and "market penetration" and "market share" amid a zero-sum game, thus reducing risk, courtesy of a "diverse" portfolio and smothering ("killing") the competition.

RW: Play from our strengths, work like hell to enhance those strengths, and survive-thrive via "organic" growth and delivering "stuff that works" and executing very, very, very well.

GF: Totally "new rules for a new game," dramatic new "management tools" that "change everything."

RW: Most of us are learning new things, but nothing that's particularly "revolutionary" as we labor mightily (full-time) "just" to "get stuff done," improve relationships, find good folks and keep 'em by showing appreciation and respect, and providing opportunities to get ahead.

GF: A fetish for the diabolically clever.

RW: Most of us know that "relentless" pounding and pounding and pounding, and then pounding some more, on those Golden Basics wins.

GF: Built to last.

RW: Most of us muddle through, trying to make it to the end of the week while keeping our customers content—and if it lasts, Thank you, God.

GF: "Changing demographics," "the new Gen X world," as many discrete market segments as there are customers.

RW (I wish): Our primary customers (85 percent of the time) are women—find the right team (lotsa and lotsa more women in senior management) and go for it. We also, to make a buck or fifty, oughta aim more at boomers and "geezers" (who collectively have pretty much all the dough), and less on callow, so-called trendsetter youth, mostly penniless.

The biggest implication of "all this," which is the thrust of this book, is that if you are . . . *really really really really really really really really really good* . . . at "basic stuff" like taking care of people, listening intently, overreacting to even the tiniest screw-up, and apologizing like crazy when you make even a wee boo-boo, a lot of good things will come your way—in good times and bad!

Which is not to denigrate the wild and wacky stuff—but, rather, to put it in perspective.

1. 2. 3. 4. 5. 6. 7. 8. **9. 10. 11.** 12. 13. 14.
15. 16. 17. 18. 19. 20. 21. 22. 23. 24. 25.
26. 27. 28. 29. 30. 31. 32. 33. 34. 35.
36. 37. 38. 39. 40. 41. 42. 43. 44. 45.
46. 47. 48. 49. 50. 51. 52. 53. 54. 55. 56.
57. 58. 59. 60. 61. 62. 63. 64. 65. 66. 67.
68. 69. 70. 71. 72. 73. 74. 75. 76. 77. 78.
79. 80. 81. 82. 83. 84. 85. 86. 87. 88.
89. 90. 91. 92. 93. 94. 95. 96. 97. 98. 99.
100. 101. 102. 103. 104. 105. 106. 107.
108. 109. 110. 111. 112. 113. 114. 115.
116. 117. 118. 119. 120. 121. 122. 123.
124. 125. 126. 127. 128. 129. 130. 131.
132. 133. 134. 135. 136. 137. 138. 139.
140. 141. 142. 143. 144. 145. 146. 147.
148. 149. 150. 151. 152. 153. 154. 155.
156. 157. 158. 159. 160. 161. 162. 163.

Crisis

9. That Which Goeth Up and Up and Up Doth Not Goeth More Up and More Up and More Up Forever and Ever and Ever.

"It ain't what you don't know that gets you into trouble.
It's what you know for sure that just ain't so."
—Mark Twain

"As I see it, the economics profession went astray because economists, as a group, mistook beauty, clad in impressive-looking mathematics, for truth."
—Paul Krugman, economist, Nobel laureate

"I can calculate the motion of heavenly bodies, but not the madness of people."
—Sir Isaac Newton

As I write (in April 2009), there's damn little to smile about in the world financial markets. And yet . . . it's hard not to giggle, in a perverse way, at all that's transpired in the last couple of years.

Just watching these Wizards of Wall Street (the ones with the 168 IQs who had the likes of Paul Simon and the Jonas Brothers performing at their kids' kindergarten graduation parties) pissing on themselves and on one another is such an incredible spectacle.

First, pissing on themselves: Former Citigroup chieftain John Reed celebrated the 10th anniversary of the mega-mega-mega Citicorp-Travelers merger he crafted by calling the deal a "mistake." As Reed told the *Financial Times* in April 2008: "The stockholders have not benefited, the employees certainly have not benefited and I don't think the customers have benefited." (Thanks, Johnny boy.) Mr. Reed and his partner in crime, Travelers honcho Sandy Weill, on the other hand, BENEFITED—all caps.

Then, pissing on each other: Weill, after deposing Reed and hand-picking Chuck Prince to take the helm of Citigroup, later blamed the mess on Prince's "poor management" rather than questioning the recipe for disaster he and Reed cooked up—a recipe that can be boiled down to: "Huge-er is better than merely huge." (Prince "retired" in 2007 but still walked away with BIG BENEFITS—all caps.) Speaking of partners in crime, the *Financial Times* also reported in April 2008 that former Merrill Lynch boss of bosses David Komansky had called the work of his chosen successor, Stan O'Neal, "absolutely criminal." Not a whole lot of restraint, or even vaguely adult behavior, there.

But as I said, it's all rather amusing, or would be, absent the global economic chaos that will bequeath a hangover that'll last a decade. (Or two. Or . . .) As an avowed enemy of almost any giant consolidation in the name of either "synergy" or the provision of "one-stop shopping," I am drowning in smugness. Also, watching these geniuses turn out to have feet of maggot-infested barnyard shit (I live on a farm) is also chortle-worthy to one who has always had trouble with the whole Superstar-CEO/Leader-as-God phenomenon.

There's such a bizarre element of "obviousness" to this fiasco that it makes me think we need some new ground rules for business:

(1) That which goeth up and up and up doth not always goeth more up and more up and more up forever and ever and ever. (You might want to write that one down!)

(2) Thou shalt not (even if thou art an economist or mathematician) buy or sell the derivatives-of-derivatives-of-derivatives if you have no idea how to value said derivatives-of-derivatives-of-derivatives.

(3) Thou shalt not believe in false prophets who proclaim that undecipherable financial instruments can banish risk from the face of the earth "forever and ever and ever and ever, Amen."

(4) Thou shalt not offer to lend money for a home to a person who showeth no proof of income, credit, or employment.

(5) If thou art tempted to lend money for a home to a person who showeth no proof of income, credit, or employment, thou must dial down the greed meter immediately. (Of course, history and the biosciences alike tell us that the greed meter is *never* dialed down in the slightest—never has been, never will be.)

(6) My favorite: In 9 cases out of 8, big mergers . . . sucketh. In 9 cases out of 7, they provideth very little imagined "synergistic value" and destroyeth lots and lots (and more lots and more lots) of "actual value" along the way—along with thousands upon thousands of jobs.

(7) Optimism, even "unwarranted" optimism, is of the utmost value for those pursuing innovation. I lived in Silicon Valley for 30 years, and if there hadn't been "unwarranted" optimism, there'd have been no Apple or Intel. But you darn well ought to have a pessimist in the office next door, or an older mentor, for whom you have the utmost respect.

> ## IT "BOGLES" THE MIND

Vanguard Mutual Fund Group founder John Bogle wrote the best "business" (LIFE!) book I've read in years. The (BRILLIANT!) title: *Enough.* Rather than expend several paragraphs summarizing the short-but-very-sweet-and-very-lucid tome, I'll let some chapter titles do the work for me:

"Too Much Cost, Not Enough Value"

"Too Much Speculation, Not Enough Investment"

"Too Much Complexity, Not Enough Simplicity"

"Too Much Counting, Not Enough Trust"

"Too Much Business Conduct, Not Enough Professional Conduct"

"Too Much Salesmanship, Not Enough Stewardship"

"Too Much Focus on Things, Not Enough Focus on Commitment"

"Too Many Twenty-First-Century Values, Not Enough Eighteenth-Century Values"

"Too Much 'Success,' Not Enough Character"

For the book's overarching theme, Mr. Bogle begins with this vignette:

"At a party given by a billionaire on Shelter Island, Kurt Vonnegut informs his pal, Joseph Heller, that their host, a hedge fund manager, had made more money in a single day than Heller had earned from his wildly popular novel *Catch-22* over its whole history. Heller responds, 'Yes, but I have something he will never have . . . **enough.**' "

Enough said.

10. Good Things (Especially in Bad Times?) Come in Threes.

Although historians will long debate the initial response to the financial market's collapse, an article in the *Washington Post* on September 19, 2008, "In Crucible of Crisis, Paulson, Bernanke, Geithner

Forge a Committee of Three," offers a fascinating analysis of Hank Paulson's management style:

> [Former Treasury Secretary John Snow] closed the Treasury's monitoring room, where staff members keep an eye on global stock, bond and currency markets around the clock, to save money. Snow's contact with Bernanke, then in office just six months, was mainly limited to formal weekly breakfasts. There was little communication between Snow and Geithner.
>
> That changed rapidly with Paulson. A creature of the financial markets prone to firing off rapid phone calls to any potential source of information, he took to calling Geithner and Bernanke at all times of day, to bounce ideas off them or discuss the latest trouble spot in the markets.
>
> "Overcommunication never hurts," Paulson said. "If it is something significant, I would just pick up the phone and call Ben. One of the things I do is I create an atmosphere where I am so direct and so open and collaborative with people I trust that it brings out the same in them."

(NB: In the power-mad D.C. environment, such casual back-and-forth is essentially unprecedented. This apparently innocuous sentence—*"If it is something significant, I would just pick up the phone and call Ben."*—is as BIG a "little" thing as one could imagine.)

Assessment of final outcome notwithstanding, this analysis—blended with my own observations over the years—yields a few tentative lessons on how to deal with emergencies:

(1) Concoct an *authoritarian* control group that numbers three. (Yes, good things, or at least *useful* things, do come in threes.) I am anti-authoritarian to the core, but there are rare exceptions to that rule.

(2) "Over" communicate. **(!!!)**

(3) **Drop all pretense of formality.**

(4) Park egos at the door. *(Boot egoists from the inner circle if they don't shape up very quickly.)*

(5) Ensure that the group is diverse. (The *Post* points out that the troika of Paulson, Bernanke, and Geithner consists of a Wall Street titan, an academic, and a career civil servant.)

(6) Ensure that each member of the group has a Towering Competence—and is perceived as having such.

(7) Foster a predilection for . . . **rapid trial and error**. First, that creates the perception that "they aren't dilly-dallyin'"—motion matters. Second, the cure is anything but sure—so one must get moving if for no other reason than to see what happens when the system is perturbed. Third, there must be a willingness to admit error and stop a failed experiment ASAP—rather than holding on as a way of not admitting the experiment was a bust.

(8) Each member must have widespread **credibility.** (Snow had virtually no Wall Street credibility and would have been impotent in the fall of 2008.)

(9) Also "over" communicate beyond the group.

Summary message:

Communicate.
Communicate.
Communicate.
Communicate.
Communicate.
Communicate.
Communicate.
Communicate.

11. Get China on Your Mind! Get India on Your Mind!

Study up on China. (And India.)

Read books.

Troll the Web.

Talk to people.

Initiate a study group.

Ponder China. (And India.)

Visit China. (And India.)

Make "meditation" about China (and India) part of your day's ritual.

This is not a "call to action" so much as a "call to awareness." Ignorance about China (or about India) is . . . **simply . . . not acceptable.**

Not acceptable . . . regardless of Age.

Not acceptable . . . regardless of Profession.

Not acceptable . . . regardless of Industry.

Not acceptable . . . regardless of Company size.

Not acceptable . . . regardless of Education.

Not acceptable . . . regardless of Wage level.

Not acceptable . . . regardless of Any Other Damn Variable You Can Name.

Hint (per me):

China is not a "problem."

China is not a "threat."

China may or may not be an "opportunity."

China (India) is a . . . **Reality** . . . a Part of Our Lives. (Period.)

Act accordingly.

1. 2. 3. 4. 5. 6. 7. 8. 9. 10. 11. **12. 13. 14.**
15. 16. 17. 18. 19. 20. 21. 22. 23. 24. 25.
26. 27. 28. 29. 30. 31. 32. 33. 34. 35.
36. 37. 38. 39. 40. 41. 42. 43. 44. 45.
46. 47. 48. 49. 50. 51. 52. 53. 54. 55. 56.
57. 58. 59. 60. 61. 62. 63. 64. 65. 66. 67.
68. 69. 70. 71. 72. 73. 74. 75. 76. 77. 78.
79. 80. 81. 82. 83. 84. 85. 86. 87. 88.
89. 90. 91. 92. 93. 94. 95. 96. 97. 98. 99.
100. 101. 102. 103. 104. 105. 106. 107.
108. 109. 110. 111. 112. 113. 114. 115.
116. 117. 118. 119. 120. 121. 122. 123.
124. 125. 126. 127. 128. 129. 130. 131.
132. 133. 134. 135. 136. 137. 138. 139.
140. 141. 142. 143. 144. 145. 146. 147.
148. 149. 150. 151. 152. 153. 154. 155.
156. 157. 158. 159. 160. 161. 162. 163.

Opportunity

12. Tough Times? Matchless Opportunity!

"This is the chance to catch your competitors napping."
"Grab your weakened competitors' customers ASAP!"
"Think positive!"
"One man's disaster is another's main chance!"

There was a lot of . . . **unmitigated crap like that** . . . going around as the financial crisis of 2007++ deepened.

On the other hand, I think there *is* an appropriate use of the word *opportunity* in tough times—and it's a million miles from the nonsense above.

That is, a crisis is a pure (yes) and "simple" (no) . . . **test of character.** And perhaps one of the most important one or two or three such tests we'll face in our adult lifetime.

And I think we should think about it that way.

Instead of leaping to "grab our staggering competitor's customers," maybe we should react with great compassion toward that competitor—not by paying his bills, but by making it clear that we have neither the intention nor the desire to rip his customers out from under him (or her).

Instead of "think positive," try . . . "think thoughtful." Mindless optimism is just that—mindless. We must deal realistically with the crisis—and, arguably, exhibit a level of decency that knows no bounds. Such behavior is neither "positive" nor "negative." It is what it is: *decent*.

You get the drift, I'm sure. It *is* a time of matchless opportunity, a matchless opportunity . . . to exhibit character. *(Or not.)*

Sneaky fact is, such a display of character is probably damn good for business when the comeback occurs—people have very long memories of thoughtful behavior!

13. Boring Is Beautiful!
(Or at Least It *Can* Be.)

I *love* Jim's Group!
I *love* Basement Systems, Inc.!

Jim Penman's Jim's Group has been around for about 25 years. It all started with Jim's Mowing—Mr. Penman's way to feed himself while pursuing a Ph.D. I don't know whether or not Mr. P. ever finished his Ph.D. But I do know that Jim's Group is going on 3,000 franchisees in its home turf of Australia, and also in New Zealand, Canada, and the United Kingdom. There are barrels of awards to attest to the superior work the company does and the amazing opportunities it offers its franchisees.

Well, what does it do?
Stuff.
What kind of stuff?
You know, stuff.
More precisely, the sort of "stuff" that busy people don't have the time or the inclination to do.

Consider:

Jim's Mowing Canada	Jim's Paving
Jim's Mowing UK	Jim's Pergolas
Jim's Antennas	Jim's Pool Care
Jim's Carpet Cleaning	Jim's Pressure Cleaning
Jim's Car Cleaning	Jim's Roofing
Jim's Dog Wash	Jim's Security Doors
Jim's Fencing	Jim's Trees
Jim's Floors	Jim's Window Cleaning
Jim's Painting	

If you want to know more, download *What Will They Franchise Next? The Story of Jim's Group* (http://www.jimsskipbins.com.au/pdf/what_will_they_franchise_next.pdf).

Basement Systems, Inc., previously mentioned, is a fast-growing, $60-million-plus Connecticut-based business. Larry Janesky runs it. He'll dry out your basement. (See his, yes, bestselling book *Dry Basement Science*.) The basement thus becomes a stellar storage area, or a non-damp, non-moldy, non-illness-inducing family room, or a spare bedroom—whatever.

Message: For would-be entrepreneurs, there's more to life than biotech and Internet start-ups and "boutique" financial planning businesses.

Think dog washing!
Think dry basements!
Think any damn thing!

Message: "Not cool" can be very very **very** very very cool.

❯ **MIND THE GURU GAP REDUX**

As I said before, there's more to life than Big, Publicly Traded, "Sexy" Businesses—but you'd never know it from reading the work of most management "gurus." Alas, I'm one of those gurus who knows the ins and outs of GE and HP—but not much about the other 80 percent or 90 percent or 95 percent or 98 percent of the economy.

For example, only recently did I bother to read Thomas Stanley and William Danko's classic *The Millionaire Next Door,* originally published back in 1996. It talks about the successful people who run companies like Jim's Group or Basement Systems, Inc. Consider, per Stanley and Danko, these attributes of the True Superstars of the World Economy whom they profile in their book:

- They . . . lived in the same town all their adult life.

- They . . . are the first generation in their family to achieve wealth (and they had no parental support).

- They . . . "don't look like millionaires, don't dress like millionaires, don't eat like millionaires, don't act like millionaires."

- They . . . prosper outside the realm of "guru" glamour: "Many of the types of businesses [they] are in could be classified as 'dull-normal.' [They] are welding contractors, auctioneers, scrap-metal dealers, lessors of portable toilets, dry cleaners, re-builders of diesel engines, paving contractors . . ."

Yup, that's the real, beyond-the-gurus economy.

And it spells **o-p-p-o-r-t-u-n-i-t-y** for any and all with guts and gumption. (And you can leave the MIT Ph.D. to the guy next door who's *not* the millionaire.) (Indeed, the MIT Ph.D.s have their valuable place— but it's not the only place. In fact, not the principal place associated with our economic welfare or excellence.)

14. "Old" Rules. (Yes, Even in the "Age of the Internet.")

"People turning 50 today have half their adult lives ahead of them."

—Bill Novelli, *50+: Igniting a Revolution to Reinvent America*

(Novelli's assertion, in today's New World of the Old, is obviously true . . . in retrospect. But I well remember first reading this—the impact was simply staggering. The "oldies" like me are just half done. That is surely not consistent with the behavior of today's product developers or marketers—with veeeeery rare exceptions.)

Americans on average own 13 cars in a lifetime; 7 are bought after the age of 50.

(How about deriving a "code" to remind you of "all this": **13/7/50.**)

People age . . . **55 or older** . . . are . . . **more active** . . . in . . . **online finance, shopping, and entertainment** . . . than those under 55 (Forrester Research).

Americans over 50 control a gargantuan share of the personal wealth in the United States. And are healthy. (And the $$$$ part remains the case post–Big Recession.)
And: **American *women* over 50** . . . control an enormous and growing share of that enormous share of our total wealth.

The aging population opportunity is staggering in . . . North America, Oceania, Western Europe, and Japan.

The beloved "18–44 demographic" is wildly overrated as a desirable market.

Furthermore, there is no evidence that brand loyalties established in youth stick. (I made a list of about 25 brands I regularly used as a twentysomething. And today's preferences. The overlap was exactly ... **Zero.**)

My take on "all this," as a Professional Observer and Card-carrying (AARP, Medicare) Member of the Modern Elderclass:

We are the Aussies & Kiwis & Americans & Canadians. We are the Western Europeans & Japanese. We are the fastest-growing, the biggest, the wealthiest, the boldest, the most (yes) ambitious, the most experimental & exploratory, the most (self-)indulgent, the most difficult & demanding, the most service- & experience-obsessed, the most vigorous, the most health-conscious, the most female, the most profoundly important commercial market in the history of the world—and we will be the Center of your Universe for the next 25 years. We have arrived!

Are you acting accordingly?

If your answer is "yes"—congratulations, you are a rare bird indeed! **(Perhaps 1 in 100.)**

If your answer is "no"—what do you plan to do about it? In the next six months? **In the next year?** Two years? (Be precise in your answer.)

Do you understand that taking advantage of this ADWT **(Amazing Demographic & Wealth Tsunami)** will require a full-bore "cultural" and "strategic" "revolution" in your company?

And do you understand that this applies as much to the small biz as to the giants?

> **DUMB MONEY**

A lot of dumb things go on in business. None dumber than these... **two big omissions:** effectively ignoring-underestimating the Women's Market Potential ... (See #100.)

And ... effectively ignoring-underestimating the Boomer/50-Plus Market Potential.

In a word (two, actually): **Stupid! Stupid!**

15. Build Green Now. (No Excuses!)

I believe it would be wise—for reasons that range from the geopolitical advantages of energy independence to the amelioration of global warming—to mostly give up our SUVs and quickly seek alternative forms of energy. But such issues remain controversial.

Green buildings are ... **not** ... controversial. (Or should not be.)

Becoming a Green Building Advocate-Practitioner is the ultimate no-brainer.

There is . . . **absolutely no excuse** . . . for not being a Green Building Advocate-Practitioner.

Thirty years ago we learned that "quality is free"—most were skeptical at first, but, done right, quality improvement saves money, as well as improving the product. Later, 3M gave us 3P. That is . . . Pollution Prevention Pays. That, too, proved accurate. The same is true for green buildings—new ones and the retrofitting of old ones, small ones and large ones. Expenditures are indeed required to achieve optimal energy efficiency and maximum green potential. But the overwhelming majority of evidence suggests that these investments will be paid back in the short to medium term. Moreover, in the spirit of manufacturing's "continuous improvement," there are a host of small steps that are free or absurdly inexpensive that move in the right direction that can be done . . .

Right now.

(On top of all the energy-environmental advantages associated with green buildings, there is also a raft of evidence demonstrating that worker productivity goes up . . . **significantly** . . . in green facilities. The long and short of it is that these facilities are more pleasant places to work.)

Admittedly, I am a trained civil engineer with an advanced degree in construction management and hence I find the topic to be great fun! But I would urge—**beg**—you to stick your toes in the water, perhaps via the written word. Here are a few of the texts I perused and enjoyed, all of which included numerous, compelling case studies:

Green Building A to Z, by Jerry Yudelson

The HOK Guidebook to Sustainable Design, by Sandra Mendler, William Odell, and Mary Ann Lazarus

Green Architecture, by James Wines

Sustainable Construction: Green Building Design and Delivery, by Charles Kibert

Enjoy!
Act!
Now!
Even if "just" your home office!
No excuses!
Immediate dividends!

⟩ BUILT TO . . . WASTE?

Here is the impact of our buildings on energy consumption, CO_2 emissions, and the like:

Share of total energy used by buildings: **39%**

Share of electricity used by buildings: **68%**

Share of carbon-dioxide emissions caused by buildings: **40%**

Share of raw materials used in buildings: **30%**

Share of non-industrial landfill related to buildings: **40%**

These figures add up to an opportunity of staggering proportions!

Source: U.S. Green Building Council (from *Green Building A to Z*, by Jerry Yudelson)

16. Bottom Line in Bad Times: Obsess Over the *Top* Line.

Horst Schulze, the legendary former Ritz-Carlton chief, came out of retirement to launch a luxury brand of small hotels. In a 2008 *Prestige* magazine interview, he directly addressed, with aplomb, the issue of starting a new business during a recession: "I [will] not accept the explanation of a recession negatively affecting the [new] business. There are still people traveling. We just have to get them to stay in our hotel."

This kind of attitude reminds us that instant, mindless cutting of R&D or training or sales force travel in the face of a downturn is often counterproductive—or, rather, downright dumb.

Bad Times?
Become Top-Line Hypermanic!

Cutting, cutting, cutting is typically Recession Obsession–Preoccupation #1. Cutting is probably necessary, but don't let it stop you from becoming Born-Again Sales Hounds. With whatever tools you can dream up, redouble your time and effort aimed at increasing your business with existing customers—and maybe bagging a few new ones.

And this advice doesn't just apply in bad times. I am obsessed with the top line. I want everything I do to scream "DISTINCTION." And so I ask how every-damn-thing I do creates Brand Value–Distinction. I do pore over my P&Ls and savagely attack costs . . . every now and again . . . but the first item I eyeball is . . . GROSS REVENUE. If "GR" is growing at a healthy clip, then I know that all is likely well. Or, at least: not "bad."

❯ WHAT'S NEW? ("LEND" AN EAR!)

You ain't gonna beat the likes of China on cost. The alternative, and there's only one, is to sharpen your focus on Innovation and provision of memorable Experiences—and hence on Top-Line Growth. Instead of waiting to launch a new idea or business until "things get better," or starting off every project with a focus on cost minimization, consider instead this quote from former Lend Lease (Australia) CEO Stuart Hornery: "Every project we take on starts with a question:

'How can we do what's never been done before?' "

Make Hornery's **Bold Question** your *automatic* Question #1:

"How will this project enhance the Customer Experience in a way that's so 'dramatically different' from our competitors that we capture new customers and retain old customers and grow our share of business with them. And markedly boost the 'top line'?"

"THINK DIFFERENT" must be a full-time preoccupation in good times and bad. For starters (**a big deal**), that means constantly and purposefully exposing yourself to, and absorbing, diverse input.

Set up a lunch . . . TOMORROW . . . with someone new, from a different line of work than yours. Or spend the evening perusing articles on a topic way off the mainstream for you. Or invite the local grocery store manager to address your team in Purchasing or HR.

Keep the new inputs pouring in; they're the best path to a sustaining top-line obsession, marked by a constant string of new products and services.

(Can you really constantly think about new and "dramatically" different? Isn't it pie-in-the-sky? Isn't it exhausting? Isn't it "guru-babble"? In four words: No. No. No. No. That is, "surrounded by new inputs-ideas-people" becomes "the new normal." It becomes odd *not* to be bombarded by new ideas and their proponents—from R&D to purchasing. Rather than "tiring," it becomes Exhilarating—and an attractant to interesting people and hence a self-fulfilling prophecy.)

1. 2. 3. 4. 5. 6. 7. 8. 9. 10. 11. 12. 13. 14.
15. 16. **17. 18. 19. 20.** 21. 22. 23. 24. 25.
26. 27. 28. 29. 30. 31. 32. 33. 34. 35.
36. 37. 38. 39. 40. 41. 42. 43. 44. 45.
46. 47. 48. 49. 50. 51. 52. 53. 54. 55. 56.
57. 58. 59. 60. 61. 62. 63. 64. 65. 66. 67.
68. 69. 70. 71. 72. 73. 74. 75. 76. 77. 78.
79. 80. 81. 82. 83. 84. 85. 86. 87. 88.
89. 90. 91. 92. 93. 94. 95. 96. 97. 98. 99.
100. 101. 102. 103. 104. 105. 106. 107.
108. 109. 110. 111. 112. 113. 114. 115.
116. 117. 118. 119. 120. 121. 122. 123.
124. 125. 126. 127. 128. 129. 130. 131.
132. 133. 134. 135. 136. 137. 138. 139.
140. 141. 142. 143. 144. 145. 146. 147.
148. 149. 150. 151. 152. 153. 154. 155.
156. 157. 158. 159. 160. 161. 162. 163.

Resilience

17. Swan Dive: A Guide to Getting On with Getting On.

I am mesmerized by the Black Swan.

Black Swan = **U**npredictable **E**xtreme **E**vent, as described by Nassim Nicholas Taleb in his book *The Black Swan*.

We must live day to day, year to year, by gettin' on with gettin' on. Surprises aplenty are not so few and not so far between—and we've mostly learned how to cope and at least muddle through. But the Black Swan is different—**a once-in-two-lifetimes affair.** Our response-behavior-character in the face thereof will, as Taleb says, determine our life's course.

Well, if we can't plan for it because of its, by definition, "difference-ness," and we can't let it distract us 24 hours a day every day, what can we do? There are no surefire remedies, but there is a line of thought—and a single word—that may be of practical use. The word is . . . **resilience.**

To deal with the absurdly unlikely, we can consciously think about and hire people and promote those with demonstrated evidence of resilience and, hence, perhaps travel at least some distance toward shaping our organization to be more or less able to respond to a Black Swan.

Below you'll find some musings (no more than that) on the idea of resilience. These are raw—"key words" really, meant to do no more than get *you* musing on this topic.

Observable attributes of resilient people (worth considering in the hiring and, especially, promoting process):

- Inner calm.
- High self-knowledge **("comfortable in one's own skin").**
- *Breadth* of out-of-the-ordinary experience—drove a cab, worked construction, ran Alaska tours, did Teach for America.
- Appetite for modestly controlled chaos **(quite literally revels in messy situations—"comes to life" in them).**
- Reaches out effortlessly to a wide variety of people (in general and on the fly).
- Exudes energy.
- Known for integrity, a "straight shooter."
- **Sense of humor!** (Critical! Able to break the insane level of tension.)
- Empathy ("I feel your pain"—not weepy empathy, but obvious human compassion; understands that some people have little resilience and treats such folk with respect, not as "losers").
- "Cruelty"! (Must make tough decisions instantaneously, without looking back.)
- Decisive, but not rigid.
- A strong individual, and an equally strong team player. (Nirvana, of course, but one can aim to find these two traits co-mingled.)
- Understands the chain of command *and* its importance—and evades it as necessary.
- Comfortable being challenged by way-out thinkers, but with a strong "doer" bias overall.
- A person of Hope. ("Religious-like"?)

Observable Attributes of Resilient Organizations:

- Conscious hiring of resilient folks at all levels and in all functions. (I.e., "demonstrated resilience" is on the spec sheet.)
- Promotion for demonstrated resilience—be explicit about so doing.
- **Decentralization!!!** (In organizational structure, physical configuration, and systems alike. Decentralization = Less hooked up. (Helps avoid "house of cards" problem.)
- Shadow "emergency organization"—ready to roll. ("Excess" resources available to throw into the breach—the "just-in-time," zero inventory–zero slack concept works brilliantly in maximizing efficiency when things run smoothly, but it can be an unmitigated disaster when uncertainty and ambiguity and confusion rule.)
- Very serious "War gaming." (But don't let it lead to false confidence. To some extent, if you can game it, it ain't a Black Swan.)
- **Redundancy!!!** (Redundancy in "trivial stuff" is a must—there is nothing "trivial" about "extra" flashlights, in reality or metaphorically, when a Black Swan appears.)
- Culture of (1) self-starting, (2) caring and respect, (3) execution as Priority #1, (4) accountability-responsibility by 100 percent of folks. (Oddly, or not so oddly, the illegal Mexican immigrant who sneaks across a guarded border successfully and is now a busboy may well have far more resilience than a Summa Cum Laude Harvard grad!)
- "Culture of Resilience" (as a de jure explicit "plank" of organizational values set).
- Focusing **obsessively** on initiative-taking at the front-line. (One of the big weaknesses of contingency planning is that it more or less depends on well and expensively equipped "first responders" to guide affairs. **Overwhelming evidence indicates that the on-the-spot participants make *most* of the**

critical decisions—*before* even the most agile of First Responders appears on the scene.)

- **MBWA**/Managing By Wandering Around—communicate all the time about everything "at the coal face."
- Transparency. **(Keeping everyone in the know, no one in the dark.)**
- Financial padding (cash on hand, etc., needed if the computer system crashes for a few days).
- Excellent equipment. (But . . .)
- Remember that . . . **Training Trumps Equipment.**
- Ability to get by for (quite) a while without IS-IT. **(This is imperative and perhaps expensive; but the odds of a serious cyber-interruption are close to 100 percent.)**
- Testing the whole organization with uncomfortable situations—sports teams routinely do it, why not your accounting department?
- Pattern of promoting an unusually high share of mavericks. (Mavericks think "weird is normal.")
- Diversity per se!!!!!!!! (Differing views and backgrounds are priceless, especially in exceptional circumstances—nothing better than having someone who at age 20 was an Army ranger.)

⟩ PLANNING FOR THE UNPLANNABLE

Four words: redundancy, slack, $$$, breathing.

Many of the meetings I attend have been planned for more than a year—and I am the sole speaker. Hence, neither snow nor sleet nor revolution nor Montezuma's revenge (nor any combination thereof) is an excuse for my not showing up. And yet, shit happens—the only question is what consistency said shit is and from whence it was hurled.

My "secret" to resilience in the face of nearly impossible circumstances lies in four words:

Redundancy. Multiple flights booked via multiple paths. Double (or treble) everything—from passports to computers to world phones. Travel clothes that could double in a pinch as "event" clothes. You name it, and, like NASA, I've got two or three of them. As a statistics buff, I constantly calculate the probabilities of treble and quadruple screw-ups—it drives my wife crazy when she travels with me.

Slack. I'm a pretty busy fella, but I bite my tongue till it bleeds and program lots of slack into the system. I aim for gaps between flight legs of four or five hours—they reduce the odds that an errant thunder squall, or two, could make a godawful mess of a Boston to Mumbai or Boston to Seoul trip.

$$$. Resilience is not free. First, there are those duplicate tools—like computers. But there are also the likes of travel-services fees associated with double- and triple-booking. (And the cost of a lot of flowers and candy for the numerous people who help make the impossible possible!)

Breathing. I am, alas, not Mr. Calm. I'm no Barack Obama. But I have taught myself some breathing rituals—and after years of practice, I can induce a pretty satisfactory calm with one or two or three minutes (no more) of "right breathing."

I share these personal "tricks" with you, not because I think you care about my flavor of paranoia, but because I think that this quartet of practices has something close to universal validity. I couldn't survive without redundancy-slack-$$$-breathing; and I really don't see how others could, either.

18. Lifetime Employment Is Dead. Your Career Is Not.

The world is flat. (Or at least a lot flatter than it was.) Outsourcing is ubiquitous. (In big companies.) "Lifetime employment" is dead. *(Period.)* You're on your own. (Not entirely, but more than has been the case in recent decades for, again, bigger company employees—there was never a *"guaranteed anything"* for those who work in tiny and small businesses.)

So if many of us are more on our own than before, then:

1. The "signature" of our work and . . .
2. The vitality of our network will determine our professional fate.

Though I introduced the idea of "Brand You" (translation: you've got to stand out to survive professionally) some 15 years ago, and although chaos in the workplace has accelerated madly since, huge numbers of people continue to have problems with the situation that, say, a local electrician faces every day: The newly precarious necessarily need to see (*must* see, per me) themselves as a "business," as a "brand" unto themselves. And many are scared out of their wits at the idea of "going entrepreneurial." Ubiquitous rejoinder: "It's not my thing." "I didn't get the entrepreneurial gene." Or some such.

I feel their pain, but as to the "missing genetic ingredient"—baloney! I stand foursquare with the father of microlending and 2006 Nobel Peace Prize winner Muhammad Yunus. He claims—and I wholeheartedly agree—that we've mostly lost the mojo we *all* once had. *"All human beings are entrepreneurs,"* Mr. Yunus states. *"When we were in the caves we were all self-employed . . . finding our food, feeding ourselves. That's where the human history began . . . As civilization came we suppressed it. We became labor because [they] stamped us, 'You are labor.' We forgot that we are entrepreneurs."*

That statement doesn't remove, or perhaps even diminish, our fears—especially if you are 53 years old, you have been laid off permanently, and your pension has evaporated as well. No, I'm not offering insufferable "tough love." *I am simply reminding us that we who made it this far along the evolutionary path are highly skilled and resilient survivors from the get-go. We do, like that very "normal" electrician down the road from me, have what it takes.*

(Yes, I keep referring to that "local electrician." Simply put, his cohort numbers in the millions—and the Ivy League degree count is minuscule. "This stuff" can be done and is done, routinely, by mortals—not just the Steve Jobses of the world.)

We've pretty much got to work full-time on buffing up our skill set, sharpening our sales proclivity* (*sorry—you've gotta learn to sell), and networking like a maniac. It won't be easy for many, but it can be done by "normal" people; and though life will doubtless appear to be more precarious, the odds are actually pretty good, *very* good in fact, that the improving skill set and enhanced network will enhance our long-term "career" viability—and will also be a damn sight more fulfilling than the lot of the cubicle slaves so aptly documented by Scott Adams's *Dilbert* comic strip.

Message: You . . . **do** . . . have the . . . Right Stuff!

> ## BRAND YOU: "INC." THE DEAL

First step (assuming you didn't take it long ago) toward building a "resilient" career: **Redo your résumé.**

To begin with, for your private consumption, put Judith Sanders, Inc., at the top of the page where "mere" "Judith Sanders" used to reside. As you rework the résumé, imagine yourself going before a panel of venture capitalists to sell your business plan. Are you *(Judith Sanders, Inc.)* a going and growing concern with a fabulous service offering and bright prospects—or not?

The gaping holes in your draft of *Judith Sanders, Inc.*, if you are bone honest, may scare the hell out of you. But, assuming you are still employed, there are immediate steps to take. For example: *Revisit immediately your current projects and spiff them up in such a way that you can imagine them* . . . **as exciting-"remarkable" entries** . . . *on your résumé one year or two years hence. Volunteer for projects that will contribute to your growth both by extending your main skill set as well as filling in holes in, say, financial management.*

I could go on—but I'll simply conclude with a mantra coined by my friend Julie Anixter:

"Distinct or extinct!"

19. "Failure"—Celebrate It!

Notes toward a Theory of Failure (or is it a Theory of Success?):

(1) To succeed, you have to try more stuff than the other guy—fast.

(2) If you try more stuff in a hurry, you'll make lots of mistakes. (It's an Iron Law of Nature.)

(3) Hence, screwing up a lot is a very good sign of progress—perhaps the only sure sign.

(4) If we aim to (more or less) maximize screw-ups, then we must do more than "tolerate" screw-ups.

(5) We must "encourage" screw-ups.

(6) We must **cel-e-brate** screw-ups!

A **(brilliant)** variation on this theme comes from successful Australian businessman Phil Daniels, who attributes a large share of his success "to six words." Namely:

"Reward excellent failures. Punish mediocre successes."

Those words belong in my "Top Five Quotes" club (from among perhaps 5,000). I believe the idea is profound, and the impact enormous . . . **if** . . . you use a literal translation. That is, if you literally . . . **reward** . . . excellent failures. And if you literally . . . **punish** . . . mediocre successes.

As Les Wexner, founder of Limited Brands, once told me:

"In fashion, your batting average is never anywhere near 1.000. Your strikeouts will always, over time, surpass your hits—especially your home runs. So a buyer with no mistakes is taking no chances—the kiss of death in this business; and cause for a poor evaluation. The buyer who will hit home runs, like power hitters in baseball, will also have a bushel of swinging strikeouts. I will in fact reward those swinging strikeouts—as the price of the home runs that are required for our growth."

Amen.

▶ "FAIL-SAFE" WISDOM

"Fail. Forward. Fast."
—High-tech exec, Valley Forge, PA

"Fail faster. Succeed sooner."
—David Kelley, founder IDEO

"Fail. Fail again. Fail better."
—Samuel Beckett, Nobel laureate, Literature

"Success is going from failure to failure without losing enthusiasm."
—Winston Churchill

Whoever Makes the Most Mistakes Wins
—Book title, Richard Farson and Ralph Keyes

"Sam was not afraid to fail."
—David Glass, former CEO, Walmart, on Walmart founder
  Sam Walton's most significant success trait

"If people . . . tell me they skied all day and never fell down, I tell them
to try a different mountain."
—Michael Bloomberg

"I've missed more than 9,000 shots in my career. I've lost almost
300 games. Twenty-six times, I've been trusted to take the game-
winning shot and missed. I've failed over and over and over again
in my life. And that is why I succeed."
—Michael Jordan

20. The World's Worst Advice (Please Ignore It).

An old friend visited me for a couple of days. Google him, and you'll be impressed. Or you would be, if I were to tell you who he is.

In the course of a dozen conversations—old-guy conversations—we shared stories of joys and sorrows, anger and pain, good fortune and ill winds, pals and foes and traitors and through-it-all supporters.

His Hall-of-Fame career includes bushels of excoriating criticisms along the way. Embarrassing and well-deserved failures. Off years—in fact, off decades.

And musing on it all reminded me of a Very Sensible Saying that I think is pure, unmitigated crap—in fact, **(the)** World's Worst Advice:

"Know when to hold 'em, know when to fold 'em."

Forget "fold 'em." Drop it from your vocabulary. Excise it. Bury it. Stomp on its grave.

If you care, really care, really really care about what you are pursuing, well, then . . . *pursue-the-hell-out-of-it-until-hell-freezes-over-and-then-some-and-then-some-more.*

And may the naysayers roast in hell or freeze in the Antarctic or bore themselves to death with the sound of their "statistically accurate" advice.

My anonymous visiting friend gave me *The Pixar Touch: The Making of a Company*, by David Price. Consider this paragraph:

"One of the curious aspects of Pixar's story is that each of the leaders was, by conventional standards, a failure at the time he came onto the scene. [Animator-superstar John] Lasseter landed his dream job at Disney out of college—and had just been fired from it. [Tech genius and founding president Ed] Catmull had done well-respected work as a graduate student in computer graphics, but had been turned down for a teaching position and ended up in what he felt was a dead-end software development job. Alvy Ray Smith, the company's co-founder, had checked out of academia, got work at Xerox's famous Palo Alto Research Center, and then abruptly found himself on the street. [Steve] Jobs had endured humiliation and pain as he was rejected from Apple Computer; overnight he had transformed from boy wonder of Silicon Valley to a roundly ridiculed has-been."

That is, shit happens. And if enough of it happens to you, then, if you are (statistically) wise, you'll fold 'em. And God (and I) will love you just as much as if you'd endured.

But we won't read about you in the history books.

Now, if you do indeed "endure"—well, we probably won't read about you, either, because the odds indeed *are* looooooooooong against you making it into that history book.

But if you really really really **(really)** really care . . . then there ain't no time to "fold 'em" until your last breath has been drawn—and even that's too soon if you've bothered along the way to inflame others about your purportedly quixotic cause.

In the (absolutely not) immortal words of Tom Peters:

"There's a time to hold 'em and a time to keep on holdin' 'em—if you really really really care."

The Recession 46

Forty-Six "Secrets" and "Strategies" for Dealing with the Gut-Wrenching Downturn of 2007++

I am constantly asked for "strategies/secrets for surviving the recession." I try to appear wise and informed—and parade original, sophisticated thoughts. But if you want to know what's *really* going through my head, see the list that follows. (Note: I introduced this list in May 2009, when all the economic statistics were gruesome. Nonetheless, many immediately pointed out that it's as relevant in good times as in bad.)

1. You come to work earlier.

2. You leave work later.

3. You work harder.

4. You may well work for less; and, if so, you adapt to the untoward circumstances with a smile—even if it kills you inside.

5. You volunteer to do more.

6. You dig deep, deeper, deepest—and always bring a good attitude to work.

7. You fake it if your good attitude flags.

8. You literally practice your "stage face" in the mirror each morning, and in the loo midmorning.

9. You give new meaning to the idea and intensive practice of "visible management."

10. You take better-than-usual care of yourself and encourage others to do the same—physical well-being significantly impacts mental well-being and response to stress.

11. You shrug off shit that flows downhill in your direction—buy a shovel or a "preworn" raincoat on eBay.

12. You try to forget about the "good old days"—nostalgia is self-destructive. (And boring.)

13. You buck yourself up with the thought that "this too shall pass," but then remind yourself that it might not pass anytime soon; and so

you rededicate yourself to making the absolute best of what you have now—character is determined, virtually in full, by one's reaction to adverse circumstances.

14. You work the phones and then work the phones some more—and stay in touch with, and on the mind of, positively everyone.

15. You frequently invent breaks from routine, including "weird" ones—"change-ups" prevent wallowing in despair and bring a fresh perspective.

16. You eschew all forms of personal excess.

17. You simplify.

18. You sweat the *details as never* before.

19. You sweat the *details as never* before.

20. You sweat the *details as never* before.

21. You raise to the sky and maintain—at all costs—the **Standards of Excellence** by which you unfailingly and unflinchingly evaluate your own performance.

22. You are maniacal when it comes to responding to even the slightest screw-up.

23. You find ways to be around young people and to keep young people around—they are less likely to be members of the "sky is falling" school. (Naiveté can be a blessing.)

24. You learn new tricks of your trade.

25. You pass old tricks of the trade on to others—mentoring matters now more than ever.

26. You invest heavily in your Internet-Web2.0-Twitter-Facebook-"cloud"-computing skills.

27. You remind yourself, daily, that this is not just something to be "gotten through"—it is the Final Exam of Competence, of Character, and, even if you're not a boss, of Leadership. (People often make great leaps in a short period during difficult times.)

28. You network like a demon.

29. You network like a demon *inside* the company—get to know more of the folks who "do the real work," and who can be your most dependable allies when it comes to getting things done seamlessly and fast.

30. You network like a demon *outside* the company—get to know more of the folks "down the line," who "do the real work" in vendor-customer outfits. (They can become, and will become, your most avid allies and champions.)

31. You offer thanks to others by the truckload if good things happen—and take the heat if bad things happen.

32. You behave kindly, but you don't sugarcoat or hide the truth—humans are startlingly resilient, and rumors are the real spirit-killers.

33. You treat small successes as if they were World Cup victories—and celebrate and commend people accordingly.

34. You shrug off the losses (ignoring what's going on in your tummy), and get back on the horse and immediately try again.

35. You avoid negative people to the extent you can—pollution kills.

36. You read the riot act to the gloom-sprayers, once avoiding them becomes impossible. (Gloom is the ultimate "weapon of mass destruction" in tough times.)

37. You give new meaning to the word *thoughtful*.

38. You don't put limits on the budget for flowers—"bright and colorful" works marvels.

39. You redouble and retriple your efforts to "walk in your customers' shoes." (Especially if the shoes smell.)

40. You mind your manners—and accept others' lack of manners in the face of their strains.

41. You are kind to all humankind.

42. You keep your shoes shined.

43. You leave the blame game at the office door.

44. You call out, in no uncertain terms, those who continue to play the "office politics" game.

45. You become a paragon of personal accountability.

46. *And then you pray.*

1. 2. 3. 4. 5. 6. 7. 8. 9. 10. 11. 12. 13. 14. 15. 16. 17. 18. 19. 20. **21. 22. 23. 24. 25. 26.** 27. 28. 29. 30. 31. 32. 33. 34. 35. 36. 37. 38. 39. 40. 41. 42. 43. 44. 45. 46. 47. 48. 49. 50. 51. 52. 53. 54. 55. 56. 57. 58. 59. 60. 61. 62. 63. 64. 65. 66. 67. 68. 69. 70. 71. 72. 73. 74. 75. 76. 77. 78. 79. 80. 81. 82. 83. 84. 85. 86. 87. 88. 89. 90. 91. 92. 93. 94. 95. 96. 97. 98. 99. 100. 101. 102. 103. 104. 105. 106. 107. 108. 109. 110. 111. 112. 113. 114. 115. 116. 117. 118. 119. 120. 121. 122. 123. 124. 125. 126. 127. 128. 129. 130. 131. 132. 133. 134. 135. 136. 137. 138. 139. 140. 141. 142. 143. 144. 145. 146. 147. 148. 149. 150. 151. 152. 153. 154. 155. 156. 157. 158. 159. 160. 161. 162. 163.

Self

21. You Are Your Product— Develop It.

Assignment. To be completed no more than 24 hours from the moment you read this.

Find a mirror. Stand in front of it . . .
Smiling.
Saying . . . "Thank you."
Doing . . . jumping jacks. (Or some equivalent thereof.)
"For God's sake, WHY?" you ask.

Smiling begets a warmer environment.
(Home or work.)
Thanking begets an environment of mutual appreciation.
Enthusiasm (the likes of those jumping jacks) **begets enthusiasm.**

Love begets love.
Energy begets energy.
Wow begets Wow.
Optimism begets Optimism.
Honesty begets honesty.

Caring begets caring.
Listening begets engagement.

How do you "motivate" others?
Take a B-school course on Leadership?
No! (Don't get me started.)
Answer: Motivate yourself first.
By hook.
Or by crook.

Call it **LBUAA: Leadership by Unilateral Attitude Adjustment.**

Are there things that can be labeled "circumstances"?
Of course.
Do bad things happen to good people?
Of course.
Is there such a thing as "powerlessness"?
Perceived powerlessness?
Yes.
Real powerlessness?
No!
No!
No!

Viktor Frankl, psychologist and Holocaust survivor, on concentration camps:

"The last of the human freedoms—the ability to choose one's attitude in any given set of circumstances."

If you can figure out how to go to work with a smile today, I (despite my engineer's training, and the resulting baggage of an MBA from a "quant school") will . . . **guarantee** . . . you that you will not only "have a better day," but will (eventually) infect others! And performance will improve—maybe even take a Great Leap Upward.

NB: As usual . . . "easier said than done." On the other hand, as a trained and avowed "behaviorist" (devotee to B. F. Skinner, his rats, and "operant conditioning"), I will indeed **guarantee** that if you can drag your sagging self as far as that mirror, the simple act of practicing your smile—no matter how apparently infantile—will, in fact, beget more smiles from you which will beget more smiles from others which will (consider Smiler-in-Chief Nelson Mandela) perhaps change the shape of the world!

Take charge now!
Task one: Work on yourself.
Relentlessly!

❯ "ME FIRST"

A few wise words on why a "me first" approach is anything but . . . "selfish":

"You must be the change you wish to see in the world."
—Gandhi

"Being aware of yourself and how you affect everyone around you is what distinguishes a superior leader."
—from "Masters of the Breakthrough Moment," *strategy + business, no. 45*

"To develop others, start with yourself."
—Marshall Goldsmith, executive coach

"Work on me first."
—Kerry Patterson, Joseph Grenny, Ron McMillan,
  and Al Switzler, *Crucial Conversations*

"How can a high-level leader like _____ be so out of touch with the
truth about himself? It's more common than you would imagine. In fact,
the higher up the ladder a leader climbs, the less accurate his self-
assessment is likely to be. The problem is an acute lack of feedback,
especially on people issues."
—Daniel Goleman et al., *The New Leaders*

22. Job One: Amuse Yourself!

I luuuuuv great customer–"end user" feedback! I am competitive to
a fault in that regard. And a slave to the market—still, "after all these
years." At a higher level of marketplace engagement, I love a hearty
business backlog, especially if it's based on repeat business—and I
carefully measure it against that of previous years. And I love a fee-
per-event yield that exceeds last year, the year before.

And yet . . . in an important way . . . I indeed put the customer–
"end user" second . . .

Second to what? To put it simply (to me, anyway):

To give a high-impact, well-regarded speech to customers, I first
& second & third have to focus all my restless energy on "satisfying"
. . . *myself.*

I must be . . . *physically & emotionally & intellectually agitated &
excited & desperate beyond measure* . . . if I want to . . . *communicate
& connect & compel & grab by the collar & say my piece* . . . about a
small number of things, often contentious and not always "crowd-

pleasing," that, at the moment, are literally a matter of personal . . .
life and *death*.

I crave great "customer feedback"—but in no way, shape, or form
am I trying to "satisfy my customer." I am, I repeat, trying instead
to satisfy *me*, my own deep neediness to reach out and grab my customer and connect with my customer over ideas that consume and
devour me.

Hence . . . my "Job One" is purely selfish and internally focused:
to be completely captivated by the subject matter at hand. That is,
to repeat in slightly different words: **Job One is . . . self-
motivation.**

As Warren Bennis, my primo mentor, to whom this book is dedicated, wrote in *On Becoming a Leader*: "No leader sets out to be a
leader per se, but rather to express him- or herself freely and fully.
That is, leaders have no interest in proving themselves, but an abiding
interest in expressing themselves."

So I'm back to my somewhat disingenuous message: To put the
marketplace customer *truly* first, I must put the person serving the
customer (me, in this instance) "more first."

Excitement & self-stimulation first!
"Service" second!
(Think about it.)

> **TAKE AN (INTERNAL) VACATION**

Stay fresh!
Stay engaged!
Learn!
Devote "adequate" time to self-development!
(That is . . . a *lot* of time!)
It is *not* self-indulgent!

Let's say you're a systems salesperson.

So ... Take the day "off."

That is: Spend the day in the lab with the scientists and engineers. Take a couple of them to lunch. Learn about their new projects—even the ones for which the payoff is five years out.

Repeat monthly: Devote at least two work days to "far-out stuff" aimed at personal battery recharging.

23. Fitness Power = Staying Power.

A moody friend, faced with high-tech employment disruption (and, partly, burnout), is now a physical-fitness trainer. She told me that she was no less than "flabbergasted" by the positive attitude of the people she worked with.

She is a keen "people observer," and says she doubts that the phenomenon can be traced to "a certain kind of person" who is attracted to the job. And she says so, in part, because of her own attitudinal transformation (right word, she insists: "transformation"). Her conclusion:

"It's simple. Men or, especially, women are 'happy' if they are comfortable with their bodies. And if they are very physically fit they are by definition at least happier with their bodies. They simply can't help being more positive and more optimistic. It's quite extraordinary."

I don't urge, or believe in, or countenance, shoving extreme physical fitness down anybody's throat. But I do suggest that having programs available pretty much free of charge, tools within reach, and "regular" folks doubling as fitness mentors will improve overall organization effectiveness—perhaps "remarkably."

(FYI: *The value of this idea goes up by an order of magnitude in tough times . . . when "attitude enhancers" are worth their weight in gold.*)

24. Mental Gymnastics, Urgency Of.

While writing the "tip" above on *physical* fitness, it dawned on me, in spite of being a voracious seeker and absorber of new ideas, how rarely I can put my head on the pillow and actually say,

"I really had my mind twisted into a pretzel today."

Or: "Holy s**t, I can't believe . . ."

Many of us have been convinced of the value of those physical stretching regimens alluded to immediately above. But what about the mental equivalent?

We may, especially in Web World, come across "new stuff" numerous times in the course of a day. In fact, the extraordinary is now so ordinary that it rarely registers.

But what about truly weird stuff, genuinely surprising stuff, counterintuitive stuff, the stuff that makes your head literally spin and sets you to digging and digging and digging some more?

If you go to bed three days in a row without some genuinely new ideas wandering around and around in your brain and kicking your synapses—well, I suggest that you let that worry you.

(And then act upon your very appropriate concern.)

25. You *Are* Your Story! So Work on It!

He/she who has the best/most compelling/most resonant story wins:

In life!
In business!
In front of the jury!
In front of the congregation!

From the local district rep seat all the way to the White House!

Stories are **100 percent** about emotion—and emotion, far more than dynamite, moves mountains. (Trust me, I just finished an excellent book on the digging of the Panama Canal. The dream, kept alive for centuries by a parade of unhinged dreamers, made the canal that changed the world—the sticks of blasting material were almost incidental.) And effective storytelling—concerning your career or your company or your current six-week project—is a refined art. Maybe it comes naturally to your 79-year-old grandpa . . . but it didn't/doesn't to me!

I WORK LIKE HELL AT IT!

Do you ever make "presentations"?
I bet the answer is "Yes."

Well . . . STOP.

No more presentations.
Ever again.

I stopped years ago.
I never give presentations.
I do . . . for pay, no less . . . **tell stories.**
Story after story after (linked) story.

As I prepare I am conscious . . . 100 percent of the time . . . of the evolving *story*, of the *plot*, of the *narrative* that I wish to follow.

For example: Regardless of the intensity of the client demand ("We need to translate your slides into Spanish"), I never submit my presentations ahead of time. That's because I rework them—keep refining the *story collection*, its *plot*, its *flow*, its *rhythm*—until moments before I go onstage. I suspect that in the last few hours before a speech, I revise my "script" well over 100 times.

Your schedule today is . . . a short story with a beginning, narrative, end, and memory that lingers on.
Your current project is . . . an unfolding story about making something better, exciting users, etc.
Your organization's raison d'être, and hence its effectiveness, is . . . a story.
Your career is . . . a story.

HE/SHE WHO HAS THE BEST STORY WINS!
SO . . . *WORK* . . . ON YOUR STORY!
MASTER—become a "professional at"—THE ART OF STORYMAKING/STORYTELLING/STORY DOING/STORY PRESENTING!

(*"Master"* is a word that, as you've doubtless figured out already, I use again and again in this book. **Storytelling "excellence" is not something you "pick up along the way."** It is an art, a craft, a discipline to be mastered—like playing the flute. If you buy my "story line" here, you will pursue its implications as that determined flutist would pursue her instrumental skill.)

On a related note, I conclude from the likes of the preceding analysis that "brand" is, though thought to be the apex of marketing achievement ("brand power"), encompassed by and in fact *subsidiary* to "the story."

"Word games," you say. "Of course the 'brand,' in effect, tells a story." Yes, of course it does, but I'd argue that semantics *do* matter.

"Brand" has to some extent become a sterile concept, wildly overused and hence almost made meaningless, that has burned itself out or is in the process thereof—no one screams that message more loudly and effectively than Saatchi & Saatchi chief Kevin Roberts in practice and in his mold-breaking book, *Lovemarks*.

Furthermore, when we say "brand," we are likely to begin with a clinical analysis of the market, competition, etc. But a story is a story is a good yarn or potboiler or thriller or whatever—it connects and changes your worldview, or it doesn't. To grossly oversimplify, by more or less erasing the word *brand* from your vocabulary and instead obsessing on "story-story-story," stories that move mountains, stories that grab, stories that shock, you will, in my opinion, end up looking at the world in a different and more useful way. "Story" is a far more animated and engaging, less clinical formulation than brand—and is a great yardstick for effectiveness. *"Does our story really enthrall?"* may be the most potent business-profitability-effectiveness question one can ask—and, besides, a question that as readily applies to a revised business process ("What's the story of this new reporting scheme?") or training course as to a more traditional product or service.

❯ A WHOLE NEW . . . STORY

Story time! Here's what a few smart folks have said about the (*business*) value of storytelling:

"A key—perhaps *the* key—to leadership is the effective communication of a story."
—Howard Gardner, *Leading Minds: An Anatomy of Leadership*

"Leaders don't just make products and make decisions. *Leaders make meaning.*"
—John Seely Brown, Xerox PARC

"Management has a lot to do with answers. Leadership is a function of questions. And the first question for a leader always is: *'Who do we intend to be?'* not 'What are we going to do?' but 'Who do we intend to be?' "
—Max De Pree, Herman Miller

"The essence of American presidential leadership, and the secret of presidential success, is storytelling."
—Evan Cornog, *The Power and the Story: How the Crafted Presidential Narrative Has Determined Political Success from George Washington to George W. Bush*

"But where to fight [after surviving the Battle of Britain], given that the British Army was incapable of engaging the Wehrmacht in Europe? Churchill's policy between 1940 and 1944 was dominated by a belief in the importance of military theater. He perceived that there must be action, even if not always useful; there must be successes, even if overstated or even imagined; there must be glory, even if undeserved."
—Renowned historian Max Hastings describing Winston Churchill as Britain's stage director, maintaining public morale during the dog days of World War II

"The last few decades have belonged to a certain kind of person with a certain kind of mind—computer programmers who could crank code, lawyers who could craft contracts, MBAs who could crunch numbers. But the keys to the kingdom are changing hands. The future belongs to a very different kind of person with a very different kind of mind— creators and empathizers, pattern recognizers, and meaning makers. *These people—artists, inventors, designers, storytellers, caregivers, consolers, big picture thinkers—will now reap society's richest rewards and share its greatest joys.*"
—Dan Pink, *A Whole New Mind*

"We are in the twilight of a society based on data. As information and intelligence become the domain of computers, society will place new value on the one human ability that cannot be automated: emotion. Imagination, myth, ritual—the language of emotion—will affect everything from our purchasing decisions to how well we work with others. *Companies will thrive on the basis of their stories and myths.* Companies will need to understand that their products are less important than their stories."
—Rolf Jensen, Copenhagen Institute for Future Studies

26. Develop Your R.POV8—ASAP!

After finishing, exhausted, a round of seminars with 500 law partners and a couple of hundred top financial planners, it was clear to me that the professionals I'd addressed are what I call "scary smart." And they've missed more than a few of their kids' soccer games; that is, 12-hour days are the norm.

But "talent" and outrageously hard work are not enough! Why? Because, among other things, there are a lot of talented people around who do what they do and do it well and who work long long days.

So what's the "secret" to differentiation? Marketing guru Seth Godin offers an important clue when he says: **"If you can't describe your position in eight words or less, you don't have a position."**

I choose to interpret this not as a "marketing tip," but as a profound statement. Hence, I spent my two seminars hammering on "Remarkable Point of View" . . . or **R.POV.** Or, to steal more or less from Seth . . . **R.POV8** . . . a Remarkable Point of View . . . captured in eight words or less.

I leave you with a "simple" question about yourself: Is what I'm up to remarkably different—and can it be captured in simple, compelling language (4, 6, 8, 10, no more than 15 words)?

(Consider: **Working on your R.POV8 is far more important than any "strategic planning" exercise!**)

> **PUTTING A FINE POINT ON IT**

Developing, maintaining, *and* refreshing an R.POV/R.POV8 is excruciatingly difficult. Trust me on this. At the Tom Peters Company, as our 20th birthday approached, we spent 18 months redesigning our logo. And after those 18 months of heavy lifting, we ended up with what? A red [PANTONE #032] exclamation point **(!)**—which was not only exactly right for us, but came *at least* seven words under Seth's maximum. Maybe you ought to follow in our footsteps—strange as it sounds, nothing concentrates the mind more than a logo redesign. You must define yourself well for years to come in a word or two, or a simple image.

Talk about essence!

1. 2. 3. 4. 5. 6. 7. 8. 9. 10. 11. 12. 13. 14.
15. 16. 17. 18. 19. 20. 21. 22. 23. 24. 25.
26. **27. 28. 29. 30. 31. 32.** 33. 34. 35.
36. 37. 38. 39. 40. 41. 42. 43. 44. 45.
46. 47. 48. 49. 50. 51. 52. 53. 54. 55. 56.
57. 58. 59. 60. 61. 62. 63. 64. 65. 66. 67.
68. 69. 70. 71. 72. 73. 74. 75. 76. 77. 78.
79. 80. 81. 82. 83. 84. 85. 86. 87. 88.
89. 90. 91. 92. 93. 94. 95. 96. 97. 98. 99.
100. 101. 102. 103. 104. 105. 106. 107.
108. 109. 110. 111. 112. 113. 114. 115.
116. 117. 118. 119. 120. 121. 122. 123.
124. 125. 126. 127. 128. 129. 130. 131.
132. 133. 134. 135. 136. 137. 138. 139.
140. 141. 142. 143. 144. 145. 146. 147.
148. 149. 150. 151. 152. 153. 154. 155.
156. 157. 158. 159. 160. 161. 162. 163.

Others

27. Kindness Is Free!

When it comes to a patient's evaluation of a hospital stay, you'd think that "getting well" was the heart of the matter, the alpha and the omega, not to mention the gammas and deltas, etc.

Wrong!

In one massive survey, Press Ganey Associates, the masters of evaluating hospital patient satisfaction, queried 139,380 former patients at 225 hospitals on that topic. After the data were collected, they teased out the 15 most powerful determinants of the patient's reaction to her or his experience.

And the winner [loser] is . . .

"Not a single one of the Top 15 sources of Patient Satisfaction had to do with the patient's health outcome. All 15, in effect, were related to the quality of the patient's interactions with hospital staff—and employee satisfaction among staff members."

None.

N-O-N-E.

Zero.

Z-e-r-o.

The study is reported in (and the quote above paraphrased from) *Putting Patients First,* by Susan Frampton, Laura Gilpin, and Patrick

Charmel. The authors are leaders at Griffin Hospital in Derby, Connecticut. Year after year it ranks near the top (Top 10 upon occasion) of *Fortune* magazine's Best Companies to Work For list—one of the rare health care institutions to do so. It also tops the charts on nearly every other measure you can name from patient safety to financial viability. The so-called Planetree Alliance, run from Griffin, is the epicenter of the "patient-centric care" movement.

The authors use the startling Press Ganey data as the jumping-off point for discussing the process and tenets that guide their work with staff and patients at Griffin/Planetree:

"There is a misconception that supportive interactions require more staff or more time and are therefore more costly. Although labor costs are a substantial part of any hospital budget, the interactions themselves add nothing to the budget.

Kindness is free.

"Listening to patients or answering their questions costs nothing. It could be argued that negative interactions—alienating patients, being unresponsive to their needs, or limiting their sense of control—can be very costly. *Angry, frustrated, or frightened patients may be combative, withdrawn, and less cooperative, requiring far more time than it would have taken to interact with them initially in a positive way."*

The Big Lessons here—and they are big—are several:

(1) *Process frequently (usually? invariably?) "beats" outcome in assessment of an "experience"*—even one as apparently "outcome sensitive" as a hospital stay. The positive quality of staff interactions were more memorable than whether or not the health problem was fixed.

(2) *Happy staff, happy customers.* Want to "put the customer first"? Put the staff "more first"! (More on this later.)

(3) *Quality is free—and then some.* We learned (well, most of us learned) when the "quality movement" dominated our consciousness

that not only was quality free—but doing the quality bit right actually reduced costs, often dramatically. Same here!

And, to repeat (and what could be more worth repeating?) . . .

(4) *Kindness is free!!!*

> **THREE OF A "KIND"?**

"Three things in human life are important. The first is to be kind. The second is to be kind. And the third is to be kind."
—Henry James (in *Choosing Civility: The Twenty-five Rules of Considerate Conduct,* by P. M. Forni)

"For many years literature was my life . . . One day, while lecturing on the *Divine Comedy*, I looked at my students and realized that I wanted them to be kind human beings more than I wanted them to know about Dante. I told them that if they knew everything about Dante and then they went out and treated an elderly lady on the bus unkindly, I'd feel that I had failed as a teacher."
—P. M. Forni, *Choosing Civility: The Twenty-five Rules of Considerate Conduct* (Forni is professor of Italian literature at Johns Hopkins University and founder, in 2000, of the Johns Hopkins Civility Project)

---

28. Civil! Civil! Civil!

This morning, as I write (in October 2008), I got a call from someone I knew a little but not at all well. He asked me to do something for a presidential candidate. (My candidate, about whom I was quite keen.) He began with a nasty, long-winded riff on how awful the other candidate was. On and on it went.

Until I hung up.

Yes, emotions run high in such campaigns.
(They have since the Adams-Jefferson slugfest in 1800.)
But that is no cause for incivility.
Ever.
I was tempted to swear like the sailor I once was at this guy—but it would have defeated my purpose.
Tempers flare in elections—and in business every day. (I possess a *very* hot temper, in point of fact—got it from my mom.) I don't object to sounding off in the privacy of a pub with two close friends. I do object to such intemperate sounding off in more or less public discourse.
It doesn't work, and makes you the idiot.
Advice:

Civil!
Civil!
Civil!

The more pissed off you are, the more you reach out to be civil.
Period.

➤ "CIVIL" RIGHTS—AND WRONGS

As a young man, George Washington copied 110 rules of civility into a notebook, Richard Brookhiser observes in his introduction to *Rules of Civility*. The principles were to guide Washington in the decades to come—and, in fact, marked him as a leader of singular character. The source text for GW was *Decency of Conversation Among Men*, compiled by French Jesuits in 1595.

Many of the 110 rules will seem—and are—dated. But even the least applicable smack of, indeed, civility and decency.

The "rules of civility" are about the attitudes one carries and the way one projects oneself. In the age of the Internet and social networking, though the words and conduits for action are different, the Big Idea is the same. (At least as I see it.) Grace, civility, decency, the determination never to disparage others, and the simple act of standing when anyone enters the room—these remain the essence of the effective leader's temperament and the driving force in achieving things through others' willing commitment. Perhaps these notions are more important than ever because they are honored in the breach more than ever, courtesy of our frenzied approach to life.

Silicon Valley, where I lived for three-plus decades, is a place in a hurry, where brusque seems to be the admired style. But thoughtfulness—a heartfelt reference to the illness of another's spouse or the recent accomplishment of another's child—goes just as far or farther in 2010 in Santa Clara County, California, as it did when the Jesuit fathers drafted their theses in 1595.

Sample rules of civility and decent behavior extracted from *Rules of Civility* (emphasis added):

#1—Every action done in company ought to be done with some sign of **respect** to those that are present.

#22—Show not yourself glad at the misfortune of another though he were your enemy.

#28—If anyone come to speak to you while you are sitting, stand up, though he be your inferior ... (Forget the "inferior" bit—I've been doing this *religiously* since I read the book; it "works.")

#49—Use no reproachful language against anyone; neither curse nor revile.

#65—Speak not injurious words neither in jest nor earnest; scoff at none although they give occasion. **(!!!!!!!)**

#110—Labor to keep alive in your breast that little spark of celestial fire called conscience ...

Brookhiser offers commentaries throughout, and he closes with this: "[#110 is] the only open reminder of what has been implicit all along, small matters and large matters are linked; there are no great spirits who do not pay attention to both; these little courtesies reflect, as in a pocket mirror, the social and moral order."

Civility 2010 = Civility 1776 = Civility 1595.
Period.

29. Listen to Ann— and "Act Accordingly."

At an all-day seminar I gave a few years ago, the late Ann Richards, former governor of Texas, was the luncheon speaker. Feisty-fabulous Ann had lots to say of value, but one "obvious" (ain't they always) item was a true whack on the side of the head. I paraphrase:

"Suppose you're waiting in a long line at an airline desk to rebook your flight after it has been mysteriously cancelled. You are in a horrid mood, and the line's imperceptible movement hardly helps. Finally, you make it to the front, and are in the physical proximity of that most loathsome of all creatures imaginable, a live airline employee.

"Take two deep breaths, smile with the smile you'd use if you were meeting Queen Elizabeth II, and say to yourself, 'This woman/man is the only human being on earth who at this moment in time can help me with my most pressing problem.' Then act accordingly."

I listened.
I tried it.

It worked.
I do it as a matter of routine.
It . . . **always** . . . works.

Behave decently because it's the decent thing to do.
Behave decently because it works.

(Thank you, Ann.)
(We miss you.)

30. "Being There." (Or: How I Learned First Principles from My Grandfather's Last Rites.)

Dale Carnegie (*How to Win Friends and Influence People*) once famously said:

> *"You can make more friends in two months by becoming interested in other people than you can in two years by trying to get other people interested in you."*

Mr. Carnegie's observation-commandment-towering truth came to mind when a good friend asked me to contribute to a compilation of "best advice I ever got" stories that he was putting together. I thought for a long time about his "simple" request. And here's where I ended up:

"My grandfather Owen Snow (my mom's side) ran a little country store in Wicomico Church, Virginia, in a part of the state called the

'Northern Neck.' As you might expect, we grandkids loved hanging out in the store—there were still barrels of this and that back in the late '40s and even the '50s. Sometimes Grampa Owen would let us measure something out—and he would turn tyrant, despite our youth and his affection, if we ever accidentally shorted someone by even a fraction of an ounce. He'd always pile a little something extra into a can of 10-penny nails, or whatever. One also noticed, to the extent that a kid could, that he always took his time with people, listened to their stories, nodded frequently, and treated everyone with the utmost respect.

"I was in the Navy in Port Hueneme, California, when Grampa Owen passed away. We were days from a deployment to Danang, Vietnam, but my commanding officer didn't hesitate for a second in giving me four days' leave, even though I was the so-called Embarkation Officer—there's a lesson for another day in that, too. Anyway, I made it to Wicomico Church in plenty of time for the service. Did I tell you it was a truly pipsqueak town, with, I'd guess, a population of 400 or 500, though my memory is cloudy? The roads were still pretty primitive, and it'd been dry for a while, as I recall. Around 8 A.M., the service was at 10, I thought I sensed the dust starting to stir. In short order, it was a veritable dust storm. (My God, I shiver, the memory is so clear.) The upshot of all this is that over 1,000 people showed up. I talked to several of them, none of whom I knew. It seemed as if Grampa Owen had lent each and every one a helping hand at one time or another—good advice, a call to someone somewhere who might help them out, an extended period of credit, a few bucks out of his pocket, whatever, and whatever, and whatever.

"The 'lesson' that funeral taught me was the power of decency and thoughtfulness. It wasn't that my mom and dad hadn't done a lot of that, but this was the Ultimate Technicolor Illustration. In the most unassuming way, Grandpa Owen had 'been there' for an entire community and beyond—and a great dust storm of people, some, who'd moved, from 100 miles away, had come to say one last thanks. If there isn't a crystal clear message, and, de facto, advice in that, I don't know where you'd find it."

To make the obvious more obvious: How do you stack up on The Great "Being There" Exam? It's the ultimate "life question"—*and* the ultimate "business-career-success question."

31. Appreciating the Great Battle: A Case for Consideration.

"Be kind, for everyone you meet is fighting a great battle."
—Plato

I ran across the above quotation two or three years ago. It's a saying that rattles around and around and around in my mind, and it has, I think, led me to Nirvana—that is, altered behavior on my part.

Consider: You are in a negotiation—or simply trying to engage one of your coworkers as an important project milestone approaches. The unassailable fact:

That other person is . . . **always** . . . *98+ percent hidden from your view.*

Her mother has vision problems and is having the devil's own time dealing with them, and is making everyone within reach miserable in the process. His teenage son has suddenly started cutting classes—getting to the bottom of it isn't being helped by Dad issuing an endless stream of "cease and desist" orders. Or maybe it's not so oceanic—she had a testy encounter with a coworker yesterday and she's simply a little off balance. He's taking the family hiking for the weekend—and he's upset about the odds that a client problem looms in the way.

Whatever.

And, yes, there are always "whatevers" piled on top of whatevers.

Even if you're a somewhat avid major-league baseball fan, one of the 162 regular-season games is pretty much like any other. But not to the manager of, say, the Mariners. His "department" (25-person roster) is a godawful mess of professional and personal problems. So-and-so can't shake a slump and needs a break—but there's no way in hell that you can give him one. So-and-so has had a nasty personal incident reported in the paper in gory detail this morning; to use the vernacular, "Where's his head at" this evening? And on it goes. And on and on and on it goes. Fact is, there are 162 scheduled events, called "games," and each is more or less . . . **totally different** . . . from the one before and the one that follows.

Having said all this does *not* mean that our baseball manager has to be, in any way, shape, or form, a soft touch. It *does* mean, if he's worth his salt, that he has to figure in all this "extraneous" (not!) stuff. And, of course, as those who know my biases are aware:

I see no essential difference between a 25-person baseball team and a 25-person IS or HR department, except that each work "season" (year) in HR or IS has about 220 "games"—that is, workdays. And each workday is different for each "player" (employee) as their "great battles," per our instructor, Plato, unfold—mostly invisible to their coworkers and bosses.

"The boss's job is not to be a shrink"—I've heard that one a hundred times. And it is utter baloney.

It is precisely the boss's job to be a shrink!
(At least if he or she gives a damn about getting things done.)

Suppose you're in charge of the President's protective detail for a speech on farm policy in Des Moines tomorrow. Don't you want to know pretty precisely "where their heads are at" for the six agents physically closest to the President? Of course, these agents are the quintessential professionals—but along with that undoubtedly come an unusually large number of personal problems, and I'm not sure I want one of the President's six closest agents to have had a knock-down, drag-out fight with her husband or 14-year-old daughter last night, and *especially* if that fight mostly took place long distance, over the phone or, God help us, IM-style.

So, *awareness* is called for—for the sake of enterprise effectiveness. And *empathy* is called for. No, not "softness," as I said, but human empathy for the plight that besets all with whom we deal. It is *reported* (I can't find the exact quote—though I've found 20 like it) that legendary football coach Vince Lombardi, a tough guy's tough guy in a brutal profession, said, *"You do not need to like your players, but you must love them."* Those precise words might not work for you, but the idea is unassailable for the effective boss, a four-star general dealing with three-star generals or the director of a community theater off-off-off-Syracuse, let alone Broadway.

Be kind, for everyone is fighting a great battle—I have redoubled my personal efforts to take Plato's advice, every word of it, on board in every situation I face. Have I made better business decisions? I'd guess so, though I have no certain evidence. Do I feel like I'm a better human being—well, maybe, just a little. But, in keeping with the theme of this book, a "little" can be a bloody hell of a BIG lot!

(We'll each choose our own route, if any, with this. In my case, I repeat more or less as mantra, before going into a meeting or making an important call, or most any call: *Be kind, for everyone is fighting a great battle.* I think it at least ups the awareness ante a notch or two.)

> **MOODY BLUE DEVILS?**

"Things don't stay the same. You have to understand that not only your business situation changes, but the people you're working with aren't the same day to day. Someone is sick. Someone is having a wedding. [You must] gauge the mood, the thinking level of the team that day."
—Mike Krzyzewski ("Coach K"), coach of the Duke University Blue Devils basketball team

32. Thoughtfulness Is Free (or Close Thereto).

I like, and value, the word *decency*—a lot. (See Steve Harrison's phenomenal *The Manager's Book of Decencies: How Small Gestures Build Great Companies*.) I like the word *respect*—a lot. (See Sara Lawrence-Lightfoot's superb *Respect*.)

But I'm stuck on, hooked on, wedded to, wild about another word these (discombobulated) days: *thoughtfulness*. I am enamored with the idea of living and then adding to our formal or informal vision & values statement:

"We are thoughtful in all we do."

I'm so taken with the idea that I suggest-urge-beg that "thoughtfulness" joins the likes of "people," "customers," "product," "profit," "action," "excellence" on the "10 Great Business Words List"—or some such.

Times are perilous.
Competition is brutal.

Hustle is essential.

Cost-cutting is imperative.

All true!

But how, in the process of getting from difficult here to difficult there in concert with our many constituents-stakeholders with whom we hope to do business over the long haul, do we "live in the world"?

Who are we?
How are we?
What are we as a human institution?
Who am I (boss, follower)?
What do I leave in my wake?

It's character, in a way, to be sure. (Another stunningly important and, alas, underused word.) But, in a sense, thoughtfulness is even more encompassing than character. It is transactional—thoughtfulness applies literally to every internal and external activity, as well as being something that resides deep within.

I like the idea of showing up for work in a place that cherishes . . . *thoughtfulness.*

I like the idea of doing business with a service provider known for its . . . *thoughtfulness.*

I like being a vendor to an outfit that's . . . *thoughtful.*

All this is X10 in troubled times.

Thoughtful is *not* "soft."
No.
No.
No.

And:

No.
No.
No.

In fact, I'd contend that "dogmatic thoughtfulness" (now *there's* a term) improves growth and profitability and long-term enterprise solidity in a pretty damn direct, high-impact, ultimately measurable cause-and-effect way.

Thoughtfulness is **key** to customer retention.
Thoughtfulness is **key** to employee recruitment and satisfaction.
Thoughtfulness is **key** to brand perception.
Thoughtfulness is **key** to your ability to look in the mirror—and tell your kids about your job.

"Thoughtfulness is free."

Thoughtfulness is **key** to speeding things up—it reduces friction.
Thoughtfulness is **key** to Business Issue #1, cross-functional communication—XF communication is 98 percent a matter of social factors.
Thoughtfulness is **key** to transparency and even cost containment—it abets rather than stifles truth-telling.

So think about thoughtfulness, think about the truth, or not, to your mind, of the list above, think about adding *"Thoughtfulness in all we do"* to your unit's (or company's) (or agency's) values statement.

But . . . do so only after you and your team have figured out exactly what thoughtfulness means in a variety of contexts. And do so only after you have made a demonstrated personal and organizational commitment to thoughtfulness. Thence, you must be unabashedly devoted to keeping one another honest in the practice of Dogmatic Thoughtfulness—with, alas, adverse consequences, eventually severe, for those who fail to take this essential attribute aboard.

Starting time?
Not "today"—but "now."
That is, thoughtfulness is an especially potent "tool" in crazy-disruptive-scary times.

Hence:

Consider the idea of: *"We are thoughtful in all we do."*
What does it mean?
How does one practice it?
Talk about it with peers, pals, vendors, customers, etc., etc.
Talk about thoughtfulness—**"The Practice of Dogmatic Thoughtfulness"**—as a powerful and pragmatic business value. (Again, especially in traumatic times.)
Keep debating.
Consider adding "Thoughtfulness in all we do," maybe "dogmatic thoughtfulness in all we do," to your formal values proclamation—or otherwise vigorously promoting the idea.

(NB: You must also come to agreement on the immense "bottom line/$$$$ value"-pragmatism of this idea before formally proceeding; it may well make you a better person, but it is not in any way a "mushy" idea.)

1. 2. 3. 4. 5. 6. 7. 8. 9. 10. 11. 12. 13. 14. 15. 16. 17. 18. 19. 20. 21. 22. 23. 24. 25. 26. 27. 28. 29. 30. 31. 32. **33. 34. 35. 36.** 37. 38. 39. 40. 41. 42. 43. 44. 45. 46. 47. 48. 49. 50. 51. 52. 53. 54. 55. 56. 57. 58. 59. 60. 61. 62. 63. 64. 65. 66. 67. 68. 69. 70. 71. 72. 73. 74. 75. 76. 77. 78. 79. 80. 81. 82. 83. 84. 85. 86. 87. 88. 89. 90. 91. 92. 93. 94. 95. 96. 97. 98. 99. 100. 101. 102. 103. 104. 105. 106. 107. 108. 109. 110. 111. 112. 113. 114. 115. 116. 117. 118. 119. 120. 121. 122. 123. 124. 125. 126. 127. 128. 129. 130. 131. 132. 133. 134. 135. 136. 137. 138. 139. 140. 141. 142. 143. 144. 145. 146. 147. 148. 149. 150. 151. 152. 153. 154. 155. 156. 157. 158. 159. 160. 161. 162. 163.

Connection

33. Only Connect . . .

Only connect!
That was the whole of her sermon.
Only connect the prose and the passion, and both will be exalted,
And human love will be seen at its highest.
Live in fragments no longer.
Only connect . . .
—E. M. Forster, *Howards End*

Only connect!

Is there a better way to sum up a life lived well?
(And lived effectively?)

Message (my translation):

It's always about relationships.

Always was.
Always will be.
Only connect.

Hence, and long before the Internet and social networking:

The business of business is relationships.
The essence of effective business is effective relationships.

The "R.O.I." (Return on Investment) that truly matters is . . .
R.O.I.R.

Return on Investment in Relationships.

Moreover, we can manage and actually measure R.O.I.R.-related activity more accurately than we can manage and measure standard "financial" R.O.I. Lying with statistics is relatively easy. Lying about the state of relationships is nigh on impossible.* (*When I was at McKinsey, senior partners would closely examine, brick by brick, the state of Client relationships per se as they evaluated junior partners—like me.)

▸ RESPECT: READ ALL ABOUT IT

I urge-beg you to ingest-form a yearlong study group around the following:

The Manager's Book of Decencies: How Small Gestures Build Great Companies—Steve Harrison

Respect—Sara Lawrence-Lightfoot

Hostmanship: The Art of Making People Feel Welcome—Jan Gunnarsson and Olle Blohm (leader as host to his-her employees)

The SPEED of Trust: The One Thing That Changes Everything—Stephen M. R. Covey

The Dream Manager—Matthew Kelly

The Customer Comes Second: Put Your People First and Watch 'Em Kick Butt—Hal Rosenbluth and Diane McFerrin Peters (no relation)

Crucial Conversations and *Crucial Confrontations*—Kerry Patterson, Joseph Grenny, Ron McMillan, Al Switzler

Influence: Science and Practice—Robert Cialdini

Emotional Intelligence: Why It Can Matter More Than IQ—Daniel Goleman

Built to Win: Creating a World-Class Negotiating Organization—Hal Movius and Lawrence Susskind

34. They Liked Ike (Because Ike Liked *Them*).

General Dwight David Eisenhower did the impossible. No, not the successful and history-changing D-Day landing per se. Nor the subsequent march to Germany. His "impossible dream"—come true—was to keep the Yanks and the Brits from annihilating each other long enough to hit the beach and get on with the real job at hand!

Turns out General Eisenhower, most keen professional observers agree, had a "secret," which he in fact understood:

"Allied commands depend on mutual confidence; this confidence is gained, above all, through the development of friendships."

Yup, that's *his* Success Tip #1!
Aggressively make friends!

Armchair General magazine (May 2008) traces the origins of this most pronounced of Eisenhower's leadership traits: "Perhaps his most outstanding ability [at West Point, decades before D-Day] was the ease with which he made friends and earned the trust of fellow cadets who came from widely varied backgrounds; it was a quality that would pay great dividends during his future coalition command."

So you're manager of an 11-person project team. Members likely come from four functions—and two or three companies.

Fact:
You are a full-bore, no-bull "coalition commander"!

Success Key #1: Make friends. Pointedly—that is, consciously *and* measurably *and* carefully—track your "investments" in friend-making; think about friend-making in the same way you would think about any investment process.

Micro-success key: You may be "one of those," large in number, who simply do not take to this "friend-making thing" instinctively. While there may be some truth to your self-assessment—it's mainly a cop-out. Eisenhower was, indeed, "naturally" gregarious. And you probably will never match him. But—and it is a big "but"—this is beyond any shadow of doubt a **"learnable skill"** that you can acquire or improve upon by Hard Work and Practice, alone or with peers.

Macro-success Key: In hiring, promoting, incenting, pay (close) attention to "friend-making proclivity-skills." It is a trait you *can* observe and, in effect, "measure"—and DDE sure as hell teaches us it ain't no "soft" trait.

▸ LONG BEFORE ANYONE "FRIENDED" ANYONE ELSE . . .

Despite our "everything is new" world of social networking, you might do worse, and could hardly do better in my opinion, than to go back to Dale Carnegie's classic *How to Win Friends & Influence People*—named by NPR as one of the top three business books of the 20th century.

35. Always Make It Personal.

A week of my life: five speeches, five different countries, five different cultures. By watching audiences respond to each speech (one can—*must*—learn to watch and sniff intently as one speaks), I relearned a few lessons. Above all:

Make it personal.

For one thing, I'm a nut about reading local papers, chatting up anyone I can grab to get a flavor of what's afoot.

Or just hitting the pavement.

So in my seminar in Stockholm, for example, I began by talking about my jaunt the day before to the giant local department store, NK, and shopping from a long list foisted on me by my wife, who did four years of her professional training as a tapestry weaver in Sweden. It didn't hurt that I called NK "the world's best department store"—which I think it may well be. Appreciating someone else's turf nabs megapoints! (Sorry, again, to trouble you with the "obvious"—but, then, that's the point of the book!) On the other hand, I've screwed this up upon occasion. I once offhandedly criticized something that went awry at the local hotel I was staying in. Though it was part of a big chain, my remarks were not perceived as generic "customer service lessons"—as I had intended—but as a frontal assault-insult aimed at my hosts in Tampa, Florida, and, effectively, each and every audience member! (Ye gads! Lesson noted!)

In Germany, I played shamelessly to my German heritage and "Germanic" engineering background—and teased incessantly about the need for my listeners, and me, to overcome rigidity of thought and behavior in a world gone wobbly with new technology and new global players.

In Italy, I showed up in a gorgeous Italian shirt and tie, purchased the afternoon before on the high street in Milano, joked about the stratospheric+ price—and then tied the whole thing to my spiel on design and new approaches to value-added.

Bottom line: A speaker (any speaker, any topic, anywhere) is always, even in a 10-minute exchange, attempting first and foremost to form a common heritage with the audience. Any speaker worth her or his salt wants to move an audience to act. That is only accomplished, in my experience, when "they" are converted into "we." "WE . . . are confronted with this challenge or that." "WE . . . must get beyond the places where WE are . . . JOINTLY . . . stuck today." "WE . . . are frail and battered . . . but WE . . . must act with dispatch." And so on.

"We" power? Amen!

Your argument may be airtight, the data unassailable, but if your message is not . . . **up close and personal and "sold" as a joint challenge** . . . if it's not . . . **coming from the heart** . . . then it can be perceived, especially in another culture, as an . . . Assault By a Thoughtless Stranger!

BTW: *To state the obvious, the tougher the sell* (and my ideas—such as "forget everything you thought you knew and that made you successful"—can be pretty tough to swallow) *the Tighter the Intimate Human Bond Must Be!*

BTW: This is hard, conscious work! (Yes, work! None, zip, zero, nada of these "little" ideas can be implemented "off the top of your head." They must be studied and worked at and practiced assiduously. I know this reminder is not the first or second or third of its sort—nor shall it be the last.)

> THE W-WORD (LET'S USE IT)

The "We-power approach" was taught to me by Jim Crownover, my first McKinsey partner-mentor back in 1974. "Tom," he said, none too gently, "when you address the Client, always use the word **'We.'** As in 'The way *we* might get at this blah blah blah.' The idea is it's us and the Client . . . *Foraging as a Mighty Team in Hot Pursuit of the Truth."*

I'll be the first to admit that this is a "trick." But beginning in those McKinsey days, I contend that I was the one being tricked: Use "we" and "us" enough . . . and you begin to feel that you *are* on the Client's team, not vice versa.

To this day, 30+ years later, by instinct, I religiously use "We" and "Us" when working with Clients—and a team of wild horses could not elicit "I" or "You."

Though it may be a trick of sorts . . . it is also a Fundamental Value concerning Groups on Joint Ventures in Quest of Better Understanding. So:

We hereby swear to use the word "us" *until we are blue in the face. (Words matter! A lot!)*

We hereby swear to use the word "partner" *until we are blue in the face. (Words matter! A lot!)*

We hereby swear to use the word "team" *until we are blue in the face. (Words matter! A lot!)*

We agree, right?

(NB: Also observe, "Trick" #2, my "religious" capitalization of Client. Another McKinsey gem that makes a big difference. Yes, it's all about **Respect** and **Teamwork** and **Common Cause**—no matter, in the case of McKinsey, how "technical" the task.)

36. Commit "Acts of Deliberate Relationship Enhancement."

During his days as Goldman Sachs boss, former Treasury secretary Hank Paulson formed a habit well worth noting. In an interview with Patricia Sellers for *Fortune*'s "How I Work" column, Paulson reported that he would call "60 CEOs in the first week [of the year] to wish them Happy New Year."

During my brief White House stint in the mid-1970s, I did something similar, spending eight or nine straight hours one New Year's Eve on my office phone. I called close to 100 people I worked with—in agencies all over Washington and in embassies around the world—to thank them for their help the prior year. In addition to enjoying the chats, which I did (I suspect Paulson did, too), I admit that I was purposefully engaging in an ADRE . . . an Act of Deliberate Relationship Enhancement.

I'm not suggesting false sincerity here, as I fully buy the argument that "If you aren't sincere, it'll come through as if you were using a megaphone." I nonetheless urge you to develop some similar ritual. Moreover, I urge you to start it in the next couple of weeks, then get into the New Year's Habit.

Think ADRE. Twelve months a year!

Flash!
Flash!
Flash!
For immediate action!
For immediate action!
For immediate action!
New Year's resolution that works any day of the year!

Call (C-A-L-L!) (NOT EMAIL!) 25 to 50 people . . . IN THE NEXT FIVE DAYS . . . to thank them for their support in the last 90 days or six months! Then, establish this, like Paulson, as a December 20 habit—25 to 50 calls in a three- or four-day period before Christmas.* **

(*Trust me: This is fun!!)
(**Trust me: This "works.")

(Two small addenda: [1] Of course, the person on the other end of the line will know what you're up to; doesn't matter—the fact that you made the effort is the big deal! [2] Call or, perhaps better yet, send a handwritten note. Not email—and that goes for twentysomethings as well as us old buggers.)

1. 2. 3. 4. 5. 6. 7. 8. 9. 10. 11. 12. 13. 14.

15. 16. 17. 18. 19. 20. 21. 22. 23. 24. 25.

26. 27. 28. 29. 30. 31. 32. 33. 34. 35.

36. **37. 38. 39. 40.** 41. 42. 43. 44. 45.

46. 47. 48. 49. 50. 51. 52. 53. 54. 55. 56.

57. 58. 59. 60. 61. 62. 63. 64. 65. 66. 67.

68. 69. 70. 71. 72. 73. 74. 75. 76. 77. 78.

79. 80. 81. 82. 83. 84. 85. 86. 87. 88.

89. 90. 91. 92. 93. 94. 95. 96. 97. 98. 99.

100. 101. 102. 103. 104. 105. 106. 107.

108. 109. 110. 111. 112. 113. 114. 115.

116. 117. 118. 119. 120. 121. 122. 123.

124. 125. 126. 127. 128. 129. 130. 131.

132. 133. 134. 135. 136. 137. 138. 139.

140. 141. 142. 143. 144. 145. 146. 147.

148. 149. 150. 151. 152. 153. 154. 155.

156. 157. 158. 159. 160. 161. 162. 163.

Attitude

37. Put the "Eye-Sparkle Factor" on Your Menu.

Some people's eyes have an engaging, infectious "sparkle." Some don't. **Hire (only???) those who "have it."**

Consider:

I gave a lecture in Switzerland on "talent selection"—and the use of "unconventional" (emotional, mostly) measures for so doing. At a break I had an exchange with a youthful participant, who wondered aloud why I would go on and on and on . . . and then on . . . about the likes of "vivacity":

"Suppose you and I were opening the restaurant of our dreams," I said to her. "We'd both put in $75,000 . . . effectively, our life's savings. We were 'betting the farm.' We were dead certain we had a great idea, and we'd bargained our way into a very good location—and through our networking even lassoed a terrific chef. Now the time had come to hire 'the others'—e.g., waiters and waitresses and busboys.

"Numerous applicants had satisfactory 'restaurant experience.'
"But several didn't.

"One young woman/man in particular was a rank amateur—but had the most compelling 'sparkle' in her/his eye. The sort about which we Americans say 'lit up the room.' How would that 'sparkle' that 'lit up the room' rank in our hire–no hire consideration? Remember, we've bet our entire stake on the restaurant."

She reluctantly agreed, lesser Swiss emotionalism notwithstanding, that the "sparkle" pretty much ruled.

In reality, the participant in question ran not a restaurant, but a 30-person unit in an IS/IT department. And my real goal was to urge her to think about how the "Eye-sparkle Factor" should play as big a role in *IS/IT* hiring decisions (or any field, for that matter) as it does in the hospitality industry! The fact is, most IS/IT projects fall way, way short of their potential—and in 9.8 out of 10 cases, they do so because of unenthusiastic users, not inferior software. Hence, as always, it is a "people thing," a "sales thing," a "soft skills thing" that derails even the most technical "internal" projects.

Message: **So-called soft factors—which are the true "hard factors"—rule!** For scientists who must convince others to spend money to support their research. For IS/IT bosses who only succeed if users become enthusiasts. And for those "betting the farm" on the restaurant of their dreams. Maybe you don't go so far as to take a pass on anyone with a less-than-overwhelming "eye-sparkle quotient," but you damn well ought to consider it 100 percent of the time! (And for "big bosses," insist that HR folks put these "soft factors" at the top of the quals list for *every* job!)

38. Pleasant, Caring, Engaged—at 6 A.M.!

There is a little bistro about 100 yards from my Boston house where you'll find me at 6:00 A.M. sharp when I'm in the city. The coffee is good to great (and 100 times better than my own), the croissants a pure delight.

And, yes, they open at 6:00 A.M.
No small thing for an early riser.
And coffee addict.

But that's not the point of this riff. Rather, I want to say a few words about a woman I dote on but whose name I don't know. And the tragedy of her leaving me for good.

Here's the story:

(1) While she worked at the bistro, she would come in about 4:00 A.M. each day to get things ready.

(2) She appeared to be very efficient at what she did.

(3) She lit up my life for a moment or two, no more, rain or snow, sleet or hail, gloomy or sunny, 90°F or −5°F.

Her style would *not* be described as "chirpy." (I'd guess she's 45, an age by which chirpiness is highly suspect, by my lights.) But she seemed to enjoy what she did, and when we'd exchange a few pleasant sentences, she brought along a good (good, not "great") attitude day in and day out.

I emphasize "good but not great" because, at 6:00 A.M., I'm not looking for "Let's go out and kick ass, guys." I'm looking for solid and engaged and sociable-friendly and gettin' the job done with everyday pleasure.

Her solidness and spirit were just the tonic I needed—as much as the caffeine. And she provided it again and again and then again.

She's gone now. And I miss her terribly, and I didn't know her name. That's not all bad either, in a funny way. It's not that "Mary's gone—alas." It's that "this person" whose name I don't know who, in a solid-quiet way, launched my days on a sound (not giddy) basis is not in situ anymore.

Message to you as shop owner or office boss: Look for, desperately pursue, settle for nothing less than such folks—they are surely not a dime, or even a dollar, a dozen. But they are out there, and if you take the trouble to seek them out and show your occasional appreciation for what they do, Excellence, I predict, will be within your grasp. (And quite possibly a bushel of profit to go along with it.)

The fact is, the workplace to a great extent is "where we live." We need star accountants. Boffo saleswomen. Over-the-top creatives in marketing and new product development. And so on. But, since we're effectively talking about "where we live," we would in general benefit mightily—including on the P&L—if we insisted on, in 100 percent of positions:

"Pleasant."
"Caring."
"Engaged."

So, let's put this . . . **Big Three** . . . in the hiring practices manual. Let's put the Big Three in every evaluation and in every promotion decision.

Let's get pleasant-caring-engaged people in every department. (Hint: If we look for "it" in accounting as much as in, say, sales and publicity, we'll have gone a long way toward making . . . **all-important** . . . cross-functional coordination more or less automatic—yes, "automatic.")

Start now.

39. Hire "Cheerful"— Or: That Damned AV Guy!

Giving a seminar.
Everything went wrong!
Small sins.
Big sins!
Unprofessional!
Unforgivable!

And I was in a deservedly, as I saw it, foul, foul mood about it all. (No way to go into a speech.)
And then I did my last stop before Showtime . . . my AV check.

That damned AV guy!

I was in a foul mood.
I savored . . . self-righteously . . . my Foul Mood.

That damned AV guy!
He was in a Great Mood!
Happy with the World!

Humming!

Can you believe it . . . **HUMMING!**

And, in spite of the blackness of the thundercloud between my ears, my damned mood started to improve. We started joking about this or that, talkin' shop, even laughin' about the mess-ups, and in short order I was bordering on . . . CHEERFUL.

You get the point, I'm sure: Despite one's Very Best Efforts to Harbor a Grudge for Various Injustices . . . another's Cheerfulness acts as a Contagion!

That damned AV guy.

He saved my speech.

He saved my neck.

Cheerful people will do that.

(Message I: HIRE CHEERFUL!)

(Message II: Avoid-Dismiss FMCs . . . Foul Mood Carriers. THEY SCREW YOU UP! AND 100 PEOPLE WHO SUR-ROUND THEM.)

(Message III: All Hail "that damned AV guy"!)

(Message IV: One "damned AV guy" can change the mood of a battalion!)

40. Which "Flag" Are You Waving?

I have some fear that you'll read this and accuse me of playing "holier than thou." Alas, I suppose I must say, "So be it."

I had gone into town to do some errands. On the way, I was delayed by a crew doing some roadside tree trimming. One lane of Vermont Route 30 was closed—and there was, naturally, a flagman at each end of the work area.

As is my habit, I waved to the flagman—not some big full-body "Yo, my man," just a little flick of the wrist. It ain't a great job, and a dollop of recognition can't hurt—right?

The guy on the front end waved back—a similar flick of the wrist, and perhaps a little nod. But as I approached the other end, I almost cringed. The flagman there had as sour-grim an expression as I've seen in a long time. Not aggressively, attack-dog sour, just sour-sour. (Presumably you know what I mean.) I waved anyway, but as expected received no response whatsoever.

Maybe Flagman #2 was fired from a two-hundred-thou-a-year job at Lehman. Maybe Walmart laid him off. Maybe his wife is pissed off at him. Maybe he has a nasty head cold. Any of those things is possible, or a hundred others—plus the job's not exactly a major career step.

Or is it?

(More accurately, could it be?)

I use a lot of quotes in my speeches; but the fact is that I commit very few to memory. But one that is etched indelibly into my synapses comes from Dr. Martin Luther King Jr.:

"If a man is called to be a street sweeper, he should sweep streets even as Michelangelo painted, or Beethoven composed music, or Shakespeare wrote poetry. He should sweep streets so well that all the hosts of heaven and earth will pause to say, Here lived a great street sweeper who did his job well."

I'm sure there are multiple interpretations of this, and for a while I had a touch of trouble with the quote: Did it mean that our street sweeper should aspire to no more than street sweeping? I decided not necessarily. To my mind, the quote means that whatever you are doing at the moment for whatever reason can be (ought to be, per Dr. King) turned into a Work of High Art and Full-blown Commitment.

I remember, on a visit to Rome at Easter a couple of years ago, racing at one point to catch a glimpse of a world-famous (!!-true) cop who stood in the center of a mid-city roundabout directing traffic with the same style-vigor-artistry with which Leonard Bernstein conducted a symphony orchestra or John Madden coached from the Oakland Raiders' football sidelines.

It's a truism, as I see it, that a Flagman's job, per Dr. King and our Grand Roman Traffic-circle Cop, could indeed be turned into High Art. Or at least the work could be performed with a positive-vigorous-engaged attitude.

My sour flagman made me sad—mostly for him, but it also put a wee dent in my day. We are in the midst of difficult economic times. Some readers are doubtless doing something "less" than they were a couple of years ago—perhaps both their ego and wallet have been dented.

But no one but no one but no one can rob you of your attitude. It's all yours, and only yours, to shape and put on parade.

Maybe tough times make it tough to sport a grin. But tough times are especially good times in their own fashion, the true measure of who we are, an opportunity (correct word), even a "golden opportunity," to stand out for your Spirit & Determination & Engagement & Comradeship, and, yes, your Unswerving Commitment to EXCELLENCE in All You Do.

Flagman, 7-Eleven clerk, or bank teller, there's always a promotion right around the corner—or at least something close to a short-term employment guarantee—if you live by the words of Martin Luther King Jr. And if the Great Attitude is still not enough, at least you retain your self-respect—which is no small thing (in fact, is a Very Big Thing).

The "bastids" can't steal your attitude!
(No matter how hard they may advertently or inadvertently try.)
Your attitude is all yours!

Are you Flagman #2?
Or Dr. King's street sweeper?
Today?
Right now?

1. 2. 3. 4. 5. 6. 7. 8. 9. 10. 11. 12. 13. 14. 15. 16. 17. 18. 19. 20. 21. 22. 23. 24. 25. 26. 27. 28. 29. 30. 31. 32. 33. 34. 35. 36. 37. 38. 39. 40. **41. 42. 43. 44.** 45. 46. 47. 48. 49. 50. 51. 52. 53. 54. 55. 56. 57. 58. 59. 60. 61. 62. 63. 64. 65. 66. 67. 68. 69. 70. 71. 72. 73. 74. 75. 76. 77. 78. 79. 80. 81. 82. 83. 84. 85. 86. 87. 88. 89. 90. 91. 92. 93. 94. 95. 96. 97. 98. 99. 100. 101. 102. 103. 104. 105. 106. 107. 108. 109. 110. 111. 112. 113. 114. 115. 116. 117. 118. 119. 120. 121. 122. 123. 124. 125. 126. 127. 128. 129. 130. 131. 132. 133. 134. 135. 136. 137. 138. 139. 140. 141. 142. 143. 144. 145. 146. 147. 148. 149. 150. 151. 152. 153. 154. 155. 156. 157. 158. 159. 160. 161. 162. 163.

Performance

41. It's Showtime! All the Time!

Joe Pine and Jim Gilmore gave us a great gift of a book. *The Experience Economy: Work Is Theater & Every Business a Stage.* Oh, how I love that title! As well as their Fundamental Hypothesis:

"Experiences are as distinct from services as services are from goods."

(NB: "Experiences" *are* as distinct from "services" as services are from "goods": A "service" is a . . . *transaction* . . . that gets the job done. An "experience" is/can be/should be a . . . *"memorable moment"* . . . no matter how apparently trivial—e.g., the receptionist greeting a Client with panache at 7:45 A.M.)

Or, relative to you and me, courtesy David D'Alessandro's unequivocal words in *Career Warfare*:

"It's always show time!"

"Showtime" for *me* =

Every speech!
Every PowerPoint presentation!
Every *individual* slide!
Every CLIENT phone call!

EVERY INTERCHANGE WITH A "FOURTH-LEVEL" CLIENT "ADMIN ASSISTANT" (who may make a negative—or positive!—comment to her boss's boss—who signs my check!—about an off-the-cuff comment I hastily made).

EVERY EMPLOYEE INTERACTION . . . especially when I'm stressed and/or grouchy.

Every post at tompeters.com!

Every tweet at Twitter!

Every SEVEN-SECOND EYE CONTACT with someone who asks me to sign a book!

And so on.

And on.

And on.

Am I hopelessly uptight-demanding-ridiculous-absurd about all this?

Absolutely.

But no, too; "it" (being "on") has become a way of life, as natural as breathing. (My wife says it takes me two or three days, after I've been on the road, to quit "preaching to 4,000 people.")

Is this "no way to live"?

Hell, no!

I am . . . Desperate to . . . **Make a Difference!**

I hope you are, too.

(That's what leadership is all about!)

(And "life," too—remember "that damned AV guy.")

If you are indeed "desperate" to make your team a World Cup IS/IT winner, remember:

It's showtime . . . all the time.

(*Every* interaction, like my life, is with a potentially vociferous ally—or foe or foot-dragger.)

▶ THIS TIME, IT'S "PERSONA"

Successful performers, for good and (sometimes) for ill, know how to play a role. They don a "persona"—a mask of leadership (for the Greeks, it literally was a mask) that commands others to follow.

Case #1: In the winter of 1776, the Continental Army was on its last legs. The British went to General George Washington's HQ in Cambridge, Massachusetts, to ask for his surrender. They confronted a man who presented himself in every way as a serious commander in chief. Bearing. Grace. Decisiveness. Uniform design. Horse. Horse's livery. It was 98 percent Dress-for-Success and Theater and Great Design that sent the British away believing they confronted a Formidable Foe—not a ragtag band of ill-equipped farmers itching to go home, and with no legal ties that prevented them from so doing.

Case #2: No one, experts report to a man, has more carefully crafted every aspect of his persona than the unlikely 44th President of the United States of America . . . Barack Obama. Talk about Insanely Great Design! (It may not all be to your liking—but he parlayed it into White House residence, no mean feat!)

Case #3: And then there's Bernie Madoff. If you're sane, you think he's a horrid human. Nonetheless, one stands in awe of his ability to bilk so many truly brilliant people for so long—make no mistake, it was a product of a very carefully concocted persona acted out without let-up or slip-up for decades. Talk about a design story with punch! Talk about "It's always showtime!"

42. Work (Like a Demon) on Your First Impressions.

First impressions are your and my personal-career keys, and the keys to the likes of a company's customer service report card. We both get that. (Of course.) And yet . . . I feel quite sure that we need Constant Reminding, reminding not just of the Power of First Impressions, but that there is a full-blown . . . **Science and Art of the Construction and Execution and Maintenance of Fantastic Beginnings.**

For example, my wife rags on me semiconstantly for not looking people directly in the eye when I'm introduced. At first, I thought she was nuts, especially as I get paid sometimes to attend post-speech "G & G" (Grip and Grin) sessions with Client execs or top salespeople or key customers. But after a short course of self-observation, I belatedly had to admit that she's mostly right—I think it's my soul-deep shyness. (No baloney; a lot of people who sparkle at a podium are withdrawn in more intimate settings—and vice versa.) Upshot: At age 67 I'm working on that eye contact—and conscious work it is, but well worth it.

Back to the overall issue. Fox News über-spin doctor Roger Ailes claims that I/you/we all have . . . **7 seconds** . . . to make a first impression. And he gives us this advice:

First: "Amp up your attitude." Some people radiate energy, some don't. But the don'ts can at least square their shoulders, and pump themselves up a bit. ("Energy" is not to be confused with aggressiveness. Energy is, in my opinion—I can't speak for Roger A.—mostly in the eyes.)

Second: "Give your message a mission." That is, if you've got something you want to get from the interaction ... STAY ON MESSAGE. I honestly think I give my best speeches when I'm tired. I cut down or cut out all the convoluted twists and turns—and stay religiously "on topic."

Third: "Recognize 'face value.'" A "poker face," Ailes tells us, works well in poker—but is a disaster in more normal human interaction, including professional settings. Call it "animation" or "engagement" (my terms, not Ailes's); but it is different from raw energy; it's something about being In the Moment. And, again, the idea is not to mimic a whirling dervish—animation to me mostly involves the intensity of concentration. (My wife—this time I think it's a positive—claims my intensity of listening-concentration scares her half to death if it's aimed her way. I wouldn't know.)

The "bottom line" here is more important than the specific points: **Pay mindful attention to how you engage! It's as important as** (or, yup, more important than) **"content"—like it or not.**

> **FIRST THINGS**

As with personal success, so with organizational success: To an exceptional degree, customers evaluate your company according to their initial brush or full-fledged contact.

The Griffin Hospital team, masters of "patient-centric care," as it's sometimes called and as described in my riff on Kindness, clearly believes that the first impression matters. Hence, prospective patients are, for starters, sent clear driving directions!

As the patient heads for the hospital, he or she is already in a tizzy; lousy directions will only fuel the angst. (Music piped into the parking lot is also part of their ... **First Impressions Theatrical.**)

No surprise, the true master of "all this" is Disney. Disney pays about as much attention to the parking lots and parking lot attendants and the parking process as to their theme rides. For example, the staffers involved are carefully selected and even more selectively trained—they are true "parking professionals."

My "simple" advice: **Beginnings are overwhelmingly important—and surely count as "strategic substance" in any interchange.**

Think through beginnings **v-e-r-y** carefully—one micro-step at a time. Invest Time **(lots of)** & Money **(lots of)** & Training **(lots of)** in creating and managing first impressions.

What about something akin to a new "C-level" job:

CFIO/Chief First Impressions Officer.

(And if "C-level" is a little much, which maybe it is, I do sincerely counsel at least a DFI/Director of First Impressions.)

NB: Study (that word again!) the Art & Craft of Packaging. For one thing, there's a literature a thousand books long. Packagers are the ultimate "spin doctors"—they have all of about **one-third of a second** (not the seven seconds Ailes says you and I have) to hook you or me to a product on the store shelves that took three years and 80 million dollars to create.

NB: *I did a vastly extensive and expensive house renovation about 20 years ago. The prospective contractor, one of three I was interviewing, was due at my house for our first meeting at 11:00 A.M. I saw him pull up in his truck at about 10:40 A.M. He sat in his truck until precisely 10:58 A.M., then came to the front door and knocked. He had, effectively, iced the job before the first word was exchanged.*

43. Work (Like a Demon) on Your Last Impressions.

Now that you've got your seven-second impression nailed, having mastered your entries, consider the other bookend . . .

Daniel Kahneman (a psychologist who won the Economics Nobel in 2002 for his groundbreaking work in the field of behavioral economics) tells us, as reported in *Psychology Today*, that our memories are very selective. In particular, no matter how extended an event (party, commercial transaction), we form our view and make our evaluation based—with *dramatic* skew—on the "most intense moments" and the "final moments."

This is just one of the many compelling arguments for what I call EEM, or Emotional Experience Management. The "final moments" evidence is particularly startling; it explains why we might attend a brilliant, four-hour dinner party, yet three months later only remember that two guests exchanged heated remarks on the way out the door. (This is not an "illustrative story." A ton of hard data supports such tales.)

The solution?

Plan-Manage-Micromanage "Last Impressions-Experiences." AGGRESSIVELY.

It's not nearly enough to avoid last impression "screw-ups." Of course we don't want anything to "go wrong" at the Experience Exit Stage. But more important, we want a . . . Planned Exit Atmospherics Strategy & Story that's . . . memorable, compelling, emotional, that goes "aggressively right," not "not wrong."

A doc's walking the patient to the door (rather than pointing distractedly to the Billing Desk, while simultaneously picking up the next patient's folder) is the **Determining Factor** in the Patient's Impression . . . more, actually, than a good or bad diagnosis. (Again, hard evidence supports this apparently ludicrous statement.) Similarly, a bad dessert can mar an otherwise 5-star meal . . . just as an on-the-edge-of-your-seat, drop-the-popcorn climax can salvage a film or play that suffered a few bumpy plot points early on in the performance.

So . . . WORK ON YOUR EXITS . . . ASSIDUOUSLY!

Meaning of "work on"?

Consider the last impression: tear it apart, tiny step by tiny step by tiny step. Diagnose it. Video it. Ask outsiders to view the video. Play-act the "exit sequence."

❯ GET 'EM COMING AND GOING

Beginnings! (See #42.)
Endings! (See #43.)

Open 15 minutes before the official opening time.
Close 15 minutes after the scheduled closing time.

Message: Good sense and hard-nosed social-psych research say:

Beginnings Matter!
(A lot!!)
Endings Matter!
(A lot!!)

Obsess on beginnings!
Obsess on endings!
Key word: **obsess.**

44. Work on Your Presentation Skills. (Or: 17 Minutes Can Change the World!)

CNN wire, afternoon, June 4, 2008: "He was an obscure state lawmaker. But after a 17-minute star-making turn as a keynote speaker at the 2004 Democratic National Convention, and a scant two years in the U.S. Senate, Barack Obama is on the verge of becoming his party's presidential nominee."

As I mentioned at the start of the introduction, my first blog post at tompeters.com, on July 28, 2004, was an encomium to Barack Obama's convention speech. Among other things, I said: "I know a good speech when I hear one. Namely the Democratic Convention keynote by Illinois Senate candidate Barack Obama. The content may or may not have been to your taste depending on your politics, but as a Work of Art there should be no dispute: Clear and compelling theme. Perfect pitch. Connection with the immediate and distant audience. Humor and self-deprecation. Memorable stories. Phrases that uplift. Timing to die for." (It's worked out pretty well for then Illinois state senator Obama. At that point, he wasn't yet even a *U.S.* senator!)

Seventeen minutes!

My God:

Seventeen minutes!

Seventeen good minutes—and you, too, can move your wife and young daughters (husband and young daughters—someday!) into 1600 Pennsylvania Avenue!

Fact, in "our" more modest worlds: Awful or poor or average or even "okay" or "pretty good" presentation skills trip up or hold back an incredible number of otherwise exceptionally talented people at *all* levels, and in *all* functions, and in businesses of *all* sizes, in *all* industries. And yet it is rare to see someone launch a martial-arts-training-style-no-bull-I'm-gonna-master-(or-at-least-get-a-helluva-lot-better-at)-this-thing-or-bloody-well-die-trying offensive on presentation skill improvement.

I . . . simply . . . don't get it.

Please.
Please.
Please.
Please.

Do me a *(personal)* favor.

At least . . . *consider* . . . an all-out-fully-professional-time-consuming-study-and-practice-sustained attack on your presentation skills.

All out.
Fully professional.
Time-consuming.
Study.
Practice.
Sustained.
Attack.

I'll look forward to the engraved invitation to your Inaugural Ball . . .

❯ "POWER POINT" FROM A POWERFUL GUY

My obsession with bugging others about primacy of top-tier presentation skills started late, after I sat at dinner, in 2007, next to a "Top 25" exec at a Fortune 25 company, an outfit known for its "just-the-facts" approach to decision making. We were chatting about this, that, and the other, and at one point he said to me, out of the blue, "I work like hell developing guys for the top, and say I've got four guys who've performed well and could move up. I'll swear, two or three, or sometimes all four, will drop off the track as a direct result of lousy presentation skills."

I know this chap reasonably well, and he's a naturally reticent genius engineer whose speaking skills were positively horrid until he applied, over a period of years, his gargantuan willpower—**and brute force**—to training/improving himself.

1. 2. 3. 4. 5. 6. 7. 8. 9. 10. 11. 12. 13. 14.
15. 16. 17. 18. 19. 20. 21. 22. 23. 24. 25.
26. 27. 28. 29. 30. 31. 32. 33. 34. 35.
36. 37. 38. 39. 40. 41. 42. 43. 44. **45.**
46. 47. 48. 49. 50. 51. 52. 53. 54. 55. 56.
57. 58. 59. 60. 61. 62. 63. 64. 65. 66. 67.
68. 69. 70. 71. 72. 73. 74. 75. 76. 77. 78.
79. 80. 81. 82. 83. 84. 85. 86. 87. 88.
89. 90. 91. 92. 93. 94. 95. 96. 97. 98. 99.
100. 101. 102. 103. 104. 105. 106. 107.
108. 109. 110. 111. 112. 113. 114. 115.
116. 117. 118. 119. 120. 121. 122. 123.
124. 125. 126. 127. 128. 129. 130. 131.
132. 133. 134. 135. 136. 137. 138. 139.
140. 141. 142. 143. 144. 145. 146. 147.
148. 149. 150. 151. 152. 153. 154. 155.
156. 157. 158. 159. 160. 161. 162. 163.

Work

45. On Being a "Professional."

Think "professional," and what words come to mind? Doctor. Lawyer. Schoolteacher. Musician. Ballplayer. Six Sigma quality guru. Cloud-computing consultant. JIT inventory management expert. Said professionals share certain characteristics.

They are . . .

- Students of their craft
- Dedicated to a "calling"
- Pursuing constant improvement
- Masters of a defined body of knowledge
- Etc.

Well, my effort in many sections of this book is to expand, or even redefine, the idea of "professional" to include several bedrock areas of behavior, the effective practice of which determines success or failure in getting things done.

For example . . .

- Saying "Thank you" (Mastering the Practice of Appreciation)
- Apologizing (Repairing frayed relationships)
- Listening (Hearing and Absorbing and Engaging with others' views)
- Questioning effectively

- MBWA (Managing By Wandering Around)/The Art of Staying Connected
- Achieving peace and prosperity among warring organizational tribes (turning cross-functional integration into Strategic Weapon #1)
- Writing and Presenting

And so on. Each of these items—and I've said it a dozen times and I'll say this a dozen more times—**can** be studied and **can** be mastered—with about as much practice as is required to achieve mastery in painting or molecular biology. Most of us take most of the things enumerated immediately above "seriously." But few of us are determined to achieve no-bull . . . **"professionalism"** . . . around these and like topics, which are the true bedrock of enterprise effectiveness.

Action: Reflect on the principal ideas discussed in these pages. Develop a Formal Study Plan for a handful of topics such as those suggested above—for yourself and for your group.

46. "Everything Passes Through Finance" (And So Should You).

I listened to a presentation by the CIO of Sysco, the giant distribution company. The topic was a transforming new system, the implementation of which he'd successfully overseen. One huge advantage he'd had, he told us, was a long stint in finance—he knew pretty much everyone there; and he'd been able to communicate in the insiders' code and with the insiders' sensibilities.

The average reader probably won't have the same experience as our Sysco friend, but the idea is nonetheless powerful. Pretty much everything we're involved in "passes through Finance" at some point. It's not true, as the joke goes, that "The finance guys have a one-word vocabulary, 'No.'" It *is* by and large true that they are typically not pushovers, and that they'll push you to answer some uncomfortable questions.

And for smooth implementation of your project, it's nice (**imperative**) to know the language—and a few of the folks as well.

Hence I recommend that you try and get on a project team that will give you a chance to learn the Language of Finance—and to begin in earnest to build a network in the department. And try a course or two in accounting or finance if you didn't major in business or get an MBA. This is a straightforward investment, and the direct or indirect return may be high as a kite—and long-lasting.

(Of course the primary "trick" is to ask questions, even simplistic ones—it shows that you want to learn and you wish for one of "them" to be your teacher—what greater mark of respect?)

Everything passes through Finance.
Their business is your business.
(Stop pissing and moaning about their world.)
(Invest in appreciation of their world.)

47. What's on the Agenda? Why Don't You Decide?

He/she who writes the Agenda and Summary Doc (innocuously called "Meeting Notes") wields . . . Incredible Power!

Believe it!

The question is seemingly innocent, "What should we cover at the Weekly Review Meeting?" The response is anything but innocent: **The "agenda" is in and of itself a group "To-Do" list.** (More important than any pretentious "strategic plan.") And: **"To-Don't" list.** (What's left off . . . to the Supreme Annoyance of many Power Players.)

Moreover . . . some stuff will be at the **Top** . . . some at the bottom. (The latter probably won't get covered, or will be given short shrift.) Hence . . . *a "mere" agenda Establishes & Determines the Group Conversation for, say, the week, or even the quarter.* (And . . . the lovely catch . . . concocting the Agenda by soliciting members is typically a "crappy task," unwanted by one and almost all.)

My message: **grab it!**

Larger message: *Social networking, group document editing, and the like aside, one of the most effective paths to power has long been interjecting oneself squarely into the middle of key information streams. While working on the creation of a Public Management Program at Stanford's business school in the early 1970s, I ended up exercising exceptional sway over events. As by far the most junior member of the team, I got "stuck" with all the record-keeping and draft-writing jobs that were beneath the grandees nominally in charge. I de facto controlled "institutional memory."*

I could not have said "Go west," if the group intended to "Go east." But I damn well could turn east into east-northeast or east-southeast at will. To pull off something like this requires complete understanding of information systems, an obsession with details, and more or less a willingness to go without sleep. As invisible puppeteer, one must be eternally vigilant in order to keep control of the "innocent" document flow that is the organization's lifeblood. It is an apparent dogsbody's job that can confer power beyond measure.

▶ NOTE WELL

No less important than agenda-setting is the grubby-demeaning work of note-taking. Talk about ... UNVARNISHED POWER!

Everybody is so damn busy preening, interrupting, bullheadedly pushing their pet peeve, etc. ... that they seldom hear what actually goes on during a meeting. Only the meek and quiet notetaker knows the story; and long after the participants have washed the memory of the meeting clean from their crowded lives, the Notetaker's Summary comes along explaining what transpired ... Carefully Edited.

You get my drift, I presume. The "powerless" soul who agrees to "develop the agenda," "take the notes," and "publish the notes" ... may just be the ... #**1 power player!**

Speaking of "notes," note this: James Madison was the notetaker at the U.S. Constitutional Convention in Philadelphia in 1787. To no small extent, his "mere" notes (incredibly detailed) were the principal driving force animating the Constitution of the United States of America!

48. We Are All in Sales. Period.

"Everyone lives by selling something."
—Robert Louis Stevenson

Some years ago, on a trek in New Zealand, I met a fellow at our lodge in the NZ Alps who'd had a very successful career as a TV producer—you'd recognize a couple of his shows. (It was vacation—ID'ing him would be improper.) He told me a lovely little story—not so "little," actually. I paraphrase, from some old notes:

"For a host of reasons, including, to be sure, cockiness, I was dead certain that I had some winning ideas. And, yet, try as I would—I busted my ass—I couldn't get funding, not even for a cut-rate pilot.

"One night I was in a hotel and the TV was on, just background noise, really. It was one of those middle-of-the-night advertorials, on make a million 'overnight' in real estate. The guy was going on at one point about collecting information from numerous sources about the person you're meeting with. [This is waaaaay pre-Google.] It wasn't tricky, but it made sense.

"To make a long story short, that show launched an intense year or so scramble to teach myself selling. I read every damn 'how to' book written. Most were shit, but even the bad ones would have a useful tidbit or two. I actually went to a handful of those all-day selling seminars; again, the yield was usually low, but a couple were real gems.

"Fact is my campaign to master selling paid off pretty damn quickly. Within six months I'd gotten my first serious funding. Maybe it was just luck, but I really don't think that's the whole thing.

"I'm a pretty good salesman these days—maybe I ought to do my own 2:00 A.M. get-rich-now seminar. What do you think?"

He was teasing about the last part, of course—but I bet it'd be a hell of a show if he did do it.

We all *do* live by selling something—the TV producer, the Presbyterian minister, the youthful IT "nerd" trying to get a user to adopt his pet system.

Accept the fact that, like it or not, you are a "career" "salesperson."

So . . . Master your craft.

1. 2. 3. 4. 5. 6. 7. 8. 9. 10. 11. 12. 13. 14. 15. 16. 17. 18. 19. 20. 21. 22. 23. 24. 25. 26. 27. 28. 29. 30. 31. 32. 33. 34. 35. 36. 37. 38. 39. 40. 41. 42. 43. 44. 45. 46. 47. 48. **49. 50. 51. 52.** 53. 54. 55. 56. 57. 58. 59. 60. 61. 62. 63. 64. 65. 66. 67. 68. 69. 70. 71. 72. 73. 74. 75. 76. 77. 78. 79. 80. 81. 82. 83. 84. 85. 86. 87. 88. 89. 90. 91. 92. 93. 94. 95. 96. 97. 98. 99. 100. 101. 102. 103. 104. 105. 106. 107. 108. 109. 110. 111. 112. 113. 114. 115. 116. 117. 118. 119. 120. 121. 122. 123. 124. 125. 126. 127. 128. 129. 130. 131. 132. 133. 134. 135. 136. 137. 138. 139. 140. 141. 142. 143. 144. 145. 146. 147. 148. 149. 150. 151. 152. 153. 154. 155. 156. 157. 158. 159. 160. 161. 162. 163.

Initiative

49. Make That "Three-Minute Call"! Today! Now!

Dealing with sticky situations isn't much fun. Particularly if, as is often the case, you think that the other party is mostly responsible for the stickiness. Hence, there's an overwhelming tendency to "wait things out," to hope that they'll miraculously resolve themselves, to await the other person's taking the initiative ("as they should"); and in the process of delay, we routinely end up idly dithering as little, salvageable messes fester into big, intractable ones.

Question: How do you stop the festering dead in its tracks?
Answer: Take three deep breaths, stop overanalyzing things, stop *thinking*, and . . . *make the damn call.*

Today.
Now!

Call it "The Three-Minute Call Axiom":

In short, a three-minute call made today (NOW!) to deal with a "slightly" bruised ego or a "minor" misunderstanding can go a long way toward helping you avoid a trip to divorce court, the loss of a billion-dollar Client (lots of evidence for this), or an employee lawsuit tomorrow.

I've learned that when it comes to most "major" "situations," there comes a moment (or two . . . or five such moments) when the underlying problem that was eminently fixable slips out of your grasp. But at that crucial, in retrospect, moment, pride or embarrassment or simple unwillingness to further mess up an already-nasty day led to evasion, delay, and "I'll do it tomorrow . . ."

Or the next day . . .
Or the day after . . .

No!
No!

Do it today! And, not so incidentally, there is good news, even wonderful news:

In 9 out of 10 cases, the call goes far, far better than you anticipated it would. (The fact that you took the initiative accounts for a lot.) Not only does "the call" help "deal with" a thorny problem, but surprisingly often it launches a new and positive trajectory for a fraying relationship.

➤ "CALL" TO ACTION

"Make the three-minute call" works. But even if you agree wholeheartedly with that idea . . . *will you make the call?* And, more to the point, *how will you make yourself make it?*

One answer is simple "self-discipline." And that will work for some of us. Congratulations if you're a member of that set.

Another answer, abetted by our desktop and handheld technologies, is Bold Reminders—flashing or beeping messages on a screen: HAVE YOU MADE YOUR "THREE-MINUTE CALL" TODAY?

A third answer is a diary devoted to self-assessment. (Ben Franklin—beating the "day timer" by 200+ years—was a master, year after year, of . . . *formal, written, daily self-assessments*. Indeed, he carefully graphed his self-assessment scores for a dozen factors! Yes, I said "daily.")

A fourth strategy is to develop some type of relationship with a professional "coach" (the good ones are priceless, the bad ones a waste); a peer with whom you discuss such things regularly; or a Support Group that keeps you honest, on the model of Alcoholics Anonymous or Weight Watchers. That last option might readily be seen as going too far, but if the behavioral trait or traits under consideration, such as the three-minute call, are of immense value, then extreme self-enforcement measures may be merited.

And last (but far from least): **P-r-a-c-t-i-c-e.** It is one of my great bugbears that we think it obvious that practice matters beyond measure if the topic is flower arranging, the piano, or soldiering, but give little or no thought to the idea of practice and mastery if the topic is "merely" the likes of "making the three-minute call."

I'd argue that "making the three-minute call" is at least as worthy of study and practice as learning to play a cello or build a fine cabinet: Nations rise or fall, battles are won or lost, based on (1) not making the call, or (2) making the call occasionally, or (3) making the call routinely, as a matter of habit, and with abiding skill.

So . . . good luck!

Wrong.
Scrap "Good luck."
Instead: Happy hard work and professional practice of "make-the-three-minute-call-now."

50. Show Up! (It's a Start.)

While editing and fact-checking one of my latest presentations, my colleague Cathy Mosca came across a slide in which I had written, "Ninety percent of success is showing up." It didn't quite ring true. She checked it and corrected it to . . . **80 percent.** Our exchange encouraged me to do some Googling. I immediately confirmed that I was wrong and she was right—no surprise—but also came across a lovely little essay by Brad Isaac at his site PersistenceUnlimited.com:

> *"80 percent of success is just showing up."*
> —*Woody Allen*

"I often think about that quotation. It may sound easy to shrug off, but not if you look a little deeper. It doesn't just mean show up for job interviews or to work for an 80 percent increase in success.

"Showing up also means . . . **starting.**

"For instance, did you show up at the gym today? **'Just showing up' means you're 80 percent of the way to a good workout.** The hard part of fighting yourself to get dressed in workout gear, dealing with traffic and the worry about pain you might experience is over. Now all that is left is to just do the workout. Pretty simple, huh? Even a child could do it.

"Same thing with opportunity. It's easier to make significant progress on a project if you simply show up to do it. Candidly, one of my hardest tasks of the day is 'showing up' for Development Visual Studio. It seems simple enough . . . just double click on an icon. But if I think too much about the seemingly 10,000 things I have to do once I launch it, I am much more likely to 'accidentally' launch my Web browser or fiddle with email.

"But once I'm in there, the work is typically easy and fun. Some days I can knock out more tasks than I planned. And I feel like a success at the end of the day.

"You can be or do whatever you want just by showing up. If you want to be an author, show up to write your manuscript every day, show up to writing classes, show up to make phone calls to editors. Doesn't it make sense that someone who arrives at the door of opportunity has more success than someone just sitting at home?

"So increase your chances by 80 percent. Show Up!"

So: Show up!

It works!

Here's a tip on ensuring that you will, indeed, show up: Make a personal "show-up" commitment—a commitment from which you can't escape without grave embarrassment. You're busy as hell, and really don't have time to go to your Smalltown Theater board meeting on Thursday. But you really ought to go, for a host of reasons. On Tuesday, email or call Mary, your board colleague: "How about I pick you up Thursday, and we'll chat on the way to the meeting." Of course, you can stiff Mary, and the world won't end. Nonetheless, your little . . . self-set "show-up-or-stiff-Mary" trap . . . vastly increases the odds of your making the painful effort to go to that meeting.

❯ SMALL STATE, BIG IMPACT

I consider it the **Ultimate Proof** that Showing Up Matters. Namely, the drafting of the United States Constitution, as reported in David Stewart's *Summer of 1787*.

We typically think of the Convention in terms of the Great Men—of Washington and Madison and Franklin. But the facts are very different:

(1) Given this, that, and the other, including a miserable summer-long heat wave, there were on average only 30 folks present on the floor at Independence Hall. Some states, like New Hampshire, didn't even bother to send delegates; other states' delegates, like New York's, were rarely in attendance.

(2) States were allowed to decide on the number of delegates they'd send to Philadelphia. The two biggest states, Virginia and Pennsylvania, sent seven. But wee Delaware sent five! Moreover, all five Delaware delegates were in attendance close to 100 percent of the time! Hence, Delaware had an *enormous* impact on the final document! (Call it the "Constitution of the Great State of Delaware, as used by the rest of us.")

(3) **Delaware's Big Secret: Showing Up!!** More or less "proof positive" of "showing up"—this is one hell of a compelling case with consequences of the utmost significance!

(This story repeats remarks in the introduction. In this instance it's merited.)

51. Get Up Earlier Than the Next (in This Case) Gal.

I was flying to Boston from London on a Saturday morning. It was a seven-hour flight. A professional woman was sitting in front of me. I duly swear, she did not look up once during the entire flight. She produced more on her laptop in those seven hours than I do in a week. Or a month.

I'm not touting workaholism here.
I am stating the obvious.

She or he who works the *hardest* has one hell of an advantage.

She or he who is best *prepared* has one hell of an advantage.

She or he who is always . . . **"over" prepared** . . . has one hell of an advantage.

She or he who does the most *research* has one hell of an advantage.

I would not have wanted to challenge that woman on that Boston-London flight in whatever presentation venue she was approaching.

Would you?

52. Make an Insane Public Effort.

The late sports superagent Mark McCormack (once voted the most powerful man in sports) condoned and even certified one of my own crazy habits.

McCormack said there are times, not necessarily infrequent . . . **when it is wise-*imperative* to . . . travel 5,000 miles for a five-minute meeting.**

It was a tactic I started using in 1974, when I was a junior White House staffer working on drug abuse issues. I discovered the startling power of being able to say, **"When I was with Ambassador Moynihan in Delhi [or Ambassador Helms in Teheran] just three days ago, he assured me that . . ."** It was, well, a showstopper—even when I was in the presence of people much more senior than I was.

It's something I end up doing probably once a year. And the power and effectiveness thereof are literally beyond measure. There's substance to this tactic—you can get a lot done in a short meeting when it's clear that you've killed yourself to be there. But it's overwhelmingly psychological. The power of making a perceived **"insane effort"** almost always breaks a logjam—and not infrequently leads to a solution on the spot.

(Incidentally, in an age of instant electronic communication, this tactic is arguably more important than ever. These days, it gets harder and harder to distinguish signal from noise. A 5,000-mile trip for a five-minute meeting . . . **ain't no tweet.**)

Advice: *When an issue is of the utmost importance and at a standstill (or in free fall), proactively look for an opportunity to "make a statement" through a gesture that unmistakably indicates great pain and engagement and urgency on your part.* (Is this Machiavellian? Sure, to some extent. But to make such an effort, you actually *must* care. The "insane gesture" simply acts as rock-solid proof that you'll go to anylength-imaginable-and-then-some to make progress.)

> ### ▶ I'LL SEE YOUR 5,000 AND RAISE YOU 7,000
>
> Max Kraus tops Mark McCormack by 7,000 miles—call it 12,000 miles to reseat a couple of screws. Max reports:
>
> "My best 'walking around' story took place many years ago when I was running Electro-Nite Company. We sold some equipment to a Chinese steel mill that would help improve their steel quality. This was just after the opening of trade with China, and we had to plow through massive red

tape with the U.S. government, get the letter of credit, etc. But we finally made the shipment; it went by air, and we waited to hear if all was well.

"Unfortunately the next word, in those days by teletype, was that it did not work. As a believer in 'walking around' sales as well as management [remember Hewlett-Packard's MBWA/Managing By Wandering Around—TP], and also intrigued by the possibility of a trip to China, I sent a reply saying that we guaranteed our equipment and that if they would provide a visa for me and an engineer, we would come to Wuhan at our expense to see the problem. In those days visas were almost nonexistent, but within twenty-four hours we had a reply accepting our offer. Again, paperwork took a couple of weeks, but off to China we went.

"We were met at the Beijing airport, escorted to our hotel, and offered a car, guide, and interpreter for three days to see the Wall, Summer Palace, etc.—and then flown to Wuhan. The steel mill was massive, with over 100,000 workers, and of course a crowd gathered to see us work on the equipment. Much to my dismay and embarrassment, the problem turned out to be two long screws that were causing a short circuit. I removed the screws and told the group that while I was embarrassed, I hoped that I had demonstrated our commitment to service and satisfaction. We stayed a week to work with them as they put the equipment in service.

"I could go on with more stories of our visit. But the bottom line was that I made several subsequent trips, enjoyed good business and many 'Chinese Banquets' for a number of years. 'Walking around' does work!"

(Full disclosure: Max is my publisher Bob Miller's stepfather. Unbidden, Max sent this to Bob, who sent it along to me—knowing I'm always a sucker for a great MBWA story. I read it and was mesmerized—Bob was reluctant, but I told him I'd blow off the book if he didn't let me use it. Go, Bob! Go, Max! Go, Mark McCormack! Five thousand miles, twelve thousand miles—what the hell! Perceived do-or-die effort, the ultimate sales tool! And, of course, the perverse part of it: A screw-up, responded to in a flash and with "overkill," usually leads to a better relationship than if nothing had gone wrong in the first place!)

1. 2. 3. 4. 5. 6. 7. 8. 9. 10. 11. 12. 13. 14.
15. 16. 17. 18. 19. 20. 21. 22. 23. 24. 25.
26. 27. 28. 29. 30. 31. 32. 33. 34. 35.
36. 37. 38. 39. 40. 41. 42. 43. 44. 45.
46. 47. 48. 49. 50. 51. 52. **53. 54. 55. 56.**
57. 58. 59. 60. 61. 62. 63. 64. 65. 66. 67.
68. 69. 70. 71. 72. 73. 74. 75. 76. 77. 78.
79. 80. 81. 82. 83. 84. 85. 86. 87. 88.
89. 90. 91. 92. 93. 94. 95. 96. 97. 98. 99.
100. 101. 102. 103. 104. 105. 106. 107.
108. 109. 110. 111. 112. 113. 114. 115.
116. 117. 118. 119. 120. 121. 122. 123.
124. 125. 126. 127. 128. 129. 130. 131.
132. 133. 134. 135. 136. 137. 138. 139.
140. 141. 142. 143. 144. 145. 146. 147.
148. 149. 150. 151. 152. 153. 154. 155.
156. 157. 158. 159. 160. 161. 162. 163.

Leadership

53. To Lead Is to Measurably Help Others Succeed.

"Managing winds up being the allocation of resources against tasks. Leadership focuses on people. My definition of a leader is someone who helps people succeed."
—Carol Bartz, Yahoo!

"The role of the director is to create a space where the actors and actresses can become more than they've ever been before, more than they've dreamed of being."
—Robert Altman, Oscar acceptance speech

"No matter what the situation, [the great manager's] first response is always to think about the individual concerned and how things can be arranged to help that individual experience success."
—Marcus Buckingham, *The One Thing You Need to Know*

The "business" of leaders at all levels is to help those in their charge develop beyond their dreams—which in turn almost automatically leads to "all that other stuff," such as happy customers, happy stockholders, happy communities.

So how do you stack up on the Bartz-Altman-Buckingham scale? I suggest that you measure yourself *specifically* in terms of the individuals you've helped succeed in the last 12 months, and, per Altman, succeed beyond their dreams. That is, review your work with a person who reports to you (that's pretty much the whole story, eh—you working with people, one at a time); write a short "case study" on her/him, and assess the degree to which you have *specifically* helped her/him grow-succeed. (Be tough on yourself—please.) (Repeat. Regularly.)

The idea here is to change the employee evaluation process into a two-part formal process, where both parts are given equal billing:

Part ONE, which you doubtless already do, is to evaluate the employee's performance.

Part TWO, just as formal and important and painstaking, is to evaluate yourself on how well you're doing in working with that employee—the idea is very granular, not your assessment of "how I do at helping my staff grow," but "How did I do in, say, the first half of 2010 in helping Sue Chen grow and succeed?"

This is one damned high standard!
(And of the utmost importance.)

54. At Their Service.

Ask yourself daily:

"What did I *specifically* do today to be 'of service' to members of my group? Was I truly a 'servant' to them?"

This all-powerful idea derives from Robert Greenleaf's extraordinary book, *Servant Leadership*.

Here are two "exam" questions that Greenleaf urges leaders to ask concerning the people on their team:

1. Do those served grow as persons?
2. Do they, while being served, become healthier, wiser, freer, more autonomous, more likely themselves to become servants?

Message (Unequivocal):

(1) Leaders exist to serve their people. Period.
(2) A team well served by its leader will be inclined to pursue Excellence.

Use the word **"Serve."** (That's what you *do*.)
Use the word **"Service."** (That's what you *provide*.)
Use the word **"Servant."** (That's what you *are*.)

55.   Have You "Hosted" Any Good Employees Lately?

Mind-bender: Consider the leader's primary job to be . . . *a host to her or his employees.* That's precisely the way Jan Gunnarsson and Olle Blohm urge us to think in their provocative book . . . *Hostmanship: The Art of Making People Feel Welcome.*

Gunnarsson and Blohm based this idea on their experience with running a hotel. Yet they convincingly demonstrate that the "hostmanship" idea applies . . . **everywhere** . . . and not just in the hospitality biz.

Here's what they did:

"We went through the hotel [soon after acquiring it] and made a *'consideration renovation.'* [My italics.] Instead of redoing bathrooms, dining rooms, and guest rooms, we gave employees new uniforms, bought flowers and fruit, and changed colors. Our focus was totally on the staff. *They were the ones we wanted to make happy. We wanted them to wake up every morning excited about a new day at work.*"

(To annoyingly repeat: Don't redo the lobby—redo the employee cafeteria!)

And here's what they discovered:

"*The path to a hostmanship culture paradoxically does not go through the guest. In fact it wouldn't be totally wrong to say that the guest has nothing to do with it.* [Again, my italics.] True hostmanship leaders focus on their employees. What drives [exceptionalism] is finding the right people and getting them to love their work and see it as a passion. . . . The guest comes into the picture only when you are ready to ask,

" 'Would you prefer to stay at a hotel where the staff love their work or where management has made customers its highest priority?' "

I love words!
I think that word choice is critical to leaders.

"Consideration renovation."
Brilliant!

Leading as "hostmanship."
Brilliant!

If a leader "hosts" his or her employees with enthusiasm, then the odds go way up that employees will do the same thing with their "guests"—aka "customers."

(My first suggested "action step" is simple: Study the words above very carefully.)

56. A Sacred Trust.

As I see it, anyone who takes on any leadership job, minor or major, assumes no less than a . . . **Sacred Trust.** I know that's apparently extreme language. But I stand by it.

This sacred trust is all about what organizations are all about: *the professional (and, to some extent, personal) development of people.* Sure, the boss's job is to "get the job done," and done effectively. But "bosshood" primarily entails an abiding responsibility for the people under your charge. (It's circular, of course: Turned-on people do turned-on work. Q.E.D.)

Consider an example from your own career: You take on, say, a leadership position. For some period, be it a four-month project or a two-year assignment as a department head, 6 or 66 people are your responsibility. And, in my opinion, each and every one of those 6 or 66 ought to leave your charge in better shape than when you arrived. They should have had a measurable, remarkable, personal, and professional growth experience.

They should have grown in their discipline—accounting, marketing, training, whatever. They should have grown through exposure to new people and new ideas. Even the most junior among them (an 18-year-old stock boy, perhaps) should have been put into some form of leadership role (organizing the logistics for a company outing, perhaps).

Here are some key steps along this "sacred" path:

- Begin (in the next 30 days) with small groups or one-on-one sit-downs, aimed at assessing the current state of things; that is, the growth experience during your tenure to date—of each and every employee, in precise terms.
- As part of, say, a three-month (no longer) phase of a project plan, establish Formal Personal Growth Goals for *each* individual—achievement of those 90-day goals will be a large part of your formal evaluation of the project.
- Along the way, talk up these goals, in private or in public. Make them, perhaps, an explicit part of your unit's mission or values statement: *"We are committed to the measurable growth of each and every member of our staff. We aspire to have every staff member say of their stay here, 'That was a remarkable period of my development.'"*

> **"LEADING" PRACTICE**

One twist on this idea, practiced by companies such as W. L. Gore and Quad/Graphics, is a formal mentoring program. Everyone *("every" is the operative word)* has a mentor, and after a few months of breaking into the job, everyone *("every" is the operative word)* will *act* as a mentor. Thus, everyone *("every" is the operative word)* acquires "leadership and people development experience" from the get-go.

("Sacred trust" for each and every one? Too much to ask? Fairy-tale rhetoric? Well, "sacred trust" is surely the operative descriptor for an 18-year-old U.S. Army private on a four-person team embedded in the roughest mountain passes in Afghanistan—eh?)

57. Rat Psych Rules!—Or: Deploying Positive Reinforcement's Incredible Potency.

"You shouldn't be looking for people slipping up, you should be looking for all the good things people do and praising those."
—Richard Branson

"I can live for two months on a good compliment."
—Mark Twain

In my Ph.D. student incarnation, I was more or less trained by a "rat psychologist"—that is, a "behaviorist." He was not a down-the-line disciple of B. F. Skinner, but he did believe in the power of basic behavioral reinforcers.

And I, as they say, swallowed the Kool-Aid.
(Or at least took a swill.)

While I was getting my MBA, in the early 1970s, one "organizational behavior" prof told us of a fascinating experiment. Students were in a bowl-like classroom, with the teacher at the bottom. Students were instructed by the experimenter to nod, not in unison but noticeably, when the prof moved, say, Stage Right. And not to nod when he was in the center or moved Stage Left. The story goes—which I passionately believe—that in short order the prof was practically glued to the corner of Stage Right, and pretty much stayed there, unaware of the circumstances.

Such is the power of deliberate positive reinforcement.

To give you "the full Skinner" in 100 words or less (or maybe more, but not so many more): Positive reinforcement, small or large, reliably induces forward motion—that is, more of the good thing you acknowledged with that simple, little, in-passing "Thanks" or "Nice job." Negative reinforcement is of questionable value. It often spurs a general slowdown, not just a course alteration relative to the behavior you attempted to correct. Moreover, negative reinforcement routinely induces clever evasion—the "bad" behavior isn't halted, instead the person negatively reinforced just concocts elaborate new habits to keep from getting caught. I'm not suggesting you stop offering course corrections—I am suggesting that you may be unpleasantly surprised by the unintended consequences.

I was, and always will be, a sucker for positive reinforcement. And you are, too—like it or not.

So???? Why the hell are we so chary with this magic potion?
I can only come up with one answer: Lunacy!

A positive comment, not gushing, just positive. A small plaque, a pin, a celebratory banquet (**or lunch!**) at the end of a small but successful project, a smile, a "thank you" or two or three or eleven. The evidence is clear—people don't get much positive reinforcement! Because you and I, as leaders, don't offer it up. I repeat: Sheer lunacy!

You may be "one of those"—one of those who believes "They've got to go well above and beyond to deserve praise—otherwise you're just rewarding them for doing their job."

Lunacy!

Of course extraordinary work deserves extraordinary rewards. But what about the little barrier removed? The small but important helping hand offered? The milestone met a couple of days ahead of time? I am damn well suggesting in the strongest terms I can muster that you . . . **constantly** . . . offer recognition (positive reinforcement) for the tiniest steps in the right direction. For example, after a meeting go out of your way to acknowledge a wee contribution from someone who is skilled but ordinarily quiet.

And so on.

People.
Any of us.
All of us.
Never get tired of "it"!
I, at 67, after a career that has not been shy of accolades, bubble over with delight when someone gives me the slightest positive feedback— "How nice of you, Tom, to bring flowers to the receptionist this morning." (I beam for hours—at 67!—for the recognition.)

This is one . . . "Mother of All Power Tools"!
Believe it!

Use it!
Liberally!
(No time like the present!)

The fact is—**fact**—that your ratio, *which you should consciously manage,* of Positive to Negative reinforcement ought to be pretty-very high. But, alas, research tells us that the opposite is the case: From child rearing to the office, the frequency of Negative reinforcement typically outpaces the Positive reinforcements by a hearty ratio— moreover, a lot of managers have the hardest damn time giving *any* positive reinforcement. As I said before . . . **lunacy.**

So fix it!

You are not a rat!
Or are you?
I sure as hell am!

> SHIPSHAPE SHIFT

Here, drawn from the recent book *Barack, Inc.: Winning Business Lessons from the Obama Campaign,* by Rick Faulk and Barry Libert, is a story that encapsulates perfectly the power of positive reinforcement:

"[Retired United States Navy] Captain Mike Abrashoff knows the importance of saying 'thank you.' In his first book, *It's Your Ship,* he related how he sent letters to the parents of his crew members on the guided-missile destroyer USS *Benfold* . . . Putting himself in those parents' shoes, he imagined how happy they would be to hear from the commanding officer that their sons and daughters were doing well. And he figured that those parents would, in turn, call their children to tell them how proud they were of them.

"Abrashoff debated whether to send a letter to the parents of one young man who wasn't really star material. Weighing the sailor's progress, he decided to go ahead. A couple of weeks later, the sailor appeared at his door, tears streaming down his face. It seems the kid's father had always considered him a failure and told him so. After reading the captain's letter, he called to congratulate his son and tell him how proud he was of him. 'Captain, I can't thank you enough,' said the young man. For the first time in his life, he felt loved and encouraged by his father.

"As Abrashoff says, 'Leadership is the art of practicing simple things—commonsense gestures that ensure high morale and vastly increase the odds of winning.' In other words, small changes can have big consequences."

1. 2. 3. 4. 5. 6. 7. 8. 9. 10. 11. 12. 13. 14.
15. 16. 17. 18. 19. 20. 21. 22. 23. 24. 25.
26. 27. 28. 29. 30. 31. 32. 33. 34. 35.
36. 37. 38. 39. 40. 41. 42. 43. 44. 45.
46. 47. 48. 49. 50. 51. 52. 53. 54. 55. 56.
57. **58. 59. 60. 61.** 62. 63. 64. 65. 66. 67.
68. 69. 70. 71. 72. 73. 74. 75. 76. 77. 78.
79. 80. 81. 82. 83. 84. 85. 86. 87. 88.
89. 90. 91. 92. 93. 94. 95. 96. 97. 98. 99.
100. 101. 102. 103. 104. 105. 106. 107.
108. 109. 110. 111. 112. 113. 114. 115.
116. 117. 118. 119. 120. 121. 122. 123.
124. 125. 126. 127. 128. 129. 130. 131.
132. 133. 134. 135. 136. 137. 138. 139.
140. 141. 142. 143. 144. 145. 146. 147.
148. 149. 150. 151. 152. 153. 154. 155.
156. 157. 158. 159. 160. 161. 162. 163.

Words

58. "What Do You Think?"

Our colleague Dave Wheeler said, in a comment at tompeters.com: "The **4** most important words in management are . . . **What do you think?**"

I agree!

And the old engineer in me screams: *Quantify!*

So: How many times . . . *today* . . . did you "use the four words"? I.e. . . . **Exactly** how many times did you utter: "What do you think?"

TRACK IT!
Count 'em.
Graph it.
Insist that every leader track it.
AND POSSIBLY PUT IT IN THE "VALUES STATEMENT":

"We obsessively ask 'What do you think?'—We understand that we rise or fall on the engagement and intelligence and constant contributions of 100 percent of us."

"What do you think?" is sooooo important because . . .

(1) "They" are in fact "closer to the action"—they know the score.

(2) It screams: **"You are an invaluable person. I respect you. I respect your knowledge. I respect your judgment. I need your help."**

(3) It demonstrates that *you* know the score—i.e., understand that you can't do it alone, that you know you don't have all the answers.

(4) It shouts, "This is a . . . **team effort.** We rise or fall together."

59. "Thank You."

"The deepest human need is the need to be appreciated."

—William James, premier American psychologist, 1842–1910
(I think I've used this in about five books—and I surely plan to use it in the next one.)

How many times . . . *today* . . . did you "use the two words"?
I.e. . . . **Exactly** how many times did you utter:

"Thank you"?

TRACK IT!
Count 'em.
Graph it.
Insist that every leader track it.

AND, YES, CONSIDER PUTTING IT IN THE "VALUES STATEMENT":

"We habitually express appreciation for one another's efforts—because we do in fact consciously appreciate everyone's 'ordinary' 'daily' contributions, let alone the extraordinary ones."

(NB: There is simply no way whatsoever that I could overestimate . . . **"Thank-You Power."** If this doesn't come naturally to you, and it doesn't for some—do it anyway. You will be so stunned by the effect "Thank you" has that you will soon embed the habit in your hourly affairs. We may well "pay them," but the good attitude people exude is 100 percent voluntary—i.e., it is *always* "above and beyond," and hence it is *always* worthy of note—and a heartfelt "Thank you.")

(NB: In #57 above, I talked about "rat psychology" and positive reinforcement. There is surely duplication here. But my point in this heartfelt riff is to narrow the discussion and focus exclusively on the two words and only the two words: **"THANK YOU."**) (They must be singled out!)

60. "I'm Sorry."

"I regard apologizing as the most magical, healing, restorative gesture human beings can make. It is the centerpiece of my work with executives who want to get better."
—Marshall Goldsmith, *What Got You Here Won't Get You There: How Successful People Become Even More Successful* (Goldsmith is perhaps the world's most prominent executive coach.)

"Apologies unmask all the hopes, desires, and uncertainties that make us human because, at the moment of genuine apology, we confront our humanity most fully. At the point of apology we strip off a mask and face our limitations. No wonder we hesitate."
—John Kador, *Effective Apology: Mending Fences, Building Bridges, and Restoring Trust*

Talk about strong and unequivocal language!
(". . . most magical, healing, restorative gesture . . .")
Could it be merited?

Well, yes. Like Goldsmith and Kador, I believe that a genuine apology (and there's a lot to write, which space here does not permit, about a hundred shades and flavors of "genuine") is of the utmost personal *and* strategic importance—and, indeed, worthy of the label "magical."

My view is long held—and mostly a byproduct, personal as much as professional, of experience. Usually and sadly, like so many (males, at any rate—there are enormous gender differences on this dimension), my signal experiences with apology are associated with my *failure* to do so—with horrid consequences.

As I have become convinced of the power (redux: personal, professional, magical) of apology, I have actually accumulated a small library, which includes, in addition to Kador's book cited above, Nick Smith's *I Was Wrong* and Aaron Lazare's *On Apology*. All three take us on a journey from deep philosophical considerations to a raft of case studies that range from "small" personal apologies to Lincoln's apology for slavery.

One is left with an encompassing sense of the extraordinary power of the . . . **Art of Apology** . . . rightfully considered. Meld that to experiences in professional contexts, and I believe we are talking about, in practical business terms, a . . . **"matchless strategic lever."** (Yes, damn it, *strategic*. Yes, damn it, *matchless*.)

In the arsenal of what *really* matters when it comes to getting things done/execution/implementation, there are few—**if any**—"power tools" that have the heft of:

"I apologize."
"I'm sorry."
"I'm to blame."
"Simply put, I screwed up."
"I bear full responsibility for this f***-up."
"I blew it. Period."
"There may have been 'other factors' involved, but I damn well did contribute significantly to making this mess—and I flat-out apologize."

Key point/Bonus: *Often as not, an Effective Apology is far more than a "bullet dodged." That is, not only is a problem cleared up, but also the cock-up brilliantly—***and overwhelmingly and unequivocally***—atoned for solidifies a relationship . . .* **and** *. . . carries it forward.*

(Some more evidence of the hardest sort: In addition to being an excellent "how to" guide, Kador's *Effective Apology* also offers ladle-dropper examples. With a new and forthcoming policy on apologies, Toro, the lawn mower folks, reduced the average cost of settling a claim from **$115,000** in 1991 to **$35,000** in 2008—and the company hasn't been to trial in the last **15** years! The Veterans Administration hospital in Lexington, Massachusetts, developed an approach, totally uncharacteristic in health care, that entailed apologizing for errors—*even when no patient request or claim was made.* In 2000, the systemic mean VA hospital malpractice settlement throughout the United States was **$413,000;** the Lexington VA hospital settlement number was **$36,000**—*and there were far fewer per patient claims to begin with.)*

Suggested bottom line:

(1) Start with Kador's *Effective Apology* **(ASAP)** and become a full-blown . . . *Student* of Apology.

(2) Talk with your mates about the . . . Commercial Effectiveness of Strategic Apology.

(3) Assuming you agree on the "strategic" power of apology, commence treating the Art of Apology as a "professional *practice*." (That's Kador's advice—and I heartily concur!)

(4) Acknowledge that this "practice" can become one of a small handful of no less than "core strategic competencies"!

❯ A "SORRY" AFFAIR

There are also matters such as the . . . **"Virtuous Circle of Apology."** Suppose a problem arises—and it's pretty clear that it's mostly your fault. Nonetheless, my actions where also contributory; there are rarely if ever cases where one party is 100 percent guilty or guiltless. So I bite the bullet, call you, and take the blame in general. (I *don't* say, "Well, I'm not blameless." I simply say, "I screwed up on that late shipment.") When I take such an initiative, experience overwhelmingly suggests that the "Virtuous Circle of Apology" will begin. You, in fact, being aware of your significant contribution to the error, will almost surely jump in with, *"No, no, no. It was me. I'm the one who screwed this thing up."* After which we will bend over backwards seeing who can accept the greater share of the responsibility. **(!!!)** Done right, in three or four minutes we will be laughing or crying about the situation—and agreeing to have lunch or a beer or two in the next few days.

61. Words of Truth— from a Fiction Writer.

"Why not just tell the truth?"
—Raymond Carver

(The late Raymond Carver was one of America's most skillful short story writers—no one knew the contours of the human psyche better.)

(The problem with lying, in addition to the moral cost, is, of course, the amount of time and effort that must go into maintaining the cover-up—and the degree to which the whole affair deadens the soul. Or deadens an entire organization's will to move forward.)

1. 2. 3. 4. 5. 6. 7. 8. 9. 10. 11. 12. 13. 14. 15. 16. 17. 18. 19. 20. 21. 22. 23. 24. 25. 26. 27. 28. 29. 30. 31. 32. 33. 34. 35. 36. 37. 38. 39. 40. 41. 42. 43. 44. 45. 46. 47. 48. 49. 50. 51. 52. 53. 54. 55. 56. 57. 58. 59. 60. 61. **62. 63. 64. 65.** 66. 67. 68. 69. 70. 71. 72. 73. 74. 75. 76. 77. 78. 79. 80. 81. 82. 83. 84. 85. 86. 87. 88. 89. 90. 91. 92. 93. 94. 95. 96. 97. 98. 99. 100. 101. 102. 103. 104. 105. 106. 107. 108. 109. 110. 111. 112. 113. 114. 115. 116. 117. 118. 119. 120. 121. 122. 123. 124. 125. 126. 127. 128. 129. 130. 131. 132. 133. 134. 135. 136. 137. 138. 139. 140. 141. 142. 143. 144. 145. 146. 147. 148. 149. 150. 151. 152. 153. 154. 155. 156. 157. 158. 159. 160. 161. 162. 163.

Networking

One Line of Code: The Shortest Distance Between "Critic" and "Champion."

"They" say that complex software implementations fall short of promised effectiveness almost all the time. "They" add that the problem is rarely the software; it's almost always less-than-enthusiastic (or out-and-out recalcitrant) down-the-line users.

I have the answer! Well, no, of course not, but I do have *an* answer: **one line of code!**

You're in IT.
The software you've got on offer will change the world!
It's perfection, in fact—an engineer's dream come true!

But the implementation will take place far from home. The answer to pulling off that implementation? Well, in large measure, if you're wise, it's sales; you hit the road and . . . sell sell sell . . . would-be users . . . retail . . . one at a time. You sit down with, say, Erik H. in marketing. He listens to your pitch, agrees on the importance of the project— **but**—has a host of concerns. You listen, you go home; and, in effect . . . **you alter . . . one . . . line of code, which deals with . . . one . . . of Erik's issues.**

Bingo!

Nine out of 10 of Erik's issues are still not addressed . . . **but** . . . you changed . . . **something . . . directly . . . because of Erik!**

In 4.2 out of 5 cases, Erik flips from thorn in your side to fellow champion! Suddenly the whole damn thing is *"Erik's* project"! In Erik's mind, the whole damn thing would have been a bust without his precious, save-*your*-ass input!

I exaggerate in the details, of course, but the "one line of code" moniker per se came from an IT guy in an Australian small-business financial service company. **("I guarantee it'll work, mate.")** (Yes, he *did* say, "mate.")

> The point is obvious:
> *Give people a chance to engage at the more or less design stage.*
> *Respond directly and visibly to a couple of their problems.*
> *Convert foe to friend (in 4.2 of 5 cases, remember).*

I wouldn't blame you if you called this approach manipulative. While obviously somewhat true, the fact is that the majority of "Eriks" actually *do* have an idea (or 7 or 10, most of which are pretty good, a few of which are gems) that makes your *own* overall implementation better!

The ultimate solution might not be quite so pretty or "perfect"— you've gunked it up with prospective-user changes. But, loss of a touch of perfectionism notwithstanding, the product *does* get better in ways that matter to the users/"customers"—and user buy-in (after all, the point of the whole bloody exercise) goes through the roof.

Message:

(1) Staff departments must . . . **"sell"** . . . their services.

(2) "Sales" success requires . . . **active user buy-in.**

(3) Active user buy-in comes from respectfully listening to the user and . . . **taking some of her issues on board.**

Today:

Examine a stalled project. (Alas, we all have them.) Make a renewed and vigorous effort to **"go consultative"** with users; go to them, yes, starting today, as more or less a humble supplicant: **A-pol-o-gize for not having listened attentively enough to date.** Remember: Apologies are worth more than their weight in gold—approximately 100 percent of the time. (See #60.) Bend over backwards to listen intently (including "reading between the lines"—this is a somewhat learnable skill that's tough for any number of technically-proficient-but-empathetically-challenged-staff-professionals), and accommodate some of their needs. And observe what happens.

▶ CONSULT! (AND CONSULT AND THEN CONSULT.)

Roger Rosenblatt's *Rules for Aging* is one of my favorite books, clearly on a very short "all-time-best" list. Among his very small number of tips for guaranteed (his word, as I recall) success at damn near anything:

"Consult everyone on everything."

Amen!

(There were actually two tips—the second was ... *thanking everyone you can think of as profusely and often as you can manage.*)
(Both tips are veeeeery near and veeeeery dear to my heart.)
(Rosenblatt, who more or less wrote the book as a 60th birthday present to himself, claims that his failure to scale the heights of some of the bureaucracies of which he was a part can largely be attributed to his less than 100 percent zeal on these two dimensions.)

Rosenblatt.
Success.
Consult everyone.
On everything.
Thank everyone.
All the time.

As I said: Amen!

63. "Suck Down" for Success.

My professional "Adventures in Gender Differences" voyage began with a conversation with an exec at the travel service giant Rosenbluth International (now part of American Express). In a wide-ranging discussion, we passed through his career as a very successful systems salesman at AT&T. He said, in effect, or exactly per my memory: *"My secret was hiring women."*

The story he told was illuminating: The fact is, in any large, or large-ish, organization "the sale" (for a significant commercial product like the one my pal was selling) takes place three or four levels "down" from the top. That is, the vetting and analysis that precedes a *"yes"* or *"no"* is likely done by a 28-year-old staff engineer in a little cube in nowhereville on whose desk the project landed.

Back to my pal and his female hires. "For guys," he said, "it's always ego. The guy is a senior salesman, and he therefore, God help us, pretty much insists on dealing more or less exclusively with senior counterparts. It's beneath his self-invented station-in-corporate-life to muck about in the bowels of the customer's operation with 'mere clerks,' or some such. But the women I hired reveled in the things that the men eschew. The women willingly invested big-time in developing a rich network two or three or four levels 'down' in the customer operation; 'down' . . . where the decision to buy or not is effectively made!"

To make a long story short, the bottom line—female or male—is what I call:

The Gargantuan Power of "Sucking Down."

Forget "sucking up"—it's a low-odds strategy. If you are willing to invest the time, "sucking down" is a high-odds affair—to paraphrase the immortal robber Willy Sutton on why he chose to knock off banks, "It's where the money is." (Oh, is it ever.) In addition to the plain fact that "down there" is where the deal is effectively done, the folks a couple of levels "down" **["down" always in quotes—" 'down' is the real 'up' " is the anthem here]** are typically bowled over by your time and attention—we all crave being taken seriously. Hence, the next thing you know (after a *lot* of work), you've got in effect a private sales network to die for in the bowels of the customer organization—and it's a network, typically, with staying power; there's not so much volatility "down there."

Suck down for success!!

(You read it here first.)

(As always, in this book, the point is not "catch as catch can" or "a good idea." It's about a well-thought-out scheme, in fact, no less than a "way of life"—*a measured, systematic effort to penetrate the working-class ranks of a Client organization and develop a set of relationships with the real deal makers!*)

(NB: Alternate formulation to "Suck down for success": **"Success does not depend on 'the people you know in high places'—it depends on 'the people you know in low places.' "**)

> **REACHING "DOWN" . . . UP ON CAPITOL HILL**

My personal breakthrough on this one came over three decades ago, working on drug issues in/near the White House. I needed congressional support—but I was a junior staffer, White House affiliation or not. Fortunately, a wise pal gave me priceless "Capitol Hill" advice: *"The secret is not getting close to the congressman—the odds of that are very, very low. The secret is finding and courting the congressman's young LA [legislative assistant] who will be the one who deals with your issue."*

I did just that!
With abandon!

And, zounds, did it ever yield pay dirt. (I still fondly recall my boss once saying, "It seems as if you've got Congressman _____ [subcommittee chairman] working for you!")

64. Formula for Success: C(I) > C(E).

This idea waltzed into my life when I was speaking to sales folks at GE Energy. (Largely big systems sales, often to public clients in developing countries.) I've long argued that the set of relationships inside your own company is almost as important as the relationships with external bill-paying customers. Although it may not be a universal truth, it struck me as I talked to my GE pals that in many cases . . . our Internal Customers/"C(I)" are in fact . . . **more important** . . . than our External Customers/"C(E)."

Again:

C(I) > C(E) (Internal Customers are more important than External Customers.)

In this case at GE . . . *to win with External Customers the systems salespeople typically want an* **"unfair share"** *(the words of one GE informant) of a host of insiders' time—engineers, the logistics team, lawyers, and the all-important ("yes" or "no") risk-assessment staff.*

Lots of GE people are selling lots of stuff—and need . . . *yesterday* . . . lots and lots and lots of time-consuming Inside Help. Which means I (the salesperson) want to be . . . *at or very near the front of the queue* . . . for the harried risk-assessment staffers' time and attention; I want to be at the head of the engineers' queue, too, as they are the ones customizing the product . . .

Hence my full set of "internal [customer] relationships" may well end up being/*will* likely end up being more important—**even far more important**—than my "external [customer] relations."

With the GE case in mind, I subsequently found myself saying to a supersuccessful systems saleswoman at a Spanish telecom company, *"Your problem is* [not "may be," but "is"—what arrogance] *that you are spending too much time with your* [bill-paying external] *customers."* She looked at me as if I lost a screw or 10, but we then got into a useful discussion about "customers" (typically meaning *external* customers) and "customers" (of the *internal* sort). Her main gripe, which had triggered her question in the first place, was that her external customers often get their orders filled after the promised date of installation—because her company's engineers routinely missed their promised deadline in configuring systems. I urged her, then, to spend more time nurturing her network *inside* her own engineering department; the reallocation of time might cost her a few quota points in the short term—but was a "guaranteed" (another arrogant term!) winner in the mid to long term.

The applications of this idea range way beyond enormous GE systems sales or the Spanish telecom company. In the past, I, for example, as a McKinsey consultant at the "Client interface," wanted an "unfair" share—*and* posthaste—of our Graphics Department's attention when a hastily scheduled presentation loomed. As a junior purchasing staffer, you want an *unfair share* of the Legal Staff's time as you prepare a medium-sized contract. As a White House staffer many moons ago, I wanted the various gatekeepers to put my memo to the secretary of state (etc.) at the front of an infinitely long queue of people who *waaaaay* outranked me.

Critical query: **What ... precisely (measure it!!) ... have you done lately (last 36 hours!) for your all-important "portfolio" of ... internal customers?????????????**

(E.g.: *When was the last time you took a C(I) to lunch or dinner? Or brought flowers to the Legal Department after they'd done you even a wee favor?*)

I repeat:

Measure it!
Track it!
Obsess on it!
E-v-e-r-y* (!!) day.

(*Every = Do Not Let a Single Day Pass Without Doing Something Notable for Some Internal Customer.)

There are literally a hundred twists and turns to this. Consider just a few:

(1) Keep your *internal* customers "over"informed—tweet them or email or IM them about the trivial and the not-so-trivial in your work with your external customers. Go out of your way to put them on your team as "in-the-loop" insiders—we *all* love to be "insiders"!

(2) Give your internal customers *"face time"* with your external customers—this, too, is a mega-turn-on!

(3) If you're the Big Boss, plan a "sales" convention-gala for top *internal* staff performers—e.g., those in logistics and engineering and finance who greased the way for giant sales and performed follow-up service miracles for key clients.

(4) *We're all (well, most of us) suckers for pens and pins and (in my case) baseball hats.* After a big sale or on-time delivery, pass out those pens and pins and hats, commemorating the success, to internal staff supporters—by the bushel.

(5) On the one hand, as customer contact people, we want C(I)s in large numbers "in our pocket." On the other hand, we want our C(I)s to join us in getting directly committed to and charged up about the C(E)s—if we are *really* smart, we will want to help our Internal Customers in, say, engineering, to develop their own *direct* relationships with *external* customers' engineers—it's all about, in the end, breadth and depth of network.

(6) Etc.

(7) Etc.

> **"JUNIOR" LEAGUE PLAY**

I owe it all to **Walt.**

Walt Minnick, exactly my age, had an extraordinary private sector career. But rather than retire, at age 66, he ran for Congress in a long-odds Idaho campaign . . . and won.

I worked for (young) Walter at the White House over 30 years ago. It truly seemed as though this then rather junior guy had half of Washington in his pocket! A lot of the reason, I'm convinced, was his abiding attention to . . . **Junior (!!!)** . . . Internal Customers. At the end of each of his six workdays, for example, at about 7:00 P.M., Walt would retire to his office and write 10 or 15 thank-you notes. Not, or rarely, to the Big People—but to the junior secretary to Mr. Big who, against all odds, had gotten Walt 10 minutes on Mr. Big's calendar. Walt's lesson took. My fanaticism on this topic for the last 30 years is largely thanks to now-Congressman Minnick's example.

65. How Does Your "Inside Game" Measure Up?

Given: Cross-functional communication is such a problem that it could fairly be called enterprise "Problem #1." (Whoops . . . that may be at least the 26th time I've said that—and we're not even halfway through the book. Maybe I'll hook you by the 50th repetition.)

Solution (one more part thereof): All *staff* departments ought to/should/**must** quickly install first-rate *internal* customer satisfaction measurement systems . . . with tough up and down incentives.

In my experience, it is the rare staff department that measures (internal) customer satisfaction religiously—and the ever more rare internal unit that ties substantial rewards and penalties to such measurements.

That must change!

So . . . start . . .

Now!

Begin your discussion about this.

Today!

(You could push back with objections such as, "The auditors are, after all, cops—they're not out to win popularity awards." True, to a point. The okay auditor discharges his duties in a thoroughly professional manner and names names if appropriate. The . . . **superb** . . . auditor also discharges her duties in a thoroughly professional manner—*but also helps the audited department appreciate the theory and practice of, say, superior record keeping.* That is, staff departments possess peculiar expertise in the likes of auditing—but they can express said expertise in the manner of a dentist pulling teeth without Novocain, or in the spirit of wholehearted hyper-responsive *partnership.* It is the latter that I'm urging as the goal of an effective internal customer satisfaction evaluation system. In fact, if I were a Big Boss, COO for example, I would insist that all departments, small or large, develop internal customer satisfaction schemes that include attention-grabbing incentives.)

❯ BANK ON IT

Case: *I met the boss of Staff Services at a large Italian bank. He was fanatic about "customer" satisfaction for his departments' internal customers. In his scheme, each staff department's internal "customers" themselves devised the measures; and the primary dollar and cents (euro) incentives for staff departments were based primarily on quantitative measures of their internal customers' satisfaction. The staff department exec called this Internal Customer Satisfaction System "my principal strategic initiative."*

1. 2. 3. 4. 5. 6. 7. 8. 9. 10. 11. 12. 13. 14.
15. 16. 17. 18. 19. 20. 21. 22. 23. 24. 25.
26. 27. 28. 29. 30. 31. 32. 33. 34. 35.
36. 37. 38. 39. 40. 41. 42. 43. 44. 45.
46. 47. 48. 49. 50. 51. 52. 53. 54. 55. 56.
57. 58. 59. 60. 61. 62. 63. 64. 65. **66. 67.**
68. 69. 70. 71. 72. 73. 74. 75. 76. 77. 78.
79. 80. 81. 82. 83. 84. 85. 86. 87. 88.
89. 90. 91. 92. 93. 94. 95. 96. 97. 98. 99.
100. 101. 102. 103. 104. 105. 106. 107.
108. 109. 110. 111. 112. 113. 114. 115.
116. 117. 118. 119. 120. 121. 122. 123.
124. 125. 126. 127. 128. 129. 130. 131.
132. 133. 134. 135. 136. 137. 138. 139.
140. 141. 142. 143. 144. 145. 146. 147.
148. 149. 150. 151. 152. 153. 154. 155.
156. 157. 158. 159. 160. 161. 162. 163.

Lunch

66. Across the Board: Cross-Functional Collaboration Is Issue #1.

Cross-functional issues are the organization's **#1** problem.

#1:

6-person logistics subdepartment.

12-table restaurant.

Auto dealership.

Therefore: **Actively going after this issue ... Daily ... is a Monster Opportunity.**

Want great cross-functional cooperation-opportunity maximization, or ... **XFX (Cross-functional Excellence)** ... as I call it?

Answer: Make *friends* in other functions! (Purposefully.)

Answer: Go to *lunch* with people in other functions!! (Frequently!) (Also see immediately below.)

Answer: Ask peers in other functions for some references so you can become *conversant in their world*. (Big deal: You'll find it interesting—and it's a helluva sign of ... **Give-a-damn-ism.**)

Answer: *Invite counterparts in other functions to your meetings. Religiously. Ask them to present "cool stuff" from "their world" to your group.* (B-i-g deal; useful *and* respectful.)

Answer: Present counterparts in other functions awards for service to your group—hold an *"All-Star Supporters [from other groups] Banquet." (Stupendous!)*

Answer: *When someone in another function asks for assistance, respond with even more alacrity than you would if it were the person in the cubicle next to yours—or more than you would for a key external customer.*

Answer: **Do not bad-mouth** . . . "the damned accountants," "the damned HR guy." Ever. *(Even in the privacy of your bathtub.)*

Answer: Share more information than you think you "need to" . . . ASAP & Always.

Answer: Whenever you are dealing with peers in other functions, ask repeatedly: **"What do you think?"** (Remember!)

Answer: Twenty more things like this that boil down to establishing and maintaining and enhancing *social–human bonds* with "the 'thems,' " as I label it.

Answer: Frequency! Repeat! Repeat! Repeat!

67. Getting Along and Going to Lunch: *Solving* the Cross-Functional Cooperation Problem.

Time and time **(and time)** again, from the battlefield to the fast-food outfit, we are tripped up by nonexistent or contentious cross-functional communications/coordination/lost opportunities for Earthshaking Change.

There's a lot to say (and I've said it elsewhere and in this book—and will keep saying it), but I want this one to stand by itself.

Do lunch!

I don't care what your "priorities" are. Ignoring my powerlessness over you, I nonetheless **demand** that you . . . **devote a minimum of . . . *five* lunches per month . . . to dining with folks in other functions.**

Tell 'em the truth when you proffer the invitation: You're tired of all the botched communications and lost opportunities—and you are determined for both your sakes to develop a . . . **Big-Activist-Intimate Network Across the Organization.**

Do it!
Schedule the first one right now!
Put the book down!
N-O-W!
(Trust me!)
(This is big!)
(Very big!)

NB: Fact is, on a personal as well as a professional level, you'll find in . . . **9 cases out of 9** . . . (okay, 9 out of 9.7) that you have a lot in common (six degrees of separation, etc.) with your first-date lunch partner from Logistics, and that he/she is also irritated by the same cross-functional maladroitness that you are. Well: The hell with your bosses and the megabuck schemes of the IT guys—fix it at lunch. *(If 70 percent of staffers would do it as a matter of routine, measured routine, the organization would have developed the sharpest competitive arrow possible!)*

> **BATTER UP! MAKE EACH "LUNCH DATE" COUNT**

Consider each workday lunch an "at bat." (I'm an unrepentant base-ball nut.) Four workweeks at five days each adds up to about 20 "at bats" each month.

20 opportunities to start *New Relationships*;

20 opportunities to nurture or extend *Old Relationships*;

20 opportunities to patch up *Frayed Relationships;*

20 opportunities to *"Take a Freak to Lunch"*—and learn something new;

20 opportunities to test an idea with a potential *Recruit-Alliance Partner*;

20 opportunities to get to know someone in *Another Function*;

20 opportunities to…PURSUE or MAKE A SALE…to gain a *Convert-Champion* for your idea or project.

I'm not urging you to ignore the pals you usually go to lunch with. And if you "use" all 20 monthly lunch "opportunities" to the utmost, I'll be tempted to call you "over the top." (Or determined to become the next Donald Trump. Or U.S. president in 2012.)

But I do urge-beg you to consider Lunches as a/*the*/your Most Precious Resource.

Each lunch gone is gone for good.

Lunch opportunity utilized effectively = High R.O.I.R. (Return on Investment in Relationships.)

20 per month. **240** per year. To a major-league baseball player, EACH AT BAT IS PRECIOUS. To a "determined-to-build-a-matchless-network-and-collect-cool-outsiders-and-useful-allies"…EACH LUNCH IS PRECIOUS.

Agree?

So?

Invite someone interesting/potentially useful to lunch…tomorrow. If it's before noon, how about lunch today…TODAY.

The Equations

**An Engineer's View of the ...
Secrets of Effective Implementation**

Engineers live for mathematical and/or algebraic representation of any and all things.

Hence, I, an unrepentant engineer, offer this set of "equations" aimed at helping you, engineer or not, boost your odds of success at implementing damn near anything.

Success at GTD/Getting Things Done Is a Function of . . .

S = ƒ(#&DR, -2L, -3L, -4L, I&E)

Success is a function of: Number and depth of relationships, 2, 3, and 4 levels down inside and outside the organization.

S = ƒ(SD > SU)

"Sucking down" is more important than "sucking up"—the idea is to have the entire "underbelly" of the organization working for you.

S = ƒ(#non-FF, #non-FL)

Number of friends not in my function, number of lunches with friends not in my function.

S = ƒ(#FF)

Number of friends in the finance organization.

S = ƒ(#OF)

Number of oddball friends.

S = *f*(PDL)

Purposeful, deep listening—this is very hard work.

S = *f*(#EODD3MC)

Number of end-of-the-day difficult (you'd rather avoid) "3-minute calls" that soothe raw feelings, mend fences, etc.

S = *f*(UFP, UFK, OAPS)

Unsolicited Favors Performed, UFs involving coworkers' kids, overt acts of politeness-solicitude toward coworkers' spouses, parents, etc.

S = *f*(#TY, #TNT)

Number of "thank yous" today, number of thank-you notes sent today.

S = *f*(SU)

Show up!

S = *f*(ID)

Seeking the assignment of writing first drafts, minutes, etc.

S = *f*(#SEAs)

Number of solid relationships with Executive Assistants.

S = *f*(%UL/w-m)

Percent of useful lunches per week, month.

S = ƒ(FG/FO, BOF/CMO)

Favors given, favors owed collectively, balance of favors, conscious management of.

S = ƒ(CPRMA, MTS)

Conscious-planned Relationship management activities, measured time spent thereon.

S = ƒ(TN/d, FG/m, AA/d)

Thank-you notes per Day, flowers given per Month, Acts of Appreciation per Day.

S = ƒ(PT100%A"T"S, E"NMF"–TTT)

Proactive, timely, 100 percent apologies for "tiny" screw-ups, even if not my fault (it always takes two to tango).

S = ƒ(UAAR, NBS-NSG)

Universal accountability-acceptance of responsibility for all affairs, no blame-shifting, no scapegoating.

S = ƒ(AP"L"S, LFCT)

Awareness, perception of "little" snubs—and lightning-fast correction thereof.

S = ƒ(ODIRAAS)

Overwhelming, disproportionate, instantaneous reaction to any and all screw-ups.

S = ƒ(G)

Grace.

S = ƒ(GA)

Grace toward adversary.

S = ƒ(GW)

Grace toward the wounded in bureaucratic firefights.

S = ƒ(PD)

Purposeful decency.

S = ƒ(EC, MMO)

Emotional connections, management and maintenance of.

S = ƒ(IMDOP)

Investment in Mastery of Detailed Organizational Processes.

S = ƒ(TSH)

Time spent on Hiring.

$S = f(TSPD, TSP\text{-}LI)$

Time spent on promotion decisions, especially for first-level managers.

$S = f(\%\text{"SS," } H\text{-}PD)$

Percent of soft stuff involved in Hiring, Promotion decisions.

$S = f(TSWA, P/NP)$

Time spent wandering around, purposeful, non-planned.

$S = f(SBS)$

Slack built into Schedule.

$S = f(TSHR)$

Time spent . . . Hurdle Removing.

$S = f(\%TM\text{"TSS," } PM\text{"TSS," } D\text{"TD""TSS"})$

Success is a function of: percent of time, measured, on "this Soft Stuff," purposeful management of "this Soft Stuff," daily "to-do" concerning "this Soft Stuff."

****

I'll conclude with three more "equations"—oriented toward organizational success-effectiveness-excellence:

O(B) = ƒ(XX)

O(B), the "blueness" of one's "ocean" [think "competitive advantage," as defined in the popular book Blue Ocean Strategy*] is directly proportional to one's eXcellence in eXecution/XX. [If one finds a "strategic" "blue ocean," one will, especially in today's world, be copied immediately; the only "defense"—possibility of sustaining success—is XX/eXcellence in eXecution. Think ExxonMobil; they and their rivals know where the hydrocarbons are—but ExxonMobil handily out-executes the competition.]*

S(O) = ƒ(XXFX)

The single most important cause of failure to execute effectively is the lack of effective cross-functional communication-execution. Hence, Organizational Success is a function of eXcellence (X) in cross-functional (XF) eXecution (X).

S(O) = ƒ(X"SIT")

In honor of HP's all-powerful MBWA/Managing By Wandering Around, the following: S(O), Organizational Success, is a function of X "SIT," eXcellence at Staying In Touch.

1. 2. 3. 4. 5. 6. 7. 8. 9. 10. 11. 12. 13. 14.
15. 16. 17. 18. 19. 20. 21. 22. 23. 24. 25.
26. 27. 28. 29. 30. 31. 32. 33. 34. 35.
36. 37. 38. 39. 40. 41. 42. 43. 44. 45.
46. 47. 48. 49. 50. 51. 52. 53. 54. 55. 56.
57. 58. 59. 60. 61. 62. 63. 64. 65. 66. 67.
68. 69. 70. 71. 72. 73. 74. 75. 76. 77. 78.
79. 80. 81. 82. 83. 84. 85. 86. 87. 88.
89. 90. 91. 92. 93. 94. 95. 96. 97. 98. 99.
100. 101. 102. 103. 104. 105. 106. 107.
108. 109. 110. 111. 112. 113. 114. 115.
116. 117. 118. 119. 120. 121. 122. 123.
124. 125. 126. 127. 128. 129. 130. 131.
132. 133. 134. 135. 136. 137. 138. 139.
140. 141. 142. 143. 144. 145. 146. 147.
148. 149. 150. 151. 152. 153. 154. 155.
156. 157. 158. 159. 160. 161. 162. 163.

Yes

My wife, Susan, and I, on short notice, invited her mom, then age 74, to come down from New Canaan, Connecticut, and join us for a Midtown Manhattan dinner.

She said "No."
Period.

I've known Joan Sargent for a long time. If she's anything, she's self-certain.
I.e., "No" = No.

When we arrived in town from Vermont, we were therefore non-plussed to find a message from Joan, saying, *"I'll be arriving at 7."*
We were pleased. (Yes, I have a great relationship with my mother-in-law.) *And surprised.* We obviously asked her why she'd changed her mind.
Short answer:

"I decided to say 'Yes.' "

Longer answer. She recalled a friend who'd had a vigorous life into her 90s. "She said she had three 'secrets,'" Joan recalled. "First, surround yourself with good books on any and every topic. Second, spend time with people of all ages. And third, say 'Yes.' "

She added that indeed she had not intended to drive down from Connecticut. (For those readers who've aged a bit, peripheral vision goes for all of us pretty early, and night driving is a pain, especially in rain or snow. And the weather was foul.) But she remembered her friend and determinedly decided to . . . "say . . . 'Yes.'"

Message, Age 24 or 74:

Engage with all sorts of folks of every age.
Keep learning new stuff.
And just say . . . **"Yes"**!

69. For the Sheer Glorious 24/7 Fun of It!

Richard Branson's idea of fun is going head to head in the ring with someone who has him by a jillion pounds. As Michael Specter wrote in his wonderful *New Yorker* profile ("Branson's Luck"), "Branson likes to enter a market controlled by a giant—British Airways, say, or Coke, or Murdoch. Then he presents himself as the hip alternative."

He allows himself to get pissed off at something stupid (pathetic airline customer "service"), and on the spot, more or less, starts an airline, or whatever. (NB: I happen to believe that . . . **all** . . . successful innovation, products or processes, are the . . . lived-out fantasies of pissed-off people.) With a fortune measured in billions, he commands a payroll of about 55,000 feisty folks in 200 very independent companies. (Think Virgin Atlantic, Virgin Blue of Australia, Virgin Limousines, Virgin Money, Virgin Active health clubs, Virgin Galactic space travel . . .)

Branson *is* his brand. He enjoys his nutty stunts that personify the brand's hipness and engages in them even when out of camera range; upon discovering the car back to his hotel after a recent party (whose guests included the Google founders, half Branson's age) was full, Sir Richard simply hopped in the trunk. Specter goes so far in his profile as to dub him the "anti-Trump," while, around the office, "Branson's nickname is Dr. Yes, largely because he has never been able to bring himself to fire people, and often has trouble saying no to even the most ridiculous and unsolicited ideas."

As I read the Branson profile I let my mind wander to Howard Schultz, Starbucks founder. I like Schultz *and* his company a lot. But it seems that when one hears of its future, it's almost always in terms of Howard's goal of adding thousands upon more thousands of new shops, or some such. Branson is surely happy when his businesses succeed and grow (though not awash in tears when one fails, as long as it was a spanking good try), but his primary goal truly does seem to be the sheer fun of doing something cool to twit a giant or, more recently, by investing big in biofuels—to save the world.

In short (and long), I wish there were many more like him.

I'm not Branson by a long, long shot; but I understand the guiding impulse. The *only* reason that I take on new stuff, and keep accumulating frequent flyer miles, has long been the unadulterated pleasure I get from always marching "the other way"—and in particular storming after those I think have let us down, from numbers-obsessed execs to health care leaders' lack of patient-safety rigor as measured by hundreds of thousands of preventable annual deaths in the United States alone.

My advice?

This is *strategic*: **Do your darnedest to "make it fun," "make it a ride to remember," "make it a bloody ball"!**

It ought to be sheer-raw-unmitigated *fun* to *scramble* and *ramble* to go two or three or six country miles out of your way to get a computer system up in a flash with a diabolically clever fix that buggers the imagination—if you're in the computer service business. It ought to be sheer-raw-unmitigated *fun* for your gang to puzzle out innovative ways, in the face of long, long odds, to deliver a quirky custom order a week ahead of time. And so on.

Aiming to upend conservatism as a cohesive-committed team of rebels, a team of brothers and sisters with a sparkling new approach to first-line supervisor training that will set-the-world-on-its-ear-it's-so-cool-and-so-good . . . now that's what I call Great and Grand and Glorious 24/7 *Fun*. And I believe that it is . . . **your job** . . . as boss-leader to set precisely this set of "outrageous" challenges to your seven-person, two-month-duration project team, or your 46-person IS department.

Sir Richard Branson "gets it."
(So do I.)
(Even though my wallet is anemic compared to his.)
And you????????

(**Please, please, please:** Don't dismiss this as "motivational bullshit." Act as if your life depended on it; in fact, your professional life—and personal sanity—does.)

❯ *DILBERT* IS *NOT* FUNNY

If you have chosen to read this book, odds are you work pretty long hours—and give a damn about what you do.

Ideas like this one, if I may be so outrageously bold, are near the heart of nothing less than ... **what it means to be human.**

From the pulpit, or the battlefield when war is absolutely necessary, there is no greater leader's calling than ... *Fully Engaging Others in Quests Toward Growth and Life with Meaning.* **(Yes?) (No?)**

Dilbert is ... **not** ... funny.

(Even though I laugh at his perfect depiction of a lot of corporate life.)

Dilbert-world is about a string of days ... **effectively pissed away.** (I haven't, at age 67, got the time for that.)

As leaders, we make an implicit pledge to "be of service" and to be "wholeheartedly committed to the growth of others"—like marriage vows, and the implicit vows of parenthood.

So, label such challenges as "make it fun"—that is, truly engaging and worthy and the source of constant camaraderie—pie in the sky if you must.

But if it's pie in the sky, then what *exactly* is the alternative?

Read the ... *Collected Works of Dilbert?*

While away another day at the watercooler laughing about the idiocy of your job?

No thanks.

(And, actually, lassitude and/or aimlessness is not really an option as the labor market becomes more and more "global" and, hence, more and more competitive. A new motto, perhaps: "Only the fully engaged will survive"?)

1. 2. 3. 4. 5. 6. 7. 8. 9. 10. 11. 12. 13. 14. 15. 16. 17. 18. 19. 20. 21. 22. 23. 24. 25. 26. 27. 28. 29. 30. 31. 32. 33. 34. 35. 36. 37. 38. 39. 40. 41. 42. 43. 44. 45. 46. 47. 48. 49. 50. 51. 52. 53. 54. 55. 56. 57. 58. 59. 60. 61. 62. 63. 64. 65. 66. 67. 68. 69. **70. 71.** 72. 73. 74. 75. 76. 77. 78. 79. 80. 81. 82. 83. 84. 85. 86. 87. 88. 89. 90. 91. 92. 93. 94. 95. 96. 97. 98. 99. 100. 101. 102. 103. 104. 105. 106. 107. 108. 109. 110. 111. 112. 113. 114. 115. 116. 117. 118. 119. 120. 121. 122. 123. 124. 125. 126. 127. 128. 129. 130. 131. 132. 133. 134. 135. 136. 137. 138. 139. 140. 141. 142. 143. 144. 145. 146. 147. 148. 149. 150. 151. 152. 153. 154. 155. 156. 157. 158. 159. 160. 161. 162. 163.

70. "To-Don'ts" Are More Important Than "To-Dos."

My friend Dennis is a prominent figure. His success in a situation that matters to us all is monumental. A few years ago he received a huge $$$ grant—and he was given the opportunity to roll out his superb program across the country. Suddenly, he was required to turn his innovative ideas into a system that could be replicated by "ordinary people." Among many other things, he is "one of those people" who has 10 ideas a minute—and one of the very very few among such folks where all 10 of them are usually *good* ideas. And so his talented staff ran around madly (they loved him—and "madly" is no exaggeration) working on exciting this or exciting that. But now, to make his bold dreams come true on a broader canvas, he had a "low variation" system to concoct and run—and things promised to be different.

I attended a meeting of his advisory committee at a critical moment. The chairman had been CEO of an enormous company. And to my last breath, I will remember a single line that emerged from the fellow's mouth:

"Dennis, you need a 'to-don't' list."

In simple language:

(1) What you decide *not* to do is probably *more* important than what you decide to do.

(2) You probably can't work on "to-don't" alone—you need a sounding board/mentor/adviser/nag you trust to act as a drill sergeant who will frog-march you to the woodshed when you stray and start doing those time-draining "to-don'ts."

I've read research claiming that, as bosses, 50 or even 60 or more percent of what we do is unnecessary. I am skeptical. Not that 50 percent of our time is poorly allocated, but I think many people who say such things have a naive view of the world. That is, a helluva lot of the "unnecessary" stuff we do is, in fact, necessary. We attend a meeting in which we have no interest, or at least no apparent interest. But in fact there is a compelling interest: The subject matter *is* irrelevant, but you are there to show *visible support* for Mary Smith— who is a potential roadblock or supporter to *your* pet project's crucial next step. That is . . . *you are there 100 percent for political reasons!* But since implementation of *anything* is about 95 percent politics, it is indeed a "must attend, must appear attentive" meeting. Hence, there are a lot of "low-yield" (substance) things you need for "high-yield" (politics) reasons. So we must search all the harder and thoughtfully for the true "to-don'ts." I will offer no advice on the choice process—I leave that to you and a library full of books more or less on the topic. I merely mean here to underscore my support for a . . . **formal-systematic hyper-high-priority " 'to-don't' management process"** . . . which, indeed, *must* include that trusted adviser.

So, top of your "to-do" list for today is immediately beginning work on your "to-don't" list!

> **STOP!—IN THE NAME OF STRATEGY**

In preparation for a short speech at a Nature Conservancy fund-raiser, I read Bill Birchard's *Nature's Keepers: The Remarkable Story of How the Nature Conservancy Became the Largest Environmental Organization in the World.* When former TNC president John Sawhill had just taken the helm, he appointed a key task force to do a ground-up look at the organization's strategy. More specifically, per Sawhill's charge:

"What areas should the Conservancy focus on and more important—what activities should we STOP?" [My caps.]

I suggest outright mimicry: In the next 90 days, work with your leadership team on a... " **'Stop Doing'** *Strategic* **Review.**" Once "stop" decisions have been made, a careful, disciplined get-out-from-under execution plan must be developed. *(Beware a "stop doing" that subsequently goes underground—every activity has its rabid and wily adherents!)*

(NB: **Keep it simple.** The sheer beauty of Sawhill's charter is its clarity—What should we do? What should we stop doing? Alas, such clarity is AWOL in most such calls for strategic review.)

71. Some Things Worth Doing Are Worth Doing Not Particularly Well.

Readers of this book are adult in fact and in their approach to life. This item may insult your intelligence. On the other hand, it may help you free up, say, **20 percent** of your time as currently spent. Hence, I will take the risk of insulting you.

The reminder came one night as I was doing dishes. (It's my thing.) I was dealing with a particularly resistant old baking pan. I cleaned up the food residue—it was fully sanitary. But there was some crusty crap left, which I went after with a vengeance—but somewhat unsuccessfully. At one point I started laughing at myself. The pan was sanitary and "clean enough," plus I really didn't need to treat the effort like a speech to Fortune 50 CEOs. That's a tough sell to an engineer with mostly German blood—namely me.

The micro-event (I *did* stop) reminded me of the Greater Truth. In a world (personal, professional) of limited resources (time, in this instance) and priorities of the utmost importance (to you and me at any rate), there's a lot of "stuff" that must be done—but for which "good enough" is in fact good enough.

There are numerous instances when obsessing on the last two inches of a 100-mile journey is of paramount importance—like writing a book. (The "two last passes" which follow the "two last passes" are all-important to me, a state of nature from which I will never be dislodged.) I am in fact an ardent fan of "perfectionism," downsides notwithstanding.

Still, there are a lot of baking pans that are clean enough. The art of deciding which things do and don't merit the "two-last-passes-following-the-two-last-passes" is an important one. There's much to do—and perfectionism concerning things that don't merit perfectionism is, for some of us, a significant resource absorber.

Suggestion?

Time is your most precious resource.
Obvious.

(But *always* worth repeating.)

There is "stuff" that you must indeed do.

(That's the point, you do have to do it—the dishes.)

But it really ain't important enough to kill yourself over.

Spend no more than **"enough"** time on that stuff.

You may well be surprised, perhaps even "stunned," by how much time you can reallocate.

(Again, sorry for insulting your intelligence, if, indeed, I have.)

1. 2. 3. 4. 5. 6. 7. 8. 9. 10. 11. 12. 13. 14. 15. 16. 17. 18. 19. 20. 21. 22. 23. 24. 25. 26. 27. 28. 29. 30. 31. 32. 33. 34. 35. 36. 37. 38. 39. 40. 41. 42. 43. 44. 45. 46. 47. 48. 49. 50. 51. 52. 53. 54. 55. 56. 57. 58. 59. 60. 61. 62. 63. 64. 65. 66. 67. 68. 69. 70. 71. **72. 73. 74.** 75. 76. 77. 78. 79. 80. 81. 82. 83. 84. 85. 86. 87. 88. 89. 90. 91. 92. 93. 94. 95. 96. 97. 98. 99. 100. 101. 102. 103. 104. 105. 106. 107. 108. 109. 110. 111. 112. 113. 114. 115. 116. 117. 118. 119. 120. 121. 122. 123. 124. 125. 126. 127. 128. 129. 130. 131. 132. 133. 134. 135. 136. 137. 138. 139. 140. 141. 142. 143. 144. 145. 146. 147. 148. 149. 150. 151. 152. 153. 154. 155. 156. 157. 158. 159. 160. 161. 162. 163.

Customers

72. It's 11 A.M.—Have You Called a Customer Today?

Never.
Ever.
Get Out of Touch.
With Customers.

Easy to lose touch.
G. W. Bush.
B. H. Obama.
Me.
You.
BigCo.
WeeCo.

Must not happen.

Stop.
Now.

**Call a Customer.
Out of the Blue.**

Ask:

"How can I help?"
"How are we doing?"
"Have we delivered on every promise,
implicit as well as explicit?"

Listen.
LISTEN.

Take notes.
Meticulously.
(Record in Special eFolder/Notebook.)

Follow-up-on-at-least-some-one-"little"-thing.
FAST.
INSTANTLY.

Repeat.
48 hours hence.

Hint: This applies to 100 percent of us. Not just "bosses." And not just to those with "external" customers.

We.
All.
Have.
Customers.

73. There's Nothing But Nothing Better Than an Angry Customer!

Bizarre but true: *Our most loyal customers are ones who had a problem with us . . . and then marveled when we went the Extra 10 Miles at the Speed of Light to fix it!*

Business opportunity No. 1* = Irate customers converted into fans.

(*Yes, No. I.)

So . . . are you on the *active* prowl for customer problems to fix?

Rules:

Make **"over"**reacting to problems a keystone in the corporate culture, a plank in the Corporate Values statement. *("We respond to customer concerns with passion and rapidity and resources in ways that stun-amaze-overwhelm those customers 100 percent of the time.")*

Reward (BIG TIME) those who unearth . . . **and report** . . . customer problems.

"Over"connect; let the customer know ASAP (!!), and update constantly—*even if there is absolutely nothing to report.*

Ensure that there are *devoted* resources at the ready to respond to problems. (This is more or less **"anti**-Just-In-Time.") (No matter how good your systems, there **will** be problems—you must be staffed adequately, and then some, to respond at lightning speed.)

Work assiduously (reward lavishly, punish harshly, promote, demote) on cross-functional cooperation; most fixes (99 percent?) require such cooperation.

Reward—BIG TIME—*great* responses to problems.

Reward—BIG TIME—responses to *"little"* problems. **(There are no "little problems" in the customer's universe.)**

Publicize great responses to problems. (Internally and externally.)

Do not on threat of dismemberment imagine that prevention is "the answer" to flubs. Prevention is great—obviously. Nonetheless: Shit happens. Regardless of the effectiveness of your systems, things will and do go wrong.

Repeat: **Business opportunity No. 1 = Irate customers converted into outspoken fans.**

74. What We Have Here Is a Failure to *Over*communicate.

I long ago promised myself I'd stop using airline service horror stories. I got tired of beating dead horses, and was boring myself to death—and doubtless boring the likes of you, as well. Still, a useful reminder is a useful reminder (hence this book's raison d'être):

I was flying home from Mexico City to Boston, on Delta, via Atlanta. The ATL-BOS leg was delayed about 75 minutes. **Never once did waiting area personnel or the pilot provide any explanation whatsoever.** I do not exaggerate. Not one bloody, frigging word.

No, this is not really news in "airline-service-sucks-significantly land"—though it was a smidgen worse than usual. Nonetheless, it serves as a not-quite-friendly alarm bell to all of us in any and every circumstance, signaling the ... **Insanely Important Value of Keeping People Informed/Over-informed 100 Percent of the Time.**

To reiterate a reiteration of a reiteration: We can almost all deal quite well with shit—we all/almost all deal very poorly with uncertainty. Tell me it'll probably be a 90-minute delay because the pilot is in the bar popping tequila shots—and I'm fine. (More or less.) Total Silence? I'm on edge, pissed off as hell—irate, in fact.

Communicate! **Over**communicate!
Communicate! **Over**communicate!
Communicate! **Over**communicate!

Whatever amounts to "sensible communication," **3X** it!

Immediate "command":
Play back the last 24 or 48 hours. Is there an instance where you have failed to Fully Inform a Client, or other stakeholder including frontline employees, of a delay (wee or grand) or glitch (wee or grand)? *If your answer is "nope, all is well"—you are a liar.* (Sorry, it just slipped from the keyboard.)

Get cracking.
Now.
Make the call.

(And if you have already let someone know about a glitch [good for you] ... **call 'em again** ... to update the status of the fix, or relay the sad but honest news that the fix is more complex than first imagined.)

1. 2. 3. 4. 5. 6. 7. 8. 9. 10. 11. 12. 13. 14.
15. 16. 17. 18. 19. 20. 21. 22. 23. 24. 25.
26. 27. 28. 29. 30. 31. 32. 33. 34. 35.
36. 37. 38. 39. 40. 41. 42. 43. 44. 45.
46. 47. 48. 49. 50. 51. 52. 53. 54. 55. 56.
57. 58. 59. 60. 61. 62. 63. 64. 65. 66. 67.
68. 69. 70. 71. 72. 73. 74. **75. 76. 77. 78.**
79. 80. 81. 82. 83. 84. 85. 86. 87. 88.
89. 90. 91. 92. 93. 94. 95. 96. 97. 98. 99.
100. 101. 102. 103. 104. 105. 106. 107.
108. 109. 110. 111. 112. 113. 114. 115.
116. 117. 118. 119. 120. 121. 122. 123.
124. 125. 126. 127. 128. 129. 130. 131.
132. 133. 134. 135. 136. 137. 138. 139.
140. 141. 142. 143. 144. 145. 146. 147.
148. 149. 150. 151. 152. 153. 154. 155.
156. 157. 158. 159. 160. 161. 162. 163.

Action

75. "Trying My Damnedest!" Wrong Answer!

For a series of reasons, I was thinking about my two deployments to Vietnam. And I recalled in particular a world-shaping (for me) event: I was out in the field, deep in the jungle-mountains west of Danang, helping to build a camp for a U.S. Army Special Forces team. I was unexpectedly accosted by a U.S. Marine Corps major who arrived in a USMC helicopter—and rushed me back to Danang. I was summoned to meet with the USMC commandant **(No. 1)**, General Leonard Chapman, who was paying a visit to I Corps, the northern part of South Vietnam, which was under USMC command—more specifically under the command of General Lew Walt.

What the hell was a Navy LTJG (very junior officer) doing visiting with a four-star general? Simple. My uncle, Lieutenant General H. W. Buse Jr., was a USMC muckety-muck back in D.C., and my aunt had insisted that General Chapman see me in the flesh. (Aunts are like that, even, or especially, at the Mrs. Several-star-general level.) (Also, her son, my cousin, was in Vietnam as well—a USMC captain, holder of the Bronze Star and Purple Heart.)

When I got back from the field, covered with mud (it was rainy season—persistent jungle rain), I was sent directly to the commandant with no time to change into a respectable uniform—a great embarrassment. General Chapman engaged in all of about 15 seconds of chitchat, and having done his duty to my aunt, sent me on my way. As I was literally walking out of his temporary field office, he summoned me back, and said, out of the blue, "Tom, are you taking care of your men?" (I had a little detachment, about 20 guys as I recall, doing the work described before.)

I replied to the general, *"I'm doing my best, sir."* To this day, with a chill going up my spine (no kidding—as I type this), I can see his face darken, and his voice harden. **"Mr. Peters*,** (*U.S. Navy junior officers are referred to as "Mr.") **General Walt, General Buse, and I are not interested in whether or not you are 'doing your best.' We simply expect you to get the job done—and to take care of your sailors. Period. That will be all, Lieutenant."**

The line still resonates with me—as you can doubtless tell. You are there to "get the job done"—not just merely to "do your best." I recall the shock of recognition, many years later, when I tripped over a Churchill quote that went like this: *"It is not enough to do your best— you must succeed in doing what is necessary."*

Reluctant as I am to use such strong and absolutist language, there is Only One Acceptable Standard: Getting done what is necessary to get done.

Proceed accordingly.
And . . . **mercilessly** . . . evaluate yourself accordingly.

> **FORMULA ONE**

"A man approached J. P. Morgan, held up an envelope, and said, 'Sir, in my hand I hold a guaranteed formula for success, which I will gladly sell you for $25,000.'

" 'Sir,' J. P. Morgan replied, 'I do not know what is in the envelope; however, if you show it to me, and I like it, I give you my word as a gentleman that I will pay you what you ask.'

"The man agreed to the terms, and handed over the envelope. J. P. Morgan opened it, and extracted a single sheet of paper. He gave it one look, a mere glance, then handed the piece of paper back to the gent. And paid him the agreed-upon $25,000.

"The contents of the note:

"1. Every morning, write a list of the things that need to be done that day.

"2. **Do them.**"

Source: NPR

76. It Is Not Enough to Care!

I sure as hell wish this one weren't necessary. But I'm pissed off. Really pissed off. As pissed off as I've ever been.

We unnecessarily kill (very strong term; a little too strong—but I'm pissed off, remember) some 100,000 to 300,000+ patients in hospitals in the United States every year. We wound millions more—"and that doesn't include the numberless victims in doctors' offices," as a senior ER doc and exec told me.

And, yes, it is by and large preventable, as any number of hospitals and hospital systems prove, like Geisinger Health System, headquartered in Danville, Pennsylvania. And many, if not most, of the cures are simple, requiring management and systems fixes, not more technology.

For example, Doctor Peter Pronovost at Johns Hopkins Hospital instituted a common checklist, an idea shamelessly stolen from airline pilots' rituals, and he cut ICU line infections to zero at Hopkins. (FYI, experiment replicated in inner city Detroit.) Now "checklisting," for any number of things, is becoming a staple in many hospitals. And, yes, many hospital employees are stretched to the breaking point—but the fact is, stressed out or not, religious hand washing creates, in 2010, near miracles in the world of patient safety.

To be sure, hospitals are "chipping away" at patient safety issues (and so-called "patient-centric care," à la Griffin Hospital in Derby, Connecticut). There are literally thousands of experiments under way.

But . . .
"Chipping away" is simply . . . **not** . . . enough.
Instead I must *dis*respectfully ask:
Where are the . . . **radicals?**
Where is the . . . **radicalism?**

Glenn Steele has pulled off a miracle at Geisinger.
Where are the Glenn Steeles?

My wife recently waited five hours in an ER with a broken ankle—she described the pain as "second only to labor." But she isn't even pissed off—it's what has happened to all her friends, it's "what you expect." As I write I've been to a "Top 10" hospital three times in the last ten days for tests. No, I was not left for hours upon more hours on a gurney in a hallway as Susan was. Nonetheless, there was a major error, two errors in one case, associated with each visit. One snafu could have had dangerous consequences for my beloved pacemaker. Yup, they batted a thousand. Three-for-three, an error **100%** of the time.

At a dinner with eight guests, I deliberately turned the conversation toward this issue. Each . . . **each and every one** . . . of the guests or their immediate families had had a serious unforced error associated with their most recent hospital incarceration. In all but one case, the error had been life threatening. (And, depending on your interpretation, one may have resulted in an unnecessary death; at the least, it made a bad situation much worse.)

This is not right.
This is wrong.

Of course there are numerous "externalities," as the economists call it. Still, if I'm CEO of a hospital, this is my house—and a 100 percent error rate is waaaaay beyond "inexcusable."

Let me be clear and crude: This shit doesn't have to happen.

Where is the . . . **shame?**
Where are the . . . **radicals?**
Where are the CEOs, systemic externalities or not, who . . . **will not rest until this is fixed?**

(As I write in October 2009, health care reform is wobbling through a dozen congressional committees. The outcome is unclear. That fact is irrelevant to this discussion. This is stuff that does not require Washington's legislative help. This stuff requires . . . **raw, rad-i-cal determination** . . . and an . . . **abiding sense of responsibility.**)

(Hospital professionals *do* care—almost to the woman and man. But, per General Chapman and Winston Churchill, it is not enough to care; you must succeed at what is necessary.)

77. Captain "Day" and Captain "Night": A Tale of Two Deployments. And Two Suggestions.

In 1966, I was an ensign in the United States Navy, serving in a combat engineering battalion ("Seabees") in Danang, Vietnam. Per the Navy Seabee routine, I was deployed to Vietnam for nine months, came home for three, and went back over for another nine. With the tooth fairy looking over my shoulder, I lucked out and had two wildly different "COs" (commanding officers); taken as a pair, their impact on my worldview remains enormous 44 years later. (Pretty close to "all-you-need-to-know" status.)

To this day, I call them "day" and "night." My first CO, Dick Anderson (CAPTAIN Anderson!), was "day." Our job was to build stuff—roads, bridges, camps, gun emplacements, etc.—mostly for the U.S. Marine Corps. Captain Andy's approach could be summarized in three words, subsequently made immortal by Nike; namely, "Just do it." Or, more accurately in our case, **"Just get the damn thing built—as fast as you can."** He made it clear to the very junior officers, including me, that we were to do whatever the hell our CPOs/chief petty officers told us to do. (These were the senior enlisted men whom, in theory, *we* had life and death authority over—as far as our CO was concerned, it was pretty much the other way around.) Above all, Captain Andy wanted no excuses of any flavor—monsoon rains that made everything impassible were our problem, not God's. **"What, do you only build when it's sunny, Mr. Peters?"** (Typical Andersonism.) Captain Andy, in retrospect, gave us a ridiculous amount of autonomy—and expected us to rise to the occasion. Oh, and when he gave us hell, which was frequently, it always ended with a smile from his weather-beaten face: "You'll sort it out, Tom, I have no doubt." The upshot was that we got a lot of work done, and done well, in short order.

Deployment #2 brought Captain "Night," whose name shall not be mentioned (sort of like Voldemort). He had a different style of "leadership" entirely. It's often called "by the book." He was a stickler for the formalities. My de facto membership at the Chiefs Club, by invitation only to officers, was frowned upon as inappropriate. **I sometimes thought and think that he was more interested in typo-free reports of jobs not yet done than hell-and-high-water-completed construction with hurried documentation.** I had a crappy time, as did pretty much the whole set of junior officers; and our track record in getting things done for our customers was less than sterling. For me, the quintessential event came when I was summoned to the CO's office and lectured on the difference between "tangible" and "palpable" in a report I'd prepared that was going up the chain of command—to this day, 44 years later, I have no idea what the difference is between the two words. **But I damn well know the difference between "day" and "night"!**

❯ AN "A.A." (ACTION ADDICTS) TWO-STEP GUIDE

There was a set of "eight basics" that were the heart of *In Search of Excellence*. The place of pride . . . #1 . . . went to: **"A Bias for Action."** After three years of research, Bob Waterman and I concluded that a proclivity for "trying it out" rather than "talking it to death" was the most important attribute of winning (EXCELLENT) companies. As competition has heated up and heated up and heated up, the validity of this finding, to my mind, has become ever more clear.

Implementing it? "A bias for action" is an attitude, not a program or a strategy. Hence there is no 10-step implementation guide. However I would recommend a two-step guide:

Step One: I know you've heard it—read it a hundred times. Here comes #101. Gandhi: "You must be the change you wish to see in the world." You want an "action attitude" in your six-person IS subunit. Be or become Mr./Ms. Hustle. An idea that sounds promising comes up in a meeting—you approve a little seed money on the spot and ask for a progress report on "stuff done" one week from now.

Step Two: A-n-y-b-o-d-y who gets s-o-m-e-t-h-i-n-g done with dispatch gets **recognition to die for** . . . ASAP. Said recognition becomes a weekly ritual, perhaps . . . **"Action Addict of the Week"**?

Try it.

(That's the whole idea, ain't it?)

78. If You Want to Find Oil, You Must Drill Wells.

There's General Chapman.
There's Mr. Churchill.
There's Captain DAY.
There's Captain NIGHT.

And . . .

While walking on the treadmill one morning—I hate treadmills, but it was −8°F outside—my straining eye caught the cover of a book I'd surveyed and taken aboard for *In Search of Excellence*. It was *The Hunters* by John Masters, a successful Canadian O & G wildcatter. Here is the excerpt I underlined 25 years ago and have battered seminar participants with ever since:

"This is so simple it sounds stupid, but it is amazing how few oil people really understand that you only find oil and gas when you drill wells. You may think you're finding it when you're drawing maps and studying logs, but you have to drill."

Message: **You have to drill!**

Yup.
You have to get done what is necessary.
You have to build come rain or shine or the presence of menacing bad guys.
And if you want to find oil, you have to drill.

I sometimes, and not in jest, call "it" "the only thing I've learned 'for sure' in the last 44 years"—since the start of my Seabee experience.

Namely:

She or he who tries the most stuff . . . wins!

44 years.
One idea.
Not bad.

> ## ❯ ACTION WORDS

Naturally I've collected a ton of supporting quotes to buttress my bias for a "bias for action."

My favorites:

"We have a 'strategic' plan. It's called doing things."
—Herb Kelleher, founder, Southwest Airlines

"Experiment fearlessly."
—*BusinessWeek*, on the #1 tactic of innovation stars

"We ground up more pig brains!"
—Nobel winner in Medicine, on his "secret" of success, performing more experiments than his peers

"Ready. Fire. Aim."
—Ross Perot (and others)

"Intelligent people can always come up with intelligent reasons to do nothing."
—NPR host Scott Simon

"Andrew Higgins, who built landing craft in WWII, refused to hire graduates of engineering schools. *He believed that they only teach you what you can't do in engineering school.* He started off with 20 employees, and by the middle of the war had 30,000 working for him. He turned out 20,000 landing craft. D. D. Eisenhower told me, 'Andrew Higgins won the war for us. He did it without engineers.' "
—Stephen Ambrose, *Fast Company*

"How do I know what I think until I see what I say."
—E. M. Forster

"Blame no one.
"Expect nothing.
"Do something."
—Locker room sign posted by football coach Bill Parcells

"You miss 100 percent of the shots you never take."
—Wayne Gretzky

Amen!
(I hope one or two of these will inspire you as they have me.)

1. 2. 3. 4. 5. 6. 7. 8. 9. 10. 11. 12. 13. 14.

15. 16. 17. 18. 19. 20. 21. 22. 23. 24. 25.

26. 27. 28. 29. 30. 31. 32. 33. 34. 35.

36. 37. 38. 39. 40. 41. 42. 43. 44. 45.

46. 47. 48. 49. 50. 51. 52. 53. 54. 55. 56.

57. 58. 59. 60. 61. 62. 63. 64. 65. 66. 67.

68. 69. 70. 71. 72. 73. 74. 75. 76. 77. 78.

79. 80. 81. 82. 83. 84. 85. 86. 87. 88.

89. 90. 91. 92. 93. 94. 95. 96. 97. 98. 99.

100. 101. 102. 103. 104. 105. 106. 107.

108. 109. 110. 111. 112. 113. 114. 115.

116. 117. 118. 119. 120. 121. 122. 123.

124. 125. 126. 127. 128. 129. 130. 131.

132. 133. 134. 135. 136. 137. 138. 139.

140. 141. 142. 143. 144. 145. 146. 147.

148. 149. 150. 151. 152. 153. 154. 155.

156. 157. 158. 159. 160. 161. 162. 163.

Change

79. Zen and the Art of Achieving Change Where It Already Exists.

*"Some people look for things that went wrong and try to fix them.
I look for things that went right and try to build on them."*
—Bob Stone, aka Mr. ReGo

Bob Stone was Al Gore's point man for "reinventing" government when Gore was VP—hence the Mr. ReGo moniker. He is also credited with, in an earlier incarnation, starting a quality revolution at the Pentagon. In the process, he effectively rewrote the book on "corporate" change in huge bureaucracies. (And he kindly wrote a superb book to explain what he'd done: *Polite Revolutionary: Lessons from an Uncivil Servant.*)

Bob, as I see it, was a Zen master, a Sumo wrestler—a Master of Indirection. He full well knew that he could not force change on the federal bureaucracy; even the President rarely succeeds by frontal assault. And as a Pentagon refugee, he knew the silliness of producing ever-to-be-unread, always-to-be-ignored encyclopedic "White Papers" and fat manuals.

So he turned to and mastered the potent Art of Storytelling—and resurrected the always faithful "accentuate the positive" strategy. Hence the GoGo ReGo Gospel According to Stone:

"I look for things that went right and try to build on them."

Stone knew from extensive experience that there were astonishingly effective, renegade Civil Servants (Uncivil Servants?) at work in the underbelly of the system—plying their effective-but-scorned trade as far from the light as possible. The trick was to discover their existence and then induce them to "come out" so that he could (1) certify (via the Public Blessing of VP Gore) their heretofore shunned approaches, (2) cast their results in Monuments of Documentary Film, (3) bring them together informally as model Cadres of Tomorrow's Enlightened Practices, and (4) shame scores of others into following the lead of their obstreperous (and now honored) peers. (There's obviously much more to the tale—see Bob's book, or my précis of it in Chapter 17 of *Re-imagine!*)

Jill Ker Conway played the much same game with matchless skill upon becoming the first woman appointed president of Smith College. She found herself not only surrounded by skeptical tenured profs (mostly male!), but also without the budgetary resources to implement the very programs she needed to make her reign different from that of the feckless old boys who had preceded her.

Enter Zen.

She nosed around the campus (like Stone had done in the federal bureaucracy) and discovered a robust Change Underground, mostly consisting of impatient members of the junior ranks. She met with them (word of a 27-year-old assistant prof lunching with the Big Boss gets around in a flash), encouraged them to keep pushing—and urged them to begin the process of proclaiming their views publicly, with her implicit blessing.

As to the dollar shortage, she concocted the Sister of All End Runs.

The hell with standard budgetary sources of bucks—she met instead with members of Smith's Change "Overground"—alumnae who were beside themselves with glee at the belated appointment of this first female prexy. She met and met and met some more—and cajoled and cajoled and cajoled some more. And after a zillion lunches, teas, and dinners, she had enough "external," "off-balance-sheet" funding to pilot several programs that eventually became the hallmarks of her wildly successful term of office.

All hail the Aussie sheep-station-born Mistress of Indirection from Northampton, Massachusetts!

Message: Powerlessness is (mostly) a state of mind! With a dab of Zen here and a Guide to the Corporate Underworld there . . . Gold can be discovered and thence Mountains Can Be Moved!

Message: Become a Master of Indirection.

Message: The "guaranteed" best way to deal with the entrenched resistors?

Absolute and determined (though abidingly civil) **avoidance.**

Summary:

(1) Comb the underground for effective "troublemakers" who are creating and living tomorrow today.

(2) Anoint them as Public Paragons of the New Deal-to-Be.

(3) Encourage others to visit them and observe palpable models of new ways of doing business.

(4) Applaud the Nouveau Copycats of the First Round Pioneers— and grow the Renegade Battalions as rapidly as possible.

> **SECRET (CHANGE) AGENT**

"Somewhere in your organization, groups of people are already doing things differently and better. To create lasting change, find these areas of positive deviance and fan their flames."
—Richard Tanner Pascale and Jerry Sternin, "Your Company's Secret Change Agents," *Harvard Business Review* (The late Jerry Sternin had a sparkling record at delivering programs and progress in some of the most downtrodden parts of the globe.)

80. The Way of the Demo.

If you keep repeating something enough times, you realize what a deeply held belief it is! I got in a discussion with several tech execs (software) about some new technologies that their major corporate users were slow to adopt. I heard myself chiding them in a familiar (to me) way:

"For heaven's sake, quit trying to sell Unilever or Fiat or P&G! Enormous companies are invariably 'late adopters.' (I.e., more or less useless, sluggish twits.) The far, far better idea is to scour the world in pursuit of 2 or 3 or 4 mid-sized, noteworthy, pioneering customers who will 'join up' with you to Make Miracles Happen. Use your work with these hotshots as . . . Demos. Once you have a passel of mid-sized 'Super-cool' Demos . . . then, and only then, go to one of the Big Guys and say, 'Don't miss the Party, Dull Davey Dimwit.'"

This I Believe!

Change in "big" places is mostly a result of showing off "demos" from modest-sized "cool" places! The on-the-make general manager of the small Irish division of BigCo thinks your new Purchasing Software is off-the-charts good; she's keen to be an early adopter. Once she's done her bit, you can say to the slugabed big-division general managers, "Why don't you go and look at what Mary O'Donnell and the Irish have done with this—it changed their world."

To succeed with "new stuff," you must find . . . Kindred Spirits . . . those who will . . . Play with You (and your "cool stuff") . . . which in turn provides you with . . . "Demos" . . . that you can Tout Far & Wide.

I call "it": The way of the demo.

And I will boldly state: *Selling-by-demo is the single-best way to accelerate acceptance of a novel (= scary) idea.*

No demo.
No deal.
Period.

First Steps: Do you have a program/product/process, the acceptance of which is diffusing at a snail's pace? Seek nominations for a "prospect list" of . . . Potential Pioneers who might be amenable to offering you a Playpen and becoming your Playmate.

This is another case of winning through *indirection*. You will be "slowed down" (relative to the "big breakthrough" sale) by your decision to work on some "little" (= not huge) demos. But in the long haul, this apparent detour is the Ultimate Accelerant for overall program/product/process success.

> **PRIMARY CLUELESS**

The Way of the Demo even applies to big-time politics. What is a primary, after all, but a candidate's chance to put out a demo?

Consider the 2008 U.S. presidential campaign for the Republican nomination for president. Rudy Giuliani, the early favorite, didn't bother to collect "demos" in Iowa or New Hampshire. He skipped directly to Big Florida as his first stop. Sans a "demo," Florida, a likely "good state" for Giuliani where he'd worked like hell, turned its collective back on him—and the low-odds John McCain, replete with his New Hampshire demo, took the Florida Trophy and then the Republican nomination.

81. Big Change—All at Once!

I am an avowed incrementalist—even if the eventual aim is stratospherically high. That is, get going ASAP—and quickly experiment your way toward/to success.

But, when my wife and I had a Grand Idea in 2008 for a landscaping project that would change the look and feel of our farm in Tinmouth, Vermont, we decided, more or less, to . . . **do it all at once.** There has been pain from biting off more than we could readily chew, but the story to this point has the mark of a real success far beyond our initial imaginings.

The power of "getting going on everything at once" with but a sliver of a master plan (a couple of "napkin" sketches) was that we could envision from the outset the vague outline of what was going to (more or less) end up happening—thence we could adjust like crazy, improvise constantly, destroy and create using the entire palette, and dramatically reshape the overall work, and even the overall concept, as we went along. Which, of course, means we didn't really reject my beloved Rapid Experimentation Method—we just did it on and amid a Grand Platform called "everything is in motion and up for grabs."

To be more specific, we essentially started by blowing everything up—sticking in a roughed-out new road that changed the entire dynamics (look, feel, flow) of the farm. From there a dozen supporting projects began, or were also roughed out "on the ground," at once. (In the space of a couple of weeks.) As a result, the place was a disheveled inchoate mess ("that only a mother could love") from stem to stern, north to south, and east to west.

And then the real "serious play" (Michael Schrage's book by this title was an inspiration—more later) began. To stick to the Basic Texts of Life, we were following Nobel laureate F. A. Hayek's "spontaneous discovery" economic-growth process.

I'm not sure I'd do things, big things, this way in every instance, but I do think there are times when such an "all at once" approach is merited—when you have a Big Idea but need to be living "in the middle of it," with all ends loose ends, to figure out what it means.

Further confirmation of this idea—and how gutsy-nutsy it is!—came from, at about the time we attacked the project, reading Wendy Kopp's *One Day, All Children . . . : The Unlikely Triumph of Teach for America and What I Learned Along the Way.*

I think Ms. Kopp's story is among the most extraordinary I've happened across. From a Princeton dorm room, in 1988, she hatched a program that has arguably become the most profound educational and public service experiment-success in America in many a year or decade.

Kopp rejected from the start the advice from the Captains of Industry and other Great Ones who intended to support her—namely, she decided that even though she really didn't know what she was up to tactically, she would mount an enormous program launch to demonstrate to the world the power of her idea. "Great, Wendy, but you need 'proof of concept.' Test it with a handful of young untutored teachers in an out-of-the-way-place off-off-off-off-Broadway"—that, in effect, was the advice she got again and again and again and without exception. (And the advice *I* would have given her if asked.) But she was adamant that if she was going to attract excellent recent top-university graduates to give up two years of their lives teaching in depressed areas, she had to create a Wave of World-rattling Momentum on Day One.

Of course we now know she pulled it off . . . Big Time. But close calls and pratfalls occupy most of the 193-page book. Everything that could go wrong—and then some—*did* go wrong. Not just tiny miscues, but enormous boo-boos—again and again and again. Her tiny staff fumbled and bumbled their way to survival, then eventually success, holding on only to the Dream and Ms. Kopp's staggering intensity and energy.

As I read the book I came to the conclusion that she had been right—that the only way for her to go had been the Big Way from Day One. Of course, her youthful energy, spirit, and naiveté certainly helped her bite off such an enormous, often contentious ("20-year-old 'girl' tackles teachers unions in Manhattan, etc., etc.") notion.

(I also had the chance to ponder "all this" on my recent trip to Korea. The Korean approach to many humongous opportunities is to eschew the master plan, or much of any plan—and just get the hell going, firing full bore on a thousand cylinders at once. I witnessed one act of their show a couple of decades ago, when they leapt, from ground zero, into electronics. From that cold start they built enormous production facilities—and

learned on the fly how to make it all work and effectively compete with the best. Their individual and collective success, and the speed thereof, was mind-boggling in aim and accomplishment alike.)

Between my little project and Wendy Kopp's Richter 8.0 project and Korea, I am wondering about the times when "do it all at once and figure out what 'it' is later" is the right answer. There is no doubt that such conditions exist—though the key, beyond the compelling dream, is the raw talent and energy and enthusiasm and obsession and resilience of the participants. It is 99.99 percent (or more) a matter of raw emotion—not a matter of analytically identifying a big opportunity, assigning "good people," and then proceeding based on state-of-the-art project management software.

Hence my bottom line: **If you've got a Whopper of an Aspiration and Determination that "this must happen" bordering on Insanity . . . cut the lifeline and leap in and start flapping around!**

Translation for "your world":

Rather than investing your precious time and energy in dotting every "i" with your current subproject, then moving rote-like to the next logical step, start, in an almost half-assed way, two or three or four other tasks/subprojects just to see how the overall thing "feels." In other words, toss several balls in the air, and see what the frenzy of action "tells you" and "feels like" on the whole. I also recommend, if the occasion is right and the determination is sky-high, more or less severing the lifeline—letting go of a lot of what you are "supposed to be doing" and plunging into the big deal. By neglecting (!) your "real work," you raise to the sky your Commitment to the Big New Deal—it becomes an approximation of "do or die," which concentrates the mind wonderfully.

(For me, in working on a book like this, the approach can mean plunging into the next chapter before I even have a decent rough draft of the current chapter. Then, when I have four or five or eight or nine half-assed chapter drafts in process, I can begin to figure out what the book as a whole is actually about—or, more important, what it might be about that I hadn't imagined.)

(By the way, I'm delighted we took the "do everything" approach to our landscaping. By cutting the lifeline, we adopted a "go for it" attitude that would never have occurred if we'd taken one measured step at a time. We would never have seen the size of the opportunity for real transformation, and we would have been scared off by the price tag if we'd known what we were letting ourselves in for!)

Action: *Look at your work-in-progress project portfolio. Is there some potentially encompassing ("change the world") "meta-goal" that you might birth if you were to get moving on three or four projects simultaneously? Or what about dropping four of your five active projects—and expanding the scope of the remaining project fivefold . . . then get going on six or seven aspects of that enhanced fifth project "all at once."*

82. Big Change—in a Short Time.

The story goes that General George Patton turned around a bedraggled U.S. Army in North Africa in a matter of a few weeks upon taking charge in 1943. (Some say a few days.)

Upon taking over a new command, Admiral Lord Nelson would change the attitude of an entire fleet in . . . *less than a week.* **(!!!)**

A close friend began his teaching career at the age of 40, introduced an entirely new teaching style into a stodgy boarding school—and was voted "top teacher" within . . . **90 days.**

The CEO of a giant transportation company completely upended his senior line officers' responsibility and authority and accountability (all increased by an order of magnitude) almost "overnight." Literally everyone, including a couple of "hapless bureaucrats," rose to the occasion, and performance spurted more or less instantly—and then kept going.

AA tells us that it takes but . . . **an instant** . . . to stop drinking. (To be sure, a lifetime to follow through.)

And in 1992, I wrote about a CEO (in *Liberation Management*) who installed self-managed work teams covering 100 percent of production activities in a famously authoritarian, Teamster-organized factory . . . **over the course of one weekend.**

Several expert analysts argue from extensive anecdotal evidence that "big change" is actually "easier" than small change. That is, it's far easier to get people excited about a Big Hairy Audacious Goal (Jim Collins's felicitous term) than "incremental improvement."

My "bottom line" after lots of thought and observation: **Change will take *precisely* as long as you think it will.**

If you "think it'll take two years to do this," well, that's more or less what it'll take. Think "two weeks'll do it"—and I'd not be surprised if you'd climbed three-fourths of the rugged mountain in those two weeks.

Don't "aim high."

Aim very, very high.

The "arrogance of absurdly high expectations" can pay off in very short order if you've got the nerve to go for it and the deep-rooted (messianic) belief that . . . **"there's utterly no reason why we can't do this in a month."**

(Think about it.)

(Please.)

83. Clever? Never!

"The art of war does not require complicated maneuvers; the simplest are the best, and common sense is fundamental. From which one might wonder how it is generals make blunders; it is because they try to be clever."
—Napoleon

I make every effort to read—or at least skim—new business strategy books and articles. In 90 percent of cases, I can dismiss neither the author's thought process nor his or her evidence—but I am always taken aback by the absence of any discussion or consideration of the ability to implement the suggestions made or implied.

There is total silence around the subject.

(I started to add "more or less" to the prior sentence, then changed my mind; the "total" actually needs no modifier.)

I did a quick analysis of the Index of one "famous" strategy tome circa 2007—words like "people" and "customer" and "leadership" and "implementation" and "execution" were literally missing. Take my bugbear, which you doubtless have figured out by now—cross-functional coordination, or full-scale cross-functional teaming to add value. There's no mention, not a hint—and yet it's the failure of such coordination or opportunism that humbles strategic initiative after strategic initiative. (90 percent?)

So my battle continues to rage. Since my Ph.D. days at Stanford, now 35 years ago, I have been a more or less lonely voice shouting . . .

But what about implementation?

It does sometimes get old.

It is always frustrating.

It is also the cause of anger bordering on fury.

It pisses me off—especially at B-schools.

(But, then, pretty much everything about B-schools pisses me off.)

Companies die of implementation fiascoes—rarely of un-clever strategies.

Napoleon tells us to beware of the overly clever ones. To trust only the simple plans that can be understood and accepted by one and all; and that by their simplicity and clarity are far more readily implemented. I am a rather serious student of Admiral Horatio Nelson and General Ulysses S. Grant. (They are the only military leaders with whom I've been totally preoccupied.) Either Grant or Nelson could have penned, exactly, the kickoff quote above. Both were known for the clarity and simplicity of their plans—and the clarity and simplicity and compelling nature of their communication of those plans to their admirals and generals and privates and seamen.

Warren Buffett said recently that if you need to analyze a company's financials on a computer—don't buy the stock. From investment to implementation of a marketing plan to the fields of battle or the high seas on which they occur, tame "cleverness" and seek clarity and simplicity and a compelling story in all you do.

The "Implementation Mind-set" Exam:

(1) Can you describe your current project and its benefits and points of differentiation in a single, compelling paragraph?

(2) Can you explain your project and why you are doing it to your 15-year-old daughter and 13-year-old son to the point that they can "get it" and ask intelligent questions about it and perhaps think it is "cool"?

(3) Can you give a spur-of-the-moment 9-minute presentation, without PowerPoint, to the CEO upon immediate request? (Less than 10 minutes prep time.)

(4) Can you go to an end user of your project, at the first level of job classification, and create some excitement on her part about the project and its benefits?

(5) Can you reconstruct the bare bones of your financials on the back of an envelope without booting your computer?

(6) Can you explain in a compelling fashion why you think you've got the talent to pull off the strategic direction you have chosen?

(7) Do your project plans and presentations devote at least . . . **twice** . . . as much space–time to the Details of Implementation as they do to market analysis and positioning or benefits?

(8) Can you list the five biggest implementation hurdles expected down the pike—and exactly how you plan to overcome them?

(9) Can you explain precisely how you plan to foster cross-functional communication and excitement about your project throughout the organization as a whole?

(10) Could you please tell me the principal implementation hurdles you have faced and overcome in your last two projects?

(11) What two big things have you learned about implementation in your last two projects?

(12) Etc.

(13) Etc.

Presumably you get the drift. These questions are obviously not written in stone—but the direction thereof is.

Put Napoleon's quote on your wall or use it as a screensaver—or chant it at the beginning of every review meeting!

Is there a more important recitation of what's essential for success between these covers? Maybe a few are as important, but none could surpass it.

(NB: I gave some thought to not including any commentary here, just letting Napoleon's quote stand alone on the page. I dearly do not want to dilute in any way the power and clarity of his words.)

➤ NO POLITICS. NO IMPLEMENTATION.

In early October 2009, several cover reviews appeared of Neil Shee-han's *A Fiery Peace in a Cold War: Bernard Schriever and the Ultimate Weapon*. It's a "one guy against the world" story of the first order. Schriever either did a very good thing or a very questionable thing, depending on the reviewer. But what he did was clear, and a BIG BIG Thing, to paraphrase myself. Against very powerful forces, such as bomber maniac and Strategic Air Command boss Curtis LeMay, Schriever proposed and developed, more or less single-handedly, America's ICBM capability—mainstay of our national defense ever since.

Fiery Peace is a story of a "good strategic idea" (in the real-world context of the nearly hot Cold War) and overcoming immense technical-engineering challenges.

But that's not why I'm writing this.

As most of you know, I think political skill is as important or more important than "strategic brilliance." And Schriever, a talented engineer, was an . . . **Über-master Politician.** The forces lined up against him amount to a list as long as your arm, with most of those named carrying far more rank than Schriever. Yet he prevailed—eventually convincing one of the most pragmatic people ever to reside at 1600 Pennsylvania Avenue, Dwight David Eisenhower.

Want to accomplish something, any-damn-thing?
Sharpen your political skills!
(And this holds for a 24-year-old non-manager working on her small part of a project almost as much as it did for Bernard Schriever.)

(Relationship to Napoleon: The engineering may have been complex, but Schriever's idea was straightforward—describable in a sentence, not even a full paragraph was needed. The "last 99+ percent" was bulldog determination and relentlessness.)

You, Me,
and Charlie Wilson's
War

George Crile's* *Charlie Wilson's War*, the tale of the defeat of the Soviet Union in Afghanistan (which led directly to its subsequent unraveling), is quite simply the most extraordinary nonfiction potboiler I have ever read. Turning to the practicalities of your and my day-to-day professional affairs, the saga is peppered with de facto analyses of how Texas congressman Wilson, pretty much solo, coaxed the U.S. House of Representatives into backing the Afghan mujahideen in their resistance to the Soviets. Wilson is, to be sure, "larger than life," yet his practical "can do" tactics—and those of his CIA cohort, Gust Avrakotos—have a lot to teach all of us in far more ordinary settings.

(*NB: The late Mr. Crile was a longtime CBS *60 Minutes* producer—legendary for winning a First Amendment court battle against William Westmoreland, U.S. Commander in Vietnam; Crile called out Westmoreland over the Vietnam "body count" fiasco.)

1. Make friends with the . . . "Invisible 95 percent."

"He had become something of a legend with these people who manned the underbelly of the Agency [CIA]."
—George Crile on Gust Avrakotos, Charlie Wilson's man in the middle ranks of the CIA

Gust Avrakotos apparently knew every "top floor" CIA executive secretary by name—and had helped many of them sort out personal or professional problems. The folks in the mailroom and in the bowels of the computer operations affairs were also the subject of Gust's intense and affectionate attentions. *In effect, you could say that Gust was "Commander in Chief of the Invisible Ninety-Five Percent" of the Agency—which allowed him to make extraordinary things happen despite furious resistance from his bosses and bosses' bosses enthroned at the top of a very rigid hierarchy.*

This story reminds us in Bold Print: 99 percent (96 percent minimum—I'm not joking) of the important work of the organization is done far, far out of the limelight. While Ms. Big may be "the decider," she is working from analyses and recommendations made by a host of largely invisible, largely unappreciated junior folks—two or three (or four) levels "down," even in today's connected, streamlined organizations.

Implication: *Have I consciously invested time and significant* **(overwhelming!)** *attention and care and engagement throughout the organization? Measure it! (Damn it.)*

2. Create a Networker-Doer partnership.

Congressman Wilson had the networking part down, but he needed help with the doing. Conversely, if you are the doer, then you

> **THREE TO GET READY**

I believe that every project team with more than a half-dozen members in fact needs/must have three flavors of leaders: (1) The Visionary, who "lives"/embodies the project's scintillating promise—and sells it "24/7" in every corner of the impacted world. (2) The Networker, who creates and oversees the "political ecosystem" and actually knits people together in order to make things happen. (3) The Mechanic, who loves and lives for the budget, the schedule, and the 1,000 admin details that are the lifeblood of day-to-day team efficiency. Remove any of the three, and the project team implodes. Also, you must acknowledge that these are three very different types of people, and all three dispositions rarely (or never) come in the same package—this issue is paramount even for the one-person project "team," where the solo will need some sort of help, on the cheap or not, with the things that are not her natural fare.

must find the politician-networker. The legendary Chicago-based community organizer Saul Alinsky pointed out the difference between "organizers" and "leaders." Leaders are the visible ones, "out there," giving the speeches and manning the picket lines. The largely invisible organizer, on the other hand, spends her time recruiting the folks who will be on that picket line, settling disputes about who goes where—and procuring the buses to get the picketers to the right place at the right time with the necessary signs and bullhorns.

(NB: *Among other things, I firmly believe that Alinsky's* Rules for Radicals, *which for years I used as my sole text in project management training, is the best "project management" manual ever written; it focuses on the "missing 98 percent" of project management effectiveness— the politics of implementation—that the traditional, technical project management texts willfully ignore.*)

3. Carefully manage the BOF/Balance of Favors.

Practice potlatch—giving so much help to so many people on so many occasions (purposeful overkill!) that there is little issue about their supporting you when the (rare!) time comes to call in the chits. "Wilson made it easy for his colleagues to come to him," Crile wrote, "always gracious, almost always helpful." Some would argue, and I think I'd agree, that conscious and organized management of one's "balance of favors" (owed and due) is a very sensible (if Machiavellian) thing to do—a mentor of mine, exceptionally successful in California politics, literally had a "little black book" of favors "given" and "owed" that others would have died to get their hands on.

(The tools are different and the reach is far greater in the Age of Social Networking—but the raw essence of trading favors is as it has always been.)

4. Follow the money!

"Anybody with a brain can figure out that if they can get on the Defense subcommittee, that's where they ought to be—because that's where the money is."
—Charlie Wilson

Getting near the heart of fiscal processes offers innumerable opportunities to effectively take control of a system—as long as you are willing to invest in achieving Absolute Mastery of those processes. From the outside looking in, this is yet another big argument for nurturing relationships a few levels down in the organization—in this case, the all-important-everywhere financial organization.

▶ SCHEMIN' THE NIGHT AWAY

Many years ago, Al Smith, who became New York's governor and the Democrats' candidate in 1928 for the presidency, arrived in Albany as a freshman state legislator. While his colleagues drank and caroused the night away, very junior Representative Smith pored from dusk to dawn over every line in the state budget. His subsequent Mastery of the State Fiscal Process led him directly to power in astonishingly short order.

Lesson: Master the "dreary" details of arcane processes (especially financial processes) that others can't be bothered with. (Master = Master. You know my drill by now.)

5. Found material. (And found people.)

Don't reinvent the wheel. It costs too much, takes too much time, and requires too much bureaucratic hassle. Again and again, Charlie and Gust took advantage of extant "stuff"—unwanted stores of less than state-of-the-art hardware, for example—that was immediately available for use, rather than waiting an eternity for "perfect" (expensive, scarce, *visible*) equipment.

And don't stop there. Search out disrespected oddball groups that have done exciting work, consistent with your aims, without being fully recognized for it. In this case, that meant teaming up with a band of absurdly talented "crazies" in the Pentagon's lightly regarded ("bothersome" to the hierarchy) Weapons Upgrade Program.

6. The enemy of my enemy is my friend. Hold your nose—and get the job done.

Charlie did this on numerous occasions. So, too, Gust. So, too, you—if you're smart.

7. Real, Visible Passion!

Create compelling evidence of the source of your passion. Charlie Wilson had one apparently insuperable hurdle to his plan—a cynical old congressman who dismissed Charlie's crusade out of hand. But Charlie did have enough chits out to enable him to cajole the skeptic into visiting an Afghan refugee camp. The live, graphic evidence, as Charlie had imagined it would, turned the foe into an emotional champion of the cause—in the space of a single afternoon. If you desperately believe in a cause, figure out some way (perhaps a little less than a 10,000-mile journey) to expose would-be converts to startling, live demos of the problem, replete with testimony from those who are on the losing end of things.

(NB: Wilson's passion about his beliefs were further and visibly magnified by tactics he shamelessly employed to make it personal—and to make sure that others knew it was personal. For example, on every visit to the refugee camps, Wilson donated blood on the spot.)

8. Passion as Deterrence!

Passion works for a lot of reasons—it is indeed infectious and attracts supporters. But one of its often ignored, incredibly strong side effects is its deterrent power. Passion suggests exhausting "staying power"—"I might as well not waste energy or chits blocking him, he's not going away and he'll hound me and absorb my time till hell freezes over." (I'd add, it worked for me in my Washington stint—I was pretty powerless, but annoyingly tenacious. The "annoying" was part of the drill.)

9. Cut red tape.

"What we did in one month with Charlie would have taken us nine years to accomplish."
—Gust Avrakotos

"Ninety percent of what we call management consists of making it difficult for people to get things done."
—Peter Drucker

These two quotes are in keeping with my longtime definition of a boss: **CHRO** . . . or **C**hief **H**urdle **R**emoval **O**fficer. Which (again) means the boss must be a Master of the Intricacies and Arcania of the Interior Systems and the Political Process. In a business project, this means, among other things, Total Mastery of the *Client's* purchasing process—including Total Comprehension of the power politics in that "outside" organization, from top to "bottom."

More often than not, the best way to get "over" the hurdles is to bypass them—it reduces energy consumption. **That is, when a project is truly odd, like Charlie Wilson's campaign, waste as little time or capital as possible going directly "up the chain of command."** Aversion to the unusual, despite protestations to the contrary, rises as one nears the top. Instead, constantly devise and try and discard and re-revise end runs that (1) build a lush "horizontal" (rather than formal vertical) network, (2) add to your knowledge, and (3) eventually create a blizzard of "small wins" that start and build momentum behind the project. Be polite to your bosses (do not gratuitously give offense), but do not waste time on them until your Small Wins and Demos and Network of Avid Supporters constitute an Irresistible Force for Change.

10. **Create a small, insanely committed "band of brothers-sisters" to act as mostly invisible orchestrators.**

When all was said and done, Gust Avrakotos and his tiny **(never more than a half dozen!)** nerve center in the nether reaches of the CIA never got a smidgen of recognition for what was arguably the Agency's biggest success ever. But his little team did the work of hundreds—and reveled in their very invisibility and keen puppeteering skills. The fact that they were out of sight, out of mind, and bringing the Soviets to their knees was the ultimate turn-on.

(Rules concerning the Wee Band of Brothers: Take chances on unusual talent, regardless of formal rank—a couple of Gust's best players were ridiculously junior. Recruit peculiar talent that has no investment in conventional solutions and no conventional "ladder climbing" aspirations.)

(NB: "Dress [*your freaks*] for success" axiom. You may well recruit "weirdos"—their ideas may well be offensive to the regnant authorities. Hence the need for the "atmospherics" to be as conservative as the ideas are radical. When I undertook a contrarian mission at McKinsey, one old pro advised, "Wear the most conservative suits in the place, never be late to a meeting—don't give them any tiny excuse to dismiss or devalue you." Good advice!)

11. **Keep the long haul in mind, too.**

Think subconsciously . . . long haul. You learn from Charlie Wilson that a *small act* of recognition toward a major in an ally's military pays off Big Time . . . **15 years later** . . . when the major has become chief of staff of the _____ Army. Passion for today's action is paramount—but always, always, *always* think consciously about . . . *Network Investment.*

(NB: Thinking about Network Investment/R.O.I.R./Return on Investment in Relationships should not be a "catch as catch can" thing. It should be subject to the same . . . planning, attention, discipline, accountability, and evaluation . . . that goes into the likes of budgeting. Relationship/Network Development should be talked about openly and constantly,

and it should be on every agenda as a *formal* item for review and discussion— i.e., "R.O.I.R. Maximization Activities.")

12. The game ain't over until the fat lady sings.

"They" (lots of "theys") call it the Law of Unintended Consequences. In this instance, after the Russians had withdrawn from Afghanistan, the United States once again returned to benign neglect of the region— the result was, indirectly, 9/11, orchestrated from Afghanistan by some of the people we had supported a decade earlier; and the continuing mess in Afghanistan today.

Of not finishing the chore, Charlie Wilson said that the defeat of the Soviets in Afghanistan, their first in the Cold War and a spur to the unraveling of the Evil Empire, was a . . . *"glorious accomplishment that changed the world. And then we f$@#ed up the end game."*

❯ SURVIVAL OF THE UNADAPTABLE

In Honor of Charlie and Gust and their ilk:

"The reasonable man adapts himself to the world; the unreasonable one persists in trying to adapt the world to himself. Therefore all progress depends on the unreasonable man."
—G. B. Shaw, *Man and Superman*

"Whenever anything is being accomplished, it is being done, I have learned, by a monomaniac with a mission."
—Peter Drucker

1. 2. 3. 4. 5. 6. 7. 8. 9. 10. 11. 12. 13. 14.
15. 16. 17. 18. 19. 20. 21. 22. 23. 24. 25.
26. 27. 28. 29. 30. 31. 32. 33. 34. 35.
36. 37. 38. 39. 40. 41. 42. 43. 44. 45.
46. 47. 48. 49. 50. 51. 52. 53. 54. 55. 56.
57. 58. 59. 60. 61. 62. 63. 64. 65. 66. 67.
68. 69. 70. 71. 72. 73. 74. 75. 76. 77. 78.
79. 80. 81. 82. 83. **84. 85. 86.** 87. 88.
89. 90. 91. 92. 93. 94. 95. 96. 97. 98. 99.
100. 101. 102. 103. 104. 105. 106. 107.
108. 109. 110. 111. 112. 113. 114. 115.
116. 117. 118. 119. 120. 121. 122. 123.
124. 125. 126. 127. 128. 129. 130. 131.
132. 133. 134. 135. 136. 137. 138. 139.
140. 141. 142. 143. 144. 145. 146. 147.
148. 149. 150. 151. 152. 153. 154. 155.
156. 157. 158. 159. 160. 161. 162. 163.

Passion

84. I Second That Emotion!

Emotion matters.
What else is there?
Ever heard of a success story featuring a

. . . dispassionate symphony conductor?
. . . bored painter?
. . . apathetic self-made billionaire?
. . . 9 to 5 entrepreneur?

That's a joke, right?
Emotion and the leader's role?

Daniel Goleman, Richard Boyatzis, and Annie McKee put it this way in *The New Leaders*:

"Great leaders move us. They ignite our passion and inspire the best in us. When we try to explain why they are so effective, we speak of strategy, vision or powerful ideas. But the reality is much more primal: Great leadership works through the emotions."

Acknowledge emotion.
Hire for emotion.
Evaluate for emotion.
Promote for emotion.
Lead by emotion.
(*Follow* by emotion.)
"Sell" emotion.

(As I said: What else?)

(NB: *Emotion is as important in a two-person accountancy as at Apple. The successful two-person accountancy lives "to be of service" to its Clients. The two-person accountancy aims to "partner with" its Client to improve the Client's understanding and appreciation of the "business equation"—along with making sure that 1+1 = 2. "Emotional accountant" doesn't in any way imply abrogation of fiduciary duties—it does imply dedication to the true meaning of service and partnership and, frankly, indispensability.*)

85. One Rule! Much Gold!!

Enterprise, public or private, small or enormous, is all about humanity—about humans serving humans, about human growth and community. That's obvious, or should be. But it's *always* worth a reminder—far more than usual as we reflect on the thought-less shenanigans that delivered to us the worst financial crisis in 75 years.

Thinking deeply about these fundamentals for good times, bad times, all times ("humans serving humans") reminded me of my old friend, the late John McConnell, founder of Worthington Industries. A pragmatist to a fault, as befits an Ohioan, John believed that growth and profitability flowed from fairness and trust. In fact, he went further, and insisted that the Golden Rule makes for a complete "policy manual"!

As far as I'm concerned, he was onto something, and Worthington's continuing success in *very* tough times in a *very* tough industry (steel!) is testimony to the validity of McConnell's "simple" beliefs, lived for decades with a passion by a cast of thousands.

Musing about McConnell in turn recalled a showstopper of a quote I recently happened upon. By Dr. Frank Crane, it goes like this: *"The Golden Rule is of no use to you whatever unless you realize it is your move."*

If that doesn't bring you up short, I don't know what the hell would—it surely leveled me!

And talk about something that is . . . **immediately operational!**

Message: **It's your move!**

So . . .

Consider . . . **right now** . . . one thorny people problem or customer problem that is driving you nuts.

Operational guidance: It's your move.

What's the right thing to do?

What are you going to do?

Lights!
Camera!
Action!
Now!

❯ IN SEARCH OF EXCELLENCE: THE McCONNELL LEGACY

Twenty-five+ years.
One idea.

Hard is soft.
Soft is hard.

Aiming for profitability?
Aiming for organic growth?

Answer: People committed to supporting one another—through thick and thin.

Answer: People relentlessly committed to personal growth—fired up by rather than fearful of change.

Answer: People determined to consistently be "of service" to their bill-paying customers.

Answer: Decency.
Answer: Kindness.
Answer: Fairness.

Answer: The Golden Rule!

Answer: Your move!

(Thank you, John McConnell.)

(Thank you, Frank Crane.)

86. **Seize the Moments.**

Business ("life," too, of course) rises or falls on the nature and character and lingering memory of what the legendary airline (SAS) boss, Jan Carlzon, called "moments of truth"—those fleeting fragments of true human contact that quite literally define our enterprise's perceived Excellence—or lack thereof.

Thus our goal, perhaps our primary goal, in every flavor and every size of business, is to "MTMMOT"—**Manage to Memorable Moments of Truth.**

Every decision—about hiring, firing, supervision, training, systems development, etc.—should be designed for and brought immediately and directly to bear on the "production" of Memorable Moments of Truth.

Start by recognizing "their" importance. Finding "them." Defining them. **(Pre-cise-ly!!)** Mapping them. **(Pre-cise-ly!!)** Testing them. Measuring them. **(Pre-cise-ly!!)** Incentivizing them. Etc.

Most important: I'd urge you to use "it"—that is, lift Carlzon's term as slightly modified by me, "Manage to Memorable Moments of Truth" per se.

Most important (Part II): Pass every **(e-v-e-r-y)** decision through the "MTMMOT Filter"—how does this system, this hiring practice, whatever, affect our MTMMOTs? If an issue on, say, a weekly operations meeting agenda is *not* somehow related to improving our MTMMOTs, ask why the issue is on the agenda in the first place, or how it can be made relevant to our MTMMOTs. If an issue under discussion does or may *negatively* affect MTMMOTs, reconsider it or reconfigure it.

Relative to the latter—negative impact—one CEO (his name and company slip my mind) is adamant that positive MMOTs are far more important, not less important, in a downturn, when every customer counts **X2.** So, regardless of the pressures, beware of excessive cost-cutting that degrades MMOT quality for our Blessed Remaining Customers!

(Let me be clear: Carlzon achieved stunning success by organizing-measuring-incentivizing-managing the whole enterprise around its "production" of "Moments of Truth.")

Show starter: Immediately begin an inventory of MMOT opportunities relative to this process or that service rendered. Evaluate, quantitatively, your MTMMOT performance at this instant. Big Idea: Engage *everyone* (literally) around the MTMMOT mind-set.

(I might ordinarily be inclined to lay off the MTMMOT abbreviation—seems a bit over the top. But I think this is an exception. If you buy this notion and if you get working on it, I strongly urge you to Manage to Memorable Moments of Truth. This one—MTMMOT—may just be worth the initial derision associated with "yet another acronym.") (I like the verb "Manage to," because it suggests that almost all our work will be directed to producing and enhancing those MMOTs.)

› EN*TITLE*MENT REFORM

Tongue only slightly in cheek, I invite your attention to the more or less proposed job titles below. And, yes, I'd actually suggest you take them more or less seriously. They are "fun"—and deadly serious. Words (e.g., job titles) scream *"We take this seriously and intend to single it out for 'strategic' attention."* Maybe these are informal titles; and obviously you'd not use anything like all of them. The idea here is mind-set and flavor.

Herewith:

- Magician of Magical Moments!

- Maestro of Memorable Moments of Truth!

- Recruiter of Raving Fans!

- Impresario of First and Last Impressions!

- Wizard of WOW!

- Empress of EXCELLENCE!

- Captain of Brilliant Comebacks!

- Princess of Perception!

- Sultan of Social Networking!

- Conductor of Customer Intimacy!

- King of Customer Community!

- Queen of Customer Retention!

- Managing Director of After-Sales Ecstasy!

I'm sure you get my intent . . .

1. 2. 3. 4. 5. 6. 7. 8. 9. 10. 11. 12. 13. 14. 15. 16. 17. 18. 19. 20. 21. 22. 23. 24. 25. 26. 27. 28. 29. 30. 31. 32. 33. 34. 35. 36. 37. 38. 39. 40. 41. 42. 43. 44. 45. 46. 47. 48. 49. 50. 51. 52. 53. 54. 55. 56. 57. 58. 59. 60. 61. 62. 63. 64. 65. 66. 67. 68. 69. 70. 71. 72. 73. 74. 75. 76. 77. 78. 79. 80. 81. 82. 83. 84. 85. 86. **87. 88. 89. 90. 91.** 92. 93. 94. 95. 96. 97. 98. 99. 100. 101. 102. 103. 104. 105. 106. 107. 108. 109. 110. 111. 112. 113. 114. 115. 116. 117. 118. 119. 120. 121. 122. 123. 124. 125. 126. 127. 128. 129. 130. 131. 132. 133. 134. 135. 136. 137. 138. 139. 140. 141. 142. 143. 144. 145. 146. 147. 148. 149. 150. 151. 152. 153. 154. 155. 156. 157. 158. 159. 160. 161. 162. 163.

Presence

87. Managing By Wandering Around—It's All Around You!

Back in 1982, as my *In Search of Excellence* coauthor, Bob Waterman, and I were preparing in our Manhattan hotel room for our brief appearance on the *Today* show to talk about "the book," we got into a friendly tussle. Turns out we both most loved the same thing in *Search*—and both wanted to utter the word/words on national TV. Having no dueling pistols at hand (even though we were right across the river from the place where VP Burr had killed Alexander Hamilton in a duel in 1804), we flipped a coin. Bob won . . . and I'm still frustrated almost three decades later!

The bragging rights at stake?

MBWA, or "Managing By Wandering Around," a concept we learned about from what was, in 1979 when we began our research, a much smaller, more intimate Hewlett-Packard.

Well . . .

Welcome to 2010. MBWA still works. And an absence thereof will still and forevermore herald . . . doom.

With MBWA, "What you see is what you get." I could go on for pages (I have in the past) about the benefits of staying intimately in touch with employees, colleagues, and the world around you. But I'll keep it simple here:

Get the hell out of the cube!
Unplug the terminal!
Put your iPhone/BlackBerry in the drawer!
Chat up anybody whose path you cross ... especially if they are not among your normal chatees.
Go strolling in parts of the organization (your neighborhood? your city?) where you normally don't stroll.
Slow down.
Stop.
Chat.

("Stop. Look. Listen."—My shrink's advice to me, courtesy old-time railroad-crossing wisdom.)

NB: Email/IM/Tweets ... DO NOT COUNT ... as "chat."
"Wander" = **Wander.**
One-foot-in-front-of-the-other-foot.

(I ran into a senior health care exec who'd attended a big-league leadership seminar. The prominent instructor asked the group, "Who is your #1 enemy?" Answers, no surprise, included "competitors," "execs who play politics," "clunky systems," "thoughtless regulations." "No," the instructor snapped, "it's your *desk*—getting stuck behind your desk and slowly, or not-so-slowly, losing touch." Amen!)

Extended Idea: *Wander Writ Large* ... generic "in-touch-ism."

Put "wandering" on your permanent-formal agenda! Consider: I was recently giving a speech to retailers. To prepare, I had studied my butt off. Read a ton. Hung on to every damn Google link for dear life. Phoned a dozen experts.

My data was analyzed. My speech was locked into "PPFinal" status. I was in my hotel room in Chicago, at 3:00 P.M. Needing a mental timeout, I decided to take a stroll and "wandered" into shop after shop, apparently aimlessly, for a little over two hours.

Got back to my room. Unlocked my PPFinal. And more or less started all over again. (Outcome: Speech "could have been worse"—the very highest grade I assign to one of my own speeches.) I can't tell you precisely what I gleaned on that two-hour excursion-wander. I can tell you it "changed everything." That is, I got "in the zone," I physically and emotionally inhabited the Retail-Client-of-Tomorrow's World . . . and I somehow infused the fruits of my wandering into almost every sentence of what I subsequently presented.

It may sound counterintuitive, but "aimless wandering" requires strict discipline. We all fall into ruts, even in our wanderlust. Same route. Same people. Same time of day. Same duration. Etc. Etc. Perhaps you should behave like a personal security planner—that is, ensure that you take a different, randomized route-of-wander. Somehow you've got to introduce spontaneity-aimlessness. Make a pledge to "just" "wander" . . . at least a half hour each day. You'll be amazed at what happens when you come back to the pile of work on your desk or the doc on your screen.

I am an MBWA zealot.
I SWEAR BY MBWA.
In any and all circumstances.
Join me?

(P-l-e-a-s-e.)

> **"PAPER OR PLASTIC?" NO, *PRESENCE***

Shopping for Easter dinner in a crowded Shaw's [market] in Manchester Center, Vermont, at about 1:00 P.M. Saturday. As I check out, I'm delighted to see a bagger—an effort to relieve congestion. I am even more delighted to see that my ... **bagger** ... is, per his badge, the ...

Store Manager!!(!!)

Four hearty cheers!
(And, alas, ever so rare.)

88. All Senses! Or Nonsense!

I swear I can hear him.
The successful community bank CEO.
(He attended one of my four-day Northern California seminars.)
I swear I can hear him!
But, actually, it was two decades ago.
But I swear I can hear him!

The topic was MBWA.
Or Close to the Customer.
Or something akin.

I remember his translation from his world to what I had been discussing. It went **(precisely)** like this:

"Tom, let me give you the definition of a good lending officer. On Sunday, after church, driving the family home, he takes a little detour past a distribution center he's lent money to. Doesn't go in, barely slows down, just takes a look, tidiness, external maintenance, whatever, takes it in with all his senses. That's all."

And that was it.
In touch.
All senses.
Fleeting but "real."

Have I just explained the alpha through omega of the financial meltdown?
Of course not!

But, to put it mildly, we could have used a few more "all-senses" "drive-bys" in the world of mortgage banking. (Maybe in a few of the Credit Default Swap shops, too!)

Don't mess around!
Don't mess with me!
No damned excuses!
Right now!
Plan this week's "drive-by"- "walkabout" schedule!
Event #1 should be within the next three hours!
Execute!
Review and adjust!
Repeat!
Forever!

89. Leave Your Wallet (or Pocketbook) at Home.

I recently forgot to take my wallet with me on a grocery trip. (When home, I'm the designated shopper in the family.) It was only after I got to the grocery store—22 miles from home, the closest—that I discovered my mistake. Luckily, I had a secret cash stash in my glove compartment, just for this sort of eventuality. Boy, did I ever decimate that (not-so-small) stash in my five or six stops around town!

So what?

I, undoubtedly like you, typically pay for stuff with plastic or keystrokes. There is many an "ouch" in the process. But the credit-card "ouch" is a far cry from peeling off $138 at the grocery store, $47 to fill a . . . *Subaru*, $78 at one of my "ordinary" stops at the bookstore, and more, more, more at a couple of other shops—for example, $68 for fresh fish for four. One's sense of the true cost of living goes up by an order of magnitude.

For those who are solos or who work in a small professional office or a retail operation, I'd urge you some month to repeat my adventure in some form or other; after paying the office supply bill in $20s, I'll bet a pretty penny or 10 that you'll be ushering in an era of tighter purse strings . . . ASAP.

In MediumCo or BigCo world, if, say, you've got departments reporting to you, what about invoicing the department heads in the old-fashioned paper way for services rendered—and demanding that he-she pay the bill by writing a check; not quite as powerful as watching the cash stash shrink, but perhaps a start.

The bigger point is obvious, if elusive—more than ever, companies of all sizes have to bring reality home in some high-impact way. Not that "work as a clerk for a day" silliness—which is just a rather fun game—but something more realistic.

Many (many) years ago I did a stint in the Pentagon, working on military construction—Navy bases, etc. One day the admiral in charge called a few of us into his office. We mostly worked on translating the needs of the field into Pentagonese. (I'm not sure I ever got entirely over it.) The sums were, even then, in the billions—and we abbreviated with $2.3B, $1.4B, etc. The admiral said we were all "too damned careless" with taxpayers' money (a wondrous sentiment in the Big Five-sided Building), and that, starting immediately, we'd be required to put in all the zeros; $2.3B would now be $2,300,000,000, and so forth. I can't promise you that this little drill in the end benefited the taxpayer; but I can tell you that it did, as the admiral intended, make us think twice. A trivial story—or not. You be the judge.

Pay for your groceries with cash next time.
Your car repair, too.
The office supply bill? Ditto.

By hook or by crook . . . drag realism in the office door.

90. Get Down from Your Pedestal—and Beware the Sound of Laughter!

In his autobiography, General Norman Schwarzkopf reveals, hardly central to his story but perhaps worth my brief recounting, that he simply cannot tell a joke effectively. Forgets stuff. Timing off. Screws up the punch line. Etc. But then a funny thing happened when he got promoted to general. The moment he pinned a . . . **star** . . . on his collar he apparently became hilarious—associates started laughing uproariously at his jokes, botched or not.

The message is obvious, and it's one for all who manage, not just general officers: *Beware underlings who laugh at your jokes.* Fact is, and an important one: Once you become a boss you will *never* hear the unadulterated truth again! **(Keyword: *Never.*)** And that's almost as true for a 20-year-old shift boss in a Dunkin' Donuts in Littlesville as for a senior middle manager or business owner or General S.

The bald truth is that if you are a manager, you are a power figure. Period. Others' success at work *is* tied to your whims and fancies—and so those others will naturally, even if reluctantly, want to please you and won't exactly be itching to disagree with you or find your jokes unfunny. (I'm not suggesting they lie—just that they sometimes aren't likely to tell the whole truth and nothing but the truth. Like reporting a "minor" screw-up with a customer.)

But the "remedies" are clear and more or less foolproof, though you must be disciplined in applying them. First, by a country mile, "being there." Former GM plant manager Pat Carrigan, the first woman to run a GM plant, caused a local revolution by walking the shop floor daily. (The prior plant manager, I was told on camera for a

PBS show, never—**as in not once in a half-dozen years**—went out to where the action was.)

A second strategy is making end runs around your own hierarchy. While president of PepsiCo, the late Andy Pearson would visit an operation such as Frito-Lay, and, after a cursory nod to the CEO, he would head directly to the bullpen where the junior sub-brand managers lived. He'd pick one at random, sit down with her for an hour, and discuss in the greatest detail imaginable what was going on in her small neck of the woods. Not only would he be judging Frito's bench strength, but also zeroing in on unmasticated data.

A third strategy, if you're up in the hierarchy a couple of notches or more, is to have a trusted "good cop" nearby. Call this spying if you must, but you're not asking this person to ferret out problem employees for retribution. Rather, the idea is to have someone friendly on hand who can sniff around and give you direct feedback on how things smell—and how *you* smell—where the rubber meets the road. Obviously, your degree of trust in him/her must be stratospheric; and his/her diplomatic skills must be damn good as well.

So I remind all bosses, courtesy General Norm: **Beware the sound of laughter when you tell a joke! Beware the admiring comment when you wear a stunning new scarf or tie to work!**

(As always in the real world, there are a host of caveats. To cite one example, when your trip to the frontlines becomes a . . . **State Visit** . . . in which all normal operations come to a grinding halt and everyone puts on their BBGs/Best Behavior Grins, not only will nothing be gained, but quite a bit may be lost as others snicker at your attempt to "be as one with the masses." To top that off, some people are simply more standoffish than others; while you can and should "work on this," change does not come easily.)

91. Big Plan? No, Small Steps (Steps *on the Ground*).

In *The White Man's Burden: Why the West's Efforts to Aid the Rest Have Done So Much Ill and So Little Good*, nation-building expert William Easterly laments, "[T]he West spent $2.3 trillion on foreign aid over the last five decades and still had not managed to get twelve-cent medicines to children to prevent half of all malaria deaths. The West spent $2.3 trillion and still had not managed to get three dollars to each new mother to prevent five million child deaths . . . But I and many other like-minded people keep trying, not to abandon aid to the poor, but to make sure it reaches them."

Easterly is the archenemy of the Big Plan (his capital letters, not mine—for once) and the fan of practical activities of "Searchers" (his cap "S") who learn the ins and outs of the culture, politics, and local conditions "on the ground" in order to use local levers, and get those 12-cent medicines to community members. He writes [with my emphasis]:

"*In foreign aid, Planners announce good intentions but don't motivate anyone to carry them out; Searchers find things that work and build on them. Planners raise expectations but take no responsibility for meeting them; Searchers accept responsibility for their actions. Planners determine what to supply; Searchers find out what is in demand. Planners apply global blueprints; Searchers adapt to local conditions. Planners at the top lack knowledge of the bottom; Searchers find out what the reality is at the bottom. Planners never hear whether the planned recipients got what they needed; Searchers find out if the customer is satisfied. . . .*

"*A Planner thinks he already knows the answers; he thinks of poverty as a technical engineering problem that his answers will solve. A Searcher admits he doesn't know the answers in advance; he believes that poverty is* *a complicated tangle of political, social, historical, institutional, and technological factors. A <u>Searcher</u> hopes to find answers to individual problems only by trial-and-error experimentation. A <u>Planner</u> believes outsiders know enough to impose solutions. A <u>Searcher</u> believes only insiders have enough knowledge to find solutions, and that most solutions must be homegrown."*

(NB: Excuse the length of this extract, but the preceding statement is among the most brilliant I have ever read about implementation of anything, anywhere. Among other things, it explains the stratospheric overall failure rate of consultants, in terms of implemented plans, and the stratospheric share in enterprises of "staff"-centric projects that end in tears.)

Herewith, some of the "lessons" I've extracted from William Easterly:

Lesson: *Show up! Stay!* "Boots on the ground," "permanently," at the loci of implementation. (No long "home leaves" if possible—"in this with you" is the message that must be sent.)

Lesson: Invest in ceaseless study of conditions "on the ground"— social and political and historical and systemic.

Lesson: Talk to the "locals."

Lesson: *Listen* to the "locals." (And *listen*.) (With perceived *patience!*) (And *listen*.) (And *listen*.) (And *listen*.) (And *listen*.) (And *listen*.) (And *listen*.) (And then *listen* some more.)

(And *listen*.)

Lesson: *Respect* the "locals."

Lesson: *Empathize* with the "locals."

Lesson: Try to blend in, adopting local customs, showing deference where necessary—and never interrupt the "big man" in front of his folks, even, or especially, if you think he is 180 degrees off. (Save your "help" for later, in private.)

Lesson: By hook or by crook, network! E.g., seek out the local leaders' second cousins, etc., to gain indirect access to their uncle twice removed!

Lesson: All things come to she or he who Masters the Art of Indirection! (The "second cousins" route redux.)

Lesson: Have a truly crappy office, and other *un*-trappings! (Make "invisibility" and humility your mantras!)

Lesson: Remember, you do not, in fact, have the answers, despite your Ph.D., with honors, from the University of Chicago—where you were mentored not by one, but by two Nobel laureates in Economics.

Lesson: Regardless of the enormity of the problem, proceed by trial (manageable in size) and error, error, error. (Failure motto: "Do it right the first time!" Success motto: "Do it mostly right, we hope, the 37th time!" And hustle through those 37 tries!)

Lesson: The process of political-community engagement must also be approached as a trial-and-error learning process. (Again, the enemy is "do it right the first—or second—time.")

Lesson: Take full advantage of systemic "variation." Some places-communities will be way ahead of others—and can act as full or partial "demos," with you playing the role of mere cheerleader and tour guide. "Found experiments" may save years and will have the merit of local adaptation! (On the other hand, political sensibilities may deter one community from adopting another's approach—again, Mastery of Local Political Process and Mastery of the Art of Indirection are imperative.)

Lesson: You may have long "losing streaks." *Be brave!*

Lesson: Always alter the experiment to accommodate local needs—the act of even *tiny* local modification per se is critical, as every community leader, in order for him to accept "ownership" and demonstrate to his constituents that "we are in charge," must feel as if he has directly and measurably influenced the experiment.

Lesson: Growth (the experimental and expansion-emulation process) must be organic, and proceed at a measured pace—nudged, not hurried beyond a certain point.

Lesson: Speed kills! (To a point.)

Lesson: Short-circuiting political process kills!

Lesson: Premature rollout kills!

Lesson: Too much publicity kills!

Lesson: Too much money kills!

Lesson: Too much technology kills!

Lesson: The opposite of the preceding six "lessons" are also true—if you can't deal with paradox, you're in the wrong business. (One more time: Beware of dogmatists!)

Lesson: Outsiders, to be effective, must have genuine appreciation of—and *affection* for—the locals with whom and for whom they are working!

Lesson: Condescension kills most—said "locals" know unimaginably more about life than well-intentioned "do-gooders," young, or even, alas, not so young.

Lesson: Progress . . . MUST . . . MUST . . . MUST . . . be consistent with "local politics on the ground" in order to up the odds of sustainability even a smidgen.

("Local politics"—"the last 95 percent"!)
(Make that "the last 98 percent"!)
(Politics: Love it—or go home!* ** ***)
(*Hint: This applies . . . everywhere!)
(**No "politics," no progress!)
(***True ab-so-lute-ly everywhere.)

Lesson: Never forget the atmospherics, such as numerous celebrations for tiny milestones reached, showering praise on the local leader and your local cohorts, while you assiduously stand at the back of the back of the crowd—etc.

Lesson: The experiment has failed until the systems and political rewards, often small, are in place, with Beta tests completed, to up the odds of repetition.

Lesson: Most of your on-the-ground staff must consist of respected locals—the de facto or de jure chairwoman or CEO must be local; you must be virtually invisible.

Lesson: *Spend enormous "pointless" social time with the local political leaders;* in Gulf War I, Norm Schwarzkopf spent his evenings, nearly all of them, drinking tea until 2:00 A.M. or 3:00 A.M. with the Saudi crown prince to assuage Saudi concerns about having heathen troops on sacred soil!

Lesson: Keep your "start-up" plan simple and short and filled with question marks in order to allow others to have the next-to-the-last word and the last word.

Lesson: And a hundred other things!!

To summarize the summary:

Show up!
Listen!
Hear!
Respect!
Empathize!
Skip the Grand Theorems!
Dive in and Try and Try and Adjust and Try Again and Plagiarize from Extant Experiments . . . until You're Blue in the Face!
Move at an appropriate pace, urgent but not a headline-grabbing pace!
Honor the local politics as your life's blood—regardless of attendant frustration!
Get the community's women heavily involved. (See immediately below.)

(Probably not many of you are working for NGOs or other agencies delivering aid. But roughly 100 percent of us are in the full-time business of . . . GTD/Getting Things Done. Simply put, Easterly's book is perhaps the best tract I've read on the topic of implementation–getting things done. There is a ridiculously small library of books on implementation per se—which is a scandal. I am quite certain that you would benefit from *The White Man's Burden*.)

> ▶ **WOMEN ARE . . . THE BALL GAME**
>
> Another lesson, of particular importance, from *The White Man's Burden:*
>
> For projects involving children or health or education or community development or sustainable small-business growth (the overwhelming majority of projects) . . . **women** . . . are by far the most reliable and most central and most indirectly powerful local players in even the most chauvinist settings—their characteristic process of "implementation by indirection" means "life or death" to sustainable project success; moreover, the expanding concentric circles of women's traditional networking processes provide by far the best path for "scaling up"/expanding a program. (Men can by and large not comprehend what is taking place.) Among other things, this networking indirection–largely invisible process will seemingly "take forever" by most men's "just tell 'em what to do" S.O.P.—and then, from out of the blue, following an eternity of rambling-discussions-on-top-of-rambling-discussions, you will wake up one fine morning and discover that the thing is done, that everything has fallen in place "overnight," and that ownership is nearly universal—while the men's "direct"-bullying approach typically leads to conflict that becomes more and more entrenched with the passage of time. Concomitant imperative: Most of your (as an outsider) staff should be women; alas, most likely not visibly "in charge."

1. 2. 3. 4. 5. 6. 7. 8. 9. 10. 11. 12. 13. 14.
15. 16. 17. 18. 19. 20. 21. 22. 23. 24. 25.
26. 27. 28. 29. 30. 31. 32. 33. 34. 35.
36. 37. 38. 39. 40. 41. 42. 43. 44. 45.
46. 47. 48. 49. 50. 51. 52. 53. 54. 55. 56.
57. 58. 59. 60. 61. 62. 63. 64. 65. 66. 67.
68. 69. 70. 71. 72. 73. 74. 75. 76. 77. 78.
79. 80. 81. 82. 83. 84. 85. 86. 87. 88.
89. 90. 91. **92. 93. 94. 95.** 96. 97. 98. 99.
100. 101. 102. 103. 104. 105. 106. 107.
108. 109. 110. 111. 112. 113. 114. 115.
116. 117. 118. 119. 120. 121. 122. 123.
124. 125. 126. 127. 128. 129. 130. 131.
132. 133. 134. 135. 136. 137. 138. 139.
140. 141. 142. 143. 144. 145. 146. 147.
148. 149. 150. 151. 152. 153. 154. 155.
156. 157. 158. 159. 160. 161. 162. 163.

Talent

92. Hiring: Do You Approach It with Unabashed Fanaticism?

In *Who: The A Method for Hiring*, Geoff Smart and Randy Street say, "In short, hiring is the most important aspect of business—and yet remains woefully misunderstood."

I agree wholeheartedly with both halves of the assertion:

"Most important."
"Woefully misunderstood."

Google's Director of Leadership and Development Paul Russell adds, **"Development can help great people become even better—but if I had a dollar to spend, I'd spend . . . 70 cents . . . getting the right person in the door."**

We *are* concerned with hiring, no doubt of it. *But* . . . do we treat it . . . strategically . . . as the "most important aspect of business"— four-person auto body shop or Siemens? My constant refrain concerning such topics: Are we . . . "professional students of" . . . hiring?? As I see it (again!): Effective *hiring* = Effective *offshore motorboat racing* = A craft, a profession with a body of knowledge to be *mastered*. (If you read *Who*, you will doubtless be challenged by the meticulous hiring rituals recommended by Smart and Street; at the least, they are worthy of the closest examination.)

93. Promotion: Are You Building a "Two Per Year" Legacy?

I once talked to leadership guru Warren Bennis, to whom I dedicated this book, about promotions to relatively senior ranks. The conversation went like this:

Suppose you hold one of your organization's top jobs for five years. Suppose, and this is typically about right, that you have two key promotion decisions per year. Then it stands to reason that just *10* decisions in five years *determine* **(not "contribute to," but, in effect, "determine")** your legacy!

For example, a U.S. Air Force four-star general I got to know had a strong point of view about where his service should be going. He did not occupy the #1 slot in the USAF, but he doubtless made as much or more of a long-term difference than did the #1. In short, he carefully selected and developed a tiny handful of generals who shared his philosophy; then, before they were scheduled to rotate, he carefully slotted them into key jobs throughout the Air Force. Hence, "his boys" became the next generation of policymakers—the tactic was remarkably effective.

Once more, I'm hardly accusing you of being a slacker. I have . . . *zero* . . . doubt about the seriousness with which you attend promotion decisions. But once more I *am* asking: **Do you give the promotion decision, if you are, say,**

BigCo CEO, exactly the same attention you give a major acquisition? That's the level of importance in terms of impact—hence, it's a pretty decent yardstick of "attention deserved." Most of us, obviously, are not "CEO of BigCo," but the idea is precisely the same in *any* boss selection process.

Promotion decision?
Fanaticism rules!

94. Development: Are You Finding and Cultivating First-Rate ("Godlike") First-Line Supervisors?

Success in the marketplace is a great thing!
Top-quality products you can be proud of are great things!
Integrity and transparency are great things!

But none of the three turns out to be the principal determinant of worker satisfaction. That honor goes, hands down, to ...
whether or not the employee gets along with his or her first-line supervisor!

(NB: This is *not* a hypothesis. The research data, from the likes of Gallup's Marcus Buckingham in *First, Break All the Rules: What the World's Greatest Managers Do Differently*, are clear. The employee's satisfaction or dissatisfaction with her first-line supervisor is the Clear & Unequivocal ... **#1 factor** ... in her state of mind about her job, and hence her performance—as checkout clerk or MIT-trained research chemist.)

So?

(1) **Are you, Big Boss, a . . . f-o-r-m-a-l student of frontline supervisor behavioral excellence?* (*Yes, again, damn it, this sort of thing can be formally studied.)**

(2) **Do you spend . . . gobs and gobs (and then more and more gobs and gobs) of time . . . selecting the first-line supervisors?**

(3) **Do you have the . . . best training program in the industry (or some subset thereof) . . . for first-line supervisors?**

(4) **Do you Formally & Rigorously . . . mentor . . . first-line supervisors?**

(5) **Are you willing, pain notwithstanding, to . . . leave a first-line supervisor slot open . . . until you can fill the slot with somebody spectacular? (And are you willing to use some word like . . . "spectacular" . . . in judging applicants for the job?)**

(Is it possible that promotion decisions for first-line supervisors are more important than promotion decisions for VP slots?) **(Hint: Yes.)**

I am, once more, absolutely . . . *not* . . . suggesting that you aren't serious about first-line supervisor selection, care, and feeding.

I absolutely . . . *am* . . . suggesting, in pretty much no uncertain terms, that you probably don't take it as seriously as you might if you saw it as precisely what it is . . . a first-order . . . *strategic* . . . decision.

Strategic!

I *am* suggesting that you assess your full cadre of first-line supervisors more or less posthaste—and start down the path to . . . **Matchless Supervisory Excellence** . . . by creating the best imaginable first-line supervisory training program ASAP and assigning each frontline supervisor a senior mentor.

ASAP = Now.

(NB: First-line supervisors selection-training-development is . . . **more important in very small businesses** . . . than in larger ones.)

▶ THE "TALENT" TRIO

The last three items (#92, #93, #94) constitute HR's "Big Three"—the true "Talent Trio":

1. *Hiring* = Most important business decisions.

2. Two *promotion* decisions per year = Legacy.

3. *First-line supervisors* = Keystone to employee morale and satisfaction and productivity.

Followed in each instance by my "Big Two" queries:

1. Are you an avid *student* of the three issues/opportunities?

2. Do you spend an appropriate (that is, *"insane"*) amount of time on these three issues-opportunities-strategic watersheds?

How about, to stretch a little further:

Hiring + Two promotions/year + First-line supervisor development = De facto business strategy + Personal leadership effectiveness.

Hmmm.

95. People Who Lead People: You = Your Development Track Record.

In New Delhi in the spring of 2009, I had a senior general officer in the Indian Army in the front row of the meeting room. I don't recall the details, but evaluating senior officers for promotion came up. I ventured, boldly, that there "was . . . **ONE** . . . issue [in the promotion evaluation] that stood head and shoulders above the rest."

Namely: What this candidate's track record is—in exacting detail—in developing people. Though hardly locked in concrete, I posited that "the ONE question" might go something like this:

"In the last year [three years, say, duration of the current assignment], name the three people whose growth you've most contributed to. Please explain in some significant detail where each was at the beginning of the year, where he or she is today, and where each is heading in the next 12 and 24 and 60 months. Please explain in some detail your development strategy in each case. Please tell me your biggest development disappointment this past year—looking back, could you or would you have done anything differently? Please tell me about your greatest development triumph—and disaster—in the last 10 years. What are the 'three big things' you've learned about 'people development' along the way?"

As I see it, it's more or less *not* the boss's role, for instance, to make strategy. **It's the boss's role to develop the best strategists.** And so on. And that notion in turn is the by-product of my abiding view that . . . Job #1 . . . of the organization is to develop the people within, to live up to the assertion of RE/MAX founder Dave Liniger:

"We are a life success company."

Finally, as I see it, this in some form applies to pretty much every promotion. And it even has a bearing on evaluating a *non*manager on, say, a three-month project. That rather junior person will, for example, in several instances doubtless be responsible for accomplishing a "mere" milestone—and to do so, and do so well, she must engage her team members, and engage them in a way that they go away with some experiential learnings that contribute a bit to their growth over a three-month (nontrivial!) period; hence, she, too, will have plunged headfirst into the "people-development business."

To reiterate: **The promotion decision should be *dominated* by the candidates' detailed track record at people development— considered one person at a time.** (The candidates' assertions should be carefully checked with the people the candidates claim to have developed and with the candidates' subordinates in general.)

Reprise:

Right Now!
As in . . .
Now!
Stop what you're doing!

**Please list.
Right now!
The five people!
Whose development you have contributed to!
Directly!**

Measurably!
And Profoundly!
In the last 24 months!

Are.
You.
Happy.
With the list?
Happy with yourself?
As a "People Developer"?

If "Yes" . . .
Great!
Congrats!

If "No" . . .
What.
Precisely.
Do you plan to do about it?
Starting Monday?
No.
Starting this afternoon.

1. 2. 3. 4. 5. 6. 7. 8. 9. 10. 11. 12. 13. 14. 15. 16. 17. 18. 19. 20. 21. 22. 23. 24. 25. 26. 27. 28. 29. 30. 31. 32. 33. 34. 35. 36. 37. 38. 39. 40. 41. 42. 43. 44. 45. 46. 47. 48. 49. 50. 51. 52. 53. 54. 55. 56. 57. 58. 59. 60. 61. 62. 63. 64. 65. 66. 67. 68. 69. 70. 71. 72. 73. 74. 75. 76. 77. 78. 79. 80. 81. 82. 83. 84. 85. 86. 87. 88. 89. 90. 91. 92. 93. 94. 95. **96. 97. 98. 99.** 100. 101. 102. 103. 104. 105. 106. 107. 108. 109. 110. 111. 112. 113. 114. 115. 116. 117. 118. 119. 120. 121. 122. 123. 124. 125. 126. 127. 128. 129. 130. 131. 132. 133. 134. 135. 136. 137. 138. 139. 140. 141. 142. 143. 144. 145. 146. 147. 148. 149. 150. 151. 152. 153. 154. 155. 156. 157. 158. 159. 160. 161. 162. 163.

People

96. It's All (ALL!) About . . . the Quality of the Workforce.

I really hate the following phrase: "the only thing you need to know." Hence, I want to talk to you about . . . *the only thing you need to know.*

The formulation that follows came from a speech I gave in Shanghai in the spring of 2009. I was part of a program that included renowned consultants, economists, etc. I began by saying, "In the next few hours you will hear many prescriptions for dealing with today's shaky times—and preparing for China's future. Many of those prescriptions will involve the role of the government in manipulating economic levers, the sorts of help that big firms and SMEs will need, etc. I will doubtless find many, probably most, of the suggestions on the money—figuratively and literally."

I meant every word of it.

But then I added that *my* role was to simplify—to boldly, and perhaps foolhardily, assert that, regardless of economic levers pulled, there was in fact only . . . **One Thing That Really Mattered** . . . in the long run to the health of the enterprise—and, indeed, the economy as a whole.

Namely:

The quality and character of the workforce. (And, concomitantly, the unstinting "24/7" devotion of enterprise leaders to developing each and every member of that workforce.)

I added that "there is only one 'winning formula.' "

People who are 100 percent, everybody, no exceptions, receptionist to EVP R&D:

Committed!

Engaged!

Growing!

Learning!

Fearless (unfailingly encouraged to try new things)!

Respected!

Trusted!

Appreciated!

Independent-minded!

Team-focused!

Focused themselves, even when fresh caught, on supporting and enabling the growth of others!* (*Huge point! Supporting and enabling others' journey to Growth and Excellence is a Day #1 part of the job of everyone. *Period.*)

Passionate about their mates and their customers!

Informed!

Open (fanatic about sharing)!

Caring!

Committed to **Excellence** in everything they do!

And that, in turn, I added, demands **100 percent** . . . **"servant leaders"** (to shamelessly steal from Robert Greenleaf) . . . who are **100 percent** devoted . . . **as**

Priority #1 & Job #1 . . . to developing people, in good times or bad—100 percent of people—who are:

Committed!

Engaged!

Growing!

Learning!

Fearless (unfailingly encouraged to try new things)!

Respected!

Trusted!

Appreciated!

Independent-minded!

Team-focused!

Focused themselves, even when fresh caught, on supporting and enabling the growth of others!

Passionate about their work, their mates, and their customers!

Informed!

Open (fanatic about sharing)!

Caring!

Committed to **Excellence** in everything they do!

I explained that, in my opinion:

This applies throughout the world—in America and Brazil and Lithuania and Estonia and Korea. And in China, as it pursues a future obviously more and more dependent on incorporating intellectual capital and creativity into its enterprise portfolio (already China bridles at being assigned a role as "the world's workshop").

This applies to 100 percent of people in the workforce. As with a football team or symphony orchestra . . . **there are no "bit players."**

This applies in *every* industry and for *every* price-point strategy therein. In Brazil, Magazine Luiza, the country's Walmart, is invariably at or near the top of the "Best Companies to Work For" list, just as Wegmans, the regional grocer, and the Container Store are at the head of the pack, peers of Google and Amgen, on the American "Best" list.

This applies to companies of *all* sizes—from microscopic to humongous.

This applies in good times—and especially in bad times. Engaged workers and an unwavering Commitment to EXCELLENCE from those workers will not make problems in the market evaporate, but such people, nonetheless, represent the best chance of weathering the storm and coming out stronger on the back end.

Strategy is important.
Systems are important.
Financing is important.

But this is . . . The Only Thing You Need to Know.
Totally Committed People Surging Toward Unimaginable Personal Enterprise Growth Opportunities Win!
I'd bet my life on it.
(I guess I have.)

> NO PIE IN MY SKY!

So I made a list of desirable workforce attributes.
So what?

Isn't the whole idea "pie in the sky"—idealism run amok?

Perhaps it is.
And, yes, it's an imposing list of desirable traits.

But...

What's the alternative to aiming in this direction?

Economic levers effectively manipulated are important.
(Witness the last two years.)
Capital expenditures are important.
(No doubt of it.)

But it is the "human capital" that matters in the end.
And the human capital development...per se...which must be our abiding preoccupation.

Our obsession.

And often it is not our preoccupation or obsession.

We spend our time on developing clever strategies.
We spend our time manipulating the numbers.

And the human-capital basics get short shrift.

Consider:

As the recession heated up in the United States, one of our major consumer-electronics retailers closed its hundreds and hundreds of doors. That would be Circuit City. Meanwhile, its principal competitor soared. That would be Best Buy.

When the recession loomed, Circuit City had raced to cut costs. It got rid of most of its best salespeople—they had the highest commissions, and hence added immeasurably to the cost side of the short-term business equation.

Best Buy, years ago, had acquired a little company called "The Geek Squad." These were the consumer-electronics SWAT teams that helped customers sort out problems setting up or maintaining their purchases. The service represented by the charged-up Geek Squad eventually became Best Buy's signature of great distinction—Mark of Excellence per me.

Bottom line:

Circuit City got rid of its best folks when times got tough.
Best Buy in the same tough circumstances reemphasized its commitment to personalized service provided by an energetic, highly nurtured workforce.

I believe you can multiply this story by a thousand or a million and apply it pretty much directly to a national economy.

Circuit City vs. Best Buy?
Hardly "pie in the sky"!

97. Up with People! Up Your People Budget!

There's a convenience store near me. Its owners undertook what I'd guess was a $500,000 renovation.

Bravo!
Except . . .
Whoops . . .

The staff attitude, previously crappy, is as crappy as ever. And it's all the more obviously crappy in what's now a great-looking space. Frankly, I feel the owners pretty much pissed away the $500,000! (Okay, drop the "pretty much.")

I'll trade a paint job for a terrific attitude any day!

It calls to mind a Very Big Issue, which holds for the three-person, walkup accountancy—and for the U.S. military. And for everything in between. It's soooooooo easy—it's soooooooooo visible—to get caught up with the capital budget/the capital expenditure:

It's "permanent"!
You can take pictures of the result!
It doesn't take sick days!

The people budget, on the other hand, is . . .

All about intangibles.
"Soft stuff."
No photo ops to speak of.

So here's what I *insist* that you do: When you've absolutely, positively, unequivocally locked down your budget for the next year, I ask/beg/*command* you to pick the lock.

Please, please, please: Cut the projected capital expenditures by 15 percent.

And: Redirect those savings to the people budget (recruiting, training, perks, pay, extra staffing, whatever) . . . penny for penny or million for million!

(If I can't convince you to follow my instructions, perhaps I can at least talk you into running a simulation. Imagine—in detail—what a 15 percent transfer of funds from capital expenditures to human resources *might* look like. Run the simulation with execs, supervisors, junior staff. Discuss the results.)

**Please!
Please!
Please!**

> **COST-CUTTING? "CONTAIN" IT**

News item, buried (almost) in a pile of bad economic news, especially for retailers:

The Container Store—best place to work in America a couple of years ago, per *Fortune*—doubles **(d-o-u-b-l-e-s)** its (already very significant) frontline employee training budget.

Logic?
Not exactly rocket science:

A lot of people still shop during recessions.
It's essential that their "Container Store experience" be better than ever to please the cost-conscious remnant.
Hence: shower attention, as never before, on the frontline stalwarts who serve that ever-so-precious customer.

(Duh.)

98. Cherish the Last Two-Percenters.

After a brutal, two-hour brushcutting-landscaping session in 90-degree heat (summer of 2008), I was "dog tired" in a way that defines the term. I was done-finito-out of gas. I had truly pushed my ancient body to the limit and beyond.

But I'd gotten the day's task I'd set done!

Or had I?

As I packed up my tools, I took a final look at the output of the completed bit. Fine and almost dandy, but . . . it was still just a tiny bit ragged here and there. Problem was, I didn't have an ounce, or a gram, of energy left. "F%^* it, I'll get to it later," I said to myself, and twisted the ignition key of my Kubota four-wheel RTV.

I sat there a minute, dripping with sweat. And then I turned off the engine. With every muscle screaming in agony (I do not exaggerate—or so it felt), I got out of the Kubota, gathered a couple of tools, and spent the next 20 minutes giving the job its final touch—and then some, and then some.

While the vignette is unmistakably self-serving, it is also one of those "reminders of the obvious" worth reminding *you* of. Namely, one cannot overestimate the value of . . . **"the last two-percenter."** That person who, at 2:00 A.M., takes one final look at the presentation to the Board tomorrow and discovers that two key numbers are transposed on the footnote on Slide 47—and then looks "one **[more]** last time" when she returns at 5:45 A.M. The carpenter who, though technically "finished," adds one final touch that alters the character of the cabinet he's spent two weeks building, and then hauls the piece back to his shop for a significant (to him) re-re-revision. Etc.

Sometimes we call the last two-percenter a "pain in the ass." True, but no one **(literally no one!)** is of greater importance to the success of what we do. Funny thing, I actually felt *less* tired and *less* achy after my "last two percent" drill than when I started it.

Reward the "pain in the ass" "last two-percenter" as if she were the Ultimate Gift from the gods!

She is!

99. The Excitement Axiom— and the People Corollary.

Axiom: *Only Excited People can excite customers over the long haul— i.e., again & again.*

Corollary: *To cause our colleagues to be Excited we must put—and keep—the maintenance of their well-being and their opportunity structure at the Top of our agenda.*

Which must necessarily mean that . . .

(1) the employee who serves the paying customer is for the leader, in fact, her primary customer;

(2) hence, the paying customer actually comes second.

(Which is what Southwest founder Herb Kelleher, RE/MAX founder Dave Liniger, and former Rosenbluth International boss Hal Rosenbluth, among others, would say. I have learned at their feet and cribbed directly from all three of them—thank you, gentlemen.)

Further corollary and pledge of enterprise allegiance:

I hereby promise to . . .
First and Foremost
Cherish and Excite the People
Who in turn Have the Opportunity to
Cherish and Excite the Customer
And Induce the Customer to Recommend Us to Others
Which is the Premier Path to Growth and Profitability.
Forever and Ever,
Amen.

1. 2. 3. 4. 5. 6. 7. 8. 9. 10. 11. 12. 13. 14. 15. 16. 17. 18. 19. 20. 21. 22. 23. 24. 25. 26. 27. 28. 29. 30. 31. 32. 33. 34. 35. 36. 37. 38. 39. 40. 41. 42. 43. 44. 45. 46. 47. 48. 49. 50. 51. 52. 53. 54. 55. 56. 57. 58. 59. 60. 61. 62. 63. 64. 65. 66. 67. 68. 69. 70. 71. 72. 73. 74. 75. 76. 77. 78. 79. 80. 81. 82. 83. 84. 85. 86. 87. 88. 89. 90. 91. 92. 93. 94. 95. 96. 97. 98. 99. **100. 101. 102. 103.** 104. 105. 106. 107. 108. 109. 110. 111. 112. 113. 114. 115. 116. 117. 118. 119. 120. 121. 122. 123. 124. 125. 126. 127. 128. 129. 130. 131. 132. 133. 134. 135. 136. 137. 138. 139. 140. 141. 142. 143. 144. 145. 146. 147. 148. 149. 150. 151. 152. 153. 154. 155. 156. 157. 158. 159. 160. 161. 162. 163.

Gender

100. Pronoun Power!—
Or: The Customer Is "She."

"Forget China, India and the Internet: Economic Growth Is Driven by Women."
—Headline, the *Economist*

"One thing is certain: Women's rise to power, which is linked to the increase in wealth per capita, is happening in all domains and at all levels of society. Women are no longer content to provide efficient labor or to be consumers . . . With rising budgets and more autonomy to spend, this is just the beginning. The phenomenon will only grow as girls prove to be more successful than boys in the school system. For a number of observers, we have already entered the age of 'womenomics,' the economy as thought out and practiced by a woman."
—Aude Zieseniss de Thuin, founder of the Women's Forum
    for the Economy and Society, rated one of the top five global
    forums by the *Financial Times*

Hey, *g-u-y-s*:

If women are your/our primary customers **(they usually are, commercial as well as consumer goods in the United States),** knock off the likes of unending football analogies. If women are your/our primary customers, always **(always!)** refer to the generic customer as . . . **"she."**

There's obviously lots and lots and lots more to this issue— it's been an obsession of mine since 1996. But **language matters.**

"She."
Starting.
Now.

Drop the football (et al.) lingo.
Starting.
Now.

▶ PURSE-POWER, MADE IN JAPAN

The fast-expanding women's market is not just a U.S., or even "Western," phenomenon. To wit:

"Goldman Sachs in Tokyo has devised a basket of 115 Japanese companies that should benefit from women's rising purchasing power and changing lives as more of them go out to work. It includes industries such as financial services as well as online retailing, beauty, clothing and prepared foods. Over the past decade the value of shares in Goldman's basket has risen by 96%, against the Tokyo stockmarket's rise of 13%." (Source: *The Economist*)

101. Women Lead! (Can Men Learn to Be Good Sports About It?)

I was writing about something or other, and . . . **"naturally"** . . . found myself referring to the comeback antics, almost unique in the history of the game, of San Francisco 49ers (NFL) quarterback Joe Montana. (I lived in or near SF during the entire Reign of Montana—and in fact my house was close to his.)

So, once again . . . ho-hum . . . **boy-uses-football-example.** It *was* a good example. (Damn it.) And a lot of women *do* watch the NFL, presumably tolerating three-hours-a-Sunday of legal brutality. But it was also a typical example—and from me, Mr. Feminist Guru—of SMP/standard male prose.

A main message of *The Little BIG Things* deals with the-"soft"-stuff-that-is-really-the-"hard"-stuff that underpins organization and individual effectiveness. Fact is, a lot of "this stuff" (e.g., primacy of relationship development) comes pretty naturally to most women—and is Big News and a struggle to most males. Hence, I wonder sometimes, mostly as I toss and turn in bed, if this book and its ilk have much or any relevance to women. (No small thing since women now constitute over 50 percent of the managerial population in the United States—i.e., "my" audience.) Or do some-many-most-damn-near-all women readers laugh themselves silly as, one more time, I treat the obvious as novel? (E.g., "Listening is a . . . Very Good Thing.")

Beats me.

A close examination of this topic, though perhaps "all important," is mostly beyond the scope of this book. But I'll at least offer up one fascinating, and, I think, compelling, example perhaps worth chewing on, for the boys at least, from "Gender Experiments Surprise Even the Experts," a boxed feature title in *Leadership and the Sexes: Using*

Gender Science to Create Success in Business, by Michael Gurion and Barbara Annis (my italics):

"In the 1990s, the Canadian Broadcasting Corporation/CBC created a short film that recorded an experiment in leadership styles between women and men. CBC didn't tell the participants the objective of the work they would do that day; the director simply divided the male and female leaders into two teams, and gave those team leaders the same directions: build an adventure camp. The teams were set up in a somewhat militaristic style at first, including team members wearing uniforms, but also with the caveat in place that the teams could alter their style and method as they wished as long as they met the outcome in time.

"Leader one immediately created a rank-and-file hierarchy and gave orders, even going so far as to assert authority by challenging members on whether they had polished their shoes.

"Leader two did not have the 'troops' line up and be inspected, but instead met with the other team members in a circle, asking 'How are we doing? Are we ready?' 'Anything else we should do?' 'Do you think they'll test us on whether we've polished our shoes?' Instead of giving orders, leader two was touching team members on the arm to reassure them.

"As part of the program, CBC arranged for corporate commentators to watch the teams prepare. Initially the commentators (mostly men) were not impressed by the leadership style of leader two; the second team wasn't 'under control,' members weren't lined up, and they 'lacked order' (or so it seemed). The commentators predicted that team two would not successfully complete the task. Yet, when the project was completed, team two had built an impressive adventure camp as good as team one's, with some aspects that were judged as better.

"When debriefing their observations, the commentators noticed that when team one was building the structures for the camp, there had been discord regarding who was in charge and who had completed which job and who hadn't. Team one exhibited a lack of communication during the process of completion that created problems (for example, 'Wasn't someone else supposed to do this?').

"Team two, on the other hand, took longer to do certain things, but because of its emphasis on communication and collaboration during the enactment of the task (such as 'Let's try this' and 'What do you think about that?'), the team met the goal of building the adventure camp in its own positive way, and on time."

Interesting, eh?

(I wonder how the guys would have done if Joe Montana had been their team leader?)

> ## ▶ BOARD SILLY

Data points (all pointing in the *wrong* direction):

- 16% of S&P 500 board members are women

- 9% of S&P 500—**45** companies—have **zero** women on their board

- "Catalyst ... just completed a study showing that companies with at least three women directors performed significantly better than average in terms of return on equity [16.7% better] and return on sales [16.8% better] and return on invested capital [10% better]." (Source: *Fortune*/2007)

102. Men, "Get the Facts": Women Are Different.

I love the writer Anita Shreve. (Most women are surprised by this fact—my wife calls her books classic "chick lit.") I just finished, as I write, her superb *The Weight of Water*. Few writers—and virtually no male writers, as I see it—deal so lucidly or movingly or in such depth, with life's painful tangles of relationships. Simple fact: Women by and large instinctively appreciate complex, inchoate sets of human relationships. Men are more or less clueless. (Research, including recent neurobiological research, increasingly supports this dichotomy.)

Translating this into the emotion-driven, *all*-important-these-days world of design, I have by and large concluded, after one and a half decades of study and writing and contemplation:

Men cannot effectively design products–services–experiences for women.
Men cannot effectively sell or market to women.
Men who disagree with this are delusional.

Men (TEND TO) approach & deal with the world in a fundamentally Linear way. Few twists. Few turns. Little reflection. (Get the facts. Act. Move on. Let the chips fall where they may.)

Women (TEND TO) see bends and twists and reversals in every path that involves the interplay of humans. Women appreciate & live for those bends and switchbacks; such convolutions are the essence of the human experience on earth—men are appalled by, or at least dismissive of, the very same things, assessing them as "soft." Reading Anita Shreve all too clearly revived my awareness that my professional approach to pretty much everything (the words I use, the stories I tell, my pace, my mannerisms) are . . . PURE 100 PERCENT MALE.

I can't change that, hard as I may try. But I can do . . . *something*. And so can you.

> ### ▶ PROMISES TO KEEP

Attention, men and boys: If you are in any way involved in developing or marketing products that some women, somewhere, might buy . . . then . . . **please** . . . take the following pledge:

I pledge . . . that I will never engage in any sort of discussion of products-services-experiences that include women as customers-clients, unless one-third or more of those present and in positions of authority are women.

I pledge . . . that I will work tirelessly to ensure that women's views are heard first & last and are clearly incorporated in a commanding way in any and all action plans involving the development and marketing of our products and services.

I pledge . . . that I will not sign off on an initiative aimed primarily at women unless women are almost unanimously in agreement.

I further pledge . . . that I will become a "pioneer" in getting women-centric views clearly into the mainstream—and will work tirelessly to ensure that women's representation in any and all leadership positions is at least consistent with the shape of the markets we serve or wish to serve.

Any fellows ready to become fellow pledgees?

(I'm not asking you to follow this slavishly—obviously there's no reason to think you would. And I know I've become a radical on this topic—not as a matter of social justice, but instead for reasons economic; namely, the enormity of the opportunity and the fact that so few "get it" "strategically" and thus "leave so much on the table." On the other hand, I think it'd be hard to argue with, on logical grounds, a more or less "pledge" that's more or less like what you see here. Your call, obviously—why not discuss it with colleagues?)

103. Dressed for Success? Or: What the History of the Women's Suffrage Movement Taught Me About Hanging In and Hanging In.

In the end it was, to be precise, Harry Burn's mother who made all the difference. A suffragette, she wrote to her son, age 24 and Tennessee's youngest legislator, saying, "Don't forget to be a good boy and help Mrs. Catt . . ." He did, tipped the scales on a 49–47 vote, and brought, effectively, to an end a struggle that in its most open form had lasted 72 years, 1 month, and 7 days. With Mrs. Burn's urging and Harry's courageous vote on August 18, 1920, some 26 million American women were franchised in one fell swoop.

Fact is, I cross-dressed for the first time on March 31, 2007. I went to a local (Dorset, Vermont) costume party and tried valiantly to represent Elizabeth Cady Stanton, rightfully called the Mother of the American Women's Rights/Women's Suffrage Movement.

But that gets ahead of the game . . .

The idea animating the party was that you had to dress as someone you admire—*and* be prepared to respond to questions as the admired personage would have responded. I thought it would be great fun, and therefore took it seriously. Franklin? Churchill? Lord Nelson? John Paul Jones? John Cleese/Monty Python? No problem, I had them all pegged. And a satisfactory costume would hardly be a challenge (e.g., Churchill, cigar and brandy; Nelson or Jones, folding telescope or bits of my mildewed 40-year-old Navy uniform; and I can do Cleese almost as well as Cleese does Cleese, at least in my own mind).

That was five weeks before the party. And now, late in the afternoon on March 31, 2007, following Susan's "sartorial" guidance and that of a close friend, Lola Van Wagenen, an eminent women's historian, I was encased in a white wig and long black dress, courtesy of a Boston costume shop, and, though tripping over my hems again and again ["Welcome to our world"—Lola], ready to go—and, courtesy a dozen mesmerizing books hastily ingested on a dozen plane trips, ready to respond to questions and declaim, among other things, on Mrs. Burn, her young son Harry, Carrie Chapman Catt, and, of course, the angry, tenacious firebrand, Elizabeth Cady Stanton.

I was indeed shamefaced—shamed, after almost fifteen years of loudly and doggedly championing change to women's still diminished role in business and government, that I was almost totally ignorant of the astounding history of the American women's rights movement. And worse yet, of the gruesome details of women's status in our society only 100 years ago—that makes the use of the loaded word *"slave"* frighteningly appropriate. It was no coincidence that the American women's movement, effectively launched in Seneca Falls, New York, on July 13, 1848, grew in tandem with the abolitionist movement in America.

But those five weeks were an absolute ball! There is simply nothing but nothing that I enjoy more than sinking my teeth and heart and soul into a new historical topic like this one. (It is still not taught in schools—inquiring in my seminars, I was nothing short of flabbergasted to discover that most women don't learn of Elizabeth Cady Stanton.) I did indeed devour a dozen books from the original, and always controversial, works of Mrs. Stanton to junior high school books on the life of Susan B. Anthony. In particular I learned from:

In Her Own Right: The Life of Elizabeth Cady Stanton, by Elisabeth Griffin
Ladies of Seneca Falls, by Miriam Gurko
Century of Struggle: The Women's Rights Movement in the United States, by Eleanor Flexner and Ellen Fitzpatrick

- I learned of the fateful luncheon meeting in Seneca Falls on July 13, 1848, that was hosted by Mrs. Stanton and attended by five "ladies," including Lucretia Mott, one of the subsequent superstars of the movement; and I learned of the hastily called convention that followed only six days later, the first of its kind— and the brutally negative and demeaning reaction to the conclave.

- I read with astonishment about the Total (as in Cap "T" Total!) absence of rights of American women and, almost as important, the contempt with which their so-called frail and vacuous and largely useless selves were held by males one and virtually all, from the ignorant to the most learned. And I learned—concluded— that, as I said before, women were de facto, and de jure, the equivalent of slaves, denied fundamental and trivial rights alike and even a modicum of respect.

- As an orator myself, I learned of the critical role of powerful women orators in the women's rights movement, especially the Grimke sisters, the first American women to speak in public to an audience with men—and the contemptible response thereto.

- I learned of the stream of small steps forward (some minor property rights established by New York State—subsequently reversed); and the first grant of the right to vote, in the Territory of Wyoming in 1870 by a "legislative" vote of 6 in favor, 2 against, and 1 abstaining (on July 23, 1890, Wyoming became the first *state* to grant the franchise to women—bravo).

- I learned of the unabated viciousness and bitterness and "dirty tricks" tactics unleashed by male legislators and media barons and "men on the street" of all classes that attended the 72-year struggle, from that five-person luncheon/cabal at Seneca Falls in July 1848 to Nashville and the ratification of the Nineteenth Amendment to the Constitution of the United States of America on August 26, 1920.

- I learned of the role of "demented" (my word) optimism and matchless relentlessness that marked the movement . . .

909 political campaigns (mostly failures) between 1868 and 1920, according to Carrie Chapman Catt (campaigns at state party conventions to include woman suffrage planks—277; campaigns in state legislatures to get suffrage amendments before voters—480; campaigns before 19 successive Congresses of the United States; etc.).

• And I learned that I was hardly alone in my own ignorance of the history of the American women's rights movement, and hence my de facto diminishment (ignorance is *never* an excuse) of the role and lot of women in our so-called egalitarian democracy. Typical of our "modern" approach to women-in-American-history was the "towering" *Oxford History of the American People*, by the "towering" historian Samuel Eliot Morison; he honors the Nineteenth Amendment with two (count 'em!) sentences in a section of his book with the exalted title "Bootlegging and Other Sports." There is a monument to Morison on Commonwealth Avenue in Boston that I routinely pass as I power walk; I now purposely snort derisively and turn my head from his bronzed gaze upon passing this contemptible male chauvinist pig (ironically there is a monument to women's rights pioneers about two blocks farther along the Commonwealth Avenue mall—I indeed accordingly genuflect).

• "The right of citizens of the United States to vote shall not be denied or abridged by the United States or by any state on account of sex." (Incidentally, it was not until 1956, a scant half century ago, that the number of women voting equaled the number of men.)

I dwell on this story because it describes a personal journey (mine) away from ignorance, a journey that was, well, a blast—and, I believe, important. (I now speak noisily for far greater attention to the history of the women's rights movement—still woefully skimpy, a condition not corrected to this day.) I also dwell on this story because innovation, including social innovation, is the "business" theme nearest and dearest to my professional heart—and the most important business issue of this and, frankly, every era.

It is my long-standing argument that all innovation is irrational, nonlinear, and anything but the product of plans and focus groups; it is instead about anger to the point of rage that eventually boils over (from suffrage to the personal computer); "a little band of brothers" (whoops, the Five Great Sisters of Seneca Falls and a slew of successors); willingness to suffer vicious smear attacks and unspeakable opprobrium of both a professional and personal nature, passion (!!!!!!!); relentlessness(!!!!!!!—**72 years, 1 month, and 7 days**—from lunch at Seneca Falls to ratification of the Nineteenth Amendment by Tennessee, the 36th state to do so; and those 909 political campaigns); tolerance for setback upon setback upon setback; and strokes of luck such as the willfulness of Henry Burn's blessed mother.

All the above made the sacrifice of wearing a wig and a long dress for five hours, in honor of Elizabeth Cady Stanton, seem like small beer! (Hmmm, should I have gone as Henry Burn's mother?)

My hero, Ms. Stanton, per Elisabeth Griffin, *In Her Own Right: The Life of Elizabeth Cady Stanton:*

"She was defeated again and again and again, but she continued the struggle with passionate impatience."

"She had survived her husband, outlived most of her enemies, and exhausted her allies. Her mind remained alert, her mood optimistic, and her manner combative." [Elizabeth Cady Stanton's 80th birthday celebration, attended by 6,000 people]

Thank you, Elizabeth Cady Stanton.

❯ CHAMPIONSHIP RECORD

Lessons?

I've got just one:

A record of 1 win and 908 de facto losses (a "batting average" of .001, in 909 political campaigns) **is just fine & dandy— and more than good enough for the Hall of Fame—if the cause is worth the effort and pain and personal opprobrium!**

1. 2. 3. 4. 5. 6. 7. 8. 9. 10. 11. 12. 13. 14.
15. 16. 17. 18. 19. 20. 21. 22. 23. 24. 25.
26. 27. 28. 29. 30. 31. 32. 33. 34. 35.
36. 37. 38. 39. 40. 41. 42. 43. 44. 45.
46. 47. 48. 49. 50. 51. 52. 53. 54. 55. 56.
57. 58. 59. 60. 61. 62. 63. 64. 65. 66. 67.
68. 69. 70. 71. 72. 73. 74. 75. 76. 77. 78.
79. 80. 81. 82. 83. 84. 85. 86. 87. 88.
89. 90. 91. 92. 93. 94. 95. 96. 97. 98. 99.
100. 101. 102. 103. **104. 105. 106. 107.**
108. 109. 110. 111. 112. 113. 114. 115.
116. 117. 118. 119. 120. 121. 122. 123.
124. 125. 126. 127. 128. 129. 130. 131.
132. 133. 134. 135. 136. 137. 138. 139.
140. 141. 142. 143. 144. 145. 146. 147.
148. 149. 150. 151. 152. 153. 154. 155.
156. 157. 158. 159. 160. 161. 162. 163.

Innovation

104. The Audacity of . . . Research!

The "Sacred R&D Axiom":

In good times and bad. There are lots of sexy innovation strategies—I've championed many of them. But there's also good old-fashioned spending on R&D. (And protecting-the-hell-out-of R&D in tough times.) $$$ may have to be reduced when the economy goes south to Antarctica. But don't "cut all the far-out projects"—retain a decent-size, if trimmed, portfolio of Truly Weird Stuff. Come hell and high water, retain your best folks—and, if humanly possible, grab some new stars from competitors who are stupid enough to let them go. (Perhaps you can offer them the chance to at least get started on some of their more or less far-out pets.) Also, in tight times, there may well be opportunity to acquire small firms that have run out of dough; this is a potential Very Big Deal.

In big firms *and* small. Aggressive R&D is not just the provenance of the big company. In fact, it is arguably more important to the two-person Professional Service Firm than the lumbering giant (**!!!**); if business is slow in that two-person mini, it might be the perfect time to get on with some study topic that you've put off; to invest four or five hours a week on interesting Webinars that might yield real pay dirt, etc.

Including big projects and small. Make sure the R&D portfolio includes many one-off, short-term projects. (Quite often, these little fellas grow to become the Biggest of the Big.)

In every department. AGGRESSIVE R&D IS AS IMPORTANT IN FINANCE and PURCHASING and HR and LOGISTICS as in IT or NEW PRODUCT DEVELOPMENT!!! (THERE IS NO WAY TO OVEREMPHASIZE THE IMPORTANCE OF THIS—"leading edge" should characterize HR as much as it does New Product Development.) **(!!!!!!)**

Throughout the "supply chain!" Having vendors, suppliers, customers, etc., whose R&D spending is top quartile in their industries is of the utmost importance and should be measured.

In Systems! Innovative systems are as important as innovative products. (Witness Dell's two-decade systems-driven run that changed the world.) Manage the hell out of this!

By giving everyone "play" money. Giving everyone in the organization the opportunity to get their hands on a few bucks (and a mentor) in order to play around (right term) with a new idea is essential. (3M pioneered this—Google is today's poster child.) (Again, this is even more sensible in tiny outfits than in large ones.)

By thinking "Venture Capital." Internal VC funds can run to billions of $$$ at an Intel, but the animating idea is to cast a wide, speculative net for potential investments. (This could mean, for a restaurant owner, the likes of a $10,000 scholarship for a star-in-the-making chef to attend a top-flight cooking course in France. The restaurant Chez Panisse practices something like this.)

By reaching out to universities. Excellent research universities are National Treasures. (The USA has an enormous share thereof.) Associations, major and minor, with such universities are an important part of the innovative enterprise's R&D strategy.

> **YOU & ME & R&D**

Innovation = Everybody's Game!

Dictum: ***Every*** **department shall be equally committed to formal R&D projects and formal comparative evaluation to peers on innovativeness and research effectiveness.**

Best-in-class/Best-in-planet R&D is *every* unit's charge. *No* exceptions.

So: Ms. Purchasing, please list your ongoing, formal R&D projects. If none, or if not "remarkable," or if not "Oh my God"... then get cracking.

Formal entry in Values Statement: **"Research Is Everybody's Preoccupation."**
FYI: This is a **"Top 10"** idea among the 163 in this book.

105. Adhocracy—Love It or Leave It.

In my experience, most truly innovative projects effectively invent themselves, as opposed to being the product of a formal planning process; and their growth, too, is mostly organic, and constantly punctuated by odd twists and turns and plateaus of frightening duration.

An effective culture of innovation is largely ad hoc—which drives many traditional senior managers crazy. To them, "adhocracy" is little better than "mobocracy."

But if they can't "get it," they don't belong.

Innovation = Adhocracy.
(Period.)

Hint: If your organization chart "makes perfect sense," then you probably don't have a particularly innovative enterprise. Adhocracy requires letting go of assumptions of linearity—substituting curves and spirals and Jackson Pollock–like tangles for straight lines and 90-degree turns.

(NB: I am not arguing that plans are dangerous. They are only dangerous if you take them seriously. Preparation is essential—but even more essential is the willingness to let go of a plan in a flash and head off in a revised direction.)

Action?

(1) Organize as much work as possible **(virtually all!)** in project teams. A project team structure, even at places like my old employer, McKinsey, tends to be more fluid, with boundaries more porous, work areas less constrained. Moreover, you have the opportunity to create—and then destroy—project teams of all shapes and sizes. Many more words would be required to usefully describe such a more or less self-inventing, self-destructing (!—"creative destruction") structure-nonstructure.

(2) Put "outsiders" by the bucketload on all teams—mixed, diverse, impermanent membership leads to more flexible organization format. (Axiom: Diversity = Innovation.)

(3) Create rich internal social-networking rituals and routines to encourage anyone to play in *any* game. Cisco Systems calls this

"emergent leadership," and has bet the future on it—leaders, based on energy and expertise, "emerge" from anywhere, lead for a while when it makes sense, and then the reins change hands more or less automatically.

(4) Hire and promote for demonstrated flexibility. (It *is* an observable trait.)

106. Beyond Excellence: The "Berserk Standard."

Amazon has changed the world.
EBay has changed the world.

Craigslist has changed the world—put about a zillion nails in the coffins of newspapers, among many other Richter 8.0+ things.
Craigslist has more traffic than Amazon or eBay.
(Though a private company, craigslist has a projected market capitalization numbering in the billions of dollars.)

Amazon has **20,000** employees.
EBay has **16,000** employees.
Craigslist has . . . **30** employees.

Message: There is more than one way to skin a cat—even a thoroughly modern cat.

"Pragmatic" action?

Among other things, every **(every!)** time you start a project, no matter how small, reach out to several S.W.P.—seriously weird people—for their views about what you are undertaking. Keep reaching until you find a couple of people who are so far out that they more or less speak gibberish.

It may indeed *be* gibberish, and indeed probably *is* gibberish—but perhaps once or twice in a lifetime, it'll be someone and some approach that amounts to a blueprint for doing the work of 10,000 with 10, à la craigslist vs. Amazon and eBay.

Never get seriously under way until you've surfaced a couple of ideas that score perfect 10s, or at least 8s, on the . . . Berserk Scale.

At the least, you will have had your mind stretched, the best exercise regimen of all; at most, you may have taken a baby step toward inclusion in the history books.

> ## WEATHER, WHETHER OR NOT WE WANT TO KNOW

I've got two books beside me as I write this:

The Weather Channel: The Improbable Rise of a Media Phenomenon (Frank Batten with Jeffery Cruikshank)
ESPN: The Uncensored History (Michael Freeman)

The idea of an all-weather channel and the idea of an all-sports channel were considered the fantasies of raving lunatics.

It took both sets of "lunatics" forever to prove their points. Yet both properties achieved matchless popularity (user-addicts by the millions and more millions) and market values of several billion dollars each.

I *love* books like these. It's not so much that they "inspire" me—rather, they "remind" me of the complete sensibility of paying serious attention to so-called nonsensical things!

107. Out of the Shadows: Skunkworks, Revisited.

Lockheed invented the term "Skunk Works" as an alias for Advanced Development Programs; while there are conflicting stories about the exact origins of the term, the official story places the birth of the first Skunk Works in the 1940s. It was a small unit, based in Burbank, California, that used a totally unconventional approach to developing essential military aircraft—e.g., the famous SR-71 Blackbird spy plane, a pillar of our Cold War tactical package—in record time at minimum cost with maximum innovation executed by an astonishingly small group of astonishingly motivated people. (Too good to be true? I agree except for one thing: It *was* true.)

I came across the Lockheed Skunk Works in the early 1980s—and immediately fell madly in love. I had long been convinced that "normal pathways" would rarely yield innovation at Big Companies. And I was on the lookout for byways—places that stunk to the reigning bureaucrats. And Skunk Works, or skunkworks as I prefer, filled the bill perfectly.

In the Introduction, I reported that this book was to a large degree a "return to basics." Well, the skunkworks idea is as basic as it gets for me when it comes to innovation. I had adored the skunkworks idea so much in the 1980s that I named my Palo Alto consultancy "Skunkworks Inc." My colleagues and I held, six or seven times a year, "Skunk Camps," five-day intensive innovation-strategy seminars, on the edge of the Pacific (fittingly), aimed at regenerating the "Spirit of the Skunk" in the bellies of tiring corporations. (Naturally, in retrospect, tired corporations rarely showed—our "Skunks" were largely from midsized companies, like W. L. Gore or Perdue Farms, determined not to calcify.) I even wore an elaborate "Skunk Suit" to conduct "graduation"—given to me by the American Electronics Association for my help in keeping them "non-stuffy."

All this (too much info?) is a long-winded way of saying that somehow, by hook or by crook, you have to figure out how to fool *yourself.* How to run a trick play—that catches *you* off guard. How to run end runs on *yourself.* I won't guarantee much in this world, or in this book. But I will pretty much guarantee—no, I *will* guarantee—that standard structures won't do the trick when it comes to innovation and renewal, even in moderate-sized companies, let alone in the Bumbling Beasts.

So the generic "skunkworks idea" is a "band of brothers and sisters," contrarian in nature and determined to do it their own way, who live in the netherworld, who stink-up-the-central-culture as they pursue what they believe is an earth-shattering dream. (Companies like Xerox and Apple have also used these units to great—yes, earth-shattering—advantage at various times past.)

There are various ways to build skunkworks–flavor operations. Here are a few, meant only to tease, and hardly an exhaustive set:

Concoct a Parallel Universe. Big firms win in large measure through focus, which can be invaluable, and also invariably leads to calcification of culture, staff, the works. One way to get around this is to create what I call a Parallel Universe. It's effectively a "shadow company" with its own staffing—its own culture, in fact.

For example, as business schools saw the attractiveness of the two-year residential MBA decline, many simultaneously sensed a sharp rise in demand for part-time executive education and continuing business education in general. But "standard" professors used to "standard" students and "standard" classes at "standard" hours frequently balked at proposed change. Several smart schools set up schools within schools, utilizing outside assets (other profs, semidistant facilities) to experiment with and deliver executive education. (Some of these "parallel universe" operations didn't even report to the B-school dean and hierarchy, but found a home in the university's generic continuing education operations. One "parallel universe" exec-ed operation actually attached itself to the university's English Department—which offered autonomy for the exec-ed operation and put bucks into the impoverished English Department's coffers!) In some cases, the school-within-a-school eventually reintegrated with the "parent," but only after it had acquired enough muscle to resist the regnant culture; in a few cases the shadow organization's success actually eclipsed that of the traditional organization. (Key idea: Don't waste time trying to change the regnant culture. Fat chance! Get on with gettin' on in another setting.)

One-off projects. All units of *all* sizes should mount at least one "one-off," more or less skunkworks—that is, a separated band pursuing no-fit, low-fit projects. Such a "band" may be as small as one person in a six-person department—i.e., this truly applies to *every* unit of *any* size. (It also applies equally to *small* businesses—in a four-person video company, one of the four ought to be spending 50 percent of her time on something "far-out," perhaps a "far-out" collaboration with another small outfit.)

Centers of Excellence. A more formal approach to important innovations involves setting up something like "centers of excellence." GlaxoSmithKline, for example, created seven CEDDs, Centers of Excellence for Drug Discovery. Previously, GSK used a huge functional organization to do its development work—as usual, functional warfare and hypercomplex processes slowed things down and often dumbed them down through lowest-common-denominator compromises. Now the self-sufficient CEDDs, led by powerful project managers, short-circuit some of the previous issues—early results are promising.

Centers of Excellence in Design. Design, writ large, is increasingly the chief route to product or service differentiation. Many companies are now beyond lip service, but a long way from fully incorporating the numerous aspects of design into the heart of the company culture. One effective approach, a variation on the theme immediately above, is a Center of Excellence in Design with the avowed goal of nothing less than becoming a "hotbed" of global excellence—for example, Samsung followed this path, renovated the entire company (great design *is* Samsung, circa 2010), and is giving Sony a run for its money; Samsung has in fact modeled the way for Korea's *national* aspirations for differentiation for an entire nation via integrated commitment to Design Excellence.

The general operational idea here is that, big business or small, retail or technology, HR or IT, you can't depend on "normal" mainstream innovation programs, even in arenas dedicated to innovation per se such as R&D, to deliver the (truly new-enterprise-redeeming) goods—a huge problem given the increasing life or death importance of first-rank innovation skills. You *must* create some sort of out-of-the-mainstream, parallel infrastructure. I repeat: For the five-person training department, where the Innovation Imperative is as strong as it is for the enterprise as a whole, this can consist of "as little as" a half-time, three-month "freak assignment" for one person. Above all (1) get cracking and, I repeat (2) don't wait for the mainstream to deliver the goods—the odds of their so doing are low, *very* low.

108. S.A.V. (No, It's Not a Kind of Truck.)

"If I had said 'yes' to all the projects I turned down and 'no' to all the ones I took, it would have worked out about the same."
—David Picker, movie studio exec, quoted in William Goldman's classic *Adventures in the Screen Trade* (cited by Caltech physics professor and author Leonard Mlodinow in *The Drunkard's Walk: How Randomness Rules Our Lives*)

If, as I fervently believe ... **Randomness Rules Our Lives** ... then your ... **only (logical)** ... defense is-must be taking refuge in the message of the so-called ... **law of large numbers.** That is, any success follows from tryin' enough stuff so that the odds of doin' *something* right tilt your way.

Conclusion:

Ultimate & Perhaps Only "Surefire" Winning Formula:

S.A.V.* ** ***

Screw Around Vigorously.
**Start today.*
***Please.*

> **SCREEN TRADE SECRET**

A shrewd observation, attributed to an unknown Hollywood script-writer:

"Ever notice that **'What the hell'** is always the right decision?"

NB: I admit it. I found the quote, not at a Harvard B-School exec program, but in a nearby Cambridge, Massachusetts, novelty shop. There's a message here—not least part of which is to consider the value of the $4.00 card vs. a $4,000-a-day program at the HBS? The card, however, cost a lot more than four bucks; I ordered a couple of hundred and give them away like candies at seminars.

109. What Have You Prototyped Lately?

Don't let yourself get stuck!

(What a silly statement.)

(But, then, my goal in this book is largely to remind you of "silly" things that fall by the wayside.)

Fact: There is . . . **always** . . . *something* . . . some *little thing* . . . you can start/do in the next . . . **30 minutes** . . . to take a tiny, concrete step forward toward solving a problem or creating a new opportunity.

My colleagues and I call this the . . . **"Quick Prototype Attitude."** MIT's Michael Schrage offers us what I think is a Very Big Truth: **Innovation . . . is . . . per se . . . the reaction to a prototype.** To move forward, you must have some eighth-baked thing to talk about and shoot at and tinker with . . . ASAP.

(Schrage also tells us the attitude-approach is one of . . . **Serious Play.** In fact, that is the title of an entire book of his—which is firmly embedded on my "ALL-TIME TOP 10 BIZ BOOKS" list.)

If you've got a Cool Idea, don't sit on it.

Don't research it to death.

Grab a pal, or three (no more).

Find an empty conference room.

Right now.

Start modeling-mocking up some little bit of where you've gotten so far.

Then show it to a half dozen other trusted pals.

ASAP.

Get their hasty input—not "considered" input; but "hasty" input.

Get on with round two . . .

Three.

Four.

Forty-four.

Lesson/Message:

Prototype.

Now.

Now = *Next half hour.*

❯ "SERIOUS PLAY" BEATS SERIOUS PLANNING (SERIOUSLY)

"Effective prototyping may be the most valuable core competence an innovative organization can hope to have."
—Michael Schrage

"You can't be a serious innovator unless and until you are ready, willing and able to seriously play. 'Serious play' is not an oxymoron; it is the essence of innovation."
—Michael Schrage, *Serious Play*

"We made mistakes, of course. Most of them were omissions we didn't think of when we initially wrote the software. We fixed them by doing it over and over, again and again. We do the same today. While our competitors are still sucking their thumbs trying to make the design perfect, we're already on prototype version **#5.** By the time our rivals are ready with wires and screws, we are on version **#10.** It gets back to planning versus acting: We act from day one; others plan how to plan—for months."
—Michael Bloomberg, *Bloomberg by Bloomberg*

110. Hell Hath No Fury: Celebrate "Disturbers of the Peace."

Writer–editor–historian–man of the world Harold Evans had problems with the movie *Aviator*. Not the acting or cinematography, but his insistent belief that the lead role in the saga of the airline revolution belonged not to Howard Hughes, but to Pan Am boss Juan Trippe, who among other things was the driving force behind the introduction of the B747. Evans makes a good case:

> *"What drove Trippe? A fury that the future was always being hijacked by people with smaller ideas—by his first partners who did not want to expand airmail routes; by nations that protected flag carriers with subsidies; by the elitists who regarded flight, like luxury liners, as a privilege that could be enjoyed only by the few; by the cartel operators who rigged prices. The democratization he effected was as real as Henry Ford's."*
> —Harold Evans, "Trippe the Light Fantastic," in the *Wall Street Journal*

I believe that the Mother of [Almost] All Innovation is . . . **fury.** Abiding anger at the way things are . . . coupled with an "irrational" (statistically inappropriate) determination to beat back the innumerable protectors of the status quo and find and implement a better way.

(The launch of the B747 is one chapter. The building of the Panama Canal another. But, typically, so is the rollout of a revolutionary new mentoring program in a 16-person HR department.)

There are a thousand articles and dozens of books on the "sources of innovation." And as far as I'm concerned, they are all pretty much . . . *baloney.*

Yes, as far as I'm concerned there is one and only one "source of innovation":

Fury.

Or . . . **"seriously pissed-off people"** . . . as I prefer to more bluntly put it.

An innovator's life, almost regardless of the size of the innovation (people fight the small ones about as tenaciously as the large ones), is pure hell. All guardians of the status quo are her enemies. That includes about 100 percent of her bosses, appointed stalwart custodians of "the way we do things around here." Why is fury required? Simple: In order to survive the onslaught of these Powerful Guardians of Yesterday, and come out the other end intact, she has to be really pumped up 100 percent of the time, and equipped with very thick skin indeed—that is, really truly pissed off with the way things are.

What is the operational message here?

If you're a boss aiming for big change, begin the search today for . . . the Pissed-Off People. (They're always there—and often in hiding.)

If the recession forces cuts, don't automatically, as one company disastrously did, use it as an opportunity to weed out the "misfits," so labeled by prior HR reviews. (Innovation dried up—not too strong a phrase.)

When you hire, look for clear evidence of times that a prospect has taken the heat as she pursued something important—if all references say "She's easy to get along with," well, worry about that.

Beware in general of people who agree with you 97 percent of the time, and 100 percent when the issue's important. Professional suckups have little time or energy left over to pursue innovation.

**All (ALL) innovation comes from fury.
Hire fury.
Find fury.
Give fury room to Disturb the Peace.**

(Can this go too far? *Of course.* But the problem in 9 out of 9.3 cases is not going far enough! So err on the side of collecting . . . the Furious Ones. Most companies inevitably slide downhill, sooner than one would imagine; and one big reason is the failure to keep bringing misfits aboard—or the unwillingness of misfits to accept job offers because of the perceived futility of attempting to do new things.)

111. The Innovation15: What We Know So Far . . .

Libraries are full of books about innovation—I've written a book or two myself. (E.g., *The Circle of Innovation*, 1997.) And I recently penned (keyboarded?) "The Innovation 122," available at tompeters.com; yes, count 'em, 122 ideas about innovation. There never has been and never will be a "last word," or last 100,000 words, concerning innovation. So what follows is not it either. Nonetheless, I felt a pressing need here to devote an item to summarizing my four decades of noodling on this subject, including some stuff you've seen in more fulsome form in these pages; and all of it in 804 words:

(1) **Try it. Repeat. Repeat.** He who tries the most stuff wins. I study the history of innovation. There's nary a Nobel Prize winner who hasn't explained his win more or less thus: "We ran more experiments." (And not a Nobel historian who's failed to trot out the word "relentless.") Prototype it: A particular form of trying—some model of some part of "it" that everybody quickly has an opportunity to shoot at. Innovation guru Michael Schrage says that a distinct competence in prototyping per se is Innovator's Advantage #1. (He even offers a measure, "mean time to prototype.")

(2) **Celebrate failure.** Keyword: CELEBRATE. Not "tolerate," but "celebrate"—if "most tries" are king, then "most failures" are necessarily crown prince.

(3) **Relentlessly decentralize.** It's "the law of large numbers"—to truly decentralize means more "statistically independent tries." With, say, six divisions or a portfolio of six discrete project teams with different sorts of leaders, the odds of at least One Big Win, or two, go way up!

(4) **Parallel Universe.** Frequently the resistance to change is so strenuous that one must, in effect, give up on normal channels. An answer: Create a pretty-damn-separate "new world" with new folks, new location, new attitude, etc., etc.—yes, a "parallel universe," or, my favored term, a skunkworks.

(5) **Searchers.** Fact is, most organizations, even rather small ones, are awash in innovation—if only you'd bother to search for them. Organization observers like Bob Stone and William Easterly urge us to forget reinventing the wheel—and concentrate on our homegrown wheel makers. But you've got to have a pretty good Intelligence Network to find 'em; most are in hiding. Your job: Find 'em. Celebrate 'em. Encourage others to visit 'em. Then let the customized replication games begin.

(6) **Hang Out Axiom.** *Every* "hang out" decision is a "yes" or "no" innovation decision: That is, hang out with interesting, get more interesting; hang out with ordinary, get more ordinary. Across the board: Employees. Customers. Vendors. Etc. E.g.: "Cool vendors" who push us hard beat "strategic vendors" who specialize in telling us what we want to hear in order to preserve their business. Case study extraordinaire: *"[CEO A.G.] Lafley has shifted P&G's focus on inventing all its own products to developing others' inventions at least half the time."* (It's worked—a near miracle among slugabed giants.)

(7) **"d"iversity.** I call it "lowercase 'd' diversity." That is, diversity on any damned dimension imaginable. (!!) In any and every situation. More variety = Higher odds of success-Wow!

(8) **Co-invent with outsiders.** Again, seeking new inputs and a great test bed is the idea—working side by side with pioneer customers gives them a leg up, and you, too. Their "exclusive use" for a while may be a small price to pay. The ultimate: Crowd-sourcing! My God, the Power of Everybody—proven every day!

(9) **"Strategic" listening.** This well-developed "core competence" is key to harvesting ideas from any and every source imaginable, creating great alliances, turning on the troops, etc. Is there *anything* more powerful or closer to the true heart of sustained innovativeness?

(10) **Hire and promote innovators.** The best test of innovation potential is . . . a track record of innovation. If you are assessing a 26-year-old candidate and there are no cases-of-innovation-of-some-sort-worth-bragging-about in his or her past—then don't expect much in the future. To some extent, considering this applies to every job—e.g., the goal is universal curiosity!

(11) **XFX/Cross-functional Excellence.** Ninety percent (95 percent?) of innovation requires or can immeasurably benefit from working across functional borders, so Border Bashing/X-border Love is key to innovation success. (Many, probably most, failed innovation efforts list lousy cross-functional behavior as a "Top 3" cause—and often a "Top 1.")

(12) **Complexity and Systems Destruction Officer.** Systems are imperative. Systems constrain and strangle—and grow and grow and grow. We must declare war on our own systems, even as we depend on them, to make sure that freedom continues to ring.

(13) **R&D Equality.** "Research" is not the exclusive charter of the new product or marketing folks. *Every* (!!!) department needs a well-funded, highly regarded R&D activity; the clear expectation is that every unit/function will be as well-known for its innovation record as for its execution of standard tasks. This, collectively, may be "value-added Secret #1."

(14) **Fun! Self-deprecation!** Innovating is about breaking the rules—often *our* rules. There is a certain *mischievousness* about innovative organizations—not fun and games, but pleasure in sticking a finger in convention's eye, especially one or more of our own conventions. (Remember: When it comes to innovation, Enemy #1 is ourselves and, frightening-but-true, our most cherished past successes!)

(15) **Good luck!** Entropy rules! Performance over the long haul deteriorates! Working on every-damn-thing-you-can-think-of to up the odds of renewal ups the odds of beating the Perpetual Entropy Surge!

There it is. *Bonne chance*—you'll need it!

1. 2. 3. 4. 5. 6. 7. 8. 9. 10. 11. 12. 13. 14. 15. 16. 17. 18. 19. 20. 21. 22. 23. 24. 25. 26. 27. 28. 29. 30. 31. 32. 33. 34. 35. 36. 37. 38. 39. 40. 41. 42. 43. 44. 45. 46. 47. 48. 49. 50. 51. 52. 53. 54. 55. 56. 57. 58. 59. 60. 61. 62. 63. 64. 65. 66. 67. 68. 69. 70. 71. 72. 73. 74. 75. 76. 77. 78. 79. 80. 81. 82. 83. 84. 85. 86. 87. 88. 89. 90. 91. 92. 93. 94. 95. 96. 97. 98. 99. 100. 101. 102. 103. 104. 105. 106. 107. 108. 109. 110. 111. **112. 113. 114.** 115. 116. 117. 118. 119. 120. 121. 122. 123. 124. 125. 126. 127. 128. 129. 130. 131. 132. 133. 134. 135. 136. 137. 138. 139. 140. 141. 142. 143. 144. 145. 146. 147. 148. 149. 150. 151. 152. 153. 154. 155. 156. 157. 158. 159. 160. 161. 162. 163.

Listening

112. Now Hear This! Listening Is the Ultimate "Core Competence."

Listening is ...

(And when you read "listening," please substitute "OBSESSION with listening.)

Listening is ... the ultimate mark of *Respect*.

Listening is ... the heart and soul of *Engagement*.

Listening is ... the heart and soul of *Kindness*.

Listening is ... the heart and soul of *Thoughtfulness*.

Listening is ... the basis for true *Collaboration*.

Listening is ... the basis for true *Partnership*.

Listening is ... a *Team Sport*.

Listening is ... a *Developable Individual Skill*.*

(*Though women are inherently *far* better at it than men.)

Listening is ... the basis for *Community*.

Listening is ... the bedrock of *Joint Ventures that work*.

Listening is ... the bedrock of *Joint Ventures that last*.

Listening is ... the core of *effective Cross-functional Communication*.*

(*Which is in turn Attribute #1 of organizational effectiveness.**)

(**I know, I keep repeating this—only because "Attribute #1" is no exaggeration.)

Listening is ... the engine of *superior EXECUTION*.

Listening is . . . the key to *making the Sale.*

Listening is . . . the key to *Keeping the Customer's Business.*

Listening is . . . the engine of *Network development.*

Listening is . . . the engine of *Network maintenance.*

Listening is . . . the engine of *Network expansion.*

Listening is . . . *Learning.*

Listening is . . . the *sine qua non of Renewal.*

Listening is . . . the *sine qua non of Creativity.*

Listening is . . . the *sine qua non of Innovation.*

Listening is . . . the core of *taking Diverse opinions aboard.*

Listening is . . . *Strategy.*

Listening is . . . *Source #1 of "Value-added."*

Listening is . . . *Differentiator #1.*

Listening is . . . *Profitable.**

(*The "R.O.I." from listening is higher than from any other single activity.)

Listening underpins . . . *Commitment to EXCELLENCE.*

Do you agree with the above?

By which I mean not a quick read and cursory nod of the head—but an examination of each statement and careful assessment of its literal meaning.

(I suspect you will superficially agree—but that ain't what I'm looking for here—for your sake.)

(I'm trying to take this "listening thing" to a whole other level.)

(These days I use the "listening list" above as the launching pad for my presentations.)

If you agree, after meticulous review and discussion, then shouldn't listening be . . . *a Core Value?*

If you agree as specified, shouldn't listening be . . . *perhaps* . . . *Core Value #1?**

(*"We are Effective Listeners—we treat Listening EXCELLENCE as the Centerpiece of our Commitment to Respect and Engagement and Community and Growth"—or some such.)

If you agree, shouldn't listening be . . . *a Core Competence?*

If you agree, shouldn't listening be . . . *Core Competence #1?*

If you agree, shouldn't listening be . . . *an explicit "agenda item" at every Meeting?*

If you agree, shouldn't listening be . . . *our Strategy—per se? (Listening = Strategy.)*

If you agree, shouldn't listening be . . . *the #1 skill we look for in Hiring (for every job)?*

If you agree, shouldn't listening be . . . *the #1 attribute we examine in our Evaluations?*

If you agree, shouldn't listening be . . . *the #1 skill we look for in Promotion decisions?*

If you agree, shouldn't listening be . . . *the #1 training priority at every stage of everyone's career—from Day #1 to Day LAST?*

If you agree, what are you going to do about it . . . *in the next 30 MINUTES?*

If you agree, what are you going to do about it . . . *at your NEXT meeting?*

If you agree, what are you going to do about it . . . *by the end of the DAY?*

If you agree, what are you going to do about it . . . *in the next 30 DAYS?*

If you agree, what are you going to do about it . . . *in the next 12 MONTHS?*

NB: There are a million more—literally—things to say. Such as the difference—**Profound**—between "listening" and "*hearing.*" And, thank God, there are a million words to read on the topic—for starters, see my suggestions on the next page.

I want to "keep it simple" in this particular formulation. Hence, I will leave you with just one "starter" operational suggestion: Begin serious discussions of the above . . . **Today.**

NB: Listening. Skill. Discipline.
Key word: **Practice.**
Practice.
Practice.

⟩ **LISTEN! ASK! READ!**

Here is a veritable "library" of books on listening and asking questions. Truth is, I haven't read every one from cover to cover—hence no "for certain" recommendations. But the very fact that there are so many books on this topic should lead to the realization that listening is no idle, passive thing. You must study it. And practice it. And then practice it some more.

- *Listening Leaders: The Ten Golden Rules to Listen, Lead & Succeed*—Lyman Steil and Richard Bommelje
- *The Zen of Listening*—Rebecca Shafir
- *Effective Listening Skills*—Dennis Kratz and Abby Robinson Kratz
- *Are You Really Listening?*—Paul Donoghue and Mary Siegel
- *Active Listening: Improve Your Ability to Listen and Lead*—Michael Hoppe
- *Listening: The Forgotten Skill*—Madelyn Burley-Allen
- *Leading with Questions: How Leaders Find the Right Solutions by Knowing What to Ask*—Michael Marquardt
- *Smart Questions: Learn to Ask the Right Questions for Powerful Results*—Gerald Nadler and William Chandon
- *The Art of Asking: Ask Better Questions, Get Better Answers*—Terry Fadem
- *How to Ask Great Questions*—Karen Lee-Thorp
- *Change Your Questions, Change Your Life*—Marilee Adams
- *Asking the Right Questions: A Guide to Critical Thinking*—Neil Browne and Stuart Keeley

113. Are You an "18-Second Manager"?

In *How Doctors Think*, Dr. Jerome Groopman tells us that . . . **the best source of evidence** . . . on a patient's malady is . . . **the patient.** And then he trundles out research reporting that docs interrupt their patients, on average, 18 *seconds* after the patient starts speaking.

I repeat: **Interrupt. 18 seconds.**

I cannot point to equivalent research (though it's doubtless out there), but I will bet you a beer, or a six-pack, or a case, or a Sam Adams truck full of beer that there are, per capita, as many **"18-second interrupters"** among managers as among docs.

So . . .

Stop.
Quit bloody interrupting.
This means you.
(And me!)

Agenda:

Practice.
Seek feedback.
Give self-feedback after *every* interaction.
Use meeting videos to observe yourself—count interruptions.
Work as a group on this.

Enlist your family and friends to help you at home or at parties or on a fishing trip. **(!!)**

(If you're a lad, your wife or significant other might . . . *pay you* . . . to let her help you!)

This is not a "big deal."
This is a . . . **b-i-g d-e-a-l.**

This is . . . **s-t-r-a-t-e-g-i-c.**

Practice.
Practice.
Practice.
Practice.

▷ BE A "SILENT" PARTNER

Referring to the protagonist, Paul Christopher, a CIA field officer in *Christopher's Ghosts*, author Charles McCarry writes: *"He [Christopher] had learned when he was still very young that if he kept quiet, the other person would eventually fill the silence."* McCarry also tells us at one point that Christopher's key to a debriefing is to shut up and not interrupt; Mr. Christopher claims that *"everyone has a story to tell, if only you have the patience to wait for it and not get in the way of it."*

The book is fiction.
The idea is solid-gold fact.

114. Get the Story. Give the Respect.

"It was much later that I realized Dad's secret. He gained respect by giving it. He talked and listened to the fourth-grade kid in Spring Valley who shined shoes the same way he talked and listened to a bishop or college president. He was seriously interested in who you were and what you had to say."
—From *Respect* by Harvard professor Sara Lawrence-Lightfoot

A wonderful (and powerful) message.
Everybody has something to say!

It's your job-opportunity . . . as consultant, boss, project-peer, whatever . . . to scoop it out!
"Scoop it out" as in extract it—and as in understand it and hence understand, a bit, the speaker.

During a trip to London I was driven around by a fellow who sometimes drives Richard Branson. Branson is famous for, among many other things, his, literally . . . **hundreds of notebooks** . . . in which he meticulously records what he hears from Virgin Clients and damn near anyone else he buttonholes.
My driver confirmed Sir R's habit, and said a trip with him is an exhausting, continuous conversation about the world as seen through the *driver's* eyes. **"He bloody well interviewed me, for 90 minutes, nonstop,"** this chap said with clear admiration, **"as we crawled in from Gatwick."** As we chatted, the driver (himself a Richard) allowed as how **"the whole bit made me feel as though I had something important to say."**

Message/s:

The Driver/Richard II *did* have something to say!
(Axiom: **EVERYBODY HAS A VALUABLE STORY, DESPERATE TO ESCAPE!**)
The Driver/Richard II *is* important!
(Axiom: **CONNECT!**)
Richard I/Branson doubtless learned a thing or seven, duly recorded.
(Axiom: **JUST ASK! AND KEEP ASKING!**)
Richard I/Branson made a friend-informant-confidant for life!
(Axiom: **EXTRACT A STORY, MAKE A FRIEND-DEVOTEE.**)
Richard II/Driver will pass on the story of Richard I/Branson to 100, if not 1,000 people . . . and thus willfully extend, free of charge, the brand mythology surrounding Richard I/Branson.
(Axiom: **CONNECT. JUST ASK. GET A STORY. MAKE A FRIEND. CREATE A "BUZZ GENERATOR."**)

All because *Sir* Richard was determined to . . . Connect & LISTEN & Get the Story!

So . . .

Connect!
Listen!
Get the Story!
(Remember: **Everyone** [every single one] **has a story.**)

So . . .

Practice!
Practice!
Practice!
Practice!

"It was much later that I realized Dad's secret. He gained respect by giving it. He talked and listened to the fourth-grade kid in Spring Valley who shined shoes the same way he talked and listened to a bishop or college president. He was seriously interested in who you were and what you had to say."

—From *Respect* by Harvard professor Sara Lawrence-Lightfoot

❯ DON'T NOD OFF, NOD *ON*

Once (in Helsinki, as I recall), I was being interviewed, through an interpreter. It wasn't an aggressive interview, but the interlocutor was trying to dig beneath the surface. And dig she did—after the fact, I was taken aback when I realized how forthcoming I'd been.

Her "weapon"? She was pleasant enough, but not overwhelmingly so. That wasn't it. The weapon was (I finally realized) . . . *nodding*. Constantly. And . . . taking copious notes. The nodding was obvious and constant, not half-hidden by any means. And the note-taking was also pronounced.

And I was a total sucker for it—doubly amazing because, as I said, there was a translator in between the two of us; and triply amazing because it was, obviously, not exactly my first, or one of my first 5,000, interviews; besides, I'm exceptionally well trained in rat psychology, B. F. Skinner–style.

What was going on? *By nodding and taking notes, regardless of my level of awareness of what was up ["She wants me to blurt something out." "She's nodding like crazy."], she was respecting me and what I had to say; and by the note-taking in particular, indicating to me that what I was saying was so brilliant that it was worth immortalizing.* No wonder I shared my previously most hidden secrets—that's an exaggeration, but, frankly, not by much.

Here then, are two "tricks" that are guaranteed—*guaranteed*—to keep a person talking:

(1) Nod your head nonstop and frequently.
(2) Ostentatiously take notes.

Both tactics/tricks shout at the other, *"You are important and interesting—I must capture for eternity the pearls of wisdom you are imparting."*

(NB: I don't like writing about things like this, but on the topic of "tricks," I'll add one more that meets the "surefire" standard. The *perfect* icebreaker is *always*: "Do you have kids? What are they doing?")

Quotations
34

Needless to say, I have one hell of a file of quotes for all occasions. From that monster set, I plucked a subset consisting of 34 "gems." Presented here, FYI. (In my opinion, each one suggests a pretty obvious "to do." Some amount to repetition—I simply wanted to offer up the set in one place.)

To wit:

"Do one thing every day that scares you."
—Eleanor Roosevelt

"Life is either a daring adventure, or nothing."
—Helen Keller

"Tell me, what is it you plan to do with your one wild and precious life?"
—Mary Oliver

"All human beings are entrepreneurs. When we were in the caves we were all self-employed . . . finding our food, feeding ourselves. That's where the human history began. . . . As civilization came we suppressed it. We became labor because [they] stamped us, 'You are labor.' We forgot that we are entrepreneurs."
—Muhammad Yunus

"The two most powerful things in existence: a kind word and a thoughtful gesture."
—Ken Langone, cofounder, Home Depot

"The deepest human need is the need to be appreciated."
—William James

"It was much later that I realized Dad's secret. He gained respect by giving it. He talked and listened to the fourth-grade kid in Spring Valley who shined shoes the same way he talked

and listened to a bishop or college president. He was seriously
interested in who you were and what you had to say."
—Sara Lawrence-Lightfoot, *Respect*

"If you don't listen, you don't sell anything."
—Carolyn Marland, MD, Guardian Group

"Everyone lives by selling something."
—Robert Louis Stevenson

"Ph.D. in leadership. Short course: Make a short list of all things
done to you that you abhorred. Don't do them to others. Ever.
Make another list of things done to you that you loved. Do them
to others. Always."
—Dee Hock, founder, Visa

"Never doubt that a small group of committed people can change the world. Indeed, it is the only thing that ever has."
—Margaret Mead

"ARE YOU BEING REASONABLE? Most people are
reasonable; that's why they only do reasonably well."
—Paul Arden, *Whatever You Think, Think the Opposite*

"BLAME NO ONE. EXPECT NOTHING. DO
SOMETHING."
—Bill Parcells, football coach

"Nobody gives you power. You just take it."
—Roseanne

"To live is the rarest thing in the world. Most people exist, that
is all."
—Oscar Wilde

"The only thing you have power over is to get good at what you do. That's all there is; there ain't no more!"
—Sally Field

"The one thing you need to know about sustained individual success: Discover what you don't like doing and stop doing it."
—Marcus Buckingham, *The One Thing You Need to Know*

"Have you invested as much this year in your career as in your car?"
—Molly Sargent, OD consultant and trainer

"The difference [between 'worthy' ambition and 'mere' ambition] is well illustrated by the contrast between the person who says he 'wishes to be a writer' and the person who says he 'wishes to write.' The former desires to be pointed out at cocktail parties, the latter is prepared for the long, solitary hours at a desk; the former desires a status, the latter a process; the former desires to be, the latter to do."
—A. C. Grayling, on Milton, in *The Meaning of Things:*
Applying Philosophy to Life

"This is the true joy of Life, the being used for a purpose recognized by yourself as a mighty one . . . the being a force of Nature instead of a feverish, selfish little clod of ailments and grievances complaining that the world will not devote itself to making you happy."
—G. B. Shaw, *Man and Superman*

"I can't tell you how many times we passed up hotshots for guys we thought were better people, and watched our guys do a lot better than the big names, not just in the classroom, but on the field—and, naturally, after they graduated, too. Again and again,

the blue chips faded out, and our little up-and-comers clawed their way to all-conference and All-America teams."
—Legendary football coach Bo Schembechler, "Recruit for
   Character," from *Bo's Lasting Lessons*

"It is not the strongest of the species that survives, nor the most intelligent, but the ones most responsive to change."
—Charles Darwin

"The most successful people are those who are good at plan B."
—James Yorke, mathematician, on chaos theory,
   in *The New Scientist*

"If things seem under control, you're just not going fast enough."
—Mario Andretti, race car driver

"You can't behave in a calm, rational manner. You've got to be out there on the lunatic fringe."
—Jack Welch, retired CEO, GE

"I guess it comes down to a simple choice, really. Get busy living, or get busy dying."
—*The Shawshank Redemption* (Tim Robbins)

"Stay Hungry. Stay Foolish."
—Steve Jobs, Apple

"You are the storyteller of your own life, and you can create your own legend or not."
—Isabel Allende

"A leader is a dealer in hope."
—Napoleon

"Nothing is so contagious as enthusiasm."
—Samuel Taylor Coleridge

"A man without a smiling face must not open a shop."
—Chinese proverb

"Before you can inspire with emotion, you must be swamped with it yourself. Before you can move their tears, your own must flow. To convince them, you must yourself believe."
—Winston Churchill

"If your actions inspire others to dream more, learn more, do more and become more, you are a leader."
—John Quincy Adams

"A year from now you may wish you had started today."
—Karen Lamb

1. 2. 3. 4. 5. 6. 7. 8. 9. 10. 11. 12. 13. 14. 15. 16. 17. 18. 19. 20. 21. 22. 23. 24. 25. 26. 27. 28. 29. 30. 31. 32. 33. 34. 35. 36. 37. 38. 39. 40. 41. 42. 43. 44. 45. 46. 47. 48. 49. 50. 51. 52. 53. 54. 55. 56. 57. 58. 59. 60. 61. 62. 63. 64. 65. 66. 67. 68. 69. 70. 71. 72. 73. 74. 75. 76. 77. 78. 79. 80. 81. 82. 83. 84. 85. 86. 87. 88. 89. 90. 91. 92. 93. 94. 95. 96. 97. 98. 99. 100. 101. 102. 103. 104. 105. 106. 107. 108. 109. 110. 111. 112. 113. 114. **115. 116. 117.** 118. 119. 120. 121. 122. 123. 124. 125. 126. 127. 128. 129. 130. 131. 132. 133. 134. 135. 136. 137. 138. 139. 140. 141. 142. 143. 144. 145. 146. 147. 148. 149. 150. 151. 152. 153. 154. 155. 156. 157. 158. 159. 160. 161. 162. 163.

Curiosity

115. If You Have to Ask . . . Then Ask (and Ask and Ask).

"I don't invest in anything I don't understand."
—Warren Buffett* **

(*Consider: Should you carry this quote around on a card??)
(**Buffett also said that if you need a computer to understand a company's numbers—don't invest.)

Is there a better way to sum up how we might have avoided the current economic crisis than Warren Buffett's simple philosophy? Probably not. (Though even Buffett made some pretty sizable mistakes—which he, unlike so many others, is the first to admit.)

One practical implication that I urge you to turn into a 2010-and-beyond set of related resolutions:

"I shall lead the league in Asking Dumb Questions."

"I shall become Questioner-in-Chief."

"I shall become 'Dumb Question'-er-in-Chief."

"I shall fill in all blanks—I'll ask until I 'get it' well enough to repeat it."

"I shall persist until I 'get it,' regardless of how dense it may make me appear at the time."

"I shall fight my ever-so-deep-seated instincts, and repeatedly say, 'Could you say that again, a little more slowly?' "

"I shall evaluate others in part on their skill and persistence at . . . Asking Dumb Questions."

"We shall hire in part on perceived or measured Instinctive Curiosity." (For every slot.)

Swallow your pride, especially if you're a "top" boss. Ask until you understand! The "dumber" the question, the better! If the askee is irritated at you or decides you're less smart than she thought, because of your "stupid" questions, well, consider that Total Victory!

Ask!
Ask!
Ask!
(Then ask again!)

Rule: Above all, "sweat the details"—the weird, incomprehensible "little" thing that appears in Footnote #7 to Appendix C that just doesn't make sense to you—probe until you find out what it means.

If I'm any good at this, I owe it all to Allen Puckett, my first boss at McKinsey & Co. Allen is clearly on the "Top 5" list of "smartest guys I've been privileged to work with." I watched Allen-the-consultant (aren't we supposed to be on top of things?) ask Incredibly Dumb Questions to CEOs who were paying him a ton of money—only to find out that Mr. $50-million-a-year CEO was clueless or misinformed. (Thanks, Allen.)

Action: Start this at your next meeting. **Today.** It'll doubtless be awkward—but soldier on. (You might make it a game—and a damn valuable one. For example, at the next meeting you run, offer in advance a banana as a reward to the person asking the dumbest question—illuminating or not. Remember, most "dumb" questions are in fact pretty dumb—that is, have straightforward answers. But 1 in 20, or 1 in 10, or 1 in 50 "dumb" questions reveal the Mother Lode of Comprehension.)

116. Reward DNK (Do Not Know).

Bosses and "brilliant" staffers are very prone to falling into the trap of not admitting when they don't know the answer or have trouble with the concept. (CEOs pocketing $75,000,000 bonuses didn't grock the superderivatives served up by their University of Chicago math Ph.D.s—welcome to Recessionus Gargantuas.) The boss thinks, "I'm supposed to know that"—and is loath to admit that he doesn't. He rarely lies outright, but he is very inclined to obfuscate his ignorance. So, too, those "brilliant" staffers who are paid large sums to be brilliant, not to not know.

Fact is, we should not only readily (gleefully?—"that's what I hired **you** for") admit when we do not know something, but also actively *seek out* things we do not know, or "DNKs." Perhaps start meetings by asking, *"What are our DNKs here?"* (And end the meeting the same way.)

We can, and should, make it positive . . . **and praiseworthy** . . . for anyone to say "DNK" when he/she/you/me DNK. Of course, that doesn't imply rewarding "I didn't bother to . . ." laziness, but instead to reward truth telling, Big Time, especially when it comes to gaping holes in our knowledge. Publicly cheer the person who admits—*in front of a boss*—that he or she "does not know" the facts here, or the answer to this or that. In fact, you might make a game (a serious game!) out of identifying the "DNKs" regarding any analysis or proposed action.

Frankly, good inventories of DNKs may be far more important to success than inventories of DKs. (Do knows, obviously.)

(NB: All good things can be taken too far. As boss, you have to take care and create an atmosphere in which the "pursuit of DNKs" does not deteriorate into a string of "gotcha moments"—as it did at McKinsey.)

117. Work the Watercooler— Or: Are You Gossiping Enough?

Big brains!
Logical thinking!
Analytic capability!
The heart of the human difference!
Right?
Wrong!

The heart of the "human difference"?
Gossip!

The human brain is about nine times bigger, on a body-size-adjusted basis, than that of mammals in general. The reason is fascinating—and mostly counterintuitive. We are, of course, a long way from being the strongest of the species. So how did we win out over the Truly Big Dudes with claws? Answer: Not by intellectual skill at calculating warhead (spear) trajectories. But by joining together in groups and outwitting and out-organizing the brutes. (*Management!*) And what brought these groups of humans together?

A brain that grew to accommodate: **Gossip!**

As British evolutionary psychologist Robin Dunbar puts it, our brains expanded almost entirely to store social information. **(Relationship stuff!!!)** To make a long, long story short short, this "relationship stuff" allowed us to manufacture the "social glue" that would underpin cohabiting in sizable bands; by developing social cohesion skills, we improved or maximized what we now call "organizational effectiveness" . . . and became Kings and Queens of the jungle and beyond.

My point here is to suggest that anyone, as so many (esp. males, esp. technically trained males with MBAs) do, who dismisses or diminishes "relationship stuff" and "communication stuff"—**and in particular "political stuff"**—as "the soft stuff" is not only an ignorant damn fool, but also denying the essence of what it means to be human.

Message I: A **(very)** high share of **"wasted"** time spent on relationship development provides by far the highest "return on investment." **(E.g.: In my experience, it's mostly fools who "don't suffer fools ['time wasters'] lightly.")**

Message II: So go "waste"! (And, often, reap.) (NB: I wasn't born yesterday. Of course there is a lot of "political bullshit." But be **very** careful: **One "no-nonsense" man's ire with "annoying bullshit" is another woman's "Winding Road to Riches and Power."**)

(Source for most of this: *No Two Alike: Human Nature and Human Individuality*, by Judith Rich Harris.)

1. 2. 3. 4. 5. 6. 7. 8. 9. 10. 11. 12. 13. 14.
15. 16. 17. 18. 19. 20. 21. 22. 23. 24. 25.
26. 27. 28. 29. 30. 31. 32. 33. 34. 35.
36. 37. 38. 39. 40. 41. 42. 43. 44. 45.
46. 47. 48. 49. 50. 51. 52. 53. 54. 55. 56.
57. 58. 59. 60. 61. 62. 63. 64. 65. 66. 67.
68. 69. 70. 71. 72. 73. 74. 75. 76. 77. 78.
79. 80. 81. 82. 83. 84. 85. 86. 87. 88.
89. 90. 91. 92. 93. 94. 95. 96. 97. 98. 99.
100. 101. 102. 103. 104. 105. 106. 107.
108. 109. 110. 111. 112. 113. 114. 115.
116. 117. **118. 119. 120. 121. 122.** 123.
124. 125. 126. 127. 128. 129. 130. 131.
132. 133. 134. 135. 136. 137. 138. 139.
140. 141. 142. 143. 144. 145. 146. 147.
148. 149. 150. 151. 152. 153. 154. 155.
156. 157. 158. 159. 160. 161. 162. 163.

Learning

118. Making the Grade: Lifelong Learning Is a Mission-Statement Must.

"The only thing you cannot afford not to do is learn."
—Hank Paulson, former U.S. Secretary of the Treasury

Gerson Barbosa, a commenter on my blog, said, "The mission statement of Johns Hopkins includes *'Cultivate their capacity for lifelong learning, to foster independent and original research, and to bring the benefits of discovery to the world.'*"

That gave me a double jolt.
(One of those . . . "I knew that. Yes, it is that important.")

In our rapidly gyrating world, learning-for-life is no longer an option; it's a professional life (or death) necessity—as more and more are beginning to realize. This is true of you at age 17 or 27 or 47 or 67—and God knows it's true of my great pal, this book's dedicatee, Warren Bennis, voracious in the depth and breadth of his quest for knowledge in his mid-80s!

(Talk about someone who puts you through your paces! You could still hear the echo of the scrape of our chairs on the restaurant floor in Santa Monica when he asked, "So what have you learned since I last saw you?"—and I acted, at 67, like a 19-year-old schoolboy as I cringed.)

Bottom line: I strongly believe that an explicit focus on "lifelong learning" for everyone on board could well be the most sustainable advantage an organization of any flavor can have!

Hence, I hereby strongly (!!) suggest that . . . **"An unstinting commitment by every one of us to accelerated lifelong learning"** . . . or some close kin be made a formal part of your mission-values statement. It deserves to be right up there in the stratosphere with the likes of superior quality and profitability.

> **LESSON PLAN**

"Syllabus" notes on organizational lifelong learning:

(1) A bedrock commitment to lifelong learning applies to . . . **the whole team** . . . in the Marriott's housekeeping department as well as in the R&D warrens at Amgen.

(2) Financial support is key—small and big. (Be careful of cutting back too far on this in difficult times.)

(3) Support for *non-work-related learning experiences* is part of the package—**we aim to instill a generic, formal, learning obsession!**

(4) Supporting this commitment throughout employees' families is also important if at all possible.

(5) Design it into the physical and electronic landscape—visibly "push" learning opportunities or imbed microlearning opportunities in your daily repartee.

(6) Support clubs, virtual and real, and any and all forms of social organization with explicit learning goals.

(7) Put **"lifelong-learning accomplishments and goals"** into the formal hiring and evaluation process—front and center.

119. Out-Study 'Em!

Tennis coach Brad Gilbert was once the #4-ranked pro in the world. But he was no natural. His breakthrough came (after a very spotty career that was about to tank early) when he acknowledged to himself that he wasn't a natural. His response could have been to kick his racket into the grandstands. Instead, it was to hit the books.

Or, rather, write one.

Gilbert was the guy who, when the other guys went for a beer after a match, hung around watching more matches, talking tennis with anyone and everyone . . . and writing it all down. (Remember Branson's hundreds of notebooks?) He began his black book, taking notes on everything, especially other players he'd faced, or players he might face. The result: that eventual #4 ranking, followed by a superb coaching career, working with the likes of Andre Agassi and Andy Roddick.

No surprise, one of Gilbert's coaching secrets has been continuing his own studies, as well as converting his players into students (sometimes no mean feat . . . with those "naturals"). Coach Gilbert acknowledges that there may be a few, like John McEnroe, who can get away without hitting the books . . . but for us mortals that's scant consolation.

This surely translates in 2010, one for one, to the World of Work you and I participate in. I loved these lines from *New York Times* columnist Tom Friedman: "When I was growing up, my parents used

to say to me: 'Finish your dinner—people in China are starving.' I, by contrast, find myself wanting to say to my daughters: 'Finish your homework—people in China and India are starving for your job.'"
Tennis or finance or engineering or bartending . . . this "simple" lesson bears repeating. (A bartender pal may, in fact, be the most assiduous student I know—and it pays off and pays.)

Study!
Study!
Study!

Age 27?
Study!

Age 47?
Study!

Age 67 (me)?
Study!
Study!
(And then study some more!)
(I'm studying harder now than I did at the beginning of my "guru" career—the market is tougher and things are moving faster!)
(And I've truly redoubled my study efforts as the recession gained a head of steam—the gigs left are frightfully competitive.)

120. **Out-Read 'Em!**

I love bookstores . . . even in the age of Amazon. And there is none I love more than London's Hatchards, on Piccadilly (est. 1797). To prepare for my annual Hatchards Christmas pilgrimage (I added a day to my voyage from Dubai to Boston expressly and solely to go to Hatchards), I emptied my backpack before heading to the store. Ha! I ended up expressing a big box home. And also ended up with a $400 book bill, high even by my standards.

THANK YOU, MOM PETERS!

She made me the marrow-sucking, reading maniac I am today. Nothing contributes more to my personal and professional well-being. The thought crossed my mind that I'd happily spend the rest of my life in a condo above Hatchards, slipping down to exchange books at a second's notice.

Read!
Read Wide!
Surprise Yourself With Your Reading Picks!
Read Deep!
Read Often!
Out-READ the "Competition"!!!!!
Take Notes!
Summarize!
Share With Others What You Read!
(Not to impress them, but selfishly, because there's no other way to imbed what you've learned.)
Create/Join a Reading Salon!
Read!

Read!
Read!
(FYI. I am *not* a fast reader—a surprise to many.)

121. Out-Write 'Em!

On a killer Houston-Bangkok trip, I read Graham Swift's *The Light of Day*. What a master! He conjured up so much emotion that I was pretty much a wreck when I reached the end of my journey. He pegs human frailty so perfectly . . .

Segue:

I'm an engineer.
Tops at all things mathematical.
(Not bragging, comes naturally.)

Writing did not/does not/never will come naturally.
(It's 3:45 A.M. in Nelson, New Zealand, as I re-re-re-edit this— laboriously.)
I'm still not worth a damn as far as I'm concerned—but at least I'm a decent journeyman. And perhaps I've found my "voice."
Want to know why?
Because I worked my ass off!
("Worked my ass off" = Wrote and wrote and wrote . . . and wrote.)
(And wrote.)

Good writing matters!
(It can move mountains.)

Odds are, neither you nor I will challenge Graham Swift's craftsmanship, but we can damn well be much, much better than we are . . . which *does* matter.

So: Work *your* ass off on your writing, from tweets to emails to blog posts to letters to your mum—each is an opportunity. (I'm amazed at how much you can learn to pack into, with some clarity, a 140-character tweet.)

> ### ➤ GRANT, WRITING
>
> Ulysses S. Grant was likely America's most effective general. He had many skills—and lucid writing, interestingly, ranked near the top. His orders to his generals before battles were masterpieces of clarity and brevity.
>
> Writing matters . . . on the battlefield in Vicksburg as well as in the boardroom.

122. Now Enrolling: "The People's MBA."

I have long been a vociferous critic of the MBA—such criticism was the de facto point of *In Search of Excellence*. Bob Waterman and I, though both engineers (Waterman in mining, me in civil) and both Stanford MBAs and both McKinsey consultants (the latter a mecca of cold-blooded business analysis), lamented business's abiding emphasis on the numbers and its accompanying de facto and de jure de-emphasis of the so-called soft "people stuff."

Well, the economic crisis of 2007++ underscores and intensifies the message of our 25-plus-year-old book. And, alas, illustrates what little distance we've come*—and how far we have to go. (*Or have we gone backwards?)

For far longer than 25 years (perhaps going on 40 years), I have made my life's work focusing on the neglected "people stuff" and "implementation stuff." Now, with tongue only slightly in cheek, I offer, here, my prospective MBA curriculum, without comment.

Core Course Menu

- **Managing People I, II, III**
- **Servant Leadership I, II**
- **Execution I, II, III**
- Creating a "Try it now" environment/Celebrating Failure
- Maximizing R.O.I.R. (Return on Investment in Relationships)
- Value-added through XFX/Cross-functional EXCELLENCE/"Sucking down," the Art of "Lower"-Level Networking
- Value-added by converting *all* "Departments" into

PSFs/Professional Service Firms/Centers of Excellence
and Astounding Value-Added
- **Sales I, II**
- Service EXCELLENCE
- Creating INCREDIBLE Customer Experiences
- Accounting I, II
- **Accountability I, II**
- Calendar Mastery/Time Management
- **MBWA I, II** (Managing By Wandering Around)
- Nurturing and Harvesting Curiosity
- Design-as-Strategy
- Giving Great Presentations I, II
- **Active Strategic Listening I, II (III?)**
- **Civility/"Thank you"-Recognition/ Thoughtfulness/Decency/Respect/ Apology-as-*Strategy***
- Knowing Oneself
- **Excellence** as Aspiration, **Excellence** as Standard for Behavioral Evaluation. **Excellence** Everywhere. **Excellence** All the Time.

Elective Menu

- Recruiting Top Talent for 100 Percent of Jobs
- **Recruiting for Smiles, Enthusiasm, Energy, Other "Soft Stuff"**
- Nurturing Talent/Helping People (Employees, Customers, Vendors, Communities) Grow Beyond Measure and Realize Their Dreams
- Building "Beautiful Systems"/Building Anti-Systems for Attacking Systems' Overcomplexity
- **Women as Preeminent Leaders**

- The Art of Finding and Nurturing Weirdos
- Building "Skunkworks"/"Black" Budgets/"Off-the-Books" Centers of Innovation
- The Art *and* Science of Influencing Others I, II
- The Preeminent Role of Emotion/Perception/Irrationality in Positively Everything
- Creating or Changing a Unit's "Culture"
- Bringing Spirit to the Workplace
- Marketing
- **Marketing to and Developing Products for Women I, II**
- **Marketing to and Developing Products for Boomers-Geezers I, II**
- Rapid Prototyping of Everything, and the Art of Serious Play
- Increasing a Unit's Metabolic Rate
- **Diversity Power Everywhere of Every Flavor**
- The Power of Universal Transparency
- Finance
- Business Strategy

While I admit that the tongue *is* within range of cheek, the *spirit* encompassed by the above is deadly serious. (If not the 10 years to get it under one's belt.) As to practicalities, at least consider these *sensibilities* when you are designing your training curriculum.

> FLIP-FLOP

Implicit in the above are a series of more or less 180-degree course reversals. Among them:

FROM:	TO:
Economics	Psychology
Marketing	Sales
Strategy	Execution
Men	Women
Finance	Accounting
Hard	Soft
Sexy leadership	Dull old management

1. 2. 3. 4. 5. 6. 7. 8. 9. 10. 11. 12. 13. 14.
15. 16. 17. 18. 19. 20. 21. 22. 23. 24. 25.
26. 27. 28. 29. 30. 31. 32. 33. 34. 35.
36. 37. 38. 39. 40. 41. 42. 43. 44. 45.
46. 47. 48. 49. 50. 51. 52. 53. 54. 55. 56.
57. 58. 59. 60. 61. 62. 63. 64. 65. 66. 67.
68. 69. 70. 71. 72. 73. 74. 75. 76. 77. 78.
79. 80. 81. 82. 83. 84. 85. 86. 87. 88.
89. 90. 91. 92. 93. 94. 95. 96. 97. 98. 99.
100. 101. 102. 103. 104. 105. 106. 107.
108. 109. 110. 111. 112. 113. 114. 115.
116. 117. 118. 119. 120. 121. 122. **123.**
124. 125. 126. 127. 128. 129. 130. 131.
132. 133. 134. 135. 136. 137. 138. 139.
140. 141. 142. 143. 144. 145. 146. 147.
148. 149. 150. 151. 152. 153. 154. 155.
156. 157. 158. 159. 160. 161. 162. 163.

Time

123. It Might Be Later Than You Think.

A "couple of minutes" late is . . . late.
Five minutes late is . . . late.
One-point-three minutes late is . . . late.
Late is . . . Late.
"Better late than never"?
Never.
Period.

Early is not late.

Early is respect.

Early = "I care."

(It matters.)

(Arriving early for a meeting is not a sign that you are "anxious." It is a sign that you are . . . PUNCTUAL.)

(Late is rude.)

(George Washington was never late.)

(I don't mean to insult you with this one, but this *is* a book about the [all-too-often-ignored] "obvious.")

124. Time Off for Smart Behavior.

Hustle rules. But the very same times that call for speed-speed-speed also call for matchless creativity, and that doesn't always match up with 90-hour workweeks—especially back-to-back-to-back 90-hour weeks. So, in the course of the day, week, year, figure out how to take a pause that refreshes.

And take it.

Some, like me, swear by two-minute meditation breaks. **(Even one-minute meditation breaks.)** Movie afternoons or whatever for a stressed-out team on severe deadline may work wonders. Vacations of more than 10 days are a must.* **(*Damn near everybody I know agrees that it takes about 10 days to get into the "relaxation zone." Period. Gates does it annually.)** Two free days at the end of or, especially, in the middle of a trying business trip make sense. The larger point is . . . work consciously at de-stressing. This idea is absolutely positively "strategic"; in no way is it merely a "nice thing to do."

NB1: Work on your breathing!!!

NB2: Trust me . . . **p-l-e-a-s-e** . . . this applies to 27-year-olds as much as or more than 67-year-olds.

NB3: Ho hum, the boss *must* "model the way."

➤ "CRACKBERRY" ADDICTS: TIME FOR DETOX

F***ING BLACKBERRY BREAKS!

THE WORLD WILL *NOT* COME TO AN END IF YOU ARE OUT OF TOUCH FOR 20 MINUTES.
OR AN HOUR.
OR A DAY.

THE WORLD HAS *NEARLY* COME TO AN END BECAUSE, IN FACT, FAR TOO MANY "BRILLIANT" PEOPLE WORKED 60/60/24/7/365–366 ... AND TOOK TOTAL LEAVE OF COMMON SENSE. (I.e., PDAs sure helped the Wall Street crowd keep us out of the tank. Not.)
IF YOU ARE CONSTANTLY ON YOUR BLACKBERRY, IT IS MOSTLY BECAUSE OF AN ... **ARROGANT, CONSUMING SENSE OF SELF-IMPORTANCE TOTALLY DIVORCED FROM REALITY.**

125. Time Out for . . . Daydreaming!

Dov Frohman is a pioneer in the semiconductor industry. Among (many) other things, he started Intel Israel and was significantly responsible for the growth of Israel's potent high-tech sector. With Robert Howard, he presented us with, surprisingly, a truly original book on leadership, *Leadership the Hard Way: Why Leadership Can't Be Taught—and How You Can Learn It Anyway*. (Nice title!)

A few of the provocative chapter titles are: "Insisting on Survival," "Leadership Under Fire" (literally—Israel, remember), "Leveraging Random Opportunities." In a chapter titled "The Soft Skills of Hard Leadership," Frohman astonishes (or, at least, astonished me) as he insists that the leader-manager must free up no less than 50 percent of his-her time from routine tasks. To wit:

> *"Most managers spend a great deal of time thinking about what they plan to do but relatively little time thinking about what they plan not to do. As a result, they become . . . so caught up in fighting the fires of the moment that they cannot really attend to the long-term threats and risks facing the organization.* **So the first soft skill of leadership the hard way is to cultivate the perspective of Marcus Aurelius: avoid busyness, free up your time, stay focused on what really matters.**
>
> *"Let me put it bluntly: every leader should routinely keep a substantial portion of his or her time—***I would say as much as 50 percent—unscheduled*** . . . Only when you have substantial 'slop' in your schedule—unscheduled time—will you have the space to reflect on what you are doing, learn from experience, and recover from your inevitable mistakes.*

"Leaders without such free time end up tackling issues only when there is an immediate or visible problem . . . Managers' typical response to my argument about free time is, 'That's all well and good, but here are all the things I have to do.' Yet we waste so much time in unproductive activity. It takes enormous effort on the part of the leader to keep time free for the truly important things."

The second unconventional, mind-ripping idea from the same chapter is "daydreaming."

"The Discipline of Daydreaming": **"Nearly every major decision of my business career was, to some degree, the result of day-dreaming** . . . To be sure, in every case I had to collect a lot of data, do detailed analysis, and make a data-based argument to convince superiors, colleagues, and business partners. But all that came later. **In the beginning, there was the daydream.**

"By daydreaming, I mean loose, unstructured thinking with no particular goal in mind . . . **In fact, I think daydreaming is a distinctive mode of cognition especially well suited to the complex, 'fuzzy' problems that characterize a more turbulent business environment.** . . .

"Daydreaming is also an effective means of coping with complexity. When a problem has high degrees of complexity, the level of detail can be overwhelming. The more one focuses on the details, the more one risks becoming lost in them . . . **Every child knows how to daydream. But many, perhaps most, lose the capacity as they grow up."**

Neither of these suggestions is easy to implement—and that's obviously an understatement. Nonetheless, I think we must try. Dov

Frohman's track record in a hypertough–lightning-fast environment is stunning. And I trust his self-assessment of the reasons for that success, the two cited here chief among them. Hence, I suggest it is well worth your time and that of your leader colleagues to ponder: **50 percent unscheduled time.** (And Mr. Frohman is doubtless busier than you and I are.) **Daydreams as Source #1 of strategy.**

(NB: If you do decide to play around with this, try to stick with Frohman's dictum—50 percent. Conjure up what that means. Not 20 percent or 30 percent . . . but 50 percent. You may not get there, but examining the idea-of-50-per-se is clearly worthwhile.)

126. Master the Art of Milestoning.

A recent trip from Vermont to Massachusetts (173.6 mi.) got me thinking of something else besides pit stops. I was running late, and noting my progress via odometer and various landmarks and highway markers. As my mood went up and down I realized (re-realized?) the power of manageable goals in every form of activity.

Amassing 173+ miles, the entire task, is of course the Big Enchilada—but a horrifying and demotivating thought at 4:00 A.M., which is often my departure time if I aim to beat Boston's morning rush hour. The sort of thing that spurs me on is . . . "scoring" the readily achievable 13-mile nugget from home to Dorset, Vermont. *(Hooray, I've made a noticeable start!!)* Likewise, bagging the 12 miles from Gill, Massachusetts (about halfway from Vermont), to Erving, Massachusetts, is downright exhilarating (it means finishing about 50 percent of the most traffic-y 27-mile stretch of road).

As I thought on this, I realized/re-realized a bunch of things:

(1) Milestones are all-important, no matter how trivial or repetitive the task.

(2) **"Milestoning"** is a real art for reasons psychological, as much as or more than for reasons of "substance."

(3) Truly trivial milestones *are* often meaningless, even if they are "accomplishments" of a sort and "milestones" of a sort—scoring the eyedrop's distance from the Dorset turn to the Stratton turn is no big deal and not really a motivator.

(4) Milestone "power" is variable. E.g., at the beginning or near the end of a task, the apparently trivial can indeed seem utterly grand. "Well, I've done *something*"—that's what I feel seconds after 4:00 A.M. when I make it to the immediate end of the farm road that starts at our

house, thus putting behind me the first click, or 0.7 miles, in numbing reality a scant 0.4 percent of the whole. (Milestone power is also variable on other dimensions. In the workday context, for instance, smallish milestones that are critical spurs to the *team's* doing the job may look pretty darned puny to the *boss*; hence, widespread publication thereof may not be a great idea.)

(5) There is a definite sweet spot . . . **"the perfect milestone."** That 13 miles from home to Dorset, or the 12 miles from Gill to Erving, is a winner—substantial enough to matter, to merit a pumped fist at 4:23 A.M., and to constitute "progress of note."

(6) There is a fine line between "trivial" on the one end and "daunting" on the other. (A 27-mile stretch, if thought of that way, is downright discouraging: "Dear God, these 27 miles of Route 2 are frigging endless.")

Each time Vermont's Loooong Winter approaches, I dread the fact that on truly rotten days I'll be forced to execute my power-walking addiction on my treadmill. I *hate hate hate* exercising indoors! But to the point of this item, I spent a pretty penny on a new treadmill a while back. Why? *Mostly because the distance accumulator indicator goes to three decimal places instead of two.* I crave constant measurable progress while on the damn machine, and nothing but nothing is "trivial." I feel like the wind is at my back as the odometer moves from **1.723** miles to **1.724.** On the old machine, struggling from 1.72 to 1.73 took approximately . . . FOREVER.

Ah, milestone power!

You are indeed welcome to dismiss the triviality of my examples here—but I do urge you to pay the closest attention to the . . . **Art of Milestoning.** It's actually of the utmost importance if, like me, you believe in the Ultimate and Abiding Power of what I call "XX," or "Double X"—the relentless pursuit of eXcellence in eXecution.

Action: Become a "milestone activist." Use milestoning as a matter of routine, but do so with the greatest care, as only partially explained above—that is, become a Milestone Professional as well as a Milestone Activist.

NB: "Milestoning" is a group endeavor, not a top-down activity.

NB: The Art of Milestone Celebration is also worthy of your (avid!) study and application.

NB: This *is* a Big Deal.

1. 2. 3. 4. 5. 6. 7. 8. 9. 10. 11. 12. 13. 14.
15. 16. 17. 18. 19. 20. 21. 22. 23. 24. 25.
26. 27. 28. 29. 30. 31. 32. 33. 34. 35.
36. 37. 38. 39. 40. 41. 42. 43. 44. 45.
46. 47. 48. 49. 50. 51. 52. 53. 54. 55. 56.
57. 58. 59. 60. 61. 62. 63. 64. 65. 66. 67.
68. 69. 70. 71. 72. 73. 74. 75. 76. 77. 78.
79. 80. 81. 82. 83. 84. 85. 86. 87. 88.
89. 90. 91. 92. 93. 94. 95. 96. 97. 98. 99.
100. 101. 102. 103. 104. 105. 106. 107.
108. 109. 110. 111. 112. 113. 114. 115.
116. 117. 118. 119. 120. 121. 122. 123.
124. 125. 126. **127. 128. 129. 130.** 131.
132. 133. 134. 135. 136. 137. 138. 139.
140. 141. 142. 143. 144. 145. 146. 147.
148. 149. 150. 151. 152. 153. 154. 155.
156. 157. 158. 159. 160. 161. 162. 163.

Design

127. Design Is . . . Everywhere!

"Everything is design."
—Richard Farson, *The Power of Design: A Force for Transforming Everything*

Design!
How Cool!
How . . . **Powerful!**
And: How pervasive!
(See the quote above.)

Sure, "design" means the string of gorgeous products from Apple or OXO or Herman Miller or John Deere. But it applies equally to the "presentation" of the training course you are about to deliver. And "design mindfulness" is at the heart of the new purchasing process about to be unveiled—in a 20-person organization. And it's the soul of the reception area in a 3-person accountancy; and the very heart of the Formal Reports that same accountancy delivers. (Long before Design became "cool"—and the "D" was routinely capitalized!—McKinsey had a full-scale department devoted to report design. Leeway on format for Client reports? ZERO.)

Hence, if you are serious about design:

(1) It becomes part of **every** (e-v-e-r-y) project, tiny to grand, in *every* (e-v-e-r-y) department.

Design *is* Sony . . . in *everything* they do.
Design *is* Apple . . . in *everything* they do.
Design *is* BMW . . . in *everything* they do.
Design *is* Starbucks . . . in *everything* they do.
Design *is* Nike . . . in *everything* they do.
Design *is* the New York Yankees . . . in *everything* they do.
Design *is* Barack Obama . . . in *everything* he does.
Design is Nicolas Sarkozy . . . in *everything* he does.
Design *should be* the four-person engineering subunit . . . in *everything* they do.
Design *should be* you . . . in *everything* you do.

(2) **Every** project has a formal "design advocate."

(3) **Everyone** is encouraged through example to become "design minded." (And it's part of their formal evaluation.) (Everyone = General management to housekeeping at the hotel, managing partner to receptionist at the accountancy or consultancy.)

(4) Design is always considered on five dimensions: (a) usability, (b) simplicity, (c) aesthetics, (d) "Cool"/"Wow"/"Gaspworthy," and (e) **Excellence.**

(5) **Every** work space is a living example of Excellence in design—it sings "our song."

(6) Design EXCELLENCE applies to **every** business process as much as to *every* product.

(7) Design per se is explicitly addressed in **every** written work plan.

(8) While design is not always "free," design-mindedness is not a cost item—and EXCELLENCE in design applies at least as much to the "low end" as to the luxury end of a market.

(9) Design Reviews are part of **all** project reviews. (I stole this from Boots the Chemist in the UK.)

(10) If you are a/the Big Boss, there should be a . . . **Chief Design Officer** . . . who lives in the "power corridor" with the Chief Financial Officer, Chief Marketing Officer, etc. (If you are a "little boss," there should be an appointed "design champion" whose collateral duty is to represent the "design view" in all the unit's work product.)

(11) "Design-mindfulness" or "EXCELLENCE in design" should (must!) be part of the organization's **Core Values Statement.** ("Design Excellence will be a trademark of all we do outside our company—and in all our internal activities as well." Or some such.)

(12) Design per se should be directly and indirectly part of **all** training programs.

(13) Etc.

(14) Etc.

> **HOPE WE SCORED!**

In my drafts of this book, and I trust it shows here, I was as concerned about design as about the prose. There is some extensive narrative, but many of our items are short and meant to be punchy—energetic, provocative, etc. I obsessed about the "look & feel"—I religiously (correct word choice) believe that "the look *is* the message"—and that I cannot deliver in any way, shape, or form on my intent for *The Little BIG Things* unless the presentation mirrors—and then pushes waaaaaaay forward—the "tone" and "soul" of the text.

I drifted this way starting with *The Tom Peters Seminar* in 1993. Then in 2003, I left inarguably one of the world's top five publishers, Knopf, to go to Dorling Kindersley—solely because they are peerless in book design, and I was keen to do no less than "re-imagine" (the subsequent title of the DK book) the business book per se to match the hyperenergetic times. If we didn't quite succeed with *Re-imagine!*, it damn well wasn't for want of grand/grandiose aspiration or lack of trying!

Have we met the same stratospheric standard here at Harper-Studio?

You alone will be the judge.

But, again, if we fall short, it won't be because we were modest in our aims, though with a far different goal for the book; there was no intent to extend the Dorling Kindersley look. Instead I hope the look and feel and text herein bring to life the idea—and *soul*—of "little BIG things"!

Design is me!
(And I'm hoping design-will-be-you.)

(Bragging moment: When I started my then inchoate design crusade, in the mid-1980s, I had but one real cohort in yakkerworld/"guruworld," the *Financial Times*'s Chris Lorenz. A few years later, it gave me the utmost egocentric pleasure when IDEO founder David Kelley publicly labeled me "the business world's leading ambassador of design"—I'd have thought Steve Jobs would have merited that descriptor. Hooray for me. Today I can say delightedly that I have yielded that "leading ambassador" moniker to literally dozens, or hundreds, of others! Design is now seen by many as "differentiator #1" in many corners of the world of commerce—albeit lip service is often the standard, which is why I'm still screaming, including right here.)

(Yes, design *is* everything!)
(As to the epigraph to #127, Farson says I said it first, I say he said it first—no matter.)

128. Is It "Lickable"?

Steve Jobs says that the definition of a superbly designed product is one you . . . **"want to lick."** (I took a chance during a speech and pulled out my sleek, black, compact WD/Western Digital external hard drive in front of over 1,000 people and licked it, and fortunately got a good response; I never would have done it outside the United States—God knows what sin it might have amounted to somewhere.)

BMW advertised a new model car as . . . **Radically Thrilling.**

Economists agree that inducing people to . . . open their wallets . . . is the cure to the recession.

And I claim it all boils down to the right kind of hammer.
A hammer you . . . want to *lick*.
A hammer that is . . . *radically thrilling*.
And a hammer that . . . induces you to make an expenditure that you hadn't intended to make.

Answer: My Tuf-E-Nuf hammer. This gorgeous little hammer, actually the . . . **Tuf-E-Nuf Mini Striker Stubby Claw Hammer** . . . is a true innovation, even an earth-shattering innovation. (By my lights.) The head looks like and has the heft of a regular heavy hammer. But the full-diameter handle is only five inches long, half the normal length. And the grip is great, up to the standard of the easy-to-hold OXO kitchen tool line. The net result is the ability to maneuver in tight spots while retaining almost all the power of a full-size hammer—and, as a bonus, owning a piece of sculptural art! I ended up buying six of the bloody things for

Christmas presents in 2008—including, Christmas spirit be damned, one as a present to myself, which I use as a paperweight or bookend when not whacking nails!

Great *design* rules!

Innovation is king!

Functionality scores!

Lickability and Radically Thrilling are the standards worth shooting for!

Excellence knows no bounds!

(And . . . there is more to design—and life—than iPods and iPhones!)

129. Design Sign: Can You Get There from Here?

The closest I've come to being late to a speech was attributable to . . . lousy directions, from the Client no less. This was at a big (!!) convention center—it ran for blocks and blocks. And I *was* running a little late. (Normally I give myself huge pads, but I was in a frenzy to make late changes, and . . .) The driver and I puzzled at the directions—and the Client's cell phone was not receiving. I finally picked a place, got out, and started hunting. Literally 25 minutes later, fit to be tied, I made it to my destination—by which time everyone was panicked, from Washington, D.C. (my speakers' agency), to Vermont (my home office) to the Client. All because of incomplete-imprecise-confusing directions and then signage.

It got me thinking: Directions, signs, manuals are life's blood, in this case and more or less in general. And most directions-signs-manuals are, well . . .

pathetic.

They confuse.

They frustrate.

They . . . *suck*.

They are decidedly unprofessional—my ultimate epithet in this book, even below "sucks."

But these guides (directions-signs-manuals) ought to be . . . **Works of Art** (damn it) . . . Pluses rather than Minuses . . . Full-scale Members of the "Value-added" Package. They should top the charts on dimensions such as these:

Clear!
Simple!
Engaging!
Beautiful!

And: **Breathtaking!** (Why not?)

I command you (or would if I could) to spend—in terms of Time & Money & Care—like the proverbial drunken sailor on Directions-Signs-Manuals.

Make your manuals (signs/directions) . . . works of art! (They *are* an incredibly important part of the Experience you provide—remember my riffs on Great Beginnings!)

The generic lesson? Check every bit of instructional material in the joint—internal as well as that with which customers and vendors interact:

Clear?

Beautiful? (!!!!)

Simple? (Yet complete?)
EXCELLENT?

Odds are VERY high that you don't put in enough effort on internal and external material. (Especially concerning "simple stuff"—ain't no such thing.)

Work on it as a group. Test it with strangers. Test it with your spouse. Test it with your kids. Test it with the guy at the auto body shop.

Mimic the Golden Gate Bridge painters who never stop, finish one paint job, then immediately start over. Likewise, pick off some single item of instructional material and evaluate it—continue on a measured basis, forever.

This is a very big deal. Here I go again adding more bureaucracy: You need a very senior person, perhaps a VP, who is titled something like Chief of User-friendly Instructional Design of Every-Bloody-Thing.

▶ PRACTICE (PEN) MAKES PERFECT

At 6:00 P.M. one summer evening, while I was out following my brush-cutting passion on the farm, I apparently woke up a yellow-jacket neighborhood buried in the mud. In short order, I was stung perhaps a dozen times—one YJ got stuck under my shirt. Luckily, I didn't go into anaphylactic shock. But in a few hours the reaction was body-wide. I went to an ER the next morning after a truly crappy night. (The doc was very pissed off that I hadn't come earlier.)

The good news was that I was on the mend in 12 hours, courtesy of an elephant-sized Benadryl injection and prednisone—thanks to the latter, I would have definitely tested positive on an Olympic doping test. The bad news: Once stung so badly, my predilection for full-blast anaphylaxis in the future soared. The additional good news: If prepared, one can handle the bad stuff with an EpiPen. (The EpiPen, to be carried with you at all appropriate times, lets you self-administer a blast of epinephrine, usually adequate protection-against-disaster until you can hustle to an ER.)

That's all prelude to my design story. (I've *always* got a "design story.") The EpiPen, upon being wanged into your thigh (through clothing, if necessary), ejects a needle that in turn injects that epinephrine. The package includes two locked-and-loaded doses. Now the instructive part: *There is a third dispenser—for practice administration.* Upon being yellow-jacketed again, God help me, there is no time to read the directions! So the practice pen, sans needle and epinephrine, lets you pull the pin as you actually would, and if you smack your thigh hard enough, it indicates that you've passed the practice test—the practice pen is infinitely reusable.

As all of us know, manuals are almost always (99+ percent of the time) infuriating. (The better term is "pieces of shit." Sorry to the über-sensitive. Tough.) This was the exception, to say the least. There was a mini-manual, but the practice injector went above and beyond. Trust me, I have a couple of testers for this and that (e.g., blood sugar measurement), and the directions merit the standard D grade . . . if I'm in a generous mood.

So hats off to the EpiPen designers—winner of my User-friendly-Design Gold Medal.

(Indicator of the enormity of the opportunity here: When you *do* come across even a single good example, it stands way out from the herd. The herd sets a very low hurdle!)

130. Love + Hate = Design Power.

Design is all about . . . **emotion.**

Moreover, it's *not* about "liking" something—or "disliking" it.

Design's . . . awesome power . . . comes precisely from the fact that it is about unvarnished emotion.

About . . . **love.**

About . . . **hate.**

I LOVE LOVE LOVE my Ziplocs—literally a million uses, I never leave home without a box or two.

I HATE HATE HATE my Cuisinart Filter Brew coffeemaker—it is nigh on impossible to pour the water in without spilling!

(I really "hate" to use "hate" to refer to a given company's product—but my defense in this case is that I really do hate it. You might love it. That's the point of this item—it's personal and emotional.)

I LOVE LOVE LOVE the simplicity of the controls on my Black & Decker coffeemaker. One switch: **On.** Or: **Off. (!!)**

I HATE HATE HATE **(HATE)** the **three(!!)** devices it takes to control my satellite TV and DVD player.

That's design.

What a **(power)** tool!

Handle with care!

And remember: "Design mindfulness" is a "cultural" trait. It is not the product of a "program." Nor is it the product of a "superstar designer"—whose services are purchased for some staggering sum.

(I am wholly in favor of superstar designers, if merited. My point here is that simply purchasing a designer does not likely alter company culture.)

First steps: Raise awareness, learn the generic language of design. Launch a widespread discussion about design in our everyday life. (Involve everyone—this is not "for artists only"; it's a **100-percent-of-us game.**) Talk about "stuff you love." And . . . "stuff you hate." Not particularly related to the company's or your department's products or services—in fact, it's best to focus on ordinary things, like restaurant experiences or cooking tools or websites. This should help heighten the awareness of the Strong Emotions that, subjectively, good and bad designs evoke. Let this ubiquitous discussion slowly merge into evaluating things closer to home—Web stuff, business processes, the quality of customer contacts, the quality of staff facilities, the quality of the flowers on the reception desk.

1. 2. 3. 4. 5. 6. 7. 8. 9. 10. 11. 12. 13. 14.
15. 16. 17. 18. 19. 20. 21. 22. 23. 24. 25.
26. 27. 28. 29. 30. 31. 32. 33. 34. 35.
36. 37. 38. 39. 40. 41. 42. 43. 44. 45.
46. 47. 48. 49. 50. 51. 52. 53. 54. 55. 56.
57. 58. 59. 60. 61. 62. 63. 64. 65. 66. 67.
68. 69. 70. 71. 72. 73. 74. 75. 76. 77. 78.
79. 80. 81. 82. 83. 84. 85. 86. 87. 88.
89. 90. 91. 92. 93. 94. 95. 96. 97. 98. 99.
100. 101. 102. 103. 104. 105. 106. 107.
108. 109. 110. 111. 112. 113. 114. 115.
116. 117. 118. 119. 120. 121. 122. 123.
124. 125. 126. 127. 128. 129. 130. **131.**
132. 133. 134. 135. 136. 137. 138. 139.
140. 141. 142. 143. 144. 145. 146. 147.
148. 149. 150. 151. 152. 153. 154. 155.
156. 157. 158. 159. 160. 161. 162. 163.

131. The Case of the Two-Cent Candy.

Years ago, I wrote about a retail store in the Palo Alto environs, a good one, which had a box of two-cent candies at the checkout. I subsequently remember that "little" parting gesture of the two-cent candy as a symbol of all that is Excellent at that store. Dozens of people—from retailers to bankers to plumbing supply house owners—who have attended seminars of mine have come up to remind me, sometimes 15 or 20 years later, of "the two-cent candy story," and to tell me how it had a sizable impact on how they did business, metaphorically and in fact.

Well, the Two-Cent Candy Phenomenon has struck again—with oomph and in the most unlikely of places.

For years Singapore's "brand" has more or less been Southeast Asia's "place that works." Its legendary operational efficiency in all it does has attracted businesses of all sorts to set up shop there. But as "the rest" in the geographic neighborhood closed the efficiency gap, and China continued to rise-race-soar, Singapore decided a couple of years ago to "rebrand" itself as not only a place that works but also as an exciting "with it" city. (I was a participant in an early rebranding conference that also featured the likes of the late Anita Roddick, Deepak Chopra, and Infosys founder and superman Narayana Murthy.)

Singapore's fabled operating efficiency starts, as indeed it should, at ports of entry—the airport being a prime example. From immigration to baggage claim to transportation downtown, the services are unmatched anywhere in the world for speed and efficiency.

Saga . . .

Immigration services in Thailand, three days before a trip to Singapore, were a pain. ("Memorable.") And entering Russia some months ago was hardly a walk in the park, either. To be sure, and especially after 9/11, entry to the United States has not been a process you'd mistake for arriving at Disneyland, nor marked by an attitude that shouted "Welcome, honored guest."

Singapore immigration services, on the other hand:

The *entry form* was a marvel of simplicity.
The *lines* were short, *very* short, with *more than adequate* staffing.
The process was *simple* and *unobtrusive*.

And:

The Immigration Officer could have easily gotten work at Starbucks; she was all smiles and courtesy.

And:

Yes!
Yes!
And . . . yes!

There was a little candy jar at each Immigration portal!!!

The "candy jar message" in a dozen ways:

"Welcome to Singapore, Tom!! We are absolutely beside ourselves with delight that you have decided to come here!"

Wow!
Wow!
Wow!
And. . .

Ask yourself . . . NOW:

What is my (personal, department, project, restaurant, law firm) "Two-Cent Candy"???

Does every part of the process of working with us/me include two-cent candies?
Do we, as a group, "think two-cent candies"?

Operationalizing: Make **"two-centing it"** part and parcel of "the way we do business around here." Don't go light on the so-called substance—but *do* remember that . . . **perception is reality** . . . and perception is shaped by two-cent candies as much as by that so-called hard substance.

Start: Have your staff collect "two-cent candy stories" for the next two weeks in their routine "life" transactions. Share those stories. Translate into "our world." And implement.

Repeat regularly.
Forever.
(Recession or no recession—you can afford two cents.)
(In fact, it is a particularly brilliant "on the cheap" idea for a recession—you doubtless don't maximize Two-Cent Opportunities. **And what opportunities they are.**)

▸ THE "RIGHT" IDEA

Minimizing TGWs/Things Gone Wrong is a (very) good thing!

("TGW" was originally one of the car manufacturers' quality measures—you enumerated for the dealer your problems in the first 100 days or so of ownership.)

Maximizing TGRs/**Things Gone Right** is a (very) good thing, too!

Focus on both.

Don't shortchange TGWs.

But don't shortchange TGRs, either.

(In an era when most things—e.g., cars—work amazingly well, TGR maximization often has more impact than a tiny, marginal reduction in TGWs.)

So: Map and measure TGRs!

It ain't a "soft" variable!

To proceed: Examine an external or internal customer's *experience* with, say, calling the company. Assume, for the moment, that in terms of operational excellence, all goes well. Now: Find **5 "TGRs"**... "little," positive, memorable "things gone right" that mark this experience.

132. If the Envelope Doesn't Fit, Forget It!

A few adventures in customer service:

- My local Starbucks stayed open a few minutes late—and the barista fetched something he had already put away—to fill my order.

- When I handed the barista at my *other* local Starbucks my thermos, she filled it up without question, even though at the time it was a nonstandard order. (I think they undercharged me—a two large-cups price for what doubtless was three large cups in quantity. Oh, and they thoroughly . . . **washed the thermos before filling it, without my asking—or even imagining!**)

- My local Whole Foods usually opens at **8:00 A.M.** But because several of us were waiting, they opened at about **7:45 A.M.** And their folks define helpful—I got a full-bore dissertation on various cuts of beef, among other things.

- The Stanford Graduate School of Business, my beloved (and I mean it) Stanford GSB, sent me a snail-mail questionnaire in prep for my MBA reunion. I took some pains to fill it out. When I got ready to mail it, I discovered that it didn't fit into the envelope they'd enclosed—I tore the questionnaire up and tossed it in the recycle bin. (Ever wonder what's wrong with MBA programs? **Lack of attention to envelopes!** Think I'm kidding?)

Do you bend over backwards to go "a little" "beyond the book" to help customers? **Do you authorize-encourage everyone (100 percent) to break the rules "a little bit" so as to stretch for the customer?** Do you solicit examples of serious stretch behavior—and celebrate it wildly? Do you open "a little" earlier than advertised? Are your envelopes the right size? Note that to give positive answers to *all* these queries requires, perhaps paradoxically, obeisance to tightly controlled operational Excellence—and at the same time openness to breaking the rules in order to be especially helpful to one's clientele or one's mates. (Creating a culture in a large corporation that's "loose" and "tight" simultaneously is no walk in the park. In fact, dealing with, rather than avoiding, this paradox is one of management's greatest challenges. One can say, with some certainty, that if you avoid it, there will be a dangerous drift toward more "safe" rule-following and less expressed initiative; thence the paradox must be addressed proactively.)

The 25 companies that made *BusinessWeek*'s first "Customer Service Champs" list in 2007 are very, very, very, **very**, very serious about the "little things" and the frontline service providers who make or break a Little Things Movement.

And you?
Personally?
Your team?
Your company?
How do you know?
For sure?
What are you doing about it?
To encourage more of it?
To . . . **reward it** . . . when it happens?

Today?

Now?

"Big aims" (I believe in them religiously!) are terrific!

Bravo!

But, people being people (see the epigraph from Henry Clay that launches this book), it's often, usually in fact, the wee things that are the basis for the remembrance of the activity; the beauty of the Dalmatian Coast of Croatia, where I hiked for a week in 2008, dims—but I'll remember for eons the Croatian along the way who, unbidden, invited me in for a cup of tea.

133. It's All About the Mud.

It's "mud season" in Vermont as I write and as we all too appropriately call it. Cars, and trucks in particular, look like flying mud balls.

While on a (muddy!) speed walk, I passed through the Equinox Hotel parking lot—Manchester Village, Vermont. They were undergoing a massive renovation. The primary contractor was Bread Loaf Construction, probably Vermont's best (in fact, tops by any standard), out of Middlebury.

Bread Loaf folks must not be as smart as I think; that is, they apparently didn't know it was mud season. Every contractor's truck in the parking lot—and the FedEx and UPS trucks, too—confirmed the "mud ball" image I just suggested. Except for Bread Loaf's. There were two BL trucks in the lot, both sizable pickups. Both, in BL tradition, were painted fire-engine red.

And neither—and here I do not exaggerate—had the tiniest apparent trace of dirt or mud or even dust.

Later in the afternoon, I was having a long interview with a top
dog at the ad agency TBWA/Chiat/Day, and, not surprisingly, the
topic turned to branding. Out of my mouth, startling me, popped,
**"Branding is a squeaky-sparkly clean
bright red contractor's truck in mud
season in Vermont."** We nattered on about the fact
that branding is, well, about . . . **Everything.** On the one
hand, that's not very helpful or operational. On the other hand, it
reminds us that nothing, absolutely nothing, is irrelevant to individual
branding—or the branding of a construction company in Vermont or
Susan Axelrod Accountants, or Megacorp Inc.

Quintessential definition of an "everything": Carl Sewell, based in
Dallas, owns a string of car dealerships, including a Cadillac "store"
in Dallas.
Carl bought a . . . **streetsweeper.**
The first thing a prospective customer sees of Sewell Village Cadillac is the road in front of the facility. Hence, **Carl decided to
take what his customer would see upon
arrival—the street!—out of the city's
hands and into his own hands;** it's fair to say
that "Project Clean Street" is a nontrivial element of his brand. That
would also explain the fantastic arrays of flowers inside—worthy of
the All-time Flower Champions, Issy Sharp's Four Seasons Hotels.
(I'd love to see Issy's flower bill—it'd make me, but not Issy, blanch.)

So **(and I command):**
Stop.
Right now.
Check the reception desk.

Check the reception area.

(Check the street—even in Manhattan.)

Check the bathroom.

Check your last Client email.

Check etc.

Check etc.

Check 10 "little things."
Right now.

Is each one stunningly, amazingly Excellent?

Does each one confirm & extend & broadcast your "brand promise"?

You, personally?

Your training department?

Your six-person insurance company on Main Street?

Your BigCo division?

(Remember, a very BIG thing: **You *are* in *absolute* control here!!!!!!!!** There are things you *cannot* make happen, to be sure; but you, no matter how "junior," or no matter what the state of the economy, *can* project Brand Excellence via a thousand "atmospherics" that in the end overwhelmingly determine Client-Employee perception.)

(I judge that there's a little bit of duplication in this point. I say: **Hooray!**)

134. **Think Billboard Sign. "We Care." "We Don't Care."**

I was walking through a giant mall—visiting a renowned retailer's space. Usually, they're one of the best, poster practitioners of "experience" design & marketing.

But . . . **the place was a mess.**

Got me thinking. I'm not a "neat freak." To the contrary, I'm a slob. But that's home. Not my profession. I select hotels in large measure based on whether or not they have 1-hour, 24-hours-a-day pressing services. (It's a fact.) I get paid (very) well for what I do. *I don't get paid to show up for a speech looking like I slept in my clothes!*

The retail space in question was crowded with customers and visitors. (Good for them.) But it'd gotten very messy in the course of the (busy) day. Stacked goods scattered about. Trash on the floor. Boxes half-opened near the checkout desk.

Etc.
(Etc.)

To me the space . . . SCREAMED . . . **"We Don't Care."**

There's a lot to Great Retailing, or great whatever. But very near or at the head of the line is: "WE CARE!" And it starts with "look and feel."

I'm not pushing passionless ultra-tidiness. That can readily be a turnoff, too. I am suggesting that you (boss) formally ask **everyone** to take **full** responsibility for keeping things "professional" 100 percent of the time . . . *to put their "We care" glasses on and eyeball* *the place.* There's but one question to ask: If I were walking in here as a customer or prospect or new hire, what would I take in—in the first 0.4 seconds? Where would it score on the 1 to 10 "We Care Scale"?

(NB: This is exactly as true for a two-person walk-up law firm as for a national retail chain.)

We care.
We don't care.
(Take your pick.)
(No in-between.)
(Really . . . no in-between. Think about it.)

1. 2. 3. 4. 5. 6. 7. 8. 9. 10. 11. 12. 13. 14.

15. 16. 17. 18. 19. 20. 21. 22. 23. 24. 25.

26. 27. 28. 29. 30. 31. 32. 33. 34. 35.

36. 37. 38. 39. 40. 41. 42. 43. 44. 45.

46. 47. 48. 49. 50. 51. 52. 53. 54. 55. 56.

57. 58. 59. 60. 61. 62. 63. 64. 65. 66. 67.

68. 69. 70. 71. 72. 73. 74. 75. 76. 77. 78.

79. 80. 81. 82. 83. 84. 85. 86. 87. 88.

89. 90. 91. 92. 93. 94. 95. 96. 97. 98. 99.

100. 101. 102. 103. 104. 105. 106. 107.

108. 109. 110. 111. 112. 113. 114. 115.

116. 117. 118. 119. 120. 121. 122. 123.

124. 125. 126. 127. 128. 129. 130. 131.

132. 133. 134. **135. 136. 137. 138. 139.**

140. 141. 142. 143. 144. 145. 146. 147.

148. 149. 150. 151. 152. 153. 154. 155.

156. 157. 158. 159. 160. 161. 162. 163.

Grunge

135. The Enemy Within— Or: There Is No Cost Higher Than the Cost of Rigidity.

In his June 2, 2009, *New York Times* column, "The Quagmire Ahead," David Brooks begins his assessment of the GM fiasco by citing an internal memo written in ... **1988** ... by EVP Elmer Johnson:

"We have vastly underestimated how deeply ingrained are the organizational and cultural rigidities that hamper our ability to execute."

That quote reminds me of another, this one by Norberto Odebrecht, head of the Brazilian-based heavy-industrial conglomerate, Odebrecht:

"Data drawn from the real world attest to a fact that is beyond our control: Everything in existence tends to deteriorate."

"Simple" fact: Accompanying GM's longtime designation of "biggest" came Olympian accompanying "rigidities." One is reminded of yet another quote, this from Walt Kelly's *Pogo*:

"We have met the enemy and he is us."

Business schools, the always helpful whipping boys in my rants, focus on the "cool" FMS troika. (Finance-Marketing-Strategy.) And yet it is the *internal* organizational "stuff," mostly MIA or very secondary in B-schools (not sexy enough), that trip companies up. Not "bad strategy," but . . . **"rigidities"** . . . that impede the ability to . . . **"execute"** . . . are the culprits behind shoddy performance in 9 out of 9.01 cases.

Toyota *didn't* do in GM.
Honda *didn't* do in GM.
Nissan *didn't* do in GM.

GM did in GM.

This is not news.
It is, however, worth restating.
And I shall do so.
Again.
And again.
And then again.

We have met the enemy.
He is us.

❯ LOOK INSIDE—AND LOOSEN UP

"Rigidities" is not just the problem of Giants.

Rigidity is a disease in three-person accountancies and 11-table restaurants only one year old.

Stop what you are doing.
Right now.

Call your best customer. Ask: *"How are we doing … compared to a year ago? Six months ago? Are we making your life more complicated? Are we more bureaucratic in any way, shape, or even tiny (especially tiny—slow accretion of sluggishness, like arterial plaque, is the issue) form? Are we slowing down? Do we ever say, 'I'd like to do that for you, but …'?"*

Call your best vendor.
Repeat the above.
Word for word.

Visit your newest employee. Ask: *"Have you run across procedures since you got here that you think are silly or overcomplicated? If so, have you passed your concerns along? If you haven't, why not—do we make it intimidating for a 'newcomer' to surface such concerns? If you have passed such concerns along, have you been praised for doing so? (Or, God help us, looked at askance?) Has more or less immediate follow-up occurred?"*

At every Exec Group meeting, set aside a 15-minute block of time to discuss a "dumbest thing we've done lately" item—insist that members bring very recent cases along for discussion. Achieve some specific resolution on the spot—and don't adjourn until you've got 7-, 14-, and 21-day Action Items with responsibility assigned.

GM grew rigid one-second-at-a-time.

You do, too.

(Your unit has become more rigid in the time it took to read this little item.)

(Believe it.)

136. Become a Decentralization Dervish!

Situation: A Sunday. Lufthansa check-in area. Logan Airport, Boston. Airport peaceful. The parent ahead of me has his young boy on a leash. The kid is energetic (i.e., boringly normal), and straining against the leash in the style of Lulu, my hypermanic Australian Shepherd.

I'm *not* keen on losing kids in airports.

(Yes, it's happened—and it's horrible.)

I *am* unalterably opposed to "kid leashes."

Frankly, it made me slightly ill, though I demurred from saying anything.

Child rearing.

Delegating.

Organization structure.

Governance in general.

In many ways, the primary issue in all the arenas just listed boils down to the classic Jeffersonian-Hamiltonian debate on centralization vs. decentralization. **(I call the centralization-**

decentralization debate ... "the all-important first 100 percent." That is, it's pretty much the whole ball game!)

Jefferson believed in "We the people"—and, in fact, perpetual revolution. Hamilton said: Centralize, enhance order, and establish a strong executive to lead the way. (We're fighting about "it," every day, 220 years or so later—as we should be; it is not resolvable by definition.)

How tight the reins?
(Order, efficiency.)
How much slack?
(Initiative, innovation.)

The child will never learn until she's on her own and has been through a full set of disasters. But you don't want any ill to come her way—so you keep the reins tight!

Stop!
Drop the "rational analysis."
Skip the "balance" argument!
Cut to the chase!

Every *person who makes it into the history books is by definition* ... **insanely disobedient.** *He or she doesn't "buy the act." He or she has contempt for his-her "betters." And yet we tell our kids in school to "sit still, follow the rules, and behave." (And if they don't, we put them on a polyester or chemical/Ritalin or metaphorical leash.)*

These thoughts are the product not only of my Logan-Lufthansa tongue-biter, but also of a recent public row with a client over the imposition (right word, per me) of "best practice" standards in a big company.

I *love* "best practices."
I *hate* "best practices."

I ... **love** ... best practices ... **if** ... they are "cool stuff" from a jillion disparate sources inside and outside the company and industry, available for each of us to learn from.

I ... **hate** ... best practices when mimicry is demanded—*"Do it the Memphis way or else!"*

(NB: *Rigidly Applied "Best Practice" = ZERO Standard Deviation = Regression Rather Than Progress.*)

True, very true, you will never get "it"/the centralization-decentralization balance *right* (nation, child rearing, your 27-person unit).

But ... I bet you (*I guarantee!*) that ... **you will s-l-o-w-l-y get it wrong.**

That is, unless ... **fanatically** (again, right word) ... managed, there is an inexorable movement toward centralization. I call it ... **ICD/ Inherent Centralist Drift.** As an ordained Bishop in the High Church of Decentralization, I humbly suggest that creeping centralization, or ICD, is the cause of the lion's share of corporate collapses!

Mostly it goes like this: *An extant decentralized structure is in place. A problem hits us between the eyes, a pretty big one. The solution is ...* **always** *(again, guarantee) ... the same. A few, or more, rules and regulations to lower the odds of a repeat. Time passes. A new problem lands. And, again, we sensibly put some more regs in place. Over time, these 100 percent ...* **individually reasonable** *... responses, and their expansive interpretation by several generations of managers flexing their "authority muscles" (call it what it is, justifying their professional existence!), lead to less and less initiative and innovation—and eventually paralysis, GM flavor. Trust me, this* **is** *the story.*

Screw up!
Tighten up!
Avoid screw-ups!
Stagnate!
Die!

So: What are the precise procedures for maintaining constant vigilance so as to limit and in fact reverse the proliferation of originally sound-procedures-collectively-become-bureaucratic-cancer?

For starters ... **Anti-ICD Police** (*please use the term*) ...

Armed ...
and Dangerous ...
and Authorized/Encouraged to Act.

(I further suggest, in addition to the Anti-ICD cops, a formal system of ... **BDs**, or Bullshit Detectors. Think of it as your network of NSA satellites. And a ... **CGRO**, or Chief Grunge Removal Officer, with an office next to the CIO and CFO and COO.)

Have you explicitly exercised any formal Anti-ICD Procedures:

This week?
Today?
(Prove it!)

(I repeat: The "action idea" is very formal procedures and specifically designated individuals responsible for blocking "ICD" as it happens. And a commitment by leadership at all levels to proactively measure and manage anti-ICD activities.)

> ALL HANDS ON DRECK

"Decentralization" is not a "CEO Thing."
It's an . . . **"everybody thing."**

Decentralization is an . . . **attitude!** "Decentralization is *not* a piece of
paper. It's *not* me. It's either in your *heart*, or not."
—Brian Joffe, CEO, BIDVest

It's a Willingness **(desire!!)** to "delegate," to give others their head, to
send them on Adventure Tours—every day.

"If it [feels] painful and scary—then you are really delegating."
—Caspian Woods, small biz owner

137. Play the . . . Great Grunge Removal Game!

Commerce Bank (now owned by Toronto-Dominion) more or less revolutionized retail banking on the East Coast of the United States. For one thing, among ever so many, Commerce computer terminals in the branches had a . . . **red button** . . . on the keyboard. When you (teller) ran into any self-(bank)-created roadblock to serving the customer . . . you'd push the red button. The impediment you discovered would be noted and formally addressed—and if action were taken, and it often was, you'd get a financial reward for having unearthed Grunge of any sort that got between the customer and an excellent service experience.

(Commerce also sported the "Two 'No' " rule. If a customer asked for the combination to the Bank Vault . . . the teller was not permitted to say, "No"! First, the teller had to go to his supervisor—if she said "No," then and only then could the teller reject the customer's request. The idea is that the bank moved heaven and earth—referring even the most outrageous request up the line—to try to say "Yes" to any-damn-thing the customer wanted. Commerce in fact called itself . . . **"Yes bank"** . . . precisely because it went to great lengths to respond affirmatively to almost any customer desire.)

My point-suggestion here is that you invent your flavor of Red Buttons (or "Two 'No' " rule) for your 3-person department, your 9-person temporary project team, your 17-table restaurant, or your 235-person division. That is, mimic Commerce Bank by creating formal processes for Identifying Grunge and Removing Grunge and getting everyone in on the . . . **Great Grunge Removal Game.** Think of it at an even higher level of abstraction as a "Strategic" "Grunge Removal Culture"—a full-blown philosophy supported by a formal infrastructure to try to keep the "inevitable grunge growth" in check or even to reverse it. A host of possibilities are there for the taking:

- An Anti-Grunge Pledge of Allegiance every morning.
  (Is this "going too far"? **No!** Grunge is the #1 Organization Effectiveness Killer—period.) (Remember . . . GM wrecked GM!)
- An anti-grunge item on *every* meeting agenda.
- A "C-level" anti-grunge exec: CGRO, Chief Grunge Removal Officer.
- Rewards for Grunge Identifiers and Grunge Removers at all levels.
- Punishments for Grunge Growers at all levels. (This, too, could be made into a game. Rather than a formal "letter to the file," giving each other a hard time for making life more difficult for internal and external others could be treated as sport—to great positive effect.)
- Devices to continually and automatically measure grunge growth and purge systems and procedures and processes of Complexity Creep/Grunge Accretion.
- Your version of visible Red Buttons for one and all and the "Two 'No' Process."
- Etc.

Get on with this . . . today!
(It's a must.)
Grunge Grows . . . **60/60/24/7/365.**

138. The I Percent Drill: Clearing Away a World of "Slop" in Just 45 Minutes.

I did an in-company seminar in the United Kingdom several years ago, for a midsized firm. ($50 million?) A generalist consultant was my copresenter; to be more accurate, he handled the first two-thirds of the day, and I provided the (I hope) grand finale.

At about 2:00 P.M. he called an abrupt halt to proceedings, and said, *"I want to make sure I earn out my full fee today, and then some. We're going to stop and do a 45-minute exercise."*

He explained that *any* operation can at *any* time cut 1 percent of its budget. (We all have flab, regardless of circumstances—not many with single-digit BMIs.) Though I in general (*vehemently*) oppose across-the-board cuts, I have absolutely no problem with the 1 percent idea—slop happens! The leader then broke the group up by function; about five functions were represented, as I recall. He gave the subgroups 30 minutes on the dot to identify their team's 1 percent. Then he had each group report in public for two or three minutes—this public recitation, he told me, raised the odds of execution; it also provided others with ideas.

Indeed, the groups readily identified their 1 percent and reported accordingly—there was actually no bitching.

I called and asked him a couple of months later how things had turned out. (He was a regular adviser to the company.) He said there was almost uniform success—and a couple of groups had decided to repeat the exercise on their own every few months. Given his closeness to the CEO, and my more general judgment, I'd guess he gave me an accurate report.

(Incidentally, the groups were not allowed to ID more than 1 percent. This was not a generic cost-cutting effort—the aim was what it was said to be, getting rid of 1 percent.)

So:
Do it!

Whether you run a two-person firm (or a one-person firm, for that matter), or a six-month midsized project team, or a 723-person unit, this afternoon . . . gather your leadership team, or everyone in the department, and take 1 percent (no more and no less) out of your budget/ projected annual costs. As my colleague said, anyone can indeed do this task—and it must not absorb more than an hour! The simple math tells us how powerful this is—with a $100,000 projected cost, you can reap $1,000 reward rather easily. (With $5,000,000 in costs you'll pocket $50K—and maybe avoid laying someone off.)

The little savings *do* add up.

(BTW, it works for personal finance, too.)
(Repeat every 90 days.)
(Bad times—or good times.)

139. Goal: To Make "Common Sense" More Common.

A lot of the giant financial-economic mess we're in can be chalked up to a failure of common sense, often by the so-called bestest of the best and brightest of the bright, egging each other on with a series of implicit "I dare yous." We are all, in fact, "insiders" in our own worlds—and we all too often lose touch with reality to a lesser or greater extent.

There are a host of things one can do to deal with this, but in this instance I only want to suggest routinely running proposals or budgets, or whatever, minor as well as major, by a **"Common Sense Ombudsman."** Said ombudsman, singular or plural, formal or informal, could be a spouse or a neighbor who owns a restaurant or the down-to-earth woman running the distribution center in South Podunk who you chatted with at the management meeting in Orlando last year. (It absolutely cannot be someone in your own organizational unit—even a "contrarian" someone; even the so-called contrarian abides by 90 percent of "the way we do things around here.")

Presumably you've got three or four projects running as we speak. Call your friend Jack, who runs finance at the local Toyota dealership. Offer him box seat tickets to next week's Royals game if he'll spend a couple of hours reviewing your project-planning docs in the next few days. Repeat this process—routinely! obsessively!—with different Jacks and Janes and Annes and Rogers. The price of the baseball or opera box seats will be trivial in comparison to value added and pratfalls avoided.

In fact, since you're saddled with a thorny problem at the moment, how about picking up the phone right now and giving Jack, Jane, Anne, or Roger a call?

1. 2. 3. 4. 5. 6. 7. 8. 9. 10. 11. 12. 13. 14.
15. 16. 17. 18. 19. 20. 21. 22. 23. 24. 25.
26. 27. 28. 29. 30. 31. 32. 33. 34. 35.
36. 37. 38. 39. 40. 41. 42. 43. 44. 45.
46. 47. 48. 49. 50. 51. 52. 53. 54. 55. 56.
57. 58. 59. 60. 61. 62. 63. 64. 65. 66. 67.
68. 69. 70. 71. 72. 73. 74. 75. 76. 77. 78.
79. 80. 81. 82. 83. 84. 85. 86. 87. 88.
89. 90. 91. 92. 93. 94. 95. 96. 97. 98. 99.
100. 101. 102. 103. 104. 105. 106. 107.
108. 109. 110. 111. 112. 113. 114. 115.
116. 117. 118. 119. 120. 121. 122. 123.
124. 125. 126. 127. 128. 129. 130. 131.
132. 133. 134. 135. 136. 137. 138. 139.
140. 141. 142. 143. 144. 145. 146. 147.
148. 149. 150. 151. 152. 153. 154. 155.
156. 157. 158. 159. 160. 161. 162. 163.

Enterprise

An Organization Is "People Serving People." (Period!)

A challenging trip to Siberia (tautology?) to give an all-day seminar got me thinking about the fundamentals of organizing and organizations. I more or less surprised myself when the definition that follows emerged from my keyboard, almost spontaneously:

Enterprise* (*at its best):

An emotional, vital, innovative, joyful, creative, entrepreneurial endeavor that maximizes individuals' growth and elicits maximum concerted human potential in the wholehearted service of others.

On the one hand, this definition is pretty high-stepping. Idealistic beyond the realm of common sense. But examine it . . . **one word at a time.** Conjure up each word's opposite, and consider the possibilities:

Do we want an emotionless organization—or an exciting one? (That's a practical enough question, eh?)

Do we want a joyless organization—is joy "impractical" in the World of Work? (Since said world is where we spend the bulk of our conscious hours as adults, I'd hope the possibility of Joy is not completely pie in the sky.)

And so on.

I have used this formulation 100 times now, literally in every corner of the globe. And to my delight, most of the people at my seminars—from Estonia to Korea to Austin—sign up for the "Siberia option." (As opposed to, "Send him home on the next plane.") Not "sign up" in the sense of taking a blood oath, but in the sense of agreeing that when you examine the words . . . ONE AT A TIME . . . and when you do conjure up the opposite of each word, you are likely to agree that although it is indeed a towering aspiration, it is not to be dismissed, either.

Organizations exist to *serve*.
The true bottom line: *People* serving *people*.

If membership in your club (organization) is not aimed at "mind-blowing" development for each staff member and "window-rattling" service for each customer and other extended family member, then . . .

just what the hell is the point?

❯ WHAT HAPPENED TO THE LAST THREE YEARS?

I cannot begin to tell you how important *and* practical I think this item is.

I cannot begin to tell you how much I would like to reach out from this page, and shake you, and shout . . .

You can do this.

To myself, I keep saying . . .

IF NOT THIS, WHAT?

You take over a department. Twenty-eight people. You aim to make it a "smoothly functioning unit." As time goes by, and you deal with brush fire after brush fire after brush fire (we all do), your aspiration-in-reality becomes "making it through the day."

And next thing you know, you've indeed "made it through the day"—about 700 times. And three years have passed. There have been no mutinies. And your annual evaluations have been consistently "pretty damn good."

But what do you really have to show for ... **three whole years of your precious life?**

Actually, not much. "Competent survival" might be an accurate description. But nobody's beating down the door to get into your unit. And you really don't have one or two ... **stupendous** ... accomplishments to brag about or sleep on.

Well, I don't think that's good enough.

For you.

For the people in your unit.

I beg you ... yes, beg ... to review the definition-aspiration with which I launched this item.

I beg you ... yes, beg ... to talk with your peers and your folks and anyone you can buttonhole about ... WHAT COULD BE.

I beg you ... yes, beg ... to "go public" with a doc called, more or less ... **"Towering Aspirations of Growth and Excellence"** ... and then use it as a litmus test against which you judge ...

... every decision, small or large;

... every project, small or large;

... every people move, small or large.

I believe there is a decent chance that, if you get moving ASAP, three years from now you will be able to look back and say ...

"Oh my God, we did that ... "

"How cool ... "

"How 'Wow' ... "

And, yes, people from all over the organization will be hammering on your door, begging (yes, begging) to sign up and become part of your ... **Greatest Show on Earth.**

141. The PSF Mandate: "Work Worth Paying For."

To understand tomorrow's value-added mandate and opportunity, let's travel back three decades: Hank was perhaps the most independent, self-assured person I'd ever met—certainly the most independent-minded under 30. He worked for me for several months in 1978, during my McKinsey days, on a distribution project for Frito-Lay in Dallas. We both had pretty similar, not particularly scintillating origins; and we'd both ended up in engineering school, he mechanical, me civil. But our paths then diverged. The U.S. Navy paid my way through school, and I returned the favor with four years' service. He had gone to work, at world's end and virtually alone, as a young—and remarkably independent and accountable—field engineer at Schlumberger, the French-founded, Texas-based, lean-mean-R&D-driven oil-field services firm.

Because of my friendship with Hank, I continued to follow Schlumberger, through some ups and downs, mostly ups, for the next 25 years. At the beginning of 2008, a *BusinessWeek* cover story reported that a brassier-than-ever Schlumberger may well take over the world: "THE GIANT STALKING BIG OIL: How Schlumberger Is Rewriting the Rules of the Energy Game." In short, Schlumberger knows how to create and run oil fields on a turnkey basis, anywhere, from searching and drilling to full-scale production to distribution. As China and Russia, among others, make their move in energy, state-run companies are locking out the major independents. Instead, they are turning to the new Kings of Large-Scale, Long-Term Project Management—and the new Kings wear the same Schlumberger overalls my friend Hank wore.

At the center of the center of the Schlumberger "empire" is a relatively new member of the family, remarkably reminiscent of IBM's enormous Global Services Unit (these days, Global Services = IBM) and UPS Logistics' teams, which run entire supply chains for enormous companies. The Schlumberger version is simply called IPM, for Integrated Project Management. It lives in a nondescript building near Gatwick Airport, and its chief says it will do "just about anything an oil-field owner would want, from drilling to production"—that is, as *BusinessWeek* put it, "[IPM] strays from [Schlumberger's] traditional role as a service provider* and moves deeper into areas once dominated by the majors." (*My pal Hank was solo on remote offshore platforms interpreting geophysical logs and the like.)

As I see it, Schlumberger is transforming itself pell-mell into what could become the biggest and most powerful "PSF" (Professional Service Firm) in history. Moreover, paths like this, from IBM and UPS and Schlumberger, are open to many, maybe even most, firms in any arena you can name. Think Best Buy's Geek Squads, the mobile service units that *are* Best Buy's competitive advantage in electronics retailing; or the "PSF" components of many giant GE "industrial" units, which produce well over 50 percent of the units' revenues; even the likes of MasterCard are getting into the act—MasterCard Advisers are running entire payment systems activities for some of their Clients, penetrating ever more deeply into the heart of the Clients' operations.

There are actually even larger ramifications of this line of thinking. In fact, one of my "Top 5" Tom Rants is urging *every* "department" in an organization to reconceive itself as a full-blown turnkey-services provider, a de facto or de jure profit-making "PSF." And, likewise, I urge companies of all flavors to consider aiming to grow through "PSF-ing." The Schlumberger-IBM-UPS-GE-MasterCard-Best Buy transformation—and it is just that—is a matter of attitude as much as "programs."

So, consider trying "the PSF idea" on for size:
- What makes for an effective "PSF"?

- Are we (department, say) at least in spirit a "PSF"?
- Do we (department) truly do WWPF—**Work Worth Paying For?** (This is essential: If the Purchasing Department sent out invoices to its internal customers, other departments and divisions, would those customers agree that Purchasing's services were worth top dollar—e.g., had they saved enough money to clinch a deal on behalf of some division in the firm, had they finagled an early delivery that had delighted the end-user customer?)
- What would be the first steps toward transforming ourselves into a de facto or de jure PSF in the next 12–18 months?

In short, I believe the "Professional Service Firm Idea" is central to the potential of many firms, including or especially *small* ones, to differentiate themselves in today's and tomorrow's increasingly competitive environment. In particular, these "PSFs" can potentially offer dramatically differentiated services limited only by their imaginations.

(To spur discussion, and I rarely make such a self-serving suggestion, you might consider perusing my book *The Professional Service Firm50: Fifty Ways to Transform Your "Department" into a Professional Service Firm Whose Trademarks Are Passion and Innovation*.)

142. Don't Let the "Enemy" Rule Your Life.

"Obsessing about your competitors, trying to match or best their offerings, spending time each day wanting to know what they are doing, and/or measuring your company against them—these activities

have no great or winning outcome. Instead you are simply prohibiting your company from finding its own way to be truly meaningful to its Clients, staff and prospects. You block your company from finding its own identity and engaging with the people who pay the bills. . . . Your competitors have never paid your bills and they never will."
—Howard Mann, *Your Business Brickyard: Getting Back to the Basics to Make Your Business More Fun to Run*

Mr. Mann also quotes Mike McCue, former VP/Technology at Netscape:

"At Netscape the competition with Microsoft was so severe, we'd wake up in the morning thinking about how we were going to deal with them instead of how we would build something great for our customers. What I realize now is that you can never, ever take your eye off the customer. Even in the face of massive competition, don't think about the competition. Literally don't think about them."

I say:
Amen!

Don't let the "enemy" rule your life. Try your damnedest to follow the exact advice of Mr. McCue: "*Literally* don't think about them." Far, far easier said than done, no doubt, but self-awareness is a start.

And, as is almost always an implementation necessity, a simple ritual: Purposely and systematically direct (with forethought, during-thought, and an afterthought "checkup") your conversations (and thoughts, if possible) away from your equivalent of "What's Microsoft doing?" ("What's the accountancy across the road doing?" or "What's the new Italian restaurant downtown doing?"); when it happens, and it will, bring the meeting to a halt. And say, as a matter of ritual, something like: "The new Honda dealership moving in is not the problem. The depth of the relationships we have with our *current* customers is the issue—and opportunity. Let's generate 10 new ideas in the next

30 minutes as to how we can renew our acquaintance with people who bought cars from us over three years ago—but haven't been back to our dealership since." (Or some such.) That is, redirect the conversation directly to performance.

I know I repeat myself.
But I'll take the risk.

We . . . are the problem.
They are . . . **not** . . . the problem.
We have one source only of Excellence: **Us.**

143. Love Your Competitors.

Oddly enough, I've run into two situations in the last 24 hours (as I write) where someone wanted to restrict the activities of a competitor. In one instance, involving a seminar I was to give, the organizer did not want a close professional friend of mine, who is in the training business, hence an indirect competitor of the organizer, to attend. In another case involving a product I'm working on, I was asked not to mention a competitor favorably. I flatly refused to accede to either request—on both moral and commercial grounds.

At the top of my *business* priority list is a desire for my overall market to grow by leaps and bounds! Sure, as the number of people giving speeches and seminars and writing books and blogging and tweeting on similar topics has leapt, my "market share" has gone w-a-y down. (It was about 100 percent after *In Search of Excellence,* when I was more or less the only *public* "management guru.") But my revenue has soared in the process—the "smaller share of a much bigger pie" axiom.

Moreover, I want (am desperate for!) my competitors to do terrific work! If they do, the "guru" industry's stock as a whole, which is sometimes wobbly, will rise.

In short, I want my competitors to thrive. *And* I welcome their presence at my events. *And* I constantly recommend to participants at my seminars that they go to my competitors' seminars. I go so far (in my blog's "Cool Friends" interviews and via book endorsements, for example) as to *enhance* their careers!

Does all this suggest an altruistic streak? Perhaps. But mostly not. To begin with, I think that when one bad-mouths or attempts to diminish one's competitors in any way, or tries to limit their activities, the "word gets around." And one develops a reputation as prickly and egocentric—and, well, as a selfish jerk.

More important:

I think (I know!) that my only effective long-term defense against the competition (think Apple versus its stalwart competitors) is to do better and unique work—and to earn and to retain the custom of those who are interested in the things I worry about.

In the original glory days of IBM, one of the legendary Thomas Watson Sr.'s Golden Rules was "Thou shalt never bad-mouth a competitor." In fact, *any* violation of this rule was a no-debate "firing offense." As IBM struggled in the 1980s, the rule slipped into disuse, and the company's sterling reputation was tarnished as a result. To return to my basic premise, IBM's real problem was the loss of its prior level of product and, especially, service distinction—their only remaining defense was to demean others.

So, I come down hard on Mr. Watson's side. It is my goal to be a highly regarded . . . **and supportive** . . . member of my professional community. Speaking crudely, I think that is an incredibly strong and sustainable competitive advantage.

"Win" with a remarkably better product.
"Win" with deeper relationships.
"Win" when your industry is prospering and has a good reputation.
Build up your competitors!!
Build up your entire industry!!

And . . . if you hear a competitor is missing deadlines, losing revenue, or experiencing any kind of failure, instead of piling on the criticism, consider lending a quiet helping hand. Trust me, it will redound to your long-term benefit.

Decency rules!

(And, paradoxically, the more "dog eat dog" the competitive situation, the more the "decency advantage" matters.)

As one of my blog's commenters, Nathan Schock, put it concerning this topic:

"This is especially important for those of us who work in professional services located outside major metropolitan areas. As our entire industry improves in our city, the large companies are less likely to look outside our city for those services. Our advertising agency believes that anything that makes the industry better in our city improves our position."

Thank you, Nathan!
Amen!

The Top 50 "Have-Yous"

While waiting in the Albany airport to board a Southwest Airlines flight to Reagan/DCA one morning, I happened across the latest *Harvard Business Review,* on the cover of which was a bright yellow "lead article" sticker. On it were the words "Mapping your competitive position." It referred to a feature article by my friend and admired colleague, Rich D'Aveni.

Rich's work is uniformly first-rate—and I have said as much publicly on several occasions, dating back 15 years. Moreover, I'm sure this article is a fine one, too—though I admit I didn't read it.

In fact, it triggered a furious, negative "Tom reaction," as my wife calls it. Of course I believe you should worry about your "competitive position." But instead of obsessing on competitive position and other abstractions, as the B-schools and consultants would invariably have us do, I instead wondered about some "practical stuff," which I believe is far, far more important to the short- and long-term "strategic" health of the enterprise, tiny or enormous.

Hence, rather than an emphasis on competitive maps or looking for a "blue ocean" (empty space, per the popular book *Blue Ocean Strategy*), I urge you to pay attention to something like my Top 50 "Have-Yous," as I call them. The list could easily be three times as long—but this ought to keep you occupied for a while. Of course, the underlying hypothesis is that if you proactively do the "small" stuff below, your "competitive position" will improve so much that mapping will become a secondary issue!

Herewith:

1. Have you called a customer . . . *today?*

2. Have you in the last 10 days . . . visited a customer?

3. Have you in the last 60 to 90 days . . . had a seminar in which several folks from a key customer's operation (different levels, different functions, different divisions) interacted, via facilitator, with various of your folks? (Goal: Fully integrates us with our key customers—and makes it clear we want to get to know them on all levels.)

4. Have you thanked a frontline employee for a small act of helpfulness . . . in the last three *days*?

5. Have you thanked a frontline employee for a small act of helpfulness in the last . . . three hours?

6. Have you thanked a frontline employee for carrying around a great attitude . . . *TODAY*?

7. Have you in the last week recognized—publicly—one of your folks for a small act of *cross-functional cooperation*? (Small, social acts enhancing cross-functional bonding may be my Obsession #1.)

8. Have you in the last week recognized—publicly—one of "their" folks (from another function) for a small act of cross-functional cooperation with your gang?

9. Have you invited in the last month a leader of *another function* to your weekly team priorities meeting???

10. Have you personally in the last week-month called-visited an internal or external customer to sort out, inquire, or apologize for some little or big thing that went awry? (No reason for doing so? If true—in your mind—then you're more out of touch than I dared imagine. Pity.)

11. Have you in the last two days had a chat with someone (a couple of levels "down") about specific deadlines concerning a project's next steps?

12. Have you in the last two days had a chat with someone (a couple of levels "down") about specific deadlines concerning a project's next steps . . . *and* what specifically and immediately *you can do to remove a hurdle*? (Remember: Boss as CHRO, Chief Hurdle Removal Officer.)

13. Have you celebrated in the last week a "small" (or large!) *milestone* reached? (I.e., are you a milestone fanatic? Are you a celebration fanatic?)

14. Have you in the last week or month revised some estimate in the "wrong" direction (i.e., acknowledged that things were more problematic than previously estimated) and apologized for making a lousy estimate? (*Somehow or other you must publicly reward the telling of difficult truths—and the reporting of bad news.*)

15. Have you installed in your tenure as a staff department boss a very comprehensive customer satisfaction scheme for all your *internal* customers? (With major consequences for hitting or missing the mark.)

16. Have you in the last six months made a weeklong, visible, very intensive *visit-"tour"* of external customers' operations?

17. Have you in the last 60 days called an abrupt halt to a meeting and "ordered" everyone to get out of the office and "into the field" *immediately* with the *order* to fix (f-i-x, finito!) *some/any* nagging "small" problem through immediate practical action?

18. Have you in the last week had a rather thorough discussion of a "trivial" "cool design thing" someone has come across—*away* from your industry or your function—at a website or in a product or its packaging? And do you urge/insist that everyone (*every* one) be on the lookout for, bring in, and present "incredibly cool stuff I've found" from "everyday life"?

19. Have you in the last two weeks had an informal meeting—at least an hour long—with a frontline employee to discuss "things we do right," "things we do wrong," and "What would it take to turn this job into something approaching his or her 'dream job' "?

20. Have you in the last 60 days had a general meeting to discuss "things we do wrong" . . . that we can fix in the next 14 days? (With follow-up *exactly* 14 days later.)

21. **Have you had, in the last year, a one-day, intense off-site with each of your principal internal customers—followed by a substantial celebration of "things gone right" on both parties' parts?**

22. Have you in the last week privately pushed someone to do some family thing that you fear might be overwhelmed by deadline pressure?

23. **Have you learned the names of the children of everyone who reports to you? (If not, you have 30 days to fix it. Nah, make that 15 days.)**

24. Have you taken, in the last month (two weeks?), an interesting-*weird* outsider to lunch? And do you keep careful track of "weird dude lunches"?

25. Have you in the last month invited an interesting-weird *outsider* to sit in on an important meeting?

26. Have you, in the last three days, discussed in a meeting something interesting, beyond your industry, that you ran across reading, etc.? (This means more than an email from you with a hyperlink or two.)

27. Have you in the last 24 hours injected into a meeting "I ran across this interesting idea in [strange place]"?

28. Have you in the last two weeks asked someone to report on something, anything that constitutes an act of brilliant service rendered

in a "trivial" situation—restaurant, car wash, etc.? (And then discussed the relevance to your work—and then implemented *on the spot* some little thing from what they observed?)

29. *Have you in the last 30 days examined in detail (hour by hour) your calendar to evaluate the degree to which "time actually spent" mirrors your "espoused priorities"?* (And had everyone on the team repeat this exercise.)

30. Have you in the last two months had a presentation to your group by a "weird" outsider?

31. Have you in the last two months had a presentation to the group by a customer, internal customer, vendor featuring "working folks" three or four levels down in the vendor/customer/internal customer organization (and in your organization)?

32. Have you in the last two months had a presentation to the group of a cool, beyond-our-industry idea by two of your folks?

33. Have you at every meeting today (and forevermore) redirected the conversation to the practicalities of implementation concerning some issue before the group?

34. Have you at every meeting today (and forevermore) had an end-of-meeting discussion on "action items to be dealt with in the next **4, 24, 48** hours"? (And then made this list public—and followed up in 4 or 24 or 48 hours.) (And made sure everyone has at least one such item.)

35. Have you had a discussion in the last six months about what it would take to get recognition in a local-national poll of "*best places to work*"?

36. Have you in the last month approved a *cool–different–very different outside training course* for one of your folks?

37. Have you in the last month *taught* a frontline training course?

38. Have you in the last week discussed the idea of Excellence per se? (What it means, how to get there—concerning a current project.)

39. Have you in the last week discussed the idea of *"Wow"*? (What it might mean, how to inject it into an ongoing "routine" project.)

40. Have you in the last 45 days assessed some major internal process in terms of the details of the "experience" that surrounds its use, as well as the measured results it provides to external or internal customers?

41. Have you in the last month had one of your folks attend a meeting you were supposed to go to, which therefore gives them unusual exposure to senior folks?

42. Have you in the last 60 (30?) (15?) **(7?)** days sat with a trusted friend or "coach" to discuss your "management style"—and its long- and short-term impact on the group?

43. Have you in the *last three days* considered a professional relationship that was a little rocky and made a call to the person involved to discuss issues and smooth the waters? (Taking the "blame," fully deserved or *not*, for letting an issue fester.)

44. Have you in the last . . . **two hours** . . . stopped by someone's (two-levels "down") office-workspace for five minutes to ask *"What do you think?"* about an issue that arose at a more or less just completed meeting? (And then stuck around for 10 or so minutes to listen—and *visibly* take notes?)

45. Have you . . . in the last day . . . looked around you ("eyeballed") to assess whether the diversity of the group pretty accurately mirrors the diversity of the market being served? (And began to act on the disparity, if it exists?)

46. Have you in the last day at some meeting gone out of your way to make sure that a normally reticent person has been engaged in a conversation—and then thanked him or her, perhaps privately, for his or her contribution?

47. Have you in the last four months had a half-day, full-team session specifically aimed at checking on the "corporate culture" and the degree we are true to it—with presentations by relatively junior folks, including frontline folks? (And with a determined effort to keep the conversation restricted to "real-world" "small" cases—not theory?)

48. Have you in the last six months talked about the *Internal Brand Promise*—i.e., what you and the organization promise employees in terms of respect and growth *opportunities*?

49. Have you in the last year had a full-day off-site to talk about individual (and group) aspirations?

50. Have you called a customer ... today?

> **HAVE YOU . . . STARTED?**

Obviously I hope you'll use this list. Perhaps as follows:

1. Circulate it to your team.

2. Agree on no more than a half-dozen items to act as a Starter Action List.

3. Pick one item.

4. Do it today.

5. Repeat once a week.

NB: Obviously, this list is meant to be suggestive, not definitive. You can develop your own, tailored to your situation. The "big idea"—which animates this book—is to go after these "small things" that collectively are the heart and soul and guts of an effective organization devoted to "Excellence in all we do."

1. 2. 3. 4. 5. 6. 7. 8. 9. 10. 11. 12. 13. 14.
15. 16. 17. 18. 19. 20. 21. 22. 23. 24. 25.
26. 27. 28. 29. 30. 31. 32. 33. 34. 35.
36. 37. 38. 39. 40. 41. 42. 43. 44. 45.
46. 47. 48. 49. 50. 51. 52. 53. 54. 55. 56.
57. 58. 59. 60. 61. 62. 63. 64. 65. 66. 67.
68. 69. 70. 71. 72. 73. 74. 75. 76. 77. 78.
79. 80. 81. 82. 83. 84. 85. 86. 87. 88.
89. 90. 91. 92. 93. 94. 95. 96. 97. 98. 99.
100. 101. 102. 103. 104. 105. 106. 107.
108. 109. 110. 111. 112. 113. 114. 115.
116. 117. 118. 119. 120. 121. 122. 123.
124. 125. 126. 127. 128. 129. 130. 131.
132. 133. 134. 135. 136. 137. 138. 139.
140. 141. 142. 143. **144. 145. 146. 147.**
148. 149. 150. 151. 152. 153. 154. 155.
156. 157. 158. 159. 160. 161. 162. 163.

Re-imagining

144. Create a "Cathedral"! (If Not, What?)

I was asked to keynote the first major conference, organized by the Australian Institute of Management, honoring the life's work of Peter Drucker. I felt an enormous responsibility—and allowed my imagination to soar on the topic of organizing fundamentals. I began with a bare-bones definition. Organizations should be . . .

. . . no less than cathedrals in which the full and awesome power of the Imagination and Spirit and native Entrepreneurial Flair of diverse individuals is unleashed in passionate pursuit of . . . Excellence.

"Cathedral/s" is a Big Word. My usage is not intended to be religious in any formal sense—hence the lowercase "c." But, in terms of human potential (quasi-religious?), I do see all effective organizations as driven . . . **first and foremost** . . . by an Unstinting Commitment to Members' Growth.

A classroom in a primary school should . . . **obviously** . . . be such a "cathedral." But so, too, an *accounting* or *training* department. No doubt of it: Organizations must effectively serve their external customers to survive, let alone thrive. But my line of logic is, at least to me, crystal clear and admits no alternatives:

We cannot expect Excellent and Imaginative and Energetic Service to be routinely provided to our Customers *unless* our frontline employees (with customer contact and in support functions) who provide that superior service are themselves engaged in a Vigorous Personal Quest for Growth and Excellence.

I don't, as I've said several times before, ask you to "buy my act." I do ask you to think about it—and the consequences **(enormous!)** thereof.

Is, in fact, your unit of any size . . .

". . . no less than a cathedral in which the full and awesome power of the Imagination and Spirit and native Entrepreneurial Flair of diverse individuals is unleashed in passionate pursuit of . . . Excellence"?

And if it is not, or if that or something akin thereto is not the aim, then tell me what the alternative is.

Please.

Cathedral.
Imagination.
Spirit.
Entrepreneurial flair.
Diverse.
Passion.
Excellence.

Or???????

(NB: This challenge—organization as cathedral devoted to human development—is simply gargantuan. And one I thought about—a lot—before issuing. And by now I've tested the idea all over the world—from Dubai to Shanghai to New Delhi to Helsinki to Joinville, Brazil, to San Antonio, Texas. In sit-down discussions there is agreement that "If not this, what?" is, in fact, a sane question—at least worthy of serious conversation. I am wholeheartedly convinced that something like this makes commercial sense.)

To "get started" in this instance is largely cerebral—talking it through with colleagues at work, with friends in small and large businesses of your acquaintance. You can make assessments of businesses close to home: One community bank plays it this way—and another doesn't. Or auto body shop A vs. auto body shop B. While doing some positive "people stuff" is good, this is of a whole other order of affairs; this is indeed a commitment to building and maintaining no less than a "cathedral."

Are.
You.
Up.
For.
It.

(And, I repeat, if *not*, what's the alternative?)

145. Enable Dreams. (If Not, What?)

Matthew Kelly's parable-based *The Dream Manager* is not ordinarily my kind of book. But Kelly's premise got to me—and it has become a centerpiece of my work. The idea is simple: *Everyone* has a dream! And if we can help him and her fulfill those dreams, then he and she will be more engaged human beings—which will, practically speaking, pay off for the organization as it strives to serve its customers. Kelly writes:

"A company's purpose is to become the-best-version-of-itself. [But] an organization can only become the-best-version-of-itself to the extent that the people who drive that organization are striving to become better-versions-of-themselves."

When you ponder that (slowly, very slowly, please!), it is both obvious and profound: "We," the team, is only as good as the engagement and commitment to *personal* growth and achievement and Excellence by each and every individual. (Obvious in football and dance—why not groceries and the accounting office?) "The question is," Kelly continues, "What is an employee's purpose? Most would say, 'to help the company achieve its purpose'—but they would be wrong. [Ponder, slowly, again.] That is certainly part of the employee's role, but an employee's primary purpose is to become the-best-version-of-himself or herself."

As stated, the book title is *Dream Manager*. In fact, Kelly asserts that explicitly helping people achieve their dreams—directly business related or not—is *a*, or even *the*, primary task a boss has. The boss, to both serve her customer or get things done in general, becomes a "dream enabler"—e.g., works with the 28-year-old maintenance man from Ghana to achieve his dream of a junior college degree. To repeat the chain of logic: If that 28-year-old feels wholly supported in his personal-growth dream, odds of his aspiring to do and doing his maintenance-man job with Excellence become very high.

So . . . are you?
That is, are you **(explicitly)** a "dream enabler"?

(Or, to start, do you *know* what your employees' dreams are?)

> **LEAD, FOLLOW, AND GET OUT OF THE WAY**

Our goal is to serve our customers brilliantly and profitably over the long haul.

Serving our customers brilliantly and profitably over the long haul is a product of brilliantly serving over the long haul the people who serve the customer.

Hence, our job as leaders—the alpha and the omega and everything in between—is abetting the sustained growth and success and engagement and enthusiasm and commitment to Excellence of those, one at a time, who directly or indirectly serve the ultimate customer.

We—leaders of every stripe—are in the "Human Growth and Development and Success and Aspiration to Excellence business."

"We" [*leaders*] **only grow when "they"** [*each and every one of our colleagues*] **are growing.**

"We" [*leaders*] **only succeed when "they"** [*each and every one of our colleagues*] **are succeeding.**

"We" [*leaders*] **only energetically march toward Excellence when "they"** [*each and every one of our colleagues*] **are energetically marching toward Excellence.**

Period.

146. Launch "Project Ray."

I very rarely "dedicate" a presentation. But a while back I launched a presentation with a PowerPoint slide that read . . . **"For Ray."**

As in: Ray Charles.

Susan and I had just watched the movie *Ray* on DVD. To be sure, it is a superb piece of work. However, the inspiration for the dedication of the presentation was not the Excellence of the film, but rather that of its subject.

In short:

Ray Charles is the embodiment of the Spirit of Re-imagining!

Time and time—**and time**—again he chose to Invent & Go His Own Way, to spit in the face of the sure thing, the assured cash flow, the powerful advisers . . . and instead march in the brand-new musical direction his Spirit willed him to march.

To be sure, the movie is an extraordinary story of overcoming adversity, from blindness to racism to drugs to fame itself. But for me it was, above all, a . . . **Matchless Tribute to the Power & Glory of Gutsy, Lonely Re-imaginings!**

To Ray Charles!

Watch *Ray*.
(Perhaps with close colleagues.)
If you are inclined, make a detailed chart of his Re-imaginings.
(I suspect they will stagger you!)

Start a "Ray File" . . . or a "Re-imaginings File."
Scribble musings about your own possible Re-imagining.

Cut out pictures.
Save blog posts.

The "problem" is so so so so so easy to state. We're already scoring 12-hour days—and keeping up is a nightmare. There's no "extra time" for . . . Project Ray! However (trust me on this one): Odds are high, very high, that if you could project forward 10 years, you'd wonder why the hell there was no . . .

Project Ray.2010.

Or, maybe, to use the designation of the times . . . **You 3.0.**

(There *is* time for Project Ray.2010/You 3.0, for the simple reason that there's not *not* time.)
(I am not the first person who's told you this.)
(I will not be the last person who tells you this.)
(But I am right.)
(And the next person who tells you will be right.)
(And maybe, just maybe, you will be spurred to action.)
(And, win *or* lose, you will be glad you were spurred to action.)

(Time flies.)
(Believe it.)

147. Realism? Not on My Watch!

Assertion:

Realism is the death of progress!
Stomp out realism!
More or less!

We recently finished a summer building project on our Vermont farm. We did our levelheaded best to budget it correctly—getting contractors to rework estimates and redesigning accordingly. (And, hey, I was trained as a construction engineer.) All that said, it looks like the carefully considered $40,000 project will come in at about $70,000. (Um, or so.)

What's new?

The Big Dig in Boston came in about four times over budget, as I recall. For the Chunnel, I think it was about three times plan. (Etc. Etc. Etc. Etc.)

I decided to do a little casual research at a dinner party, asking several people about their homebrew projects. Three questions:

(1) How did you do vs. budget for projects completed a couple of years ago?

(2) If you'd known the real price tag when you started, would you have gone ahead?

(3) In hindsight, was the eventual price tag worth it?

To Q1, the answer ranged from about 5 percent over plan (if you can believe it—I'm skeptical) to five times plan (which I *do* believe).

As to Q2, four of the six I queried said "no way" would they have started if they'd known what they were getting into—the other two were on the fence.

Concerning Q3, after-the-fact satisfaction, five said, in effect, "Yes! We'd do it again"—all five of those five "yups" were dogmatic that, **"Yes,"** they would do it again. And one said, "Maybe, maybe not."

It's obviously dangerous to extrapolate from such a tiny sample and trivial topic, but my reading of history, business, and in general says this phenomenon is as ordinary as it gets. Furthermore, in the back of one's mind, one damn well *knows* that the price tag will be far in excess of what's planned.

And my point? Yes, you'd better have a superb number-crunching CFO, but if you let him-her rule the roost, there won't be much left to roost on. Of course I know it's "Damned if you do, damned if you don't." On the other hand . . .

Progress (all progress) clearly hinges on illusion and delusion!

As for me, the Cornell master's degree holder in construction engineering, I'd vote yes in hindsight for every one of my major home projects—even if, as is true, paying for them has added in a nontrivial way to my speechifying "nights on the road" tally.

Cherish your dreamers!
Master "dreamer nurturing."

Practical translation:
Do you insist that every project team, even a small one, has an "unrealistic" dreamer on board?
Do you, as boss, make sure that as you necessarily hold the dreamer's toes to the fire, you stop short of putting out her or his fire?

Bottom line: **2.476 (range, 2.218 to 2.886) hearty cheers for dreamers' fantasies! Screw it . . . THREE hearty cheers for those dreamers and their fantasies,* lose or win, dead or alive.**

(*My opinion? A fantasy pursued **is** a "win"—100 percent of the time.)

1. 2. 3. 4. 5. 6. 7. 8. 9. 10. 11. 12. 13. 14.
15. 16. 17. 18. 19. 20. 21. 22. 23. 24. 25.
26. 27. 28. 29. 30. 31. 32. 33. 34. 35.
36. 37. 38. 39. 40. 41. 42. 43. 44. 45.
46. 47. 48. 49. 50. 51. 52. 53. 54. 55. 56.
57. 58. 59. 60. 61. 62. 63. 64. 65. 66. 67.
68. 69. 70. 71. 72. 73. 74. 75. 76. 77. 78.
79. 80. 81. 82. 83. 84. 85. 86. 87. 88.
89. 90. 91. 92. 93. 94. 95. 96. 97. 98. 99.
100. 101. 102. 103. 104. 105. 106. 107.
108. 109. 110. 111. 112. 113. 114. 115.
116. 117. 118. 119. 120. 121. 122. 123.
124. 125. 126. 127. 128. 129. 130. 131.
132. 133. 134. 135. 136. 137. 138. 139.
140. 141. 142. 143. 144. 145. 146. 147.
148. 149. 150. 151. 152. 153. 154. 155.
156. 157. 158. 159. 160. 161. 162. 163.

WOW

148. If No WOW, Then . . . No Go.

Does "it" Pop?
Does "it" Sparkle?
Does "it" make you Grin?

Is "it" . . . **Wow?**

If "it" (grand or mundane) isn't WOW . . . redo it!
Or don't do it!

This is . . . Your Day.
Not "their" day.

This Day belongs . . . ULTIMATELY . . . to You.
Not "them."

Cubicle slaves unite!
Technicolor Titans rejoice!
Throw off the Shackles of Conformity!

Just say/shout a throaty "No!" to Non-WOW!

So . . .

WOW!
Now!

No bull.
This *is* doable.

(I own no rose-colored glasses. Few 67-year-olds do. I have crappy days—and crappy months. And, for that matter, crappy years. And, alas, I give lousy speeches—or, at least, not-so-great ones. But I am unable, in *anything* I do, to be satisfied with less than an 8 on the 1-to-10 WOW-o-meter. That's as true for the brush-cutting micro-project I do most every day in summer on my Vermont farm as it is for the speeches-for-profit . . . and this book. Why not WOW-as-"ordinary"-goal????)

Yes.
This is . . . **your** . . . life.
This is . . . **your** . . . moment.

▶ NOW YOU'RE COOKING!

Think about WOW/non-WOW in apparently trivial terms: Odds are reasonably high you'll cook dinner tonight. And odds are you're tired; among other things, you had a fight with your piss-head boss this afternoon. And besides, your significant other is rarely appreciative of your culinary efforts on those occasions that you do bust your back. So you heat up a can of chili. (I *love* canned chili.)

Or you can stretch. And if you do stretch, even just a couple of times a week, even once a week, odds are very high you'll become a pretty damn good cook, and terrific meals will become a centerpiece of your relationship with your significant other. And the more you follow the virtuous circle, the more you'll enjoy screwing around with your cooking and the more . . .

Fact is, guaranteed, the world will be a different place a year from now, thanks to spicing up a routine activity with a few tablespoons of Wow. That's WOW in a nutshell. (Although I do, as I said, love canned chili.)

149. What Makes You So Special?—Or: "Only" Beats "Best."

I guarantee that any reader—from anywhere, in any business—can learn something from the following book:

Retail Superstars: Inside the 25 Best Independent Stores in America, by retail guru George Whalin.

Guarantee?
Yup!

These are stores that, literally, give new meaning to the words "special"—and "Gaspworthy" & "WOW"! That personify one of my "Top 10 Favorite Quotes," from Jerry Garcia (The Grateful Dead):

"You don't want to be merely the best of the best. You want to be the only ones who do what you do."

Retail Superstars begins, naturally (**!**), in Fairfield, Ohio, home to Jungle Jim's International Market. The adventure in *"shoppertainment,"* as Jungle Jim's calls it, begins in the parking lot and goes on to 1,600 cheeses and, yes, 1,400 varieties of hot sauce—not to mention 12,000 wines priced from $8 to $8,000 a bottle; all this is brought to you by 4,000 vendors from around the world. Like virtually all the stores in this book, customers flock to the doors from every corner of the globe.

There's Abt Electronics in Chicago, Zabar's in Manhattan, and Bronner's Christmas Wonderland in Frakenmuth, Michigan—a town of just 5,000. Bronner's 98,000-square-foot "shop" features the likes of **6,000** Christmas ornaments, **50,000** trims, and anything else you can name if it pertains to Christmas.

There's the Ron Jon Surf Shop in Cocoa Beach, Florida.
And Junkman's Daughter in Atlanta.
And Smoky Mountain Knife Works in Sevierville, Tennessee.

We finish the tour where we started—in Ohio. This time we visit Hartville Hardware in Hartville, Ohio.

These stores demonstrate-prove so many things:

You can create a worldwide attraction and thrive as an independent in the Age of the Big-Box Retailer!
You can do anything!
You can be from anywhere!
You can make *anything* . . . **bizarrely-amazingly-stupendously special!**

"Customer care" finds a new definition!
"Showmanship" finds a new definition!

If you run a *training* department . . . you can learn from this book.
If you run a *sales* department of 1 or 101 people . . . you can learn from this book.
If you run a *purchasing* department . . . **dedicated to "bizarrely-amazingly-stupendously-**

special" internal customer care . . . you can learn from this book.

You can learn about . . . *Special.*
You can learn about being . . . *"the only ones who do what we do."*
You can learn about . . . *"experience marketing."*
You can learn about . . . the *irrelevance* of Supersized Competitors . . . if you are special enough.
You can learn about . . . *Sustaining EXCELLENCE.*

Inside the 25 Best Independent Stores in America gives new meaning to my trademark phrase:

EXCELLENCE. Always.
If Not EXCELLENCE, What?
If Not EXCELLENCE Now, When?

As I said, with such outrageous self-certainty: I *guarantee* that any reader engaged in any activity, who wants to, can learn from this book.* (*And you really should visit some of these stores—call it a Tour of Excellence.)

So:

Is your product or service offering . . .
Special?
So . . . **bloody damned special** . . . it takes your and your customers' "breath away"?

Live the super-amazing-incredible-WOW-only-ones-who-do-what-we-do FLAVOR of SPECIAL.
(Or die—professionally—trying.)
(Why not!)

❯ **WOW AS LEGITIMATE ASPIRATION: MY EXCELLENT ADVENTURE**

"They" say WOW! is "too much." Life is pretty ordinary from day to day. Perhaps that's true—but the "impossible" is true, too. In my short six-decade visit to the planet, a few monumental things that couldn't possibly happen did in fact happen:

- Hitler and Tojo were defeated; and the defeated nations became great democracies and great economic powers. (I was born the day American soldiers landed in North Africa.)

- India gained its independence and became the world's largest democracy—and eventually started on the path toward economic preeminence.

- China's peasants revolted—and 35 years later embraced capitalism.

- Europe became a huge and shining symbol of peace and prosperity and democracy after centuries of being earth's bloodiest real estate.

- Though the path was and is bumpy and setbacks have occurred, various flavors of democracy bloomed around the world.

- African Americans saw the Civil Rights Movement achieve breakthrough after breakthrough—and an African American became President of the United States.

- The Berlin Wall was erected—and 30 years later, to the surprise of almost all, fell virtually overnight.

- Nelson Mandela was jailed and persevered and was freed and forgave and became President of post-apartheid South Africa—with virtually no bloodshed.

- Yuri Gagarin traveled into outer space.

- Neal Armstrong set foot on the moon.

- The sky became filled with satellites—transforming communication.

- Computers, generation after generation after generation, changed effectively everything.

- The cell phone changed our basic way of communicating.

- The Internet changed our basic forms of communication—and much, much else.

- Numerous diseases were conquered—and many were contained.

- An organ was successfully transplanted.

- America made peaceful transition after peaceful transition after peaceful transition as the presidency changed hands, from political party to political party.

Each adventure above required traveling a long, long road—with potholes galore. But the "impossible" did become possible and then reality . . . again and again and again and again.

"Wow" as "too much"?

Shame on you.

Think again.

150. Is It "Gaspworthy"?

Will your plan for addressing today's "mundane" task make others "gasp" at its audacity?

As an alumnus of McKinsey and Co., I received an email from the firm in 2004 reporting its response to the tsunami in Southeast Asia. I read it, nodded, and cast it aside. (But did not "delete" for some unknown reason.) I returned to it a few hours later—and was moved to send McKinsey's managing partner an email. I said that the response was "perfectly adequate," but I added that business has a tawdry rep these days (and that was *before* the financial meltdown), and that McKinsey is viewed far and wide as the home of the premier Counselors to Global Top Management; so, I chided, I saw it as a missed opportunity in that McKinsey's response failed to . . .

"make me gasp by its audacity."

No surprise, I got no response from McKinsey's top dog. But I also copied my old McKinsey pal and *In Search of Excellence* coauthor, Bob Waterman—who offered his hearty support. (Thanks, as always, Bob.)

Forget McKinsey. The Bigger Point is that in our "responses" to tragedy and opportunity alike, "good enough" is a less than scintillating way to pass through life.

How about, instead, as aspiration, my cobbled-together term . . .

"gaspworthy"?

So, does your response to today's principal "chore" qualify for a . . . Medal of Certified Gaspworthiness?

(Surely, you say, I [Tom] live in the land of make-believe. There's a lot of stuff that just needs doing—and need not produce a "gasp." I acknowledge that's apparently true, and indeed the default state of nature. Yet this book is mostly dedicated to the idea of little things that aren't in fact little at all—so-called "little things" that are in actual fact "gaspworthy." They range from Singapore's two-cent candies at the incoming immigration desk (#131) to the power of a "simple" "Thank you." These "small acts," consciously considered, are, collectively, the difference between success and failure at anything from waiting tables to running for President of the United States. In short, I sincerely believe that damn near anything can be made . . . "gaspworthy.")

When in doubt, make your default position the Steve Jobs Standard. Ask: How does your, say, project score on a scale topped by his . . .

"Insanely Great!"

Well, is it?

> **BEAMER POETRY**

From a BMW print ad, September 2009:

Joy

On the back of this three-letter word we built a company.

Independent of Everyone.

Accountable to no-one but the driver.

We don't just build cars.

We are the creators of emotion.

We are the guardians of ecstasy, the thrills and chills,

The laughs and smiles and all the words that can't be found in the dictionary.

We are the joy of driving.

No car company can rival our history.

Replicate our passion, our vision.

Innovation is our backbone, but Joy is our heart.

We will not stray from our three-letter purpose. We will nurture it.

We will make Joy smarter. We will push it, test it, break it—then build it again.

More efficient, more dynamic.

We will give the world the keys to Joy and they will take it for a drive.

And while others try to promise everything, we promise one thing.

The most personal, cherished and human of all emotions.

This is the story of BMW.

This is the story of Joy.

So can you match that in describing your process reengineering project?

151. Extremism in the Defense of WOW Is No Vice.

Corporations are falling like dominoes. Chief executives are getting the axe at a record pace. Why? Incremental solutions in discontinuous times seldom, if ever, work.

The axiom applies to a great enterprise and to a tiny two-person accountancy alike. And to me. And to you. Take a look at Tomorrow's Calendar. Today's, for that matter. Find and underscore something—**anything**—on that calendar that represents a small step toward something extreme. Something big. Something monumental. (And worry like hell if there's nothing!)

Ask yourself how you're going to take your "portfolio" to the next level . . . and the level after that. For starters, perhaps:

- "Do" lunch sometime this week with a potentially important/ interesting new friend/colleague.
- Revise a project—today!—to increase its novelty. Then take the first new step—today! Ask yourself, **"Can I imagine talking about this project—to a prospective employer or Client—two years from now?"** If the odds seem low, keep revising that project prospectus.
- Launch a Society of Radicals—an informal group that assesses one another's projects in terms of their audacity.

Bottom line: Never let your portfolio of prospective tasks become the home to bland, blander, blandest!

› FILE AWAY THIS IDEA . . .

The "portfolio" idea is quite powerful. Your set of 10 most recent assignments (discrete, identifiable projects with readily describable outcomes) is a "portfolio." Your current list of five active projects is a portfolio—just like the slide set of her work that a painter sends off to a gallery owner or director. "Manage" that portfolio. For example, make sure that every project sparkles—when it comes to execution. But also make sure that one drags your learning in a very new direction. Make sure one or two really push the limit—as described immediately above. Make sure that every project in the portfolio includes at least something "remarkable."

So . . .

Take the "portfolio idea" literally and seriously.

Review your portfolio with a friend—or your boss. Craft it to maximize your selfish (growth) ends and your selfless (maximum contribution to the group) ends.

If you're a boss, use employee Project Portfolios as a primary resource allocation and execution tool.

1. 2. 3. 4. 5. 6. 7. 8. 9. 10. 11. 12. 13. 14.

15. 16. 17. 18. 19. 20. 21. 22. 23. 24. 25.

26. 27. 28. 29. 30. 31. 32. 33. 34. 35.

36. 37. 38. 39. 40. 41. 42. 43. 44. 45.

46. 47. 48. 49. 50. 51. 52. 53. 54. 55. 56.

57. 58. 59. 60. 61. 62. 63. 64. 65. 66. 67.

68. 69. 70. 71. 72. 73. 74. 75. 76. 77. 78.

79. 80. 81. 82. 83. 84. 85. 86. 87. 88.

89. 90. 91. 92. 93. 94. 95. 96. 97. 98. 99.

100. 101. 102. 103. 104. 105. 106. 107.

108. 109. 110. 111. 112. 113. 114. 115.

116. 117. 118. 119. 120. 121. 122. 123.

124. 125. 126. 127. 128. 129. 130. 131.

132. 133. 134. 135. 136. 137. 138. 139.

140. 141. 142. 143. 144. 145. 146. 147.

148. 149. 150. 151. **152. 153. 154.** 155.

156. 157. 158. 159. 160. 161. 162. 163.

Now

152. Welcome to the Age of Metabolic Management.

We all know the fabled race eventually goes to the Tortoise. Well, times change, Google-speed or Alibaba-speed is the new limit (until the record is broken, which it will be soon enough), and we are now officially living in the Age of the Hare.

Period.

As Larry Light, McDonald's Global Chief Marketing Officer, put it in *Advertising Age*: **"Today, you own ideas for about an hour and a half."**

My "moniker" for dealing with and thriving in the Age of the Hare is . . .

Metabolic Management.

I believe it's one of the boss's . . . *prime tasks* . . . to Purposefully and Consciously and Perpetually work on Accelerating the Corporate (project team, etc.) Metabolism.

How can you pump up your Corporate Metabolism? Some thoughts:

- Exhibit personal urgency . . . *hourly-daily-consciously.*
- Hire for it. *(My car dealer pal Carl Sewell says he looks for antsy people "who literally can't sit still" during an interview. One well-known headhunter takes candidates to lunch in Manhattan—and frowns if they don't jaywalk.)*
- Promote it.
- Reward it. *("Speed Demon of the Week" recognition at the Monday Morning Huddle.)*
- Lavish visible rewards on people . . . *who voluntarily drop what they're doing to help others make deadline* . . . even if the others are largely responsible for their plight.
- Display perpetual . . . **fanaticism** . . . about simplifying processes—and keeping them simple and not allowing them to grow barnacles. **(Simplification = Speed.)** *(You need, literally, a CSO—Chief Simplification Officer.)*
- Display perpetual . . . fanaticism . . . about friction-free cross-functional coordination. *(Reward and promote those who "get it." Demote or detach those who don't.) (Cross-functional friction is . . . always . . . "Speed Issue" #1.)*
- Measure & Measure & Measure. (Highly visible measures, broadly published.)
- Put speed *per se* on meeting agendas.
- Set aggressive targets—forget "incrementalism," go after a **75 percent or 95 percent or 98 percent** reduction in the time it takes to do X or Y or Z. *(Bold targets inspire—and are indeed possible in Speed World. In fact, I suggest something like never accepting a "speed up" suggestion of less than 50 percent.)*

⋗ CALL YOUR "SPEED" BROKER

Consider Progressive Insurance, one of my favorite High Metabolic Rate companies:

- "[CEO Peter] Lewis has created an organization filled with sharp, type-A personalities who are encouraged to take risks—even if that sometimes leads to mistakes."

- **"One thing that we've noticed is that they've always been very good at avoiding denial. They react quickly to changes in the marketplace."**
  —Keith Trauner, portfolio manager who follows Progressive

- "When four successive hurricanes hit Florida and neighboring states in August and September [2004], Progressive sent more than 1,000 claims adjusters to the Southeast. Result: 80 percent of 21,000 filed claims had been paid by mid-October, an impressive figure. This pleased policy holders and probably helped Progressive because delays in claims payments typically mean higher costs."

- And . . . my favorite Lewis-ism: **"We don't sell insurance anymore. We sell speed."**

153. Walls of "Yesterdays." Walls of "Tomorrows."

What do your walls look like?
Do they look like "yesterday"?
Or do they look like "tomorrow"?

Yesterday = Plaques from past awards and group pictures from past parties. Etc. Etc.

Tomorrow = Work-in-Progress pictures for ongoing projects. Interesting press clips on new products just launched. Customers landed or vendors signed up in the last 30 days. Six new hires who reported in the last 30 days. Etc. Etc.

Obviously, one is delighted with those great awards, and I'm hardly suggesting that they be tossed in the ash can. It's the "spin" I'm interested in—what does the outsider or, say, a new employee see? A museum? Reverence for the past? Or inklings of an exciting future? In my case, do I have covers of old books on the walls? Or the mocked-up cover of this book? The premier slot should go to this book—right?

(NB: This idea is de facto stolen from Steve Jobs. When he returned to Apple from the wilderness in 1997, one of his first acts was to remove all traces of old glory from his office and Apple facilities in general. He felt the product line he inherited was unscintillating, and he wanted the affect of the place to reflect work in progress, not icons of yesteryear.)

154. Pissing Away Your Life: Like It or Not, Work *Is* Life!

Some say I use words like **"Wow"** tooooooooooooooooooo much. "You damn well can't," they say, "turn every 'day at the office' into some 'Adventure in EXCELLENCE.'"

Well, "they" have a point—to a point.
But it ain't much of a point.

Let me be crude, rude, and short but not sweet.

Let's do no more than a simple calculation:

By the time you're nearing 30, let's say, the stay-up-every-night-'til-2:00-A.M. era is pretty much behind you. So, let's say you awaken on average at 6:30 A.M. . . . and turn in around 11:00 P.M. (More or less.) That's 16.5 waking hours—call it 17. You just plain lose, say, two hours a day—a little over one hour on your two-way commute, and 45 minutes on whatever. So now we're at 15 "usable" hours.

Suppose your ordinary workday is 8:15 A.M. to 5:30 P.M.—that seems about right to me. (I'm not citing research here, other than years and years of casual observation.) So the workday amounts to 9.25 hours—or 8.75 when lunch is subtracted.

Which is to say, you are spending, Monday through Friday, about 8.75/15ths . . . or **60 percent** . . . of your usable hours at work.

Which means . . . *if you piss away your work time, you're pissing away well over half your "conscious" "life."*

That's one helluva penalty to pay if you are dogging it at work, doing the minimum, and not turning the workday into any kind of a growth (or high-achievement) experience.

Well, no, I don't think you're going to score a "Wow" on every project.

Or hit the "perfect 10" on the Excellence scale.

But I do suggest that if you aren't pretty regularly pursuing something like "Wow," or Excellence, with your work, you are well and truly . . .

Pissing over half your life away.

(No matter how I do the calculations, I can't come up with any other answer.)

1. 2. 3. 4. 5. 6. 7. 8. 9. 10. 11. 12. 13. 14.
15. 16. 17. 18. 19. 20. 21. 22. 23. 24. 25.
26. 27. 28. 29. 30. 31. 32. 33. 34. 35.
36. 37. 38. 39. 40. 41. 42. 43. 44. 45.
46. 47. 48. 49. 50. 51. 52. 53. 54. 55. 56.
57. 58. 59. 60. 61. 62. 63. 64. 65. 66. 67.
68. 69. 70. 71. 72. 73. 74. 75. 76. 77. 78.
79. 80. 81. 82. 83. 84. 85. 86. 87. 88.
89. 90. 91. 92. 93. 94. 95. 96. 97. 98. 99.
100. 101. 102. 103. 104. 105. 106. 107.
108. 109. 110. 111. 112. 113. 114. 115.
116. 117. 118. 119. 120. 121. 122. 123.
124. 125. 126. 127. 128. 129. 130. 131.
132. 133. 134. 135. 136. 137. 138. 139.
140. 141. 142. 143. 144. 145. 146. 147.
148. 149. 150. 151. 152. 153. 154. **155.**
156. 157. 158. 159. 160. 161. 162. 163.

Impact

155. Forget Longevity— Think "Dramatic Frenzy."

I occasionally speed-walk while listening to one or another of the Reverend Martin Luther King's most prominent speeches. I do so for reasons spiritual as well as, frankly, professional. No declamations, including Churchill's, are so moving. (And I listen to a lot of speeches . . .)

I could easily expend 5,000 words on the details of Dr. King's speaking Excellence—from the emotion to the brevity to the excruciating slow build to the storytelling to the matchless use of alliteration to the urgent call to action to the shaming of those supporters who would sit on the sidelines and not act. One of King's most extraordinary speeches took place in Memphis, immediately before he was assassinated. In it, he anticipates the tragic event. I stopped and listened to a brief section three or four times, scribbling as I did:

"Well, I don't know what will happen now. We've got some difficult days ahead. But it really doesn't matter with me now. Because I've been to the mountaintop. And I don't mind. Like anybody, I would like to live a long life. Longevity has its place, but I'm not concerned about that now. I just want to do God's will. And He's allowed me to go up to the mountain. And I've looked over. And I've seen the Promised Land. I may not

get there with you. But I want you to know tonight, that we, as a people, will get to the Promised Land. So I'm happy, tonight. I'm not worried about anything. I'm not fearing any man. Mine eyes have seen the glory of the coming of the Lord."

I get chills . . . again . . . as I write this—and I am loath to trivialize it, but I want to make another point.

"Longevity has its place, but I'm not concerned about that now . . ."

I simply don't buy "built to last" in any way, shape, or form—and this passage reinforced that abiding belief. **"Built to Impact"** is/has been/will be my Rallying Cry. Dr. King changed the world—and died at 39.

To continue the trivializing of Dr. King's words, here's my business translation: Netscape is my favorite company. Netscape was born, changed the world . . . and died, at about age six. I am desperately trying to change the world in some ever so wee way; I have but a few years left to do so, and I have purposefully chosen not to create any "institution" to attempt to move my case forward when I'm gone; the world will take care of spreading the ideas I care about (or not!) without me. I frankly don't give two hoots about longevity. I've done what I can and what I care about as well and as hard and as loudly as I can. And that's what I'll keep doing as long as the breaths keep coming.

And that's that.

I have utterly no interest in longevity.

Kjell Nordström and Jonas Ridderstråle make this point particularly well in *Funky Business:* "But what if [former head of strategic planning at Royal Dutch Shell] Arie De Geus is wrong in suggesting, in *The Living Company,* that firms should aspire to live forever? Greatness is fleeting and, for corporations, it will become ever more fleeting. **The ultimate aim of a business organiza-**

**tion, an artist, an athlete, or a stockbro-
ker may be to . . . explode in a dramatic
frenzy of value creation during a short
space of time, rather than live forever."**

Progress, to my mind, and doubtless significantly influenced by
a quarter century's residence in Silicon Valley, is a series of such
explosions—many, many duds and a few, like Apple or Netscape or
Google, that change the world. Bravo.

One last expression of this idea, from Simone de Beauvoir: "Life is
occupied in both perpetuating itself and in surpassing itself; if all it
does is maintain itself, then living is only not dying."

Again:

"I may not get there with you [but] mine eyes have seen the glory . . ."
—King

"Explode in a Dramatic Frenzy of Value Creation."
—Nordström and Ridderstråle

"If all it does is maintain itself, then living is only not dying."
—de Beauvoir

Does "dramatic frenzy of value creation" sound too exotic?
Impractical?
I think not.
(And for your sake, I hope not.)

Right now: Ask yourself and your mates . . .

How can we alter our current project to approach/encompass the
idea of "dramatic frenzy of value creation"? How do we make sure that
on some dimension or dimensions the project aims to make a break

from conventional practice—even from identified "best practices"? Would an outsider, who knows our turf in general, read our project description as it is at the moment, then reread part of it, and say, "Now that thing you're talking about trying in the hiring interviews, now that's new to me. Hmmm, very interesting. Yeah, interesting, interesting . . ."

I contend that this is a v-e-r-y **practical** idea. I contend that it is practical in that if you *don't* attempt to do such a thing, I'll *guarantee* that your eyes will not see the glory—but might well see the unemployment or "outsourced" line.

"Long-term" success? I'd take the years of 1994–1998 at Netscape over any damned alternate you can name!

▶ IN "MESS," THERE IS A MESSAGE

The famed Austrian economist Joseph Schumpeter claimed that economies advance via . . . **"the gales of creative destruction."**

Free-market Nobel laureate F. A. Hayek described capitalistic creativity, the essence of progress, as a . . . **"spontaneous discovery process."**

Urban economist Jane Jacobs (*The Death and Life of Great American Cities*) said vital cities have a rich mix of commercial and residential spaces cheek by jowl; she called the mix at its best . . . **"exuberant variety."**

Progress, per the likes of Schumpeter-Hayek-Jacobs, comes directly from the boiling, seething mess. The instability per se is the key. I not only wholeheartedly agree, but I also think "exuberant variety" as "corporate culture," or even *"departmental* culture," is the key to organic growth, success—and attracting and retaining vigorous, restless talent bent upon frenzies of value creation.

156. How About Replacing Your "Wish It Were" List with a "Do It Now" List?

"I can't wait until spring."

"I can't wait until football season!"

"I can't wait until I've finished preparing this damn presentation."

"I can't wait until So-and-So makes up his mind, so that we can get moving."

Fact is, we say this kind of thing a lot.

Yuck!

Bad!

Awful!

Horrifying!

Your correspondent (me) has reached the Sweet 16 mark . . . whoops, make that the BIG 67. And since I don't expect to live to 134, I can say with assurance that I'm playing in the second half. And therefore I refuse to allow myself to fall into the "I wish it were next Wednesday" trap—even though I often more or less do.

I have at least disciplined myself to the point of giving myself a verbal slap in the face when the "can't wait until . . ." thought crosses my mind.

One does, reasonably, wish the surgery were over, that final exams were past, that his/her daughter would get back from Iraq. Nonetheless, and I'm no Zen practitioner, the goal, as in *the* goal, is always, as in always, to make the absolute most of the moment—because, to state the obvious but often ignored-in-practice truism, *the* moment, *this* moment, is the *only* damn thing we ever have.

And it is absolutely positively as true at 27 or 37 or 47 or 57 as it is at 67.

I am *still* not very good at maintaining this perspective—and often "wish this trip were over" so I can get back home. Well, I do want to be at home, but my life for the next few days is *here, not* there—and I damn well don't want to piss away a moment of it.

Neither should you.

So: How are you going to get past the "wish-it-weres," and make the next, yes, *meeting,* the next 15 minutes special? **(Please, please, ask yourself that question. Right now.)**

(I'm trained in part as a behavioral scientist—I believe that B. F. Skinner's rats in mazes have a lot to teach us. Hence I firmly believe in behavioral rituals. I believe in routinely asking myself, "Hey, Bubba, how are you going to make . . . **the next 15 minutes** . . . matter?")

The Heart of Business Strategy

We usually think of business strategy as

some sort of aspirational market-positioning statement: "We aim to be the foremost management consultancy serving middle-size technology firms in the Southwest." Or some such. Doubtless that's part of it. But I believe that the No. 1 "strategic strength" of any firm-organization is . . . "interior superiority." That is, superiority in the likes of talent recruitment and development, execution, sparkling relationships (i.e., with everyone with whom we come in contact), and in the universal desire to "relentlessly pursue . . . Excellence . . . in everything we do." Hence I humbly offer the following 51 pieces of "commonplace advice"–"reminders of the obvious" (as opposed to marketing "cleverness" or "devious 'strategic' maneuvers" or financial legerdemain) for creating a "winning" "strategy" that is inherently sustainable. Several have been included subjects of prior items. The goal here is to provide somewhat of an alpha-to-omega set, as succinctly as possible.

Herewith:

1. "Thank you." Minimum several times a day. Measure it!

The rarest (*and most powerful*) of gifts:

"Thank You!"

Recognition for contributions or support is of inestimable value in cementing relationships—and inducing future contributions and word-of-mouth support. By the way, you can practice "thank-yous"—proffering thereof is a *learnable* skill. *And* a *measurable* one.

Bottom line: This must become habit-ritual in order to be successful.

Bottom line: Measure it!

2. "Thank you," "Thank you," and "Thank you" again. "Thank all of you!"

Message: Thank everyone even peripherally involved in some activity—especially those "deep in the hierarchy." *There are no "small" acts of support.* The "real work" of organizations happens several levels below the "top." Recognition and inclusion of "support" members of a team, no matter how indirect, has multiplicative value when it comes to getting things done—perhaps *nothing* is of greater import.

3. Smile. Work on it.

Smiles change the world—think Nelson Mandela, Dwight D. Eisenhower. Their smiles kept Allies together at D-Day in Eisenhower's case (his was called "an irresistible grin") and washed hatred away to an astounding degree in Mandela's. Smiles are key to customer retention—think Starbucks. And, no joke, you *can* work on it/at it.

4. Apologize. Even if "they" are "mostly" to blame.

Apologize if you are 10 percent to blame. Or 1 percent. Apologize especially if it hurts, especially if the person you're apologizing to is an "enemy." Keep track of your efforts. "Apology power" is, literally, without peer. Accurate term: "without peer."

5. Jump all over those who play the "blame game."

And if they play it constantly, and can't let it go, then let *them* go. The blame game slows things down, savages cooperation across internal borders (all-important!!), and can sour the entire organization.

6. Hire enthusiasm.

Enthusiasm is the ultimate virus. Its power is stunning. It can and has literally moved mountains. The likes of our Transcontinental Railroad and the Panama Canal are built on the back of enthusiasm as much as hard labor. Measure this trait in hiring and promotions. As to yourself, never let it flag—especially when it's apparently "impossible" to sustain.

7. Low enthusiasm. No hire. Any job. No promotion. Ever.

Bottom line: The VERY FIRST ITEM on EVERY job criteria list shall (should) be: *"Enthusiast."*

8. Hire optimists. Everywhere.

Don't confuse a "positive outlook on life" with mindless optimism. As Harvard psychology professor Tal Ben-Shahar told *Time,* "Healthy optimism means being in touch with reality. It certainly doesn't mean being Pollyannaish and thinking everything is great and wonderful." *Time* adds, "Ben-Shahar describes realistic optimists as 'optimalists'— not those who believe everything happens for the best, but those who make the best of things that do happen."

Again, my mantra: Such "soft" traits aren't—"soft," that is. They are in fact, collectively, of the utmost "strategic" importance. Take them seriously. Make looking for them (hiring, promoting) formal practice.

9. Hiring criteria for 100 percent of jobs: Would you like to go to lunch with him-her?

We must test "personable" in every serious candidate for any and all jobs. You need not "fall in love" with a candidate, but good chemistry and "falling in like" matter. After all, it is social glue that leads to a team's success—in field hockey or HR. (And. *Repeat.* In working across functional and internal-external barriers!)

10. Hire for good manners.

If any success I've had has a singular cause, it is the obsession with good manners that my mother conveyed. I bridled then, I get down on my knees and give thanks now. (And, hey, it worked for George Washington!)

11. Do not reject "troublemakers"—that is, those who are uncomfortable (furious) with the status quo.

Hire for manners. *And hire for rude.* Pissed-off people are the prime (perhaps sole) source of innovation, small and large. There's a fine line between the chronic complainer and the entrepreneur (internal or external) aiming to fix things that bug her. The entrepreneur turns her anger into action.

12. Expose all would-be hires to something unexpected-weird. Observe their reaction.

Somehow or other we have to get a handle on *resilience*. A staged weird occurrence is admittedly a pretty lame strategy; the suggestion is just meant to raise the issue. Another possibility is looking for major glitches and setbacks during a person's voyage—and assessing the agility and strength of character exhibited in their response.

13. Overwhelming response to even the smallest screw-ups.

Overwhelm = Overwhelm! Track/measure this. Spend $$ on it. Spend time on it. Talk about it. Set an absurdly high standard for response time and intensity. Remember the Iron Law, the Holy Axiom: **The problem is rarely/never the problem. The response to the problem invariably ends up being the real problem.**

14. Perception is everything!

Engineers hate this. (And I am one.) There are a million academic studies (or at least several thousand) that measure man's irrationality. Our reaction to things is, pure and simple, emotional. I can handle a two-hour flight delay if you keep me informed—and grow furious at a 30-minute delay if you leave me in the dark. We must always—first and foremost—give thoroughgoing consideration to "perception."

Repeat the mantra: *PERCEPTION IS ALL THERE IS.*
Hint: It is.

15. **Life is theater!**

All the world *is* a stage. Every one of us *is* an actor. (100 percent of the time.) This is as true in the provision of logistics services as in running a hotel—and is the reality of the third-grade classroom and in the U.S. Army at war and focused on creating community stability in Afghanistan's remote mountain villages. "Getting" the "theater bit" is the essence of strategy. (One analyst said that the remarkable success of Pope John Paul II stemmed in part from his youthful training in theater—he used the matchless pageantry of his papacy to reignite faith around the globe.)

16. **Call a customer.**

Right now. (Stop reading this—make the call now!)

17. **Call another customer.**

Right now. (Stop reading this—make the call now!)

18. **Call an-oth-er customer.**

Right now. (Stop reading this—make the call now!)

19. **Hiring is probably the most important thing you do.**

Hiring, say some, is simply the most important thing an organization does. Hence and pure and simple, it must become an *obsession!* (We all agree it's "damned important"—but I am indeed insisting on "obsession"; and, remarkably, that is rare.) You (every leader) must pursue a de facto Ph.D. in hiring. Message (redux): You *can* become a "Very Serious Student" of such "soft stuff."

20. **Hire "weird."**

For innovation's sake and for the sake of perpetual renewal, we need a heavy dose of oddballs. "Odd," as in far from the "normal" trajectory—e.g., spent three years in the Peace Corps in Africa after university; is a sailing champion; sings in a BBC choir. Beware sameness in hiring and promoting! (And beware being unaware of said sameness—which is frequently the case.)

21. Become a student of all with whom you meet.

Nelson Mandela studied his string of Robbins Island wardens as assiduously as someone aiming to become a doctor studies anatomy. Harvey Mackay brilliantly describes the process of becoming an expert on others with whom we interact in *Swim with the Sharks Without Being Eaten Alive.* The "business" of effective leaders is first and foremost relationships. The best, like Bill Clinton, were obsessive students of people from a *very* early age. (Clinton kept notes on virtually everyone he met.) *Work* assiduously on your Ph.D. in relationships! Never go in "cold" even to the most informal of meetings—mimic Clinton, and see every contact as a "strategic" opportunity!

22. Become a student of yourself.

"To develop others," says executive coaching guru Marshall Goldsmith, "start with yourself." Sound self-absorbed? To an extent it is, but it is a cornerstone of any leader's success. Bosses, especially senior bosses, tend to be woefully ignorant about how they come across to others. E.g., Richard thinks he's maybe too easygoing; most of his colleagues think he's constantly short-tempered. Richard also thinks he's a good listener; "they" think he interrupts constantly. Language like this sounds like a caricature—trust me (don't trust yourself!), it's not.

23. It ain't "soft," baby!
Decency pays off. Big time.
Thoughtfulness pays off. Big time.
Kindness pays off. Big time.
Integrity pays off. Big time.
Respect pays off. Big time.

**Appreciation pays off. Big time.
Courtesy pays off. Big time.
Listening pays off. Big time.**

**"Decency," "thoughtfulness," etc.
are the true language of Excellent-
Sustainable Relationships—and
hence the true language of "profit
maximization."**

Period.

24. **"d"iverse always wins.**

I call it "lowercase 'd' diversity." I'm not talking about social justice—my shtick is enterprise effectiveness. Or, at least, that's the part
you've come to these pages for. More and more research is discrediting
overdependence on experts. (And that was *before* the current financial
fiasco, born on the backs of the very best and very brightest.) Bottom
line: *Any* decision-making or execution process simply must include
every form of diversity you can conjure up—M, F, black, white, top
university, no university, preachers, teachers, short, tall . . . whatever.
Measure it! (I repeat: The evidence supporting this notion is 10 miles
wide and 10 miles deep.)

25. **"New Diverse"—welcome the Crowd.**

"Crowdsourcing" is shaping up to be the most powerful innovation
and execution and marketing tool—ever. From Wikipedia to finding
new gold fields, working-the-electronic-crowd is a priceless WMC—
Weapon of Mass Creation. Application: Everyone. Every business.
Everywhere.

26. **Do lunch with folks in other functions.**

For the umpteenth time in this book (and, yes, a bit more to come):

I hereby re-re-declare that screwed-up cross-functional communications, or "silo-ing," are invariably Cause #1 of execution problems and Cause #1 of missed innovation opportunities.

(Repeat! Yup!)

I have come to believe, almost "religiously," that the "simple" "social" remedies are far more important than formal systems and fantabulous-sexy-slick software. It's a religious devotion to lunch with folks in other functions. It's having folks in other functions at every weekly review meeting. It's awards ceremonies for those in other functions who've helped your team. Send "thank-you" notes heaped atop "thank-you" notes to those in other places who've helped out. (OVER 50 PERCENT OF YOUR THANK-YOU NOTES SHOULD BE TO OTHER FUNCTIONS' FOLK. MEASURE IT.) Do not let a single solitary day pass without *proactively* fostering the dismantling of the functional walls via "social tools."

27. **Lunch "down"—"wire" customer operations and you will win the sale and keep the business.**

Most of the decision making concerning the purchase or implementation of a new system (telecoms, software) is heavily influenced by "down-the-line" prospective users—and the "go"–"no go" analysis of your service or widget is usually more or less, mostly more, made three levels "down" in the Client organization. Your goal is to patiently ferret out and cultivate these "three-down" folks. (Hint: Women are much better at this than men; women tend to be more willing to ignore formal rank and invest anywhere and everywhere according to prospective value.)

28. Lunch "down"—"wire" your own operation two or three or more "levels" "down," and watch your implementation success soar!

The "real work" in *any* sizable enterprise is done two or three or four levels "down"—even in today's hyper-wired somewhat flattened organizations; quash your ego, and invest "down there." Among other things, those "down there" tend not to be appreciated; hence, your attention will be very welcome—and your DTN (Down There Network) will pay huge dividends. (I'd be tempted to put this on my personal "Top 1" list when I review my successes in big organizations such as the U.S. Navy, the White House, and McKinsey & Co.)

29. Manage the "Hang Out Axiom" as if it were a life or death issue—it is.

We are—unequivocally—who we hang out with. Hang out with "interesting"—get more interesting. Hang out with "dull"—become more dull. Hang out with those in other functions—improve cross-functional communication. Hang out with weird customers and vendors—get dragged into the future. Hang out with 19-year-olds—and watch your use of the Web get more interesting and extensive. Little, if anything, is more important for innovation than precise "hang out management." *Manage it! Measure it!* (Scary thought of the day: "You will become like the five people you associate with the most—this can be either a blessing or a curse."—Billy Cox)

30. You are where you sit.

The way you lay out your office's physical space can help erase barriers and (*wildly*) alter communication patterns—and critical outcomes. Talk about a "power tool"—and one that's woefully underutilized and misunderstood. A CEO hires her first corporate head of design—and plants the new Chief Design Guru next to the CEO's office; soon, everyone in the senior management ranks is humming "the design anthem." Oddball task to be done that challenges conventional wisdom—put the work team in an office 6,000 miles away. (Or at least 60.)

31. Work on everyone's listening skills.

Effective listening should be near the/at the top of everyone's skill set. It is indeed as "strategic" as it gets! Most of us, especially bosses of long standing, are terrible listeners—almost all men, bosses or not, are pretty terrible. The good news, as Stephen Covey and others have taught us: Listening is a learnable and improvable skill. The Golden Equation:

Better Listening = Better Managing = Better Selling = Better Implementation. Believe it!! Learn it—if it kills you!!

32. Become a serious student of interviewing.

You've seen great interviewers on TV. They seem to be able to extract anything from anybody. A keystone of professional life is extracting information effectively. Beyond general listening skills (see immediately above), work on interviewing skills—once again, a topic worthy of formal *study* and significant *investment*.

33. Become a serious student of presentation giving.

Listen! Talk! We spend much/most of our time on these two activities. *So, why are there so damn few of us who are Serious Students of these two Fundamental Human Skills?* Getting good, really really really good, at either one is as tough as getting good, really good, at neurosurgery. Failure to give superb presentations—two minutes or two hours, planned for a month or spontaneous—has stopped a jillion high-potential careers dead in their tracks. As "D.A.W." put it in *The [Martha's] Vineyard Gazette*: "Pens are mightier than swords. But nothing compares with vocal cords."

34. Aim for no less than the "world's best" first-line managers.

The evidence is extensive—and clear. Employees' satisfaction (retention, etc.) is most influenced by the quality of their supervisor—particularly their first-line supervisor. *Hence, one could accurately say that first-line supervisor selection and development is one of the most important "strategic" activities a firm undertakes.* Although few take the promotion decision to first-line supervisor lightly, very few *obsess* on it to the extent they should, given the importance score. Moreover, the general observation is that the quality of frontline supervisor *training* and *mentoring* is by and large appalling, slapdash at best.

35. Leaders from day one. "Everybody a leader"?

This is entirely possible—and of inestimable value. Whether it's a lead role in a small bit of a Memorial Day employee picnic, or responsibility for logistics for a field trip, give the most junior folks in the place leadership responsibility from the outset—if not Day #1, then within the first month. Hence "leadership development" becomes an overarching theme-activity from the get-go, "24/7." This is so, so, so important—leading even tiny tasks teaches (1) responsibility for others and results, (2) "breaking the rules" when necessary, (3) accountability, (4) the power of teamwork, (5) plain old hustle, (6) etc., (7) many etc.!

36. You = Your (few) promotion decisions.

The boss-of-bosses gets, on average, two serious promotion decisions a year, maybe just one. Suppose you're in a job five years. That's no more than 10 promotion decisions. Premise: *Those decisions more or less determine your legacy.* At the end of a career, your most important "product" is the people you develop. The "bottom line" is obvious: You cannot put too much effort into these decisions!!

37. "People people." Period.

"There are two kinds of people." What a foolish statement! Yet on one dimension I believe it's more or less true: There *are* people who "get off on" people, and those who don't. The latter can be incredibly important "individual contributors," but by and large should not manage others. I have tried this hypothesis out on numerous very successful leaders, especially business owners; simply put, they agree—100 percent would not be much of an exaggeration. Ms./Mr. X should be a talented financial person to run a finance department, or talented logistician to run a logistics department. But the *great* logistics *leader* will achieve superb results by developing superstars, a super team—and getting things implemented throughout his/her superior "people network" in the organization as a whole.

38. The "life success" business.

The customer is served well exactly to the extent to which the person who is serving the customer is served well. Or not. This is obvious—and as often as not, or more often than not, honored in the breach. Recall that RE/MAX founder Dave Liniger says he's in the "life success" business—his goal is to break his back enabling his real estate agents and brokers to become successful. Matthew Kelly, in *The Dream Manager*, says that making your customers' dreams come true is dependent upon making the dreams of the people who serve the customer come true—hence, helping the latter realize their dreams becomes the manager's appropriate preoccupation. In general, then, commitment to the growth of those who serve your customer, rather than the customer per se, becomes the boss's true Job One—and, in turn, the ultimate "profit maximizer's" task.

39. Hire-promote for demonstrated curiosity.

Curiosity is a remarkably important individual trait. But more encompassing is the idea of making "curiosity" part of the organization's "culture." For example, in your general approach to hiring, you can go a long way toward evaluating curiosity by observing the candidate's style of answering questions (wide ranging, or narrow), and the eclectic nature (or not) of one's demonstrated background. One exceedingly successful business owner in professional services insists, when hiring, that the candidate have at least one substantial *deep* interest beyond the "required" skill set—particularly, interestingly, for his engineers, most of whom are involved in overseas community development activities.

40. **Womenomics 101**

Women everywhere buy over 80 percent of consumer goods. And in the likes of the United States, women also purchase about 50 percent of commercial goods and services (women fill over 50 percent of U.S. managerial slots). More broadly, Aude Zieseniss de Thuin, founder of the Women's Forum for the Economy and Society, refers

> ## ❯ NOT-SO-SECRET FORMULA

$W = 2(C + I)$

Commit that equation to memory. Interpretation: The size of the "women's market" is twice the size of the Chinese market and the Indian market combined. (Actually, *more* than twice.) (And it is growing growing growing.)

Most companies don't get it—including, amazingly, according to Michael Silverstein and Kate Sayre (*Harvard Business Review*, September 2009), most of the companies who *think* they "get it."

How do you explain the lack of effort directed to this . . . **Monstrous and Matchless . . . Very Un-Secret . . . Worldwide . . . opportunity?**

Don't know.
Or: Stupidity?

Look!
Here!
Women!
World's largest market opportunity!
All yours!

to the arrival of "Womenomics . . . the economy as thought out and practiced by women." One obvious (should be obvious!) consequence is that women's representation on the Exec Team and Board should roughly mirror their purchasing power. Fact is, men are woefully ignorant about women's marketplace needs in terms of product development, marketing, and distribution—that is, pretty much everything. Bizarrely, this largest of all market opportunities is still grossly underattended all around the world.

41. Passing the "Squint Test."

"To be a leader in consumer products," says former PepsiCo CEO Steve Reinemund, "it's critical to have leaders who represent the population we serve." Pepsi does. How about you? My test: *When you squint at the pictures on the page in an annual report featuring the Executive Team and/or Board, do the gender, skin tone, age distribution, and nationalities roughly match the demographics of the market being served?* If you fail the "squint test," the obvious question is: What is your six-month, one-year, and two-year program, including immediate "next steps," for addressing the issue?

42. The next 25 years' big-humongous (and lightly regarded) marketplace story.

Focus for the next quarter century: *creating products and services for and selling and distributing to the absurdly large, ridiculously wealthy, and growing-at-hyperspeed post-50-years-of-age market. ("Boomers," born between 1946 and 1964, and "geezers," the boomer+ horde.)* We talk ceaselessly about using "revolutionary Web-based tools" to turn the world into "market segments of one." Fine, but do not ignore the two, by far, largest markets (not "segments," but "markets")—both of which are pathetically misunderstood and woefully underserved. One: women. Two: boomers and geezers. (And "2A," combining the best of the above: Boomer-Geezer Women.) The rise and rise (and rise) of boomers and geezers is simply the single most significant "demographic trend", in history. Yet marketing and product-service development remains squarely focused on the young-youngish—"the all-important 18–44 demographic" in particular. *The lost opportunities are staggering. The boomer-geezer tsunami is absolutely-positively-unequivocally* the *"marketing megatrend" of the next 25 years!*

43. Try it! Try it! Try it!

As the basis for *In Search of Excellence*, Bob Waterman and I looked at management practices at 40-odd top-performing companies. Out of this work came what we called "The Eight Basics." No. 1 was "A bias for action." More generally I claim that I've only learned one thing "for sure" in the last four and a half decades: "He/she who tries the most stuff wins." I mean it—not a dollop of hyperbole. Hence, there is nothing more important to business success than a " 'try it' culture." Alas, inculcation thereof is a devilishly difficult task. A "try it" mentality is like breathing at 3M or Google or Alibaba, and anathema at GM—even though the latter has been trying to change things on this dimension for over 25 years.

44. Screw it up! Screw it up! Screw it up!

If "try it" is enterprise Success Factor #1, then "screw it up" is Success Corollary #1. To try lots of stuff, fast, is to screw lots of stuff up, fast. And the "cultural" "trick" is learning to *love* those rapid failures—to *reward* them and *celebrate* them.

45. Simplify systems. Constantly.

Internet or no Internet, Web 2.0 or no Web 2.0, computing in the cloud or using the abacus, all organizations over time choke on the growing complexity of their systems. Systems: Can't live without them. Systems: Can't live with them. My advice: Literally, not figuratively, create a "War Department"—an "official" arm of the organization dedicated to making war on our own systems! We must work as hard at *de*-organizing as we do at organizing. (And reward the effective "de-organizers" accordingly!)

46. Simplify. One page. Max. Everything.

Become a fanatic about 10-word summaries. One-page plans and policies. Etc. The art of boiling things down is an art of the utmost importance. Strategic plan? Sure—but no more than one page long. (You can have 10,000 pages of appendices—but the "it" should go on for no more than a page.) (Maybe all major corporate docs should follow the Twitter rule—140 characters max.)

47. Simplify.

Period. (Soooooooooo important—overcomplexity and gunk in general bring about 1 out of 1 giant companies to their knees—think second law of thermodynamics, think entropy. But never stop trying to reverse the tide—or at least to hold the forces of evil/complexity at bay.)

48. The calendar never lies!

Your glorious world-changing priorities must somehow be kept in line with the "real world" in which you live. *Time is your only true resource.* (I know it's been said before and before that—so what? It always needs repeating.) And the way you divvy time up—visible to one and all—is the only true statement of what really matters to you. Distractions are life. But you must somehow to some extent override that tawdry "reality." Hence: Manage your calendar *religiously* and *rigorously*. Nothing but nothing is of greater "strategic" importance.

49. You need a "calendar buddy."

Aligning your time with your priorities—in the face of a zillion distractions—is hard work and calls for a straight-shooting accompanist who will call you out when your espoused priorities and time allocation become dangerously misaligned. (Hint: That's most of the time.) This is a *daily* "strategic" task—weekly and monthly assessments are fine, but the Single Day—TODAY—is the metric that matters! (TRUST ME! PLEASE! YOU NEED "OUTSIDE" HELP! "WILLPOWER" IS NOT ENOUGH!)

❯ BE A "CALENDAR GUY (GAL)"

Axiom I: You = Your calendar.
Axiom II: Calendars *never* lie.
Axiom III: "Don't do" decisions = Most important decisions.
Axiom IV: Time control is not a solo task.

50. We all need a "truth teller."

It's true of the president and the general—but also of the 26-year-old supervisor. Bosses never hear the "unvarnished truth." Therefore, we need a special pal who will tell it like it is. And *does* tell it like it is. This is true X100 after the second or third promotion!

51. EXCELLENCE in all we do.

In my not-unbiased view, the value of relentlessly pursuing EXCELLENCE *per se* is literally infinite. My Mantra: EXCELLENCE is a mind-set of unmatched power.

Once asked how long it took to "become excellent," legendary IBM CEO Tom Watson apparently answered . . .

"One minute."

(This was decades before *The One-Minute Manager*.) In that one minute, you promise yourself that you will never again do something that is other than Excellent—it's the Excellence version of Alcoholics Anonymous. And like AA, the "answer" is that it takes but an instant to quit (the good news), but, then, "one day at a time"—forever.

On the one hand, there are "systemic approaches" to embedding various forms of "Excellence" in an organization. So-called Six Sigma quality programs are an example. Yet at the end of the day, this "Excellence thing" is no more and no less than personal. One person, one decision, one minute: Never again anything other than Excellent. Excellence, the unvarnished pursuit thereof in good times and, especially, trying times, is the true and immutable . . . **Heart of Strategy.**

➤ OUR CREDO/A WORK IN PROGRESS

Johnson & Johnson's Credo has stood the test of time, been of pragmatic value (e.g., during the Tylenol crisis), and has proven to be worth its weight in something far more valuable than gold. Consistent with the views encompassed in the Heart of Strategy, I tried my hand at a credo—too wordy, to be sure, but perhaps suggestive.

We are thoughtful in all we do.

We are excellent listeners—to each other and to all members of our extended family (vendors, customers, communities, etc.).

We will make the four words "What do you think?" an automatic instinct in all of our internal and external dealings; moreover, "What do you think?" will precede the explication of our own view in 99 out of 100 instances.

We are dedicated to and measure our success to a significant degree by our unwavering commitment to the extreme personal growth of every one of our employees.

We will only be "delighted" with our managers if their employees are universally surprised by the level of their personal and professional growth.

We will be clear that we view leadership at every level as a sacred trust—and that leaders are indeed the servants of their employees just as the effective classroom teacher is servant to the lives and growth of her or his students.

We believe in the "inverted organization chart"—with the "leaders" at the "bottom" of a reverse pyramid.

We will construct leaders' incentive schemes so that measurable progress in human development is weighed as highly as marketplace success.

We will be a leader in research and development in every aspect of our business—and we will work primarily with vendors who are also fanatical about research and development; and work to attract a set of core customers willing to play at the edge of things and become our codevelopers.

We will aim to make our customer engagements adventures beyond the comfort zone, or adventures in growth, to use a less intimidating phrase—we will aim to add value in novel ways that surprise and stretch our customers and ourselves.

We will use the three words "Try it! Now!" almost as often as "What do you think?" We revere the experimental method, and believe success is mostly correlated with the number of things one tries.

We wholeheartedly acknowledge the value of analysis, but in the end swear by "Actions speak louder than words."

We "encourage" and "celebrate" failures; that is, we acknowledge that a near-religious devotion to "Try it! Now!" necessarily invites the failures that are part and parcel of trying new things.

We will in fact look askance at those whose records include few or no failures—such a spotless record suggests an unwillingness to brave the unknown.

We will, to summarize the last few items, all view ourselves as explorers-adventurers, proceeding toward individual and collective growth by actively engaging at the edge of things; we unstintingly believe that our customers will reap enormous value from our commitment to our constant, restless exploration.

We will encourage and insist upon constant and vociferous disagreement, but we are absolutely intolerant of disagreement in the form of personal attacks.

We will cut "overhead" to zero—instead every "department" shall aim to be best-in-class in its arena, and hence a full-scale participant in our concerted effort to add value in all we do.

We will exude and "model" integrity, individually and collectively.

We will exemplify the word "transparency" in all of our internal and external dealings—and bend over backwards to give new meaning and breadth to the term "information sharing."

We will individually and collectively accept blame for our mistakes, or even our rather minor contribution to others' mistakes—and apologize accordingly and with dispatch.

We will bring to bear overwhelming and instant and collective force to redress any customer problem, real or imagined.

We will under no circumstances bad-mouth a competitor.

We will aim to turn every customer contact into a memorable experience, remembering that all of life is indeed a stage.

We honor the word "design" in all we do, in every nook and every cranny of our organization; every system, every Web page, every customer invoice, every employee restroom is part of our purposefully designed "signature," and we intend to stand out and exude exceptionalism in one way or another.

We understand that difficult decisions must be made, but we will bend over backwards to implement such decisions with kindness and grace—the dignity of the individual will always be uppermost in our minds.

We will not intrude into our employees' lives, but we are committed to aggressively helping employees achieve a healthy lifestyle.

We will master the art of appreciation and be profuse in our use of the words "thank you" to honor assistance of even the most minor sort.

We will acknowledge through celebration even small successes—and always cast a wide net in our "thank-yous" to include bit players, especially from other functions.

We aim for others to always be surprised by our "vibrancy" and "vitality"—we view enthusiasm as the key to success in anything, and take particular care in leader selection to ensure that every one of our leaders is a "remarkable" "carrier" of enthusiasm through thick and, especially, thin.

We will drop whatever we are doing and rush to the aid of those involved in tight-deadline activities—even if those involved caused some of their own problems.

We will be meticulous in our planning, but also understand that nothing ever unfolds as planned—hence we will be known for our ability to muster resources in an instant, without fuss and from everywhere, to deal with the unexpected; participating in these ad hoc response activities will not be seen as a distraction from our "real work," but as a significant part of our "real work" and an opportunity to contribute to others and build our own skills in ways we might not have imagined.

We fully acknowledge that other units-departments-functions have other points of view than ours, but we will bend over backwards and perform handsprings to develop social connections with those in other functions so that dealings over warring perspectives are dealings among friends.

We acknowledge that agreed-upon deadlines are holy writ, and will attempt to balance requisite urgency and requisite realism in all of our commitments.

We will fight tooth and nail to minimize the ravages of hypercomplexity that "necessarily" come with growth and the mere passage of time.

We will declare total war on our own systems to ensure that they do not strangle us.

We gladly acknowledge that anyone in the organization has the duty as well as the right to challenge anyone else when he or she believes they have a valid and useful perspective to offer—this is particularly true regarding any issue that has to do with safety, quality, or meeting agreed-upon deadlines; such challenges may be firm but not rude.

We will be civil in all our dealings with one another.

We will bend over backwards to bring truly (not superficially) diverse views of every stripe imaginable to bear on plans and decisions of all sorts.

We will pursue "diversity" in part so that the composition of our workforce and leadership from top to bottom is a "pretty good" reflection of the demographics of the markets we serve or aim to serve.

We will use new technology tools to extend the definition of "our family" to every corner of the globe—we will welcome ideas and participation in our affairs from anyone and everyone.

We will aim for gender balance in all we do and from tippy top to bottom—for reasons commercial more than reasons moral.

We will never, in any way, compromise on the quality of our products or services—regardless of difficulties in our marketplace and economy.

We wholeheartedly acknowledge that in the short term (as well, obviously, as the long term) we must be profitable and exhibit stellar financial performance that is consistent with the audacious efforts to serve our people and our clients as described above.

We aim to be seen by others as "conservative" in our financial practices.

We shall talk about EXCELLENCE constantly.

We shall unfailingly aim for EXCELLENCE in all we do.

We shall use EXCELLENCE as the principal benchmark in the assessment of ourselves and our work and our community.

We shall never forget that the bedrock of EXCELLENCE is the unwavering commitment to growth of 100 percent of our employees—and in fact all of those we come in contact with.

1. 2. 3. 4. 5. 6. 7. 8. 9. 10. 11. 12. 13. 14. 15. 16. 17. 18. 19. 20. 21. 22. 23. 24. 25. 26. 27. 28. 29. 30. 31. 32. 33. 34. 35. 36. 37. 38. 39. 40. 41. 42. 43. 44. 45. 46. 47. 48. 49. 50. 51. 52. 53. 54. 55. 56. 57. 58. 59. 60. 61. 62. 63. 64. 65. 66. 67. 68. 69. 70. 71. 72. 73. 74. 75. 76. 77. 78. 79. 80. 81. 82. 83. 84. 85. 86. 87. 88. 89. 90. 91. 92. 93. 94. 95. 96. 97. 98. 99. 100. 101. 102. 103. 104. 105. 106. 107. 108. 109. 110. 111. 112. 113. 114. 115. 116. 117. 118. 119. 120. 121. 122. 123. 124. 125. 126. 127. 128. 129. 130. 131. 132. 133. 134. 135. 136. 137. 138. 139. 140. 141. 142. 143. 144. 145. 146. 147. 148. 149. 150. 151. 152. 153. 154. 155. 156. **157. 158. 159. 160.** 161. 162. 163.

Success

157. The "3H Model" of Success.

The 3Hs:
Howard.
Hilton.
Herb.

Three men, three principles.
(A lot of "life"/"success" explained.)

1. Starbucks has hit a rough patch, but as "they" say, we should all have **Howard** Schultz's problems—a guy who took a cup of java and grew a business of over 10,000 iconic shops worldwide. (And the one I visited in Al Khobar, Saudi Arabia, was as busy as my local on Charles Street in Boston.)

There is no doubt that running an international show as big as Starbucks is quite a chore, and the staff is tops, and there's data by the ton. Yet the boss, Mr. Schultz, aims (and usually succeeds) to visit—hold on to your hat—**25 shops per week.**

He believes you've gotta see the real deal up close with all your senses (after all, Starbucks sells an all-senses "experience") to know the score.

2. If there's ever been a more prominent and successful hotelier than Conrad **Hilton,** I'd like to know who it is. One Hilton anecdote: The story goes that at the conclusion of a gala honoring his career, Mr. Hilton was finally called to the podium to "share his success secrets." He made his way to the front of the house, stood very formally at the podium, and intoned . . .

"Remember to tuck the shower curtain inside the bathtub."

And that was it, and back he went to his seat.
(Oh, my heavens, how I love that quote!)

3. In 2009, American Airlines and Southwest Airlines held their annual meetings on the same day in Dallas, headquarters to both. APA, the Allied Pilots Association, picketed American's meeting. The Southwest meeting marked founder **Herb** Kelleher's retirement after 37 years. Like Mr. Hilton, Herb was asked to reveal his full set of secrets, and, like Mr. Hilton, he severely limited his remarks:

"You have to treat your employees like customers."

Apparently Mr. Kelleher has been asked that please-tell-all question a raft of times, probably thousands of times—and has always answered with the same one-liner, same eight words. And no more.

(Whoops, I forgot to mention that on the same day APA picketed American, Southwest's pilots' union paid a small fortune to take out full-page ads in the likes of USA Today *thanking Herb for his years of service—and support of the union and its pilots. Quite a contrast, eh?)*

Bottom line from the 3Hs:

(1) Stay in touch! (Howard)
(2) Sweat the details! (Hilton)
(3) People first! (Herb)

Stop.
Right now.

Put down the book.
Assess *only* the *last* 24 hours.
(I'm not interested in your grandiloquent "lifelong concerns." Last 24 hours. Period.)

On a scale of 1–10, how do you rate . . . **in the last 24 hours** . . . *on each of the 3H elements?*

158. A 5-Word, 5-Point "Complete" "Excellence Manifesto."

Maybe it's an "age thing," my apparent obsession with summarizing stuff. Or maybe it's an engineer's passion for lists.

Whatever.

Here goes, my "summary of everything" . . . in five words, generated for a seminar in which I wanted to leave behind a truly punchy message:

Cause.
Space.
Decency.
Service.
Excellence.

Cause: An objective worthy of our commitment. An aim that supersedes the need for an alarm clock and that we can brag about to our friends, our family, and our mirror.

Space: Room to roam. Constant and insistent encouragement for taking the initiative. An expectation that everyone will perceive herself or himself as a Change Agent-Entrepreneur.

Decency: Thoughtfulness to a fault in everything we do. Fairness to a fault in everything we do. Sky-high respect for every person with whom we come in contact.

Service: We unfailingly aim to "be of service." Our leaders at all levels are "in service" to their staff. Each staff member is "in service" to her or his peers and internal and external customers.

Excellence: Our ultimate aim is always . . . Excellence. Nothing less. In our treatment of one another. In the products and services we develop. In our relationships with customers-vendors-community.

Amen!
(At least as far as I'm concerned.)
(And if you agree . . . how are you doing, on each of the five points, in your six-person insurance brokerage on Main Street, Small Town? In your three-person executive development unit in Biggish Co?) ("How are you doing" I: How are you doing on each point in general? "How are you doing" II: How have you done on each of the five . . . *today?*)

159. The Full Nelson— Or: 13 Lessons on "Navigating" Excellence.

Lord Horatio Nelson, to me, an old navy man and avid student of naval history, epitomizes EXCELLENCE. And, near the 200th anniversary of his singular victory at Trafalgar, I happened upon a new biography (I've probably ingested a dozen over the years), Andrew Lambert's *Nelson: Britannia's God of War*. It looked worthwhile; and, incidentally, I was to give a speech on Leadership in Dubai 48 hours hence. So I made the purchase, devoured the book during a subsequent six-hour flight from Heathrow, where I'd picked the book up . . . extracted 13 Lessons . . . *and* foisted them on my UAE friends. (No great friends of the Brits—sorry. But it was, I thought, a helluva useful list.)

Following this set of lessons is obviously far easier said than done. Still, they offer an intriguing model worthy of our examination if Excellence is your or my aspiration. Moreover, it is particularly interesting to consider the way in which each of the 13 reinforces the other 12. Effective leadership and the achievement of Excellence (in this rare case, "achievement of," rather than "aspiration to achieve," is merited) are the result of the interaction among a complex set of characteristics:

1. *Simple scheme.* Nelson's orders of battle were paragons of simplicity and clarity—he was a damn good writer among other things. **(Doable for you or me? Yes. Damn it.)**

2. *Soaring/Bold/Noble Purpose.* Nelson pursued total victory. Many of his peers were willing, essentially, to rate surviving as victory enough. Though scary, bold goals are motivating as hell—even

if you're an involuntary sailor, at least if the likes of Nelson is your commander. **(Doable for you or me? Yes. Not on a Nelsonian scale, of course, but in the context of our more pedestrian pursuits.)**

3. *Engage others.* Nelson made his captains full partners in the process as he devised plans—unheard of in those days. **(Doable for you or me? Yes. Damn it.)**

4. *Find great talent, at any age, let it soar!* Nelson gave his best captains, young or old, far more leeway than his counterpart admirals—and he eschewed seniority as the primary measure of assigned responsibility; if your star had shined brightly, you were given a choice assignment regardless of seniority. **(Doable for you or me? Yes. Damn it.)**

5. *Lead by Love!* The sailors, every biographer agrees, loved Nelson, and he them. (Last clause in the sentence is crucial.) His concern for their well-being, regardless of the rough nature of the sailor's life in those days, was legendary. **(Doable for you or me? Yes. Damn it. Mostly. Assuming you "get off" on people who do the real work.)**

6. *Seize the Moment!* Nelson's sixth sense about enemy weakness was remarkable. He would skip to "Plan B" in a flash if merited by changing circumstances. **(Doable for you or me? Yes. Damn it. More or less—"good instincts" are the indirect product of insanely hard work. And adaptability is, alas, not a universal trait.)**

7. *Vigor!* His energy was palpable! **(Doable for you or me? Yes. Mostly. Low-energy folks probably aren't top picks for leadership positions in general; but we can at least get better in terms of our conscious projection on this dimension.)**

8. *Master your craft.* Nelson was the best damn sailor in the Royal Navy—sailors and officers appreciated that beyond measure. **(Doable for you or me? Yes. Damn it. We are not all created equal—but often "the best" is not the one who tops the charts on raw talent.)**

9. *Work harder-harder-harder than the next person.* No explanation needed. **(Doable for you or me? Yes. Damn it.)**

10. *Show the way, walk the talk, exude confidence! Start a Passion Epidemic!* Nelson led from the front—visible, in full dress uniform as the cannons roared. (**Doable for you or me? Yes. Damn it. With practice! "Practice" passion? Yes, in the sense of a willingness to express what's inside that often you try to hide or suppress. The Churchills and Roosevelts and Nelsons express emotion—of course it starts with caring about what you do; can't fake that. NB: "Express emotion" does not mean bellowing!**)

11. *Change the rules: Create your own game!* Nelson *always* took the initiative—thus forcing rivals, from the beginning and throughout maneuvering during battle, to be constantly in a reactive mode. Back to No. 1, his simple schemes and the autonomy given his commanders made taking and holding the initiative much easier than it otherwise would have been. (**Doable for you or me? Yes. Mostly—if you can measure up on several of the earlier points; as I said, it's all connected.**)

12. *Luck!* Believe it! Always necessary! Not "desirable"—but necessary. (**Doable for you or me? Anybody can get lucky—and preparedness ups the odds of getting lucky. But, truthfully, lucky is lucky.**)

13. *Be determined to come out on top, come hell or/and high water!* Lambert:

"Other Admirals were more frightened of losing than anxious to win."

This last is a big deal—it belongs as either #1 or #13. (**Doable for you or me? Yes. Damn it.**)

As noted, the value of this set of Nelsonian traits goes beyond the particulars—it is the totality, the pieces reinforcing one another, that matters. My "action" suggestion is simply to review the whole—and perhaps try laying out your own philosophy, as a whole. Such an exercise, I find, is invaluable—at the least it may lead me or you to realize and then emphasize the missing links; at most it could cause me or you to rethink what the heck we're doing with our life—e.g., are we trying to avoid messing up (avoid losing), or are we determined to personify the positive-proactive Aspiration of Excellence in our chosen field (pursue winning)?

❯ NELSON'S TWIN: U.S. GRANT

As a lad raised in the near-South of the United States, I was taught of the greatness of the Confederate general Robert E. Lee. And taught equally to dismiss the man who garnered the Union Army's initial victories and then led that army to ultimate victory—General Ulysses S. Grant.

Hence it was not until recently that I became a full-fledged Grant fanatic. Though not suggesting that I am a thoroughgoing student of military history, I now put Grant on a pedestal, much the same pedestal as Admiral Horatio Nelson. For me the two have few peers.

(NB: Theodore Roosevelt called Grant one of the three greatest Americans; Washington and Lincoln were the other two.)

Grant's obsession with action and simplicity of plan, and his genuine affection for his troops (and vice versa), are, indeed, in my mind, matchless—and rank with Nelson. Consider these quotes I've extracted from several biographies.

Action. Execution. Offense. Relentless. Opportunistic.

"The only way to whip an army is to go out and fight it." (Grant)

"Grant had an aversion to digging in."

"The one who attacks first will be victorious." (Grant)

"dogged"

"simplicity and determination"

"quickness of mind that allowed him to make on the spot adjustments ... his battles were not elegant set-piece operations"

"[other Union generals] preferred preparation to execution"

"If anyone other than Grant had been in command, the Union Army certainly would have retreated."

Lincoln (urged to fire Grant): "I can't spare this man; he fights."

"instinctive recognition that victory lay in relentlessly hounding a defeated army into surrender"

"The art of war is simple enough. Find out where your enemy is. Get at him as soon as you can. Strike at him as hard as you can and as often as you can, and keep moving on." (Grant)

"One of my superstitions had always been when I started to go anywhere or to do anything, not to turn back, or stop, until the thing intended was accomplished." (Grant)

"Grant had an extreme, almost phobic dislike of turning back and retracing his steps. If he set out for somewhere, he would get there somehow, whatever the difficulties that lay in his way. This idiosyncrasy would turn out to be one of the factors that made him such a formidable general. Grant would always, always press on—turning back was not an option for him."

Simplicity. Clarity. Room for Others' Initiative.

"The genius of Grant's command style lay in its simplicity. Grant never burdened his division commanders with excessive detail ... no elaborate staff conferences, no written orders prescribing deployment ... Grant recognized the battlefield was in flux. By not specifying movements in detail, he left his subordinate commanders free to exploit whatever opportunities developed."

"Grant's moral courage—his willingness to choose a path from which there could be no return—set him apart from most commanders ...

[Grant and Lee] were uniquely willing to take full responsibility for their actions."

Bond with Soldiers

"Above all the troops appreciated Grant's unassuming manner. Most generals went about attended by a retinue of immaculately tailored staff officers. Grant usually rode alone, except for an orderly or two to carry messages if the need arose. One soldier said the soldiers looked on Grant 'as a friendly partner, not an arbitrary commander.' Instead of cheering as he rode by, they would 'greet him as they would address one of their neighbors at home. 'Good morning, General,' 'Pleasant day, General'...'"

After Grant's victory at Chattanooga:

"The [Union senior] officers rode past the Confederates smugly without any sign of recognition except by one. 'When General Grant reached the line of ragged, filthy, bloody, despairing prisoners strung out on each side of the bridge, he lifted his hat and held it over his head until he passed the last man of that living funeral cortege. He was the only officer in that whole train who recognized us as being on the face of the earth.'* [*quote from diary of a Confederate soldier]"

(NB: This is in no way to dismiss the military leadership qualities of General Lee. And while I know that some of my great friends will never forgive me, I do admit that I have indeed become rather unstintingly admiring of the man from Galena, Illinois.)

160. A Cheat Sheet for Tough Times (and Other Times, Too).

Amid all of the advice "out there" on dealing with difficult circumstances, how do you ... boil it all down? Some thoughts:

(1) Be conscious in the Zen sense—that is, learn to and **exhibit extreme sensitivity to one's immediate surroundings.** Carefully consider, far more than you normally might, how you project: Does your "energetic" approach, for example, look more like panic? Is your smile in place? Nothing is amusing about tough economic times, but a permanently grim demeanor, even if it's merited, is a guaranteed demotivator.

(2) **Meet . . . daily, first thing** . . . with your leadership team—to discuss whatever, check assumptions. Perhaps meet again late afternoon. Meetings max 30 minutes, maybe 15.

(3) If you are a "big boss," use a 100 percent trusted, private **sounding board**—check in daily, whether you "need to" . . . or not.

(4) Concoct scenarios by the bushel, test 'em, play with 'em, short term, long term, sane, insane. (Not necessarily a formal exercise—but a constant "playful" exercise.)

(5) MBWA (Managing By Wandering Around). Wander. Sample attitudes. Visible but not frenzied. But visible . . . **VISIBLE** . . . visible.

(6) Work the phones, chat up experts, *non*experts **(!)**, customers, vendors. Seek *enormous* **(!!)** diversity of opinion. (NB: Big bosses invariably spend too much time with "experts"! Expert = Blinders = Particularly bad in uncertain/ambiguous times.)

(7) **"Over"communicate!!!!!**

(8) **"Over"communicate!!!!!**

(9) Exercise—encourage your leadership team to double up on their physical exercise; physical sharpness is insanely important to mental evenness.

(10) Underscore **"Excellence** in *every* transaction"! **(Now, more than ever!)**

1. 2. 3. 4. 5. 6. 7. 8. 9. 10. 11. 12. 13. 14.
15. 16. 17. 18. 19. 20. 21. 22. 23. 24. 25.
26. 27. 28. 29. 30. 31. 32. 33. 34. 35.
36. 37. 38. 39. 40. 41. 42. 43. 44. 45.
46. 47. 48. 49. 50. 51. 52. 53. 54. 55. 56.
57. 58. 59. 60. 61. 62. 63. 64. 65. 66. 67.
68. 69. 70. 71. 72. 73. 74. 75. 76. 77. 78.
79. 80. 81. 82. 83. 84. 85. 86. 87. 88.
89. 90. 91. 92. 93. 94. 95. 96. 97. 98. 99.
100. 101. 102. 103. 104. 105. 106. 107.
108. 109. 110. 111. 112. 113. 114. 115.
116. 117. 118. 119. 120. 121. 122. 123.
124. 125. 126. 127. 128. 129. 130. 131.
132. 133. 134. 135. 136. 137. 138. 139.
140. 141. 142. 143. 144. 145. 146. 147.
148. 149. 150. 151. 152. 153. 154. 155.
156. 157. 158. 159. 160. **161. 162. 163.**

161. Retirement Sucks.

My college fraternity brothers have a wonderful ritual: an annual newsletter that we all contribute to. A few years back (I was 62 at the time), I vented about the topic of "retirement," which appeared to be on the minds of many:

"You've all doubtless heard the Churchill yarn. The old man was transiting the Atlantic by ship. An aide made a mental calculation and turned to WSC, 'Sir Winston, I've calculated how much brandy you've drunk. It comes to about here,' he said, pointing to a spot about half-way up the wall of the cavernous ballroom in which they were seated. WSC leaned in toward the chap, pointed to his de facto marker on the wall, and purportedly said, 'So little time, so much to do.'

"I am a troubled 62. Why?

"So little time, so much to do.

"I have no idea whether this brief missive will attract contempt or mere indifference. Just let me say that I am appalled by the idea of retirement . . . or slowing down in any way, shape, or form. I write from New Orleans. It's 5 A.M. I've been up for three hours, working on today's speech.

"I am blessed. I have a chance (in just 4 hours) to influence 3,500 lives. I dare not f*** it up.

"I am often tired (I'm 62, not 22), but I Love & Appreciate the Opportunities I've been granted to take part in in the Universal Dialogue about the Meaning of Work & Life & National Purpose.

"Put simply, 'retirement' to me means being dragged off a stage and slipped into a simple pine box inscribed with these words: 'He gave a shit.' "

Stay angry!
Change the World!

Never give up!
Never give in!

Die trying!
Literally!

162. Think Legacy!

"My life is my message."
—Gandhi

LEGACY!
It can be a beautiful word!
(Why I/you mattered.)
(What I/you left behind that lasted.)

But I urge you also to think of it as a lifelong goal. And to consider your current assignment as head of a seven-person branch in an IS/IT department. (Or whatever.) Suppose you move on in 6 or 12 or 18 (or 21) months: What ... **one sentence** ... will summarize your "term"?

Please!
Take this exercise seriously!

Consider this a variation on a debate at tompeters.com over the number of priorities a person can have at one time. Well, I'm settling it.

One!

Here's the logic. As I write, I have a day crammed full of miscellaneous (that dreaded word!) activities ahead, ending with a flight from Boston/Logan to London/Heathrow. But the ... THE ... Pressing Question is: **What will the (One Sentence) legacy of *this* day have been for me?**

Yes, I believe a Single Day can have as much of a "legacy" as a life-time. In fact, that had better be the case! Why? Because this day . . . stretching out before me . . . is filled (at the moment) with limitless opportunities . . . and it is . . . **all I have!**

Right?
Just another day?
Hardly!
THIS IS . . . it!

All those things . . . the grand and the mundane . . . that I want to do with my life will either be abetted or thwarted or put off or ignored in the course of . . .

This.
One.
Unfurling.
Day.

So: What will Today's Legacy be . . . for You?

My (hoped for) answer . . .

Despite all the "stuff" I've got to do to prep for my trip, I will make sure that I've got the books, papers I need to work on some "learning project," beyond my seminars, that will move me, exhausted or not, an eighth-step down some novel path that I think is important; also, no matter how busy, I will spend an hour outside absorbing and appreciating, without distraction, the world around me.

(That's a damn tall order—on a lot of days, maybe even most days, I flunk or score no more than the terrifying "Gentleman's C." But by holding up and at least glancing at . . . **"the legacy**

mirror" . . . daily . . . at least I am checking in with my-self—and trying to stay aligned with my longer-term aspirations.)

Your turn . . .

> ❯ **ART—FOR *YOUR* SAKE!**
>
> "Make each day a masterpiece."
> —John Wooden, basketball coach extraordinaire
>
> (This sounds so wretchedly "motivational"—the nastiest thing I can say; but, to repeat, this day *is,* indeed, in the end . . . *all we have.*)

163. Don't Forget Why You're Here!

I was talking with a young lawyer, Harvard trained, now putting in her time at a big firm. She allowed as how her life at the firm was mostly a whirl of trivial activities. On the one hand that's very normal, and part of the time-honored apprenticeship process. But it's also true that in the midst of all the BS, you may gradually lose sight of why you chose to follow this worthy path (as you saw it and passionately felt it) to begin with—and, alas, you may if you're not careful never again capture the wondrous, naive (lovely word!) enthusiasm of your youth.

I've heard doctors and other professionals say the same thing as my new lawyer friend. At the very top of the pyramid, former secretary of state George Schultz mused, and I paraphrase, on how you come to public service with the highest of ideals, but "you get so caught up in the game, that you forget why you came in the first place, you forget those grand aspirations."

(Alas, many CEOs epitomize this. They become so ensnared by the growth-for-growth's-sake game and earnings-for-earnings'-sake game that they forget the fact that they are meant to be "of service" to some Olympian objective—e.g., develop their industry's equivalent of the next iPod or iPhone, or miracle drug or synthetic fuel. GM's bosses are a classic case. Somewhere, somehow they forgot along the way how to make great cars!

I have a little ritual I follow to help get back on track, when I feel myself slipping away from those "naive" aspirations of yesteryear. I take a moment or five and skim *In Search of Excellence*—and remember what I aimed to do in the first place. And how far I have sometimes strayed; it helps me get centered, or recentered. (It's not a matter of trying to revisit the past; it's about trying to recapture the *spirit* of taking on the whole-damn-world while shouting, "Damn the torpedoes, full speed ahead.")

I suggested to my newfound lawyer acquaintance that she invent some like ritual, perhaps re-read once a month the essay answers she provided on her law school admissions form. And I suggest the same to you:

"Why did I take this assignment, or choose this profession? Am I doing everything possible in my current project to hold to the principles that got me into all this? Can I renew? Can I recapture the spirit of 'a glorious calling' that I had when I started?"

Or some such.

My suggestion: Do a like exercise of your own invention every 90 days. *Better yet, a micro-version every evening!* Or, maybe, once a week, actually try to give an honest and complete answer to your spouse's question, "How was your day?" So how *was* your day? Is it what you thought it might be 10 years ago when you started this supposedly virtuous journey?

> ## "THE WORLD IS A GREAT LIAR!"

"In a way, the world is a great liar. It shows you it worships and admires money, but at the end of the day it doesn't. It says it adores fame and celebrity, but it doesn't, not really. The world admires, and wants to hold on to, and not lose, goodness. It admires virtue. At the end it gives its greatest tributes to generosity, honesty, courage, mercy, talents well used, talents that, brought into the world, make it better. That's what it really admires. That's what we talk about in eulogies, because that's what's important. We don't say, 'The thing about Joe was he was rich.' We say, if we can, 'The thing about Joe was he took care of people.' "
—Peggy Noonan, "A Life's Lesson," on the astounding response to the passing of Tim Russert, the *Wall Street Journal*, June 21–22, 2008

I wish you a long life, but if tragedy were to have struck you yesterday, what do you think "they" might say at your memorial service? This maudlin question is not to be dwelt on "24/7," but it is worth considering on an irregularly regular basis.

Amen.
And good luck.

Dedication

One (me) would hardly denigrate the importance of Peter Drucker's work in developing modern management practice. For better, and sometimes for worse, Drucker and Frederick Taylor gave us the superstructure, more or less in full, for thinking about managing enterprise as we know it today. But I was, as I sat down to write this dedication, reminded of a finger-puppet/finger-wiggling exercise we performed as children: "This is the church, this is the steeple; open the doors and see all the people." If Drucker and Taylor gave us the church, Warren Bennis and his mentor and colleague Doug McGregor gave us the people. They added the blood and sweat and tears, that "all-important last 99 percent," as I call it, to the grand production called human organization.

Warren is a humanist.
Warren is a polymath.
Warren is a scholar in the grand and classic sense of the term.
Warren is a principal combatant in the history of ideas that shape humanity.
Warren is a teacher without peer.
Warren is a mentor without peer.
Warren is a friend without peer.

I believe without hesitation that an encompassing history of ideas about the nature of humanity and our ceaseless efforts to organize and to govern ourselves would note Warren's singular contributions. But Warren's matchless efforts in the arena in which I, too, have chosen to skirmish is not the primary reason I have dedicated this book to him. I have dedicated this book to Warren Bennis primarily for selfish reasons; namely, because he has been a wonderful friend in the truest and deepest sense of the word. He has "been there" intellectually and emotionally, nonstop, for the last 30 years of my life.

It was my quirky good fortune to write (cowrite) a popular management book at a rather important juncture in U.S. business history. To say that I was not prepared for what followed would be gross understatement. After a few jolly moments of deafening huzzahs came decades of sniping and out-and-out attacks. To be sure, I have purposefully put (and kept) myself in harm's way; I have been no shrinking violet. Nonetheless, one could not be prepared for the strength of the onslaught or the vats of blood that spatter the field of intellectual battle.

Enter Warren.

He was highly regarded by one and almost all, and, for reasons still unclear, he interceded with the world at large on my behalf and became my intellectual and emotional rock-guardian-soulmate. His repeatedly expressed declaration that I was following a useful track, and that come hell and high water I should persist, gave me the gumption to stay the course. I'm honestly not sure I would have survived without him. It's really that simple.

In effect, Warren offered me the steady and warm assurance, from his Olympian loft, which I needed to keep going. And which I needed to hold my ground. And for better or for worse, I did and do just that.

I stand in awe of Warren's contributions to our world at large.
And I am truly humbled by his friendship and support.

Thank you, my dear friend.

Acknowledgments

First, Justin Hall. This book is derived from my blog, tompeters.com; and Justin Hall is, per Wikipedia, knowledge arbiter on such topics, perhaps the first "modern" blogger. His Weblog was birthed in his Swarthmore College dorm room in 1994. (Usenet and BBS and the like were progenitors, and the overall lineage is, needless to say, murky.)

Next, Bob Miller. Bob is my publisher (HarperStudio), to whom I am eternally grateful; but in this instance Bob also has the unusual distinction of having informed me that I had written a book, unbeknownst to myself. That is, in the nature of current communications anthropology, Bob was an occasional visitor to tompeters.com, and read a few of the "success tips" that I posted from time to time. He emailed to say he thought there was a book at tp.com that had mostly been written—and that he would like to publish it.

(The "book-like" material, as I could have-should have guessed, was in fact only about 10 percent along the path to publishable manuscript—but that's another story. Fact is, Bob offered, I signed up—and here we are.)

Carolann Zaccara and Jon Miller. We start with a story of clean restrooms in Gill, Massachusetts, at Wagon Wheel Country Drive-in. The heroes of this book are the people whose tales I report. My heartfelt thanks to Wagon Wheel owners Zacarra and Miller and the rest of their ilk who appear in these pages.

Dave Wheeler. Several of the success tactics herein started with comments at tompeters.com. E.g., Dave Wheeler's, "The four most important words in any organization are 'What do you think?'" I will let Dave act as surrogate in this acknowledgments section for those commenters whose work I've referred to—I hope in each case with attribution.

David O. Stewart. David is a D.C.-based constitutional lawyer. His 2007 book, *The Summer of 1787*, was in many ways the chief inspiration for the "little BIG Things" idea. Astonishingly at first blush, it turns out that many, probably most, of the critical decisions at the U.S. Constitutional Convention were determined by such profoundly un-profound things such as "showing up." (Wee Delaware's delegation was invariably present—and its efforts were decisive time and again, despite representation by rather ordinary souls.) In the same vein, one could hardly do better than John Carlin's *Playing the Enemy: Nelson Mandela and the Game That Made a Nation*; then-President Mandela used the 1995 Rugby World Cup match as political theater of the most extraordinary sort. This pair and a host of others, like a reread of Barbara Tuchman's magnificent *The Guns of August*, provided fodder for this modest effort.

Erik Hansen. I have no idea what Erik's "job description" is, because he doesn't have one. I do a lot of speaking—and I do a lot of writing and videos and the like. Erik manages-creates-makes happen all that "stuff" that's not speaking in my life. We have been working on books together since 1994—this is book #11 for the two of us. (Yup, we regularly finish each other's sentences.) Erik works with publishers and finds designers and edits and has done about 150 superb "Cool Friend" interviews for tompeters.com and runs around from hither to thither and does a wonderful job somehow or other doing every-damn-thing you can imagine and then some and then some more; and all with great skill and a priceless sense of humor. (Except when he's pissed off—it's been known to happen.)

Cathy Mosca and Shelley Dolley. Cathy and Shelley aren't quite on their 11th book with me—but they're closing in! The meticulous and creative and caring duo are our day-to-day Web managers-editors-etc. And so much much much much more. Cathy, for instance, has the thankless but all-important (!!) fact-checking job; no amount of begging by me in the corner-cutting department does the least bit of good. Thank God! Also an integral part of our Web—and now book—"home team" is Joy Panos Stauber. I have spent 20-plus years screaming, initially against the wind, about the power of design. We try our best to live that message in our work—and Joy's magic touch is a huge part of that.

(FYI: Erik and Cathy have been through this manuscript as many times as I have, and as thoroughly as I have. Hence any errors are theirs. Sorry, just kidding. All screw-ups, of which we hope there are few if any, are, of course, ultimately my fault and mine alone! But it is true that C & E could probably recite the whole manuscript from memory!)

Sarah Rainone and Michael Slind. If editors are all-important, then we are lucky beyond measure. Sarah took the first crack at my inchoate mess. In addition to doing a fine job in general, she in fact is the one who gave us our title: *The Little BIG Things*. I don't know whether the book will measure up or not—but it starts out ahead of the game with one helluva title. Thanks, Sarah! Mike was the editor of my book *Re-imagine!* in 2003. It was a monster task, and to my mind he did a magnificent job. In particular, we were messing around with a whole new business-book format, which dramatically affected the text. Mike was the hero who made it up as he went along—and made it all work. On a slightly smaller canvas, he did it again here. We were unhappy with the logic of the book. Mike did great overall editing, but it was his reorganization of the material into smaller, coherent chunks that made the difference. Mike compared it to a musical score—and I think that's exactly right.

Harry. My continuing source of ideas—and idea test bed—is my several dozen seminars each year. These days, 80 percent beyond the U.S. border. (Angola and Saudi Arabia and Ecuador and India on a recent fall 2009 jaunt.) The speaking opportunities come courtesy of my friends of three decades at the peerless (word merited, no hype) Washington Speakers Bureau in Alexandria, Virginia. In particular, among so many who have been of so much help, cofounder Harry Rhoads, perhaps my best pal, and Georgene Savikas and Christine Farrell and Bernie Swain. One step further along the chain are my most regular of seminar creators—HSM from São Paulo, Brazil, and the Institute for International Research, part of London-based Informa. José Salibi Neto at HSM and I go back 25 years now. And Eduardo Braun at HSM and Peter Rigby and Jessica Sutherland at Informa/IIR and I have a lot of good history as well.

Team Harper and friends. It's good to be "home"! As some of you doubtless know, Harper & Row published Bob Waterman's and my *In Search of Excellence* in 1982. I moved on to Random House-Knopf-Vintage and then Dorling Kindersley. And now, over a quarter of a century later, Harper, in the form of the new HarperStudio, is my publishing home base—courtesy of Bob Miller, mentioned (and thanked) above. Bob of course has a lot of help from his friends! Among them: Kim Lewis, Nikki Cutler, Helen Song, Leah Carlson-Stanisic, Eric Butler, Mary Schuck, and Katie Salisbury.

Then there is the "life" part. Day to day in my professional affairs I am blessed (good word choice!) by the dedication and excellence of Abbey Bishop and Charlie Macomber. Abbey does have a job title, Executive Director of Events, but it is as misleading as Erik's non-title.

That is, she is events queen—and does an amazing job of dealing with everyone from audio visual experts in the Ukraine to CEOs in Silicon Valley. And then there is "the rest"—a hodgepodge of anything you can think of and then some. (In the last year her effectiveness is even more magnified, as she's done her job while her husband, U.S. Army Sergeant First Class Keith Bishop, has been on deployment to Afghanistan.) Charlie is our Chief Operating Officer—though I am the "management guru" (God help us all), Charlie manages every damn thing that comes under the heading of "running the business." New Hampshire-ite Charlie has a streak of no-nonsense pragmatism-conservatism that rounds off my irregularly regular flights of borderline insane fancy. Not so incidentally, speaking of sanity and insanity, I am also aided immeasurably in somehow surviving my life-on-the-road-approximately-everywhere by friend and travel goddess-miracle worker Nancy Paul.

And then the bedrock beneath the bedrock. My partner and best friend and wife, Susan Sargent. Susan is a brilliantly successful textile artist. And a home-furnishings entrepreneur whose unique approach to color in the home has literally changed America's living style. I am somewhat known for my hustle and intensity. She puts me to shame on both scores. "I don't wait" is her ever-so-apt motto. On top of that she has turned our somewhat sizeable Grey Meadow Farm in Tinmouth, Vermont, into a simply amazing place; a few pictures have appeared from time to time at tompeters.com. I have no idea what else to say—either 10,000 words or a simple "Thanks for everything and then some!"

And then there are my two amazing stepsons, Max and Ben Cooper. While the situation is hopeless, I do more or less sorta kinda try to keep up with the whacky new world of technology emerging around me. Among other things, "Multimedia Ben" is doubtless indirectly responsible for my blogging-tweeting efforts; and Max-the-artist pushes me, as does Susan, on all things aesthetic.

(Also in the "bedrock" category is our neighbor and chief of all things farm-related, Gary Gras. If the world comes to an end, Gary will survive; I have yet to discover anything he is not capable of doing. His wonderful family—wife Jane and daughter Emma and future motocross champion Austin—are also part of our hearty-gang-on-the-mountaintop-in-Tinmouth-Vermont.)

Finally, Frank Galioto and Lisa Galioto and Steve Hersh. They know why they are on this list. And I know why they are on this list. And I know they know there would probably be no book without them.

Index

O

Obama, Barack, xix, 115, 121

Odebrecht, Norberto, 397–98

Odell, William, 41

office politics, 61

"old" rules, 37–39

Oliver, Mary, 339

On Apology (Lazare), 158

On Becoming a Leader (Bennis), 67

O'Neal, Stan, 26

One Day, All Children (Kopp), 225

"one line of code," 163–65

one-off projects, 315

one percent drill, 407–8

One Thing You Need to Know (Buckingham), 143, 341

opportunity, 33–43

  boring is beautiful, 34–36

  bottom line in bad times, 42–43

  building green, 39–41

  "old" rules, 37–39

optimism, 27, 33–34, 468

opt-in retirement accounts, 6

"organizers" vs. "leaders," 238

others, 77–91

  "being there," 83–85

  civility toward, 79–83

  consideration of, 85–88

  kindness toward, 77–79

  thoughtfulness toward, 88–91

outcome vs. process, 78

out-reading, 355–56

"outside the box," 21

outsourcing, 19

out-studying, 138–39, 353–54

out-writing, 356–57

overcommunication, 29–30, 204–5, 499

Oxford History of the American People (Morison), 303

P

packagers, 118

PanAm, 320

Panama Canal, 320

parallel universe, 314–15, 323

Parcells, Bill, 217, 340

passion, 240–41, 247–53, 495

  seizing the moments, 251–52, 494

patient-centric care, 77–79, 117, 209–12

Patterson, Kerry, 66, 94

Patton, George, 228

Paulson, Hank, 28–29, 100, 351

Pearson, Andy, 263

pedestal, getting down from the, 262–63

Penman, Jim, 34–35

people, 281–91

  budget for, 286–88

  excitement axiom, 290–91

  quality of workforce, 281–86

  two-percenters, 289–90

"people leading people," 277–79

"people serving people," 411–13

"People's MBA" (education curriculum), 358–61

PepsiCo, 263, 479

Trauner, Keith, 455

trial and error, 30

Trippe, Juan, 320

trivial stuff, 2, 3, 47, 370

troublemakers, 221, 469

truth, 161, 251–52

"truth tellers," 482

"trying my damnedest!", 207–9

"try it" culture, 322, 480

Tuf-E-Nuf hammer, 377–78

Tversky, Amos, 4–5

Twain, Mark, 25, 149

Twitter, 357, 481

two-cent candies, 385–87, 448

two-percenters, 289–90

U

uncertainty, 47, 205

universities and R&D, 308

unpredictable extreme events, 45–49

unscheduled time, 366–68

UPS, 415

user buy-in, 163–66

user-friendly design, 378–82

"us" vs. "we," 98–99

V

vacations, 364

value creation, dramatic frenzy of, 459–62

Vanguard Mutual Fund Group, 27

Van Wagenen, Lola, 301

venture capital, 308

"Virtuous Circle of Apology," 160

visible management, 58

Visionary, the, 237

vivacity, 103–4

voice messages, 3

volunteer work, 58

Vonnegut, Kurt, 28

W

Wagon Wheel Country Drive-in, xxi, 1–2

walls of "Tomorrows" and "Yesterdays," 455–56

Walmart, 5, 54

Walt, Lew, 207

Walton, Sam, 54

wandering around, 20, 48, 140–41, 255–59, 499

war gaming, 47

Washington, George, 80–81, 115, 363

Washington Post, 28–29, 30

Waterman, Robert H., Jr., xxi–xxii, 9, 214, 215, 255, 358, 418, 448, 480, 506

Watson, Thomas, 10–11, 419, 482

Weapon of Mass Creation (WMC), 472

Weather Channel, The (Batten), 312

Wegmans, 284

Weight of Water, The (Shreve), 298

Weill, Sandy, 26

weirdos, 19, 243, 470–71

Welch, Jack, 342

"we-power approach," 98–99

About the Author

Tom Peters is the coauthor of *In Search of Excellence*, the business book that changed the world. He continues to write and speak about Excellence—join the conversation at tompeters.com.

The 19 **E**s of Excellence ❯